TRAILBLAZER

TRAILBLAZER

BARBARA LEIGH SMITH BODICHON
The First Feminist to Change Our World

JANE ROBINSON

doubleday

TRANSWORLD PUBLISHERS
Penguin Random House, One Embassy Gardens,
8 Viaduct Gardens, London SW11 7BW
www.penguin.co.uk

Transworld is part of the Penguin Random House group of companies
whose addresses can be found at global.penguinrandomhouse.com

First published in Great Britain in 2024 by Doubleday
an imprint of Transworld Publishers

A CIP catalogue record for this book
is available from the British Library.

ISBN 9780857527776

Typeset in 12.5/16.1pt Bembo Book MT Pro by Jouve (UK), Milton Keynes
Printed and bound in Great Britain by Clays Ltd, Elcograf S.p.A.

The authorized representative in the EEA is Penguin Random House Ireland,
Morrison Chambers, 32 Nassau Street, Dublin D02 YH68.

Penguin Random House is committed to a sustainable future
for our business, our readers and our planet. This book is
made from Forest Stewardship Council® certified paper.

To Ed

Contents

Barbara Leigh Smith Bodichon: the Trailblazer.

Charles Dickens

Adelaide Procter

Elizabe

Hilaire Belloc

Bessie Parkes

Charles Darwin

Anna Mary
Howitt

John
Chapman   Elizabeth Gaskell

Charlotte Brontë

George Eliot

Gertrude Jekyll

Hercules Brabazon Brabazon

C.-F. Daubigny

Henri Rousseau   J.-B.-C. Corot

Berthe Morisot

Édvard Manet   D. G. Rossetti

Christina Rosse

Lizzie Siddal

Lewis Carro

Jane Burden

Mary Som

John Ruskin

J. M.

William Morris

Bar
Leigh
Boo

© Jane Robinson

Barbara was a consummate networker with an extraordinarily impressive circle
of friends and connections.

Harriet Beecher Stowe   Lucy Stone

Lucretia Mott

arrett
Anderson   Emmeline Pankhurst

lizabeth Blackwell

                    Millicent Fawcett
    Emily Davies

Bertha Ayrton   Emily Faithfull

                         Queen Victoria

        cousin Florence Nightingale

        Eugène Bodichon   Alfred Lord Tennyson

            aunt 'Ju'   Louis Blanc
            Smith

                brother Ben Leigh Smith

                         Arthur Conan
                         Doyle

ra
nith
on   Benjamin Smith
            'the Pater'

                    Sir John Franklin

    Grandfather Wm. Smith

        Harriet Martineau   Wm. Wilberforce

                    Mary Wollstonecraft

lle

urner   Mary Shelley

                    Lord Byron

The Trailblazer

IMAGINE THE SCENE. IT'S THE EARLY SUMMER OF 1866. WE are standing in the spacious entrance hall of Aubrey House, a Georgian mansion in Holland Park, west London, belonging to Clementia Taylor and her husband Peter. 'Mentia' is a radical social reformer who hosts various clubs and support groups for the dispossessed: the uneducated, for instance, the poverty-stricken or women. Aubrey House is rarely quiet, but today it's even noisier than usual. Someone has left the door of the dining room ajar, and the ringing sound of excited female voices fills the air. So, surprisingly, does a strong smell of glue.

We push the door open — it's heavy — and twenty or more women are revealed, gathered around a vast table covered by heaps of paper. In my mind's eye, this looks like nothing so much as a session for superannuated nursery-school children, complete with scissors, messy paste-pots, grubby aprons and genial chatter. Yet it's obvious that they are concentrating, engrossed in their work, and there's some method in the chaos. The piles of paper are gradually diminishing while some women cut and others paste. They cheerfully take turns.

All of them are more or less conventionally clad in dresses with corseted bodices and full skirts in unexceptional colours. But one stands out. She is tall, with red-gold hair worn not pinned up neatly, as is the custom, but billowing down her back from a green velvet headband. She wears a loose, medieval-looking gown in green tussore silk, which rustles as she moves and sets off her shining hair, her forget-me-not eyes and fair complexion, to startling effect.

Her voice is easily distinguished from the others'. It's quite deep for a woman, but musical, with the merest hint of a soft Sussex accent. And she laughs more than anyone else in the room. It's not the brittle trill of the socially insecure, but warm and spontaneous. She has a natural authority; the others don't defer to her, but ask her advice and obviously value her opinion. She looks as though she's thoroughly enjoying herself.

At the far end of the room, by a window, there's a huge scroll spread out on the carpet, weighted open with fancy candlesticks and other treasures raided from the mantelpiece. The woman with the red-gold hair walks over to it, kneels down and takes over the fiddly job of picking countless scraps of pasted paper from the table and sticking them on to the scroll.

Her name is Barbara Leigh Smith Bodichon, and this whole enterprise is her idea. The papers on the dining-room table are printed petitions, signed and returned by hundreds of women around the country of different classes and varying circumstances, asking the House of Commons to consider giving them the vote. Nearly 1,500 signatures are being snipped from the forms and glued one by one to the scroll, which Barbara is due to present to a Member of Parliament on 7 June with her activist friends Emily Davies and Elizabeth Garrett. Once that first massed petition for suffrage reaches Westminster, the long fight for women's enfranchisement will begin. And Barbara – already a pioneer in so many fields – will turn to her next crusade.

Introduction

IFIRST MET BARBARA IN *BLUESTOCKINGS* (2009), MY BOOK about the first women to go to university. She featured in *Hearts and Minds* (2018), about the suffragists. And she influenced *In the Family Way* (2015), about the experience of illegitimacy, and *Ladies Can't Climb Ladders* (2020), about women reforming the law and breaking into the professions. Several years ago, I saw some of her paintings at Girton College (which she co-founded) and realized that as well as being a feminist pioneer, responsible for kick-starting the women's rights movement in Britain, she was a successful professional artist. Chancing upon a modern edition of the letters she wrote on her honeymoon in the southern states of America, I realized she was an ardent abolitionist. I read a biography of George Eliot and realized she was the writer's closest friend. Visited a Gertrude Jekyll garden and realized Barbara gave the designer – another of her close friends – one of her first commissions. Met a scholar researching the life of Dante Gabriel Rossetti and realized she was closer to him than almost any other woman outside his family. Read some of her family letters and realized how kind, cheerful and utterly un-Victorian she was. Researched Florence Nightingale's life and realized they were first cousins. And on it goes.

So why isn't she famous? Why has someone fundamental to British social, cultural and political history been so successfully sidelined? It's partly because she blazed so many different trails. Historians are fond of labels, but Barbara defies categorization, both in the breadth of her work and influence, and in the catholicity of her personality. She was handicapped by her illegitimacy. And she never sought the spotlight. Her role was to work out how to unlock doors for people and then stand aside as they stepped through. She was often too busy doing something else when the big moments occurred (when her petition was finally presented to Parliament in 1866, for instance, she was unexpectedly needed elsewhere), so she tended to miss the party.

She's not entirely unknown. There have been three full-length biographies in the past. The first, by Hester Burton, was published in 1949 and is chatty and anecdotal. The American academic Sheila Herstein produced another in 1985. Both are useful, but the third one, written by Pam Hirsch in 1998, is indispensable. (All three titles may be found in 'Select Bibliography' at the end of this volume.) The level of detail Dr Hirsch includes in contextualizing Barbara's life and achievements is wonderful, and I owe her a huge debt of gratitude. But after reading all three books at the beginning of my research, and knowing something of her through my own work, I still felt as though there was more to be discovered about Barbara. I was beginning to form a good idea of the remarkable things she did, but not why she did them. Nor who she really was.

The first step was to track down the Leigh Smith descendants. This is when I realized just how lucky I was. It was the stuff of a biographer's dreams: having picked the perfect subject, I was invited to a vast, beautiful house where members of her family have lived for five generations, with permission to sort through anything useful I could find. There were boxes and boxes of documents there; wooden chests full of paintings and sketches; happy surprises everywhere I looked. Waiting for me on the table when I arrived was a bright green Clarks shoebox, circa 1965, packed with the first consignment of what would turn out to be hundreds of letters. I recognized Barbara's chaotic handwriting on a note at the front of the box. It simply asked: 'How long is the longest earthworm?'

I unwrapped a little tissue-paper parcel sitting next to the shoebox. There, strangely heavy in the palm of my hand, was a bracelet woven from once-lustrous tresses, with an engraved clasp. There was a long, braided necklace made of hair, too. Barbara was so proud of her crowning glory. I opened a huge coffer and began to peel away layers of watercolours, luminous and vivid, one after the other, like giant petals. Beneath them was an enormous, dark-blue garment of some kind. It turned out to be a pair of Barbara's husband's bloomers, worn by him – occasionally – under his burnouse, or long hooded North African cloak, and cherished ever since. (To be honest, he preferred to wear nothing at all under the burnouse, but sometimes duty called.)

I spent days at the house, reading and carefully cataloguing Barbara's papers; luxuriating in her art; learning about her idiosyncratic relations at first hand; trying to keep Jeoffry the cat at arm's length; and counting my blessings.

With various inevitable interruptions due to the pandemic, I spent the following months in the UK and America studying Barbara's correspondence, publications, paintings and family connections. The legwork stage of a book can be something of a chore for a writer, but Barbara had such an invigorating personality, and seemed so *modern*, that I never wearied. The more I learned about her strengths and (just as importantly) her vulnerabilities, the better I understood her, and the more I relished her company.

This is by no means a foregone conclusion for biographers. You can start a book in love, and finish it desperate for the divorce. Living with Barbara was not always straightforward, either for me or for her friends and family. But I would love to have been with her, round that dining table in 1866, fashioning a better, fairer future. How could you fail to warm to such a connoisseur of human happiness? Who was known and loved by more eminent men and women than you can shake a stick at, even though she was essentially an outsider. Who treated all comers with respect and compassion. Whose chief ambition in life was to improve the lives of others. And who never took herself too seriously.

Barbara was one of the kindest, least judgemental people I

have come across, as well as one of the most inquisitive (how long *is* the longest earthworm?). She accomplished so much, changing her world and ours in the process. But I have come to the conclusion that her greatest accomplishment of all was being – and remaining – herself, in spite of everything.

She deserves her moment in the sun.

Names and No Names

Up until 1834

Oh, those free wild spirits the Smiths always seem to have,
how glorious to feel their rush into one's own heart.[1]

FEW SMITHS CAN CLAIM A BLUE-BLOODED HERITAGE. THE
clue is in the name: a smith is a maker, not a consumer; someone
who earns rather than inherits a living. Barbara Leigh Smith
Bodichon came from a line of such people. Despite being a Whig
Member of Parliament and a wealthy man, her grandfather William Smith (1756–1835) was in many ways, like her, an outsider.
William's family background was in trade; his politics were radical, and as a Unitarian, holding deist beliefs in conflict with
orthodox Christians', he was categorized as a Dissenter. Dissenters were forbidden to hold government office, or to receive a
degree from Oxford or Cambridge University. They could be
members of the Establishment by association only, not by right.

Far from disabling him, these restrictions galvanized William.
Eighteenth-century Unitarians were Christian but professed a
rational belief in humanity rather than the Trinity; in the power
and duty of people of good conscience to improve society for
everyone. Opportunity was the key to equality, in their view,
and a love of liberty, tolerance and justice the bedrock of democracy. It appears that Unitarians were also pragmatists. William
recognized the necessity of political influence to effect social

change, so bought himself a seat in Sudbury in Suffolk for £3,000 in 1784, where, handily, less than 5 per cent of the population was eligible to vote. Fifty years later, Sudbury became the model for Charles Dickens's 'Rotten Borough' of Eatanswill in *The Pickwick Papers* (1836–7), famous for electoral corruption.

Next came Camelford in Cornwall. Even better: only seventeen electors there. It cost him another £2,000 to secure them by way of their patron, the local landowner. By 1802, he had a sound enough parliamentary reputation to win Norwich fair and square, though election expenses were always considerable. It was a seat he kept – with one year's absence – until 1830.

His £5,000 for both seats equate to about £450,000 in terms of purchasing power. This was big money, yielded by the Smith family's interests in the food and drink industry. They owned a large wholesale grocery business, the Sugar Loaf, which had grown over the generations from an ironmonger's shop run by a long-gone Mr Smith on the Isle of Wight to an import depot and emporium in the City of London. Through marriage, the family also acquired one of the largest distilleries and breweries in London, on the bank of the Thames.

The affection of good friends does not always come with the territory for people of political heft; even less so if they are rich. But William was both loving and well loved. His loyal social circle included reforming politicians, philosophers, artists and writers; men and women of influence, and of none. He was both open-minded and open-handed. At home or on their family travels during the parliamentary recess, the Smiths were appreciative connoisseurs of strong character, keeping company with and providing an idiosyncratic commentary on, among others, 'the wittiest man in England',[2] William Wilberforce; languid William Wordsworth (disappointingly grubby); his sister Dorothy, who spent her latter days gently dementing in a bath chair in her garden; a distracted Samuel Taylor Coleridge, who used to pace up and down on his visits in an opiate haze, chasing fugitive poems and ignoring everything else; the 'married' Ladies of Llangollen; high-profile abolitionists Thomas Clarkson and the unfeasibly rotund Charles James Fox; grumpy Sir Joshua Reynolds; incomprehensibly clever Erasmus Darwin and William Herschel; fiery Mary Wollstonecraft; and the determined young social reformer and journalist Harriet Martineau, who wielded her ear trumpet like an offensive weapon. Many of these people were Unitarians and Liberals like William, but not all of them. He collected eccentric friends like exotic animals in a free-range menagerie, accepting their differences while admiring their common sense of purpose.

In turn, they warmed to his cheerfulness, love of art, devotion to a growing family of ten surviving children and, most of all (Sudbury and Camelford notwithstanding), his integrity. He was Wilberforce's staunchest ally in the fight against the slave trade. So passionately did he believe in the cause that he renounced the Sugar Loaf's historical connections with plantations in Georgia and Antigua, declaring a total boycott on slave-related imports. He made personal as well as commercial sacrifices, giving up sugar despite an addictively sweet tooth. 'A family that uses five pounds of sugar per week with the same proportion of rum,' he maintained, 'will by abstaining from the consumption of West Indian produce for 21 months, prevent the slavery or murder of ONE fellow creature.'[3] A passionate crusader for human liberty, he was mortified by any association with slavery in the past, and dedicated his life to the ethical reform of politics, economics and civil rights. That sense of natural justice was inherited by his granddaughter Barbara. 'Am I not a man and a brother?' ran an abolitionist declaration of solidarity with the oppressed. And am I not a woman and a sister?

In Parliament, William was often the last to leave any reforming debate, conscious of his self-appointed duty as spokesman for those with no voice. A contemporary described his assiduity in verse:

> At length, when the candles burn blue in their sockets
> Up gets William Smith with both hands in his pockets,
> On a course of morality fearlessly enters
> With all the opinions of all the Dissenters.[4]

The warmth of his personality radiates from the letters he wrote to his family. He and his wife, Frances Coape (1759–1840), married for love. He would sometimes smuggle a note to her during the day from the House of Commons, complaining that an overrunning debate was annoyingly interrupting his 'golden dreams' of spending time with the family. He was uxorious, a fond papa, but no soft touch. In a letter to a daughter who showed signs of laziness and petulance, the message was clear: get a grip. 'I do wish you to be in this as in every other instance, Mistress of yourself, governed by reason, and not by Humour. But be thoughtful of others and share things . . . You have only to show yourself considerate & attentive, & you may be certain of finding me kind.'[5] One can imagine the little girl immediately changing her ways, mortified by her beloved papa's displeasure – except that the daughter in question, Martha (known as Patty), was about forty when this was written. Obviously, her behaviour remained a work in progress.

Patty, who never did quite master her social skills, was the eldest of William and Frances's children, born in 1782. She never married. Benjamin – Barbara's father – came next, born the following year, then Anne, later Mrs Nicholson; Frances, or Fanny, who married William Nightingale and bore Frances Parthenope and Florence; William Adams, usually called by his second name and considered something of a disappointment; Joanna, who became Mrs John Bonham Carter, mother of artist Hilary Bonham Carter; Samuel (Sam), who married Mai Shore, sister to

William Nightingale; Octavius (Oc), who with his wife Jane Cooke and brothers Benjamin and Sam became the engine driver of the Smith family's business enterprises; Frederick, who was hardly ever spoken about; and finally Julia (Ju), the second spinster bookending a productive family. They lived in comfort on the edge of rural Clapham Common, then in Park Street, Westminster, and – until a series of financial misadventures caused William to sell it – in Upper House, a modest stately home they mischievously called the Mount. It lay in two hundred acres of parkland in the village of Little Parndon in Essex, one of England's flattest counties.

In the early 1820s, William disposed of most of his library and fine furniture to meet election expenses and rebuild the under-insured Thames Bank distillery after a fire. He had unfortunately overreached himself in his love of collecting beautiful pictures and important books. The auction catalogues read like guides to a major museum. Barbara's father, Benjamin, bought some of the less opulent lots to furnish his own properties in Sussex; the rest was presumably sold to strangers.

William's art collection was remarkable, if a little fluid, depending on his fluctuating solvency. It included notable paintings by Rubens, Rembrandt, Angelica Kauffmann, Claude, Van Dyck and Stubbs. The apple of his eye was Reynolds's larger-than-life canvas *Mrs Siddons as the Tragic Muse*: it hung above the fireplace in the drawing room at 6 Park Street. It cost £700 – much more than a Rembrandt or a Rubens at the time – and the actress was so delighted with the likeness that she used to sneak into the house when the Smiths were away (courtesy of Mrs Frost, the star-struck housekeeper) to worship it in secret.[6]

Benjamin, William's eldest son, was brought up to think for himself. As a good Unitarian, thinking for himself would ideally result in a wish to follow in his charismatic father's footsteps. And indeed he did. He was an astute director of the family businesses – more successful than William – and, in time, a

Liberal politician noted for his commitment to social reform. Both father and son represented Norwich in Parliament at different times; William made his name as an abolitionist, Benjamin as a campaigner against the Corn Laws, and for wider access to education and legal representation for all, including women. Benjamin had more money than William, and kept hold of it longer, spending it on good causes, business investments, country estates, his friends and family, and his children.

On the face of it, he appeared a cheerful, generous, responsible member of society. There is no doubt that, in many ways, he was all of these. When William was threatened with bankruptcy following the financial upheavals resulting in the sale of the Mount and its contents, it was Benjamin who bailed his father out. He assumed financial responsibility for Patty and Ju, and gave away to Joanna and her new husband, John Bonham Carter, his own Mayfair townhouse as a wedding present. He was witty, colourful, a good sportsman, a loyal friend and committed politician, ready to help anyone short of money or luck. But there was another side to this genial gentleman, far more complex and troubling.

Benjamin visited Paris in 1821, taking his sisters Patty and Ju with him to escape the trauma of losing the Mount. He was in his late thirties, unmarried and apparently highly eligible. While there, the three of them called on their aunt Fanny Nightingale. She and her husband William had paused in Paris on their way home from Italy, where their daughters Parthenope and Florence were born in 1819 and 1820 respectively. Also visiting them at that time was Mr Nightingale's sister Mary, known as Mai. She was twenty-three. Within days, it seems, the Byronic Mr Smith had swept Mai off her feet. Without consulting the family, they announced their engagement.

The stunned silence greeting this news was followed by a clamour of outrage, first from Mai's parents and then from the Nightingales. Despite his close family connection, his wealth (albeit from trade) and his firm political principles, Benjamin was *not* considered the right man for Mai. It was hinted darkly that he was an adventurer with years of wild-oat sowing behind him, a heartbreaker, irresponsible and immature. In a letter to his wife, Mr Nightingale made his views clear. Though fond of both Benjamin and Mai,

> I should wish her almost to swear that she will never listen to him for a moment – he is just as agreeable as ever, but so easily disturbed, & so completely the opposite of simplicity – good taste & what may be suited to a peaceable life that no good can come of his union with anybody, but a woman as high-spirited & determined as himself.[7]

Mai was of age to marry without her parents' consent, but was too meek to defy them, and Benjamin too proud.

In later life, Florence Nightingale recalled her dashing uncle Benjamin with affection. Mai married his more conventional brother Sam a few years after this family kerfuffle, by which time Benjamin's attentions had turned even more scandalously elsewhere. But Sam could only be second best, according to Florence. 'Ben was such a large nature, with a touch of genius in him, such a delightful companion.'[8] In contrast to the smallness of her domestic circumstances as a young woman, the frustration of measuring out her life in platitudes with a mother and sister who, she remarked, 'did nothing but lie on 2 sofas in the drawing-room, calling to each other: "don't tire yourself"',[9] perhaps Florence had secretly dreamed of someone like Benjamin coming to whisk *her* off in a whirl of unconsidered romance. How might that have changed history?

LEA HURST IS A graceful sandstone building near the town of Alfreton in Derbyshire. It has a Jacobean core, but Florence Nightingale's father rebuilt it around the time of Benjamin and

Mai's courtship as a substantial (rather than showy) country house where his young family might enjoy the salutary benefits of pure air, picturesque views and deep roots. There had been Nightingales in the area for generations, whose considerable prosperity grew from lead mining and, latterly, the cotton-spinning industry.[10]

One of Benjamin Smith's most remarkable characteristics was an ability to function for much of his life as at least two people in one. Despite the fracas over Mai, William Nightingale never lost his instinctive liking for the man. The latter may have been something of a romantic – or unhappy in his 'domestic arrangements', as Nightingale put it coyly – but he remained an unpretentious and affable member of the clan. Benjamin appears not to have borne a grudge either; and indeed, up he turned at Lea Hurst between 1822 and 1827 as one of the Nightingales' welcome family visitors, approved and disapproved of at the same time. He occupied himself in Derbyshire by prospecting for new mining enterprises to add to a growing portfolio of business interests; helping to run a charitable school at the nearby village of Creech; and getting to know a local miller's daughter by the name of Anne Longden.

The Longdens lived at Alfreton Mill: widowed John (c. 1763–1838) and his two younger children, Dorothy (Dolly) and Anne, whose exact date of birth is not known but who was baptized in 1801. His wife Dorothy (née Gratton) had died in 1819, and a son, John, in infancy. Their eldest daughter, Jane, lived close by, married to Mr Smedley, the local postmaster. It has always been said within the family that Anne was a milliner's apprentice, though there is no evidence for this. How would Benjamin have met her if she were? Chaperoning Patty or Ju to Mary Simpson's Straw Bonnet shop in Alfreton, perhaps? Maybe he visited John Longden's watermill on Mr Nightingale's business, or spied her – described as 'ravishingly pretty'[11] – taking the air in Alfreton Park?

This is the stuff of costume drama and indeed, given her heavily censored story, it is difficult to imagine Anne as anything but a fictional character. A mixture of miller's daughter Maggie Tulliver from George Eliot's *Mill on the Floss* or Esther in Elizabeth Gaskell's *Mary Barton*, perhaps. Historically, 'milliner's apprentice' was a common euphemism for 'prostitute', which says more about the vulgar concept of a young woman working for a living than about the immorality of making hats.[12] It comes as no surprise, therefore, to learn what Benjamin's sister Patty thought of his concubine. Anne was assumed by Patty to be a cynical seductress who ensnared her brother and deliberately mired him in a relationship he could neither acknowledge, as a man of honour, nor escape.

In fact (and there are few facts available in Anne's history, so I am sticking to this one), the Longdens were a respectable family. John had a high-enough profile to merit notice of his death in the county newspaper, the *Derby Mercury*.[13] His wife Dorothy came from a well-established and relatively prosperous line; her cousin Joseph Gratton, for example, was a corn broker in London, and a chairman of the cutting-edge Independent Gas Company. Whether he became Benjamin's friend before or after Benjamin met Anne is unclear, but friends they certainly were. There is a worn stone tablet on the wall of St Martin's Church in Alfreton commemorating in faint lettering John Longden's wife and daughters: a public sign of local status. But little about Anne's life has escaped suppression, except for the odd passing mention by those who loved her best or who hated most what she represented in an outwardly respectable family narrative.

Anne fell pregnant in the summer of 1826. Benjamin did not deny that he was the father. Nor did he ever explain – in writing, at any rate – why he declined to marry her. It is generally assumed by historians that this was some sort of high-minded statement about the inequity of marriage laws; his protest – a little like William Smith giving up sugar – at the iniquitous concept of a wife being her husband's chattel. Wasn't that what William's crusade against slavery had been all about? People as property? Ideologically, it has been argued, Benjamin was demonstrating his respect for Anne as a fellow – or sister – human being: they were partners.

But what about Anne? It would have taken enormous courage to agree to Benjamin's social experiment, if that is what it was. Which of her acquaintances would appreciate the political niceties? To them, she would simply be one more pretty little milliner's apprentice put in the family way by a powerful man almost old enough to be her father, with no intention of making an honest woman of her. And her infant would be a bastard, without legal rights, social standing or even a name. At this time, an illegitimate baby was classed as 'filius nullius', literally 'son of no one', or nobody's child. The stigma for a mother of bringing such a child into the world was ineradicable. The shame of being that child could last for generations.

Benjamin's refusal to marry was possibly more a matter of expediency than ideology. His later conduct suggests that how he treated the women and children in his life was not, after all, part of some noble activism in the service of political reform. He *was* a reformer and practised what he preached in terms of empowering the dispossessed, as we shall see. He was also a man of principle, admired by his peers and beloved of his family. But we are back to the two-in-one person again: his treatment of Anne and her successor indicates a personality so strong that he felt entitled to ignore the inconvenient rules of society as irrelevant. Despite his parents' loving relationship, after his courtship of Mai he developed a distaste for marriage: it could and often did demean the wife, but it could also constrain the husband, and curb his personal liberty. Instead of attempting to reform from within the safe confines of the institution, he persuaded Anne that their family could survive intact in the moral wilderness, because he was Benjamin Smith. She was swept along in his wake.

There is yet another interpretation. When I was a young teen, one of my favourite Shakespeare plays was the *The Taming of the Shrew*. That is not an easy confession for a feminist, given the theme of chauvinistic subjugation, but when I first saw it I was convinced that Kate only pretended to give in to Petruchio at the end. She was actually in complete command of her actions, and therefore of her unsuspecting husband, who thought he had broken her spirit. She loved him on her terms, not his (though I wasn't quite sure why). What happened *after* the play, in my Pollyanna-ish imagination, was a fiery reckoning in which Kate explained her strategy; Petruchio, smitten by her feistiness, fell genuinely in love with her, whereupon they lived happily ever after.

I am not suggesting that Benjamin was cruel or unkind, like Petruchio; quite the opposite. But what if Anne were the 'high-spirited and determined' young woman Mr Nightingale had envisaged as the only fit mate for Benjamin? Is it conceivable that she, like my version of Kate, was in control? That she refused to marry Benjamin, not vice versa, and that it was *her* fight for social justice that inspired their daughter Barbara to change the world for women? Given Benjamin's later behaviour, however, it would appear not.

Much of the confusion over what Benjamin and/or Anne were trying to prove by 'living in sin' arises from mixed messaging. She did not take his name, but neither did she keep her own. Benjamin called her Mrs Leigh, after an ancestor from the Isle of Wight who eloped with a shopkeeper. In 1823 Benjamin had acquired a country estate in Sussex, Crowham Manor, but he never installed Anne in the big house. Instead, he put her in a rented, tile-hung picture-book cottage next to the water mill (to remind her of home?) in the nearby village of Whatlington. Their daughter was born there at 11.30 a.m. on Sunday 8 April 1827. 'Barbara' means 'stranger' or 'visitor from a different place'; her surname was a conflation of Anne's pretend 'Leigh' and

Benjamin's real, though undistinguished, 'Smith'. But all her life, she was known by family and close friends simply as 'Bar'.

One wonders who welcomed her into the world. Benjamin and Anne, of course, and Anne's nurse (or nanny) Hannah Walker. But the Smiths were tight-lipped. This was a family scandal, best cancelled by silence. There is no record of any letter of congratulation, any visit or any acknowledgement at all from either the Smiths or the Longdens. Benjamin had managed to remain on good terms with his open-minded father, William, and while Patty was splenetic at the shame he had visited upon them all by association, she insisted that he was more victim than villain. 'Oh, how it grieves me to think of his thraldom,' she wrote to her sister Fanny Nightingale, 'for he is truly as clever a man as can usually be met with, and to think to what converse he is confined.'[14] How lonely Anne must have been. She and Benjamin were still living apart, though he did spend time with her in the doll's house cottage at Whatlington. What converse did *she* enjoy?

On 12 March 1828 – less than a year after Barbara's birth – young Benjamin Leigh Smith arrived. Henceforth, the elder Benjamin was known as 'the Pater', and the younger as 'Ben'. By now, the Pater had made his first attempt to enter Parliament. In December 1827, he stood for Maldon in Essex, but because he was not proposed as a candidate until the very last minute, he polled only a single vote. This amused rather than depressed him. There were other things he wanted to do before settling down to a political career. He dissolved the various business partnerships held with his brothers and began planning a new adventure. Patty, predictably, was aghast. She blamed Anne. 'After 20 years exertion & so much done for other people, to find himself in his present situation.'[15] What was to become of him?

She need not have worried. The Pater had a talent for making money. He relished a challenge and thrived on defying expectation. Hence the next chapter in an unpredictable life: a year's sabbatical in America. On 1 April 1829, he and his young family embarked on the *Columbia*, a state-of-the-art steam packet of the Black Ball Line, bound from Portsmouth to New York. A steam packet was a new kind of ship, a courier vessel designed to operate a shuttle service between specific ports. In those days, newspapers printed the names of passengers on high-profile transatlantic voyages. Twenty-seven are listed aboard the *Columbia* 'and 20 in the steerage'.[16] Among the twenty-seven are 'Benj, Barbara and Benj Smith' but no Mrs Leigh, or even Mrs Smith. Certainly no Miss Longden. We know Anne was aboard, as she is mentioned in the Pater's journal. Surely she was not in steerage, like young Abraham Buss, his older sister Kezia and a Mr Brewer, the Pater's servants from Sussex?[17] It is more likely that she was ignored by the purser who provided the names to the press, because of her equivocal status. Yet again, it is as if she did not exist.

Choosing the *Columbia* for the passage to America was akin to booking a flight on Concorde in the 1980s: a signal of wealth and some flamboyance. Her captain, Joseph Delano, was a celebrity, admired for his ability to sail at ridiculous speed. In fact the ship broke the record during this very crossing, making the voyage in fifteen days and eighteen hours.[18] Vessels under sail could take more than twice that time. She was not large: there were eight staterooms on either side of the main cabin (a stateroom could accommodate a family of four) with each berth costing the equivalent of around £4,000. That's each *berth*, not each stateroom.

The food was lavish, served by Captain Delano's wife Alice at a thirty-foot table in the main cabin.[19] Meals increased in volume throughout the day, starting with a breakfast of broiled fish and meat, bread and butter, tea and coffee. 'Tiffin' at twelve noon was a cold buffet of beef, oysters and cheese with biscuits and porter (a rich, dark beer). The main event was dinner at 4 p.m. – a four-course feast of soup, roast meat, boiled fowl, puddings, tarts, fritters, fruit, nuts and raisins, and wine. Two and a half hours later, passengers began to wind down with a tea of bread and cheese, cold meats and cake, until at 10 p.m. they were sent to bed with whiskey punch and more cheese and biscuits to keep them ticking over until everything began again at nine o'clock the next morning.

The Pater's journal of the American trip is scribbled and sketchy, but a fascinating read.[20] It implies why he was there: this was a fact-finding tour, a quest in search of Utopia. Like the philanthropist and social architect Robert Owen, whom he admired, the Pater believed in the possibility of remodelling society. Before leaving for America, he expressed an interest in establishing an experimental colony there, like the two Owen founded in New Lanark, Scotland, and New Harmony, Indiana. These were designed as untraditional settlements where families could grow together in a cooperative and self-sufficient community, unshackled by inveterate institutions such as organized religion and traditional marriage. The idea was that industry, education, health, happiness and social responsibility would flourish in an equitable atmosphere of mutual trust and benefit.

Finding somewhere to stay when the family arrived in New York was almost impossible. The city was too full of foreigners, complained foreigner Benjamin Smith. Eventually they discovered a hotel on Broadway, where they lodged until the middle of May. Then their travels began. The Pater was determined to miss no opportunity to learn about the social mechanics of what was still a relatively young republic. He looked round a progressive college in New Brunswick and a cotton-printing factory in Trenton, New Jersey. In hot, hot Philadelphia – 30° Celsius – he observed the teaching at local infant schools before turning north to upstate New York.

He met some naval cadets at their base in West Point; at Albany he chatted with a member of the state legislature and inspected a poorhouse; he stood for ages in the rain at Saratoga to watch a procession of saturated military and civil authorities, and marvelled at a salt works there before going by canal boat to sightsee the picturesque village of Little Falls. From Utica, south of the Adirondack Mountains, he chartered a stagecoach for the 110-mile journey to Rochester, where he paused to draw breath.

Near Buffalo he watched people he called 'Indians' being taught by missionaries – something about which he had mixed feelings, being both an educationalist and a Dissenter – and noticed large parties of Irish navvies building a canal, the Protestants and Catholics among them blatantly refusing to work together. This did not bode well for Utopia. After crossing into Canada, he attended a rape trial ('justice very respectably administered', he commented) and interviewed British emigrants about their new lives.

This is all interesting and demonstrates the Pater's modern appetite for sociological research and development. But it is the personal details he betrays in an otherwise business-like diary that illuminate this extraordinary period in the life of little Barbara and her family. For example, not only did the Pater travel with Messrs Buss and Brewer, and Kezia Buss to help look after the children (though she suffered from fever which put her *hors de combat* for a while), but he also brought his Sussex gun dogs. And why not? Shooting was by far his favourite sport. He intended to do as much as he could in America, both in terms of time and volume. The journal faithfully records each day's bag, with only an occasional plaintive 'killed nothing'.

It is not clear how often the whole family travelled together. The Pater was certainly on his own when taken for a boat trip on Lake Ontario. The wind turned, and he ended up being out all night, 'contrary to promise'. Another time, he suggests that he forbade Anne to accompany him somewhere, which made her cross. 'Mouse went back in stage[coach] sulky,' he notes. All of a sudden, the woman comes alive: she is his 'Mouse', fed up with travelling, yet fed up with being left behind. With good cause, perhaps: when the Pater went to Buffalo he was excited to share the stagecoach with 'Mr Stuart Mollan and his lovely sisters, black or hazel eyed'. However, he adds sadly, they were also 'yellow phized', meaning jaundiced and sallow. What a pity.

By the end of September 1829, Anne was pregnant again. Barbara was nearly two and a half and Ben eighteen months old. The Leigh Smith itinerary continued relentlessly, meanwhile, taking in Montreal, Quebec, Dartmouth College, Boston, Rhode Island, Baltimore and Washington, DC, where the family came to a halt for the winter before returning north to New York City.

One of the trip's highlights was a visit to Niagara Falls: stupendous. But surely the novelty of America soon wore off for Anne? The whole enterprise must have been exhausting, both physically and emotionally. Travelling at home was a risky business in the late Georgian period; to travel abroad, especially for women and children, was reckless in the extreme. Her health was certainly affected. Benjamin notes that the 'Babies' suffered diarrhoea at one point, but never mentions Anne's growing discomfort as the date of their voyage home – and her third confinement – approached. Nor does he mention the new-colony idea again: Utopia was put on hold.

Barbara and Ben's sister Isabella (known as Bella) was born in Liverpool on 28 June 1830. The family arrived at the port on 10 May; Anne was obviously in no state to travel further, even as far as her own family in Derbyshire, relatively close by. When she and the children eventually returned south, the Pater gave up the lease on the Whatlington cottage and settled them into Brown's, an elegant farmhouse nearer to the small town of Robertsbridge, where a fourth child, Anne (Nannie), was born in 1831. He visited them frequently, dividing his time between Sussex and London, but they did not live together.

BARBARA REMEMBERED AN UNTROUBLED childhood, singing Sussex songs taught to her by the nurse Hannah (whom the Pater retained for Anne's sake) and learning to love the countryside. She kept some of the secrets of her early upbringing all her life, but it is obvious that she felt cherished by her parents, and by her beloved grandfather William. She adored the Pater, who taught her and the other children to ride, play charades, draw, and take nothing for granted. She witnessed his jubilation when the Great Reform Act was passed in 1832, partly drafted by her uncle John Bonham Carter, and the Slavery Abolition Act – the fruit of William's labours – the following year. Politics was a live subject in the Leigh Smith household.

Paradoxically, so was death. Infant mortality was high; it has been estimated that around one in three children born in the early nineteenth century died before their fifth birthday.[21] The Leigh Smiths did well, though Anne's confidence can hardly have been high when she fell pregnant yet again in 1832. A cholera pandemic had killed thousands on its inexorable westward progress from India; now it was doing its lethal work in London and beyond. It could strike people dead within hours. And few families were spared some sacrifice to the 'white plague' of consumption, or tuberculosis of the lungs, which might take years to claim its victims, but was usually fatal.

The Pater was well aware of the importance of good health. He and his nine siblings had all been vaccinated against smallpox when young: a newfangled idea still generally regarded at best as eccentric and, at worst, downright dangerous. When Anne began to show signs of TB, he moved her and the children – joined in the spring of 1833 by baby Willy – to a recently built and rather grand apartment on the seafront at Hastings, a few miles south of Robertsbridge. There was no known cure, but bracing fresh air and outdoor exercise were supposed to help. The first was plentiful in Hastings; the second, for the ailing mother of five young children, not so much. Still, she could gaze out of the window at the English Channel and watch the fishing boats as they came in to land their catches. The children were happy playing on the beach and running around, and the Pater was rarely far away. Nurse Hannah took care of them all.

Adversity often brings families together, but not in this case. Grandfather William never lost touch with the Pater and his children, and William Nightingale was supportive. His wife Fanny and her sister Patty, however, were relentless in their condemnation of the shameful Leigh Smiths. When news of the gravity of Anne's illness filtered through, they were not surprised. What else could she expect? The wages of sin, after all, is death.

Patty wrote a letter to Fanny about the situation at Hastings that is difficult to read, not just because of the lacy handwriting. News has recently broken of their brother Frederick, the one no one talks about. He has left England to join the army in India where – horror of horrors – he is apparently living with a woman who is not his wife, with a string of little bastards. Two black sheep in one family is a bit much, but at least Fred is far enough away to remain out of the public eye. It is unlikely any of their friends will hear about him. She implies that his is a weak character, beyond salvation. The case of the Pater, whom she calls Ben, is altogether different. He is a great man, who could have done – may yet do – great things, if only he can disentangle himself from his bizarre domestic situation.

Having discussed Fred, Patty moves on.

And now about Ben – I expect he will act without much plan & without telling me any more about it – But if the mother there [in Hastings] dies, then I think the children <u>might</u> be placed in a better situation than Fred's – & in one less injurious to the next generation of this family – & this must be thought of, because nobody can cast off Ben, and Ben will never cast off his children – He would indeed be a villain if he could – after living with them & for them exclusively to a degree no people in the world have

opportunity for till the eldest is now 7 or 8 years old [Bar-
bara was six] – but think of the actual state of the case. The
Mother [Anne] <u>I am told</u> is a married woman – At least
someone used to come after her & <u>it is supposed</u> in order
to be paid off – the Sister vulgar and cunning & dependent
even for her Clothes, then <u>lived</u> with them!

Who Anne's wronged husband is meant to be, I have no idea.
There is no evidence that he ever existed. He is either a malicious
fabrication, or a member of Anne's family mistaken for a black-
mailer; perhaps her unimpeachable London cousin Jo Gratton.
Anne's sister was Dolly Longden, a much-loved figure who
loomed large in the lives of all the Leigh Smith children.

The Upper nurse has had 3 natural children [that's Hannah
Walker, who devoted her life to the Pater's sons and daughters. There is no record that she had any of her own] – Judge
of the thrall & the mire in which Ben has lived & into
which the children will sink deeper if he does not take
some decided steps of separation from the relations & old
servants when the Mother is dead – indeed whether she
dies or not, I expect to find he is gone abroad – in order
to educate & separate the children from this mess, altho' to
hear him speak no one would think there was <u>anything to
detach them from</u>, except the Sussex dialect – The bent of
his thoughts, <u>he wd else be too miserable</u>, seems to be to
the innocency of the life he has led . . . I cannot think that
with all his sophistry – even he, can look back thro' the
last 25 years, & consent to see his sons & daughters do
likewise – with all the hideous environment of other sins
& crimes that accompany this Way of going on [she's
becoming incoherent now] . . . It would become too bad
to last. He will give them all his money unless he marries I
don't doubt & provide well for them if he does marry &

has another family – but this money & the stile they have lived in (travelling with 2 or 3 carriages & 6 or 7 servants gamekeepers & hounds – & with everything that is called handsome about them at Brighton [she means Hastings]) joined to the morals around them will be ruin, the lowest & most degrading, if they are put among low people. I see nothing for it but for him to take them to some part of Switzerland & isolate them among honest pious educated instructors to give them new habits & above all to save them from the cruelty of cutting those whom they have been taught to love.[22]

In other words, Ben's children have tainted blood. The only chance of hiding this dreadful truth is to isolate them from their present friends and the Longden family, sanitize them and then return them to polite society as redacted individuals, with a made-up history, no memory of their mother and a bland smile for all occasions. The glimpse Patty gives of the Pater's boundless love for his family is touching, but one cannot imagine either he or his children ever wanting to speak to Patty or Fanny again, had they read this letter.

'The mother' grew steadily worse. In November 1833, she and the family tracked even further south to the resort of Ryde on the Isle of Wight. There she was wheeled through the winter and following spring in an invalid chair along the promenade and the newly opened pier, becoming steadily weaker, until, on 30 August 1834, she died. She was a worn-out woman of thirty-two.

Anne was buried at St Edmund's Church at Wootton, just outside Ryde. It is a peaceful, pretty medieval church; her grave is in a prime position, nestling against the east wall, a few feet away from the altar inside. It has three Italianate arches in bas-relief, and a long, bevelled gravestone. The two outer arches frame long inscriptions which, sadly, like the one at Alfreton, have crumbled into illegibility.[23] The Pater once wrote of Anne as the least selfish person he ever knew; no doubt her memorial was along those lines. A simple white urn set into the central arch is inscribed with her name – only it is not really her name at all: Anne Smith.

Was that the Pater's last gift? Posthumous respectability? If so, it came too late.

2

Planted in Sussex Soil

1834–1848

Dear Barbara, your cheerful spirit
Never needs a stick to stir it.[1]

PATTY WAS CONFIDENT THAT THE PATER WOULD TAKE HER advice and swiftly send his bastard brood abroad, now that Anne had accomplished the only graceful thing she ever did for the Smith family by dying. She assumed he would be glad to edit out this unfortunate episode in his life's story. So when he, the children and, worse still, their working-class nurse Hannah Walker returned to Brown's in September 1834 with no sign of leaving, Patty began to panic. She wrote to Fanny Nightingale again.

He appears to be entirely in the power of this old Nurse – won by her . . . attachment real or assumed for the deceased person [Patty still cannot bring herself to say Anne's name] . . . His judgement on this point seems quite decayed – Nothing for the present seems to touch him but marks of regard towards the deceased . . . It does but prove into what blindness he has fallen . . . He thinks that if everybody were as compassionate as Nightingale he might carry his points in England. In short he is quite tempest-tost.[2]

William Nightingale was one of the few members of the wider family who supported the Pater, in defiance of his wife Fanny. What his daughter Florence thought of her Leigh Smith cousins is something we shall return to; she played no direct part in Barbara's early childhood.

Pausing only to dip her pen, Patty continued her campaign against the status quo in October. If the Pater still refused to go abroad, she suggested that the unflappable Aunt Ju be drafted in to look after him. They could always take the children 'over the water' and out of the way. Without Ju's bracing influence, she warned Fanny, 'you may feel sure this Old Woman [nurse Hannah] will throw some new attraction in his way, & the last business will be worse than the first'.[3]

It would be easy to write Patty off as an interfering prude. Suggesting that the grief-stricken Pater would succumb to the charms of a 'new attraction' pimped by Hannah is outrageous. Surely that could never happen? But the idea about Aunt Ju was inspired and bore fruit. Julia Smith (1799–1883) was everyone's favourite. She was in her mid-thirties when Anne died, petite, vivacious, mercurial but full of common sense. Florence Nightingale called her 'tempestuous Ju . . . enough to set a whole family by the ears'.[4] Most important of all, she was warm and loving. She was at the centre of a progressive circle of friends and acquaintances inherited from her father William, including the mother of sociology, Harriet Martineau; Elizabeth Reid, who founded Bedford College in London; the polymath and artist Mary Somerville (once irresistibly described as 'Isaac Newton in a bodice'[5]); American suffragists Lucretia Mott and Elizabeth Cady Stanton; and the feminist pioneer Anna Jameson. A member of ladies' abolitionist and Anti-Corn Law committees, Ju was present at the first World Anti-Slavery Convention in London in 1840 – or would have been, had the organizers allowed the women delegates physically through the doors of the meeting hall. She was a mover and a shaker, but not an iconoclast like the Pater.

Despite her activism, Ju remained permanently on call for domestic duties. Whenever a brother, sister, nephew or niece needed looking after, she would be there. Whenever they did not, she bustled about visiting friends, canvassing for various causes or travelling through Britain and abroad. The Pater was her favourite brother. He was sixteen when she was born, and she idolized him. 'I was so very fond of him,' she remembered, that 'the touch of his little finger as I walked beside him was happiness.'[6]

It is rumoured that Patty was so fervidly snobbish that she slept with a copy of the Peerage under her pillow.[7] Ju was as open-minded as her sister was not. As well as her highbrow friends, she was particularly close to her former nanny, her laundry-maid, and the housekeeper from Little Parndon days. The last will and testament of one Elizabeth Blades, dated 10 December 1830, beautifully demonstrates the degree of affection in which Ju was held by all manner of people. Miss Blades was a housekeeper at 5 Blandford Square, another of the Pater's properties. Prudently, she managed to amass savings of over £75 during her working life. She disposed of this sum in legacies to her sister to buy mourning gowns for the family, and to fellow domestic staff in the Smiths' and their friends' households, including Fanny Nightingale's maid Frances Gale, and the novelist Mrs Gaskell's servant Mrs Wood. She also left £5 to Julia Smith. Ju is the first beneficiary mentioned in the will. There is a reminder in Elizabeth's untutored hand at the end of the document: her brother James can do what he likes if there is any money left over after the various dispositions, but whatever happens, Miss Smith must have her £5, at 'the first opportunity after my Decease'.[8]

Miss Smith did not need money. But I am sure she treasured that £5 as if it were £500. This was the sort of person the Pater was looking for to teach the children about life's priorities. So Ju joined the Leigh Smith team, with Hannah and a governess, Catherine Spooner. Miss Spooner was a linen-draper's daughter from north London, born in 1817. It is unclear how she came to the Pater's attention, but she stayed connected to his children for at least twenty years.

Intriguingly, an 1837 affidavit associated with Elizabeth Blades's will was witnessed in London with a signature looking very much like 'J. M. Longden'.[9] This gives hope that Anne's father was welcomed by the Pater as one of the family. His middle daughter Dorothy certainly was. Dolly Longden (1797–1868) lived with her well-to-do, unmarried cousin Jo Gratton in London. She was four years older than Anne; obviously educated and socially confident, which suggests Anne was similarly self-possessed. Like Ju – but without the family connections – Dolly had a keen interest in politics and an inexhaustible fund of energy. The Pater chose well: this was a formidable double act of aunts. On finally making the decision to stay in England and defy whatever opprobrium society (and Patty) threw at them, he planted five Scots pine trees in the grounds of Brown's, one for each of the children. Scots pines are noble trees; they grow lofty, straight and true.

In 1836 the Pater bought two houses in an ultra-fashionable development in Hastings, very close to where he had taken Anne in the middle stages of her illness. Numbers 8 and 9 Pelham Crescent stand next to the church of St Mary in the Castle, right in the centre of the crescent. They are graceful, five-storey townhouses with tall, balconied bay windows looking out to sea. Behind them, the cliffs rear up to Hastings Castle, and the shoreline is just across the road. Barbara loved Hastings all her life. Any sad associations with Anne were dispelled in the salt air, the shifting light and colours of the sea and sky, and the endless activity of the fishermen who sold – still sell – their fresh catches on the shingle. Ships came and went, sailing further along the coast, or over the horizon to who knows where. It is not too fanciful to suppose that Barbara found comfort in being where her mother had been and seeing what she would have seen.

When I was a little girl, my father built me a house in what (for

obvious reasons) we called the banana-sandwich tree. It was just a
couple of planks wedged across clefts in the trunk, but to me, it
seemed a miniature palace, entirely my own. More conventional
friends of mine had Wendy houses in the garden. The Leigh Smith
children enjoyed the same sort of thing, but on a different level. The
Pater designated one of the Pelham Crescent houses for grown-ups,
and the other just for them.

Were the Leigh Smith children spoiled? They were indulged,
certainly, but taught to acknowledge their good fortune. It is
hard to think of anyone with less of a sense of entitlement than
Barbara. In an age when wealthy little boys and girls were ideally
seen but not heard; when an iron-bosomed nanny reigned
supreme in the nursery and her charges barely recognized their
own parents; when cleanliness was positioned next to godliness
and raising one's voice was vulgar, the Leigh Smiths ran wild.
They were encouraged to chatter and argue (rather than bicker).
The Pater was as closely involved in their lives as possible, helping to dress his children, joining in with charades and games of
chess. They roamed the beaches, lanes and woods around
Hastings and their other Sussex homes[10] all day long, with dogs
and ponies, exploring, paddling, hop picking, fishing and collecting curiosities. A neighbour described the children as
buoyant, affectionate, amiable, and radiant with good health.[11]
So much for tainted blood: there was no indication – yet – that
the little Leigh Smiths had inherited either their mother's weak
lungs or moral frailty.

Buoyant, affectionate, amiable and radiant just about sums up
the young Barbara. She was considered a notable beauty in her
youth: tall, with bright blue eyes, rosy cheeks and sumptuous
red-gold hair, colouring she inherited from Grandfather William.
That hair was famous; it was her crowning glory. Slightly spooky
bracelets and brooches woven from it still exist; its lustre has
faded now, but its silken richness remains. Family tradition has it

that she was a bold and daring girl, quick-witted and never far from laughter. The Pater praised her 'cheerful spirit / [Which] Never needs a stick to stir it' (best pronounced 'stirrit'): it was a gift to them all.

I have made it my mission while researching this biography to find a photograph or painting of Barbara smiling. In real life, a smile was her default expression, but decorum – or boredom – uncharacteristically got the better of her in front of the camera or the easel. I suppose the long exposure required for a portrait in either medium didn't help: better a serious gaze than a rictus grin. The only exception is a self-portrait in a sketch she did of a minimalist family production of *Twelfth Night*. Her brother Ben is playing Malvolio, Bella is Olivia and Barbara is the cheerful servant Maria. She is kneeling at Olivia's feet, looking as though she is just about to corpse.[12]

Barbara's sketch of a family performance of Twelfth Night.

Home-loving as he was, the Pater did not abandon his political ambitions. Anne had been in her grave for just four months
when he stood as a candidate for his father William's old seat of
Norwich in December 1834. The press reported a speech by one
of his agents at the hustings:

> Gentlemen, if you search the whole of England through, I
> say it is impossible you could find so fit a man to whom
> your interests could be entrusted as my Hon. Friend ...
> Mr Benjamin Smith – one who has the integrity and abil-
> ity, and not only the virtue, but the disposition to serve his
> country with the same truth, and on the same high prin-
> ciples as did his respected father.[13]

Integrity? Virtue? The man had five illegitimate children at
home. He was not selected for Norwich on this occasion but
went on to represent the constituency for ten years. Did people
not realize that he and Anne were unmarried? If that is the case,
then what was the point? Political statements carry little weight
if no one hears them. There is only one feasible explanation of
the Pater's risky choice to live a double (and later a triple) life: he
enjoyed it. And he was charming enough to succeed: intelligent,
engaging and apparently entirely genuine in his determination
not to conform.

To some extent, he was a gentleman of his time. The Regency
period was studded with garish examples of masculine impropri-
ety; signals of privilege and power. High-profile male transgressors
were hardly considered transgressors at all, just grown-up scally-
wags with too much force of character to be contained by
convention.

The Pater lived at a time when Regency excess was beginning to give way to Victorian prurience. There was a little
neo-Gothic window of opportunity between the two extremes,
when immorality (for men) could still just about be taken for

eccentricity. A portrait from around this period projects him as a picture of respectability. His gaze is direct; he looks self-aware but kind. *I* would trust him. But the stigma of illegitimacy was more toxic to women than men (think of Mary Wollstonecraft, vilified for bearing an illegitimate child in 1794), and more damaging to his children's generation than his own. His decision not to wed Anne was at best unfortunate.

It had no impact upon his political career, however. In 1835, following that hiccup in Norwich the previous year, he was selected for and won a seat in William Smith's former battleground of Sudbury. As it had for his father, in May 1838 this Suffolk constituency proved a stepping stone to victory at Norwich. The Pater involved bright-eyed Barbara in his campaign; she was taken out canvassing at the age of ten, dressed in a frock and sash in the traditional Whig colours of buff and blue. This was before elections were relatively seemly, private affairs involving polling booths and secret ballots; the hustings were notoriously rowdy and often violent, and votes were only counted if shouted loudly enough, in public, for the teller to hear. Barbara enjoyed herself no end.

FAITHFUL WILLIAM NIGHTINGALE CONGRATULATED the Pater on winning Norwich. 'Long life to your Honor [*sic*],' he wrote, '& may you find the Norwich folk ready to fight for you to the last day of your political existence.'[14] The Pater's father William had died in 1835; no doubt he would have been delighted. Frances Smith was similarly pleased for her son, but apprehensive.

> The next thing I have to wish you is a good wife, now that you will be so much in Town (I trust for the remainder of your life) & must have your Children near you; & now that they are becoming old enough to require something better than common Governesses and servants what a

blessing it would be to them & to you to have such a
woman as Fanny Martin or Mrs Duckworth (Miss Benyon
as was) to take the care of them – without some such Friend
to whom they can look up in your frequent absences, one
upon whom you can continually depend, I do feel that
you have little chance of comfort from them as they grow
older. I know I am very impertinent to be thrusting my
advice upon you without being asked for it.[15]

The charms of Fanny Martin and Mrs Duckworth did not
prevail. The Pater kept hold of Catherine Spooner, the 'common
Governess', and Hannah the uncouth nurse. Aunts Ju and Dolly
were usually available when needed, and there was a perfect solu-
tion to the problem – if problem it be – of topping up the
children's education: they could go to the London school he had
been helping to run for the past twenty years.

Westminster Infants' School was founded in 1818 by a group
of moneyed abolitionists and social reformers including Henry
Brougham, who became Lord High Chancellor, and James Mill,
father of John Stuart. They were inspired by Robert Owen – the
same Robert Owen whose utopian dreams had prompted the
Pater's American expedition. The school Owen set up in his
New Lanark cotton-mills complex in Scotland was groundbreaking. It was not an entirely altruistic enterprise; to increase
his workforce, Owen realized that mothers needed to be relieved
of childcare. The resulting school was part workplace nursery,
part pedagogical experiment.

Owen had little time for books, and none at all for corporal
punishment. His philosophy, informed by the eighteenth-
century Swiss pioneer Johann Heinrich Pestalozzi, was all about
kindness, with plenty of play, music and physical exercise. School
should be fun. Girls and boys learned together, developing a
sense of responsibility to their community as they did so. Who
their parents were, and how much they earned, was irrelevant.

After a short period in premises that were too small, Westminster Infants' School opened in a purpose-built hall in Vincent Square in 1826. It is now one of the most desirable addresses in London, with an expanse of sheeny green grass at its centre; then, it was sandwiched between two prisons (Tothill Fields and Millbank), not far from the Smiths' huge Thames-side distillery and brewery. The Pater paid £1,000 for the building, which afforded him a say in its design. There was one large, light schoolroom, a bath-house and a playground. Around a hundred children paid a penny a week to attend, a sum matched, and more, by the Pater. For that, they were educated, fed, even washed if necessary, and their ragged clothes repaired.

A venture like that stood or fell on the charisma of its teacher. James Buchanan (1784–1857) was a former weaver from Edinburgh. He ran Owen's infant school before being headhunted by the Pater, who travelled to New Lanark to see him in action. The Pater was so impressed that he somehow lured Buchanan south of the border. No doubt money came into the equation; it usually did with the Pater. But Buchanan was not an acquisitive man. He was just as likely to have been attracted by the love of the job, and the challenge of bringing enlightenment to new communities. He had a genuine vocation.

Buchanan was an extraordinary creature. He was tiny, rather fey, and totally impractical, married to a good-hearted, hard-working housewife (according to Aunt Ju) who looked after the quotidian while he busied himself on a higher plane. Like his role model, the eighteenth-century theologian and mystic Emanuel Swedenborg, he maintained that childhood was a time of innocence, which must be carefully curated. Another more abstruse strand of the Swedenborgian philosophy assumed a direct connection between the material and spiritual worlds: a stone was a physical representation of truth, for example, while anything circular was a direct manifestation of harmony. The soul had its own anatomy, just like the body, and, to thrive, needed the sort of spiritual exercise and fresh air that comes of free-thinking, charity and optimism. What this boiled down to was a creed of respect for the natural world and for fellow humans, a thirst for spiritual development, and demonstrable love.

That was the theory. In practice, Buchanan simply enchanted his pupils. While his wife beavered away in the background, bathing them and cooking their meals, he trotted about like the Pied Piper, tootling his flute with a string of dancing infants in his wake. He boasted that he could keep any number of children amused for any length of time, with nothing more than a ball of string. There was no poring over books or learning by rote at Westminster Infants' School; instead, the classroom walls were papered with gorgeous Smith-commissioned murals of animals and other natural wonders. He composed rhymes for the children to chant, to teach them not just about facts, but life. Here is one about a cow, and what we like to think of as the modern concept of 'nose-to-tail' environmentalism.

> Come, children, listen to me now,
> And you shall hear about the cow.
> You'll find her useful, live or dead,
> Whether she's black or white or red.
> When milkmaids milk her morn or night,
> She gives us milk, so fresh and white,
> And this we little children think,
> Is very nice for us to drink.
> The milk we skim and shake in churns,
> And then it soon to butter turns.
> The curdled milk we press and squeeze,
> And so we make it into cheese.
> The skin, with lime and bark together,
> The tanner tans, and makes it leather,
> And without this, what should we do

For soles for every boot and shoe?
This is not all, as you will see:
Her flesh is food for you and me;
Her feet provide us glue and oil;
Her bones tend to improve the soil;
And last of all, if ta'en with care,
Her horns make combs to comb our hair.
And so we learn, thanks to our teachers,
That cows are very useful creatures.[16]

In 1826, the Pater temporarily seconded Buchanan to
Derbyshire, to run a charitable village school near Lea Hurst for
a while. That would explain the Pater's extra visits to the
Nightingales – the Longdens' neighbours – that year, resulting in
the birth of Barbara the following April. By then, Buchanan's
methods had proven too eccentric for Brougham, Mill and the
other co-founders of the Westminster school. They bailed out;
he was too much of 'a queer fish' for them. Unfazed, the Pater
took over entire financial responsibility for the school himself.

By the time the Leigh Smith children were old enough to go
to school, the Pater chose Buchanan as their teacher. Queer fish
or not, Barbara and the others loved him dearly. Not only did
they attend the school with the local 'ragamuffins' (compared
with whom they were unimaginably wealthy), but the Pater
appointed Buchanan as their private tutor for school holidays.
All five of them took advantage of his good nature, recalled
Barbara, but he never resisted or lost patience. 'We used to make
him carry us upstairs [at Pelham Crescent] & I believe if he were
in the house I never walked up three flights of stairs even when I
was nine years old unless I was frisky enough to run up.'[17] They
made him read aloud to them at mealtimes, so he had no time to
eat himself. Nurse Hannah objected, pleading him to leave the
little ones and come to dinner, but he always refused, as long as

they listened and learned from whatever story had been chosen that day.

Barbara's favourite tales were from *One Thousand and One Nights*, popularly known as the *Arabian Nights*.

> That story of Perizade the princess who did not mind the black stones when she was bent on getting the living water, the talking bird & the singing tree has made an impression on my whole life. Wasn't I glad she got to the top of the hill! Wasn't I glad she could do it though her brothers failed.[18]

Perizade rashly embarked on a competitive quest to find three wondrous, magical objects; she triumphed over the boys – despite her inferior gender – because she thought of practical solutions to the obstacles in her way. When the 'black stones' that were once dead men tried to trap her, she had the self-control to keep looking forward; never back. When screeching voices threatened to strike terror into her heart, she stuffed her ears with cotton. She rode her horse as well as any man, and climbed a mountain with courage and stamina to find the objects. And whenever she came upon anyone in her way, she was unfailingly polite, but utterly determined to succeed.

Meet Barbara Leigh Smith.

It comes as something of a shock to realize, on reading some of his letters, that Buchanan was no scholar. Perhaps that is what put off Brougham and his colleagues: a teacher who wrote about 'atendance' at 'Evning school', the importance of good 'humer', the uselessness of the 'multificcation table' and the kindness of the 'Nightengale' family, did not inspire confidence.[19] Barbara could never spell well either, and wasn't too hot on punctuation (the linguistic equivalent of wearing stays, as far as she was concerned). Her handwriting was the despair of her correspondents and this biographer – but what Buchanan taught her about how to live one's life, she never forgot. 'Oh,' she once wrote, 'that man had genius of a rare kind. My life was better for his life.'[20]

IN 1839, BUCHANAN LEFT Westminster Infants' School for New Zealand. He was appointed an educational adviser to the British colony, but never arrived. The attractions of Cape Town, where he paused en route, were too strong. His son William lived there already; Buchanan, his exhausted wife Isabella and their daughter Anne joined him, and the family settled there for the rest of their lives, entertained periodically by cheerful, ill-written letters from Barbara.

She was twelve in 1839. By now, both her grandfathers had died. She missed William, who passed away less than a year after her mother, and would no doubt have missed John Longden too had she known him. I hope she did know him. Governess Catherine Spooner was still part of the family but seems to have been engaged more as a companion – or babysitter – than a teacher. None of the children mention her much, though she does feature in Barbara's journal of a trip to Wales: 'It was excellent fun helping Miss Spooner across rivers and up hills and down hills and over walls and through hedges. How it did make me laugh to see her scrambling about!'[21] Barbara was rarely unkind. So what riled her about Catherine Spooner? Perhaps they were not kindred spirits. Miss Spooner might have been glad to relinquish this boisterous and unfashionably energetic family – but she stayed. The Pater had other duties in mind for her.

As they grew older, the children were educated more formally: the boys at Bruce Castle in Tottenham, north London, and the girls at an establishment close by in Upper Clapton, owned by the Misses Wood. Both were run by Dissenters but, even in progressive schools, boys got a better deal than girls. Bruce Castle taught young men to think for themselves, while Upper Clapton taught young women to be bored. The

Misses Wood were everything Buchanan was not. Pupils learned mechanically, without understanding gained through application or explanation. We have no definite dates, but Barbara does not appear to have stayed there longer than two or three years between 1838 and 1841.[22]

More tutors arrived in the holidays: a Mr Harry Porter for Latin and history, and Mr Willetts for horse riding, which was just as important. All the girls were encouraged to draw and paint, but Barbara excelled. Inspired by the masterpieces she remembered from her grandfather's house in Park Street, she filled sketchbooks with scenes from family holidays in Wales, the Lake District and Scotland.

This is the period in her life at which we begin to appreciate Barbara as a distinct individual, limned in correspondence with her two close friends Bessie Rayner Parkes (1829–1925) and Anna Mary Howitt (1824–84).

The Parkes family moved to London from Birmingham in 1833. Unitarian Joseph Parkes was a solicitor. His American-born wife Elizabeth had a solid political heritage, being the granddaughter of Joseph Priestley, a founding father of Unitarianism in England. Bessie was proud of her radical roots.

She and Barbara used to play together as children; Barbara was invited to Bessie's parties – there was a particularly splendid one at her family's house in Great Smith Street on the occasion of Queen Victoria's coronation in 1838 – but they did not become like sisters, as Bessie put it, until 1846. In the autumn of that year, Mrs Parkes, Bessie and her consumptive brother Priestley rented one of the Pater's houses in Pelham Crescent. They resorted to Hastings, just as the Pater had thirteen years previously, to exorcise the spectre of tuberculosis. Barbara was nineteen, Bessie seventeen. The age of majority then was twenty-one, so the girls were technically still children. Both were avid readers, and precociously enjoyed discussing their concept of social justice.

They were also naturally affectionate, delighted by one another's thoughts and company.

Anna Mary Howitt was to become the mildly famous daughter of famous parents: a professional painter and illustrator whose mother Mary and father William both earned their living, somewhat precariously, as popular writers, translators and journalists. Between them they produced scores of publications; they were minor celebrities in literary circles, but never made big money. In 1840 the family moved to Germany for three years. Their sons would be better and more cheaply educated there, they reckoned; Anna Mary, who had a clear talent for art, could learn from some of the best, and Mary and William hoped to pick up interesting copy and commissions. Mary was a remarkable linguist, translating the modern novels of Fredrika Bremer from the original Swedish and Hans Christian Andersen's fairy tales from Danish, both of which languages she learned by herself.

Apparently, anyone who was anyone visited Hastings, whether or not they happened to be ill. It was an authentic alternative to Brighton, especially when the railway from London arrived in 1846: stylish without being brash. The Howitts headed there on their return to England in 1845, and soon came across the charismatic Leigh Smiths. Anna Mary was the opposite of Barbara in so many ways: anxious, unworldly, quiet and wan (a complexion set off disastrously by her mother's insistence on her wearing scarlet). Nevertheless, the two young women became devoted to one another. At one stage, Barbara declared herself in love with Anna Mary.

A sure measure of the level of intimacy in any friendship between unrelated women in the mid nineteenth century was the time it took for each to use the other's Christian name. In most cases, that day never came. When Anna Mary writes to Barbara in January 1846, trying to persuade her to join an art class in London, she addresses her as Miss Smith. They have only known one another for a few months. In an undated letter a short time later, after Barbara has sent some partridges to the Howitts to help out with the family budget, and Anna Mary has spent a dazzling week staying with the Leigh Smiths, Miss Howitt extends the all-important invitation, or 'proposal', an invitation to dispense with her surname, which Barbara accepts. She lends Anna Mary her cherished copy of *One Thousand and One Nights*; they discuss Tennyson's newly published poem *The Princess*. The heroine, Princess Ida, reminds Anna Mary of Barbara: a prescient observation, given that Ida founds a college for women, full of 'sweet girl-graduates in their golden hair'. 'I do indeed feel a very, very great happiness to know you,' writes Anna Mary, 'and still a greater one to believe you love me.'[23]

The Parkeses were perhaps less thrilling than the Howitts, but what Bessie lacked in glamour she made up for in enthusiasm, a quality Barbara always rated highly. An early letter from Bessie, written in 1847, sets the tone of their friendship. It is a poem, a sprightly parody of Alexander Pope and his prejudiced attitude to women.

> I grant the present age may find a sample
> To prove of all his censures an example,
> Wherein high life the Daughter of a house
> With misdirected zeal ensnared a spouse
> And then employs that precious time her morning
> Between gay worsted work and gay adorning [. . .]
> 'Tis a one sided picture; earth has shown
> We have <u>some</u> brains among our Sex, our own.
> Some kindly woman heart, some female mind
> To swell the chorus which uplifts mankind [. . .]
> Who strong and earnest, good and gentle too,
> Would both by law and reason give us scope
> To fine for libel Alexander Pope.[24]

Years later, Bessie recalled Barbara during the late 1840s as radiant, ardent, 'bright with the light of dawn'.[25] Bessie was the one to whom Barbara told her secrets. Barbara confessed to her, early in their relationship, that though Aunt Patty was no doubt an excellent person, she was not Barbara's cup of tea, or 'not fitted' to her 'individually', as Barbara put it with unwonted tact. A mild enough secret to modern ears, but then, family loyalty was paramount and aunts were supposed to be pathologically irreproachable. In February 1847, Bessie shared a longing to earn her own living: a subversive ambition at the time for a solvent, upper-middle-class woman.

> I should not mind losing caste at all. First all the worthless friends would be horrified and leave and the true remain. What a <u>Sieve</u> such a step would be. Of course one must be a woman grown to do such a thing [she is seventeen], but it is feasible ... There would be many hours in the evening and early morning to read and write you know. Now you might perhaps paint for a livelihood but writing tho' it may be as effectual for a purpose and aim is a very bad <u>business</u>.
>
> What [a] pity Englishwomen do nothing but be governesses [this was just before *Jane Eyre* was published] or milliners; I mean the tolerably educated: milliners![26]

Did Barbara respond by explaining about her mother? There is a pause in the surviving correspondence for a few months; some have attributed that to Barbara's indignation at Bessie's casual ridicule of her mother's craft. I suspect it has more to do with censorship. I think Barbara told Bessie about Anne and the Pater after receiving Bessie's letter, and – understandably – asked for the evidence to be destroyed, out of respect to Anne as much as for her own sake. There are far fewer letters in the world from

Barbara to others than vice versa; she was a famously poor correspondent, but she was also a cautious one, anxious not to leave comments for judgemental readers to misconstrue. 'Burn this,' she would scrawl at the top of what appear to be quite inoffensive letters. However, she was sure enough of Bessie's integrity and tolerance to risk indiscretion, and it must have been a considerable relief to share the secret at last. Bessie was a rational young woman. Her parents' marriage was not an idyllic one. Joseph Parkes is known to have been unfaithful to his wife;[27] perhaps she traded that mortifying confidence in return for Barbara's.

When Barbara herself learned the truth, and when the Leigh Smiths' illegitimacy became common knowledge, we shall never know. An early biographer claimed that she was seventeen, but offers no evidence.[28] George Eliot, who became one of Barbara's closest friends, famously described the family in 1852 as 'tabooed'.[29] In 1860 the novelist Elizabeth Gaskell wrote about meeting Barbara for the first time. 'She is – I think in consequence of her birth, a strong fighter against the established opinion of the world – which always goes against my – what shall I call it? – taste ... but I cannot help admiring her noble bravery, and respecting [her] – whilst I don't personally like her.'[30]

The secret of her birth should have been Barbara's gift to bestow on chosen friends. Instead, hardly surprisingly, it followed her through life like a grotesque familiar; ignored by some, while others recoiled in disgust. Because of her strength of character, most who met Barbara fell into the former category. It is impossible to overestimate what an achievement this was on Barbara's part.

Both Anna Mary and Bessie shared Barbara's growing interest in human and civil rights. The Pater, supported by aunts Ju and Dolly, encouraged the children to look about them and call out injustice when they saw it. That is something they also learned from James Buchanan, who, according to Barbara, was 'never ashamed to stop people in the streets and exhort them if he thought they were doing anything wrong . . . and used to lecture my father considerably'.[31]

On a family expedition to Ireland in 1845, Barbara was appalled to see the effects of potato blight. Around a million people died directly or indirectly from lack of food; another million were forced to leave home to search for a living else-where. The entire population of Ireland at the beginning of the famine was 8.5 million; by the end, it had diminished by almost one-quarter.

The Irish, like any weakened people, were easily exploited. The writer Sarah Mytton Maury, who left Britain aboard an emigrant ship for America, witnessed a heartbreaking incident in 1848.[32] An Irishwoman had been too late to board the ship with everyone else and had tried to find a boat to take her alongside. It was only a short distance, but the ferrymen demanded three shil-lings for carrying herself and the precious sack of potatoes that represented her entire capital for investment in a new life. She possessed only a few halfpence; when she offered these, they laughed in her face and rowed off with the potatoes.

Because of the British government's controversial Corn Laws imposing heavy tariffs on imported grain, the Irish could not afford wheat, oats or barley to plant in place of potatoes. The injustice angered Barbara – just as the slave trade had angered her grandfather. As an impotent nineteen-year-old young lady, she expressed that anger in the only way she could think of. While the Pater made his last speeches in Parliament (he stood down in 1847) and Aunt Ju organized meetings of the Ladies' Anti-Corn Law League, Barbara painted a picture. It is deeply impressive: an intense narrative in opaque watercolour captioned *Ireland 1846*.[33] The sunset filling much of the image is tinted with the fires of hell; a ruined monastery rises in the distance (no succour from religion there); a derelict cottage stands without its thatch in the middle ground, and a lone woman weeps in front of it by a bleak and sterile stretch of water. Partly erased is the painting's original title: 'hungery [*sic*]'.

Barbara recognized that what was happening in Ireland was devastating; not just politically, but at the most basic human level. Ever afterwards, she did what she could to draw attention to the effects of political decisions on those who had no power; on *consequences*. Activism also informed her personal relationships: if she could improve others' lives collectively by changing the system, she would; if she could do it individually by raising someone's spirits, she would gladly do that too.

3

Ye Newe Generation

1848–1851

A free-minded Albion's daughter.[1]

ON 10 OCTOBER 1848, BARBARA WROTE A LETTER TO James Buchanan in South Africa. It is full of family news. Her sister Bella – the next one down after Barbara and Ben – is making a purse, which promises well. It already looks very pretty. Anne, known as Nannie, is copying a painting of the Pater and little brother Willy playing chess, which hangs in the dining room at Pelham Crescent. Nannie is shaping up to be a good artist. Both purse and picture will be sent to the Buchanans as soon as they have been completed.

The Pater is well and cheerful, except when he reads the newspapers. Ben has just gone up to Cambridge, where he hopes to distinguish himself in mathematics. 'Bella is a beauty, and as good as beautiful.' She regularly plays chess with the Pater, while Nannie practises her drawing and the piano. Willy is a bright and merry soul who loves shooting and riding, like his father. He is a handsome lad, 'the life of the house'. During the week he goes to the same boarding school that Ben has just left, at Brede, within sight of the family seat, Crowham Manor; he comes home to Hastings at weekends, though, and is looking forward to Christmas, when he will start attending the new Royal Agricultural College at Cirencester (the Pater had shares in the

college, which opened in 1845). Aunt Patty is not here at present:
she is at Blandford Square (which implies something of a rapprochement between the Leigh Smiths and their fiercest family
critic), planning a winter excursion to the Welsh resort of Tenby.
All is well.[2]

It sounds as though Barbara is in a Jane Austen novel. This
letter served its purpose, however, in implying to her beloved
former mentor that the family was behaving as he would hope,
in a perfectly respectable, amiable manner. Goodness knows, the
Leigh Smith children were used to presenting an acceptable face
to the world in defiance of inconvenient truths.

In reality, 1848 was a remarkably turbulent year. The Smith
clan was still recovering its pride and finances after a catastrophe
on the river Thames in the summer of 1847, involving the Pater's
brother Octavius (Uncle Oc). There was a fatal accident aboard
the *Cricket*, one of the 'halfpenny steamship' fleet of which he
was a proprietor. The *Cricket* and her sister ships were essentially
commuter vessels plying a shuttle service between the Adelphi,
near Charing Cross, and London Bridge. On Friday 27 August at
9.30 a.m., with about 150 passengers aboard, she ran aground at
low water. When the engineer tried to power her free, her boiler
exploded. Some of the passengers leapt into the mud to escape
the deluge of boiling water, steam and shrapnel; others were
flung into the air by the force of the blast. Six people died and
scores were injured.

At the inquest, it emerged that the *Cricket* had recently been
fitted with new engines, patented by Oc, which were said to save
a ton of coal a day. Unfortunately, the ship's engineer had tied
the engines' safety valves down, to increase speed. The resulting
pressure caused the disaster, intensified by the extra power
needed to shift the vessel off the mud bank.

This was a terrible experience for all concerned, but the
Smiths were further distressed by questions raised during the
subsequent investigation. Did Oc know the valves were fastened

shut? He insisted upon his ignorance, but evidence was given that he used the steamer service two or three times a day on his way to and from his distillery at Thames Bank, and he was known to be hands-on, having a keen interest in engineering. How could he have missed the fact that his smart new engines had been tampered with? Well, offered Oc rather weakly, he did lose the sight in one eye the previous year . . .[3] Arguably, had he known the dangers, would he have been such a frequent passenger himself?

The judiciary was unsympathetic. At the end of September, the *Cricket*'s engineer was charged with manslaughter. Oc, as proprietor, was censured for 'shamefully neglectful' conduct in silencing and suspending a stoker who had recently reported the engineer for his dangerous habit of securing the valves. What is more, it was whispered that 'several of the jury were disposed to pronounce a more severe expression of their opinion with regard to Mr Smith than that which was eventually adopted in their verdict'.[4] In other words, there was a lingering suggestion that Oc had made use of some friends in high places.

In February 1848, one of the *Cricket*'s casualties took Oc to court for compensation. The plaintiff, Alphonzo Redgrave, was described in press reports as 'a child . . . who would probably be a cripple for life'[5] (he was thirteen at the time of the explosion); Oc was identified as the 'gentleman of fortune' whose gross negligence in failing to suspend his engineer had resulted in avoidable death and destruction.

Redgrave sued for £500; in the end, Oc was fined £200 – some £16,000 today. He also paid out undisclosed sums to others affected by the accident; readily, it appears, and with remorse. There was wide coverage of the disaster and the following litigation, much of it debating the embarrassing question of whether Mr Octavius Smith was, indeed, a gentleman. This shook his family and shocked his friends. But his reputation, and his pocket, survived intact. He was genuinely likeable, as were so many of the multi-faceted Smiths.

No doubt the Pater's gloom on reading the papers was partly due to the *Cricket* affair. But what was happening in Europe also worried him. It worried all politically aware families. When France sneezes, commented the Austrian statesman Metternich in 1848, the rest of Europe catches a cold. France did indeed 'sneeze' when a republic was declared in Paris in February; this triggered the rise of populism in Germany, and anti-government revolutions in Vienna, Milan, Prague, Dalmatia, Transylvania, Budapest and Venice. In France, 20,000 people died before the Second Republic's president was elected in December: Louis-Napoléon Bonaparte, later to become Emperor Napoleon III. Many feared the British might also turn against their leaders, especially when riots broke out in Glasgow in the spring, and demonstrations by working-class protesters such as the Chartists grew in number and profile throughout the year.

The Pater was not in government any more; all he could do to show solidarity with those he saw as politically oppressed was to support them on a personal level and welcome them into his home. It is intriguing to think that, had circumstances been different, he might also have welcomed an exiled comrade of the famous French Republican Louis Blanc (a friend of the Pater's) by the name of Eugène Bodichon. But Bodichon had travelled south to Algeria during the unquiet 1830s and would not play his part in Barbara's story for another eight years.

Barbara was as disturbed as her father by the news from the continent. She wrote a bitter poem about the hypocrisy of those who called for peace in Europe at any cost. 'The Question' was published in the leading radical periodical *The Examiner*, signed simply 'B.L.S.'. To quote it all would be too much — it is strong stuff — but a few lines give the gist.

> This is the Question, — Body's Peace, or Soul's?
> Who cares for quiet walks thro' street and road,
> For so-called law, and order, quietness —

Quiet to eat in, drink in, sleep in —
If the mind's torn with wrong and inward war?
Battles that rage within, are they not real?
Despots make very quiet, peaceful places!
They sweep away all agitating things:
They love to see their people eat and drink:
They make them peaceful [...]
Is this a peace we love? Yes! If we're brutes:
No! if our souls are mightier than flesh.[6]

Barbara was no poet (she knew it, and soon gave up), but the passion behind the verse is undeniable.

Closer to home, Barbara was forced to confront the Pater's mortality: a sobering prospect. She and Miss Spooner were asked to witness a codicil to his will in November. Neither of them read what it was they were witnessing; they simply signed their names, and then tried to forget about it. Besides, one of them already knew what the codicil was about. When the other found out, she would be devastated. We shall come to that.

Even though Barbara's friends were constantly celebrating her robust health and spirits, she was troubled in her early twenties by eye problems, which she feared might blind her. It is not clear what caused the ophthalmia, or inflammation (if that is what it was), but it appears to have been improved by the loan of some extraordinary blue-lensed glasses by Anna Mary Howitt, who wrote to Barbara soon after sending them.

Dearest, do not trouble yourself about keeping my spectacles! I am so happy to believe they may be of service to you — Mamma possesses two pair [sic] — one violet coloured pair I have been wearing today and [in] spite of the hot, glaring sun have believed it cool, every object being soft and cool to my eyes — I have looked a great object but have felt very comfortable.[7]

Barbara must also have looked 'a great object' with her glowing hair loose or casually braided around a velvet band; her voluminous gowns, sometimes in plain jewel colours, sometimes jauntily striped; her favourite 'Balmoral' walking boots with coloured laces; and her little round shades. Her voice was low and sweet but rarely, I suspect, demure; her frame was still 'buoyant' and her manner disarmingly direct. Once encountered, this imposing young woman was unlikely to be forgotten.

EIGHTEEN FORTY-EIGHT WAS ALSO memorable for being the year that Barbara officially reached adulthood. She turned twenty-one in April. We should bear in mind what was expected of a typical 21-year-old woman of fortune (like Barbara) and good breeding (unlike her) at the time. Having finished her education, parasitized from a governess not much older than she was, our stereotype heroine would be armed with all the necessary accomplishments to face one of two destinies. Able to draw, sew, sing, play an easy sonata on the piano, write legible letters, make unexceptional conversation, smile prettily and sit still while she was corseted and coiffed by her maid, she would either be launched on to the marriage market or – if success seemed unlikely – reclaimed by her family for domestic and charitable duties at home.

One of the best ways to gauge the expectation of women in any era is to look at contemporary instruction books. They tell the reader everything society thinks she should know. In her manual subtitled 'The Art of Social and Domestic Life', Mrs Mary Holland gives us a dizzying array of lifestyle tips for the early Victorian period, directed at young ladies ostensibly like Barbara. A quick trawl through the index reveals articles – among hundreds – on, for example, the best method of preventing hysterics; how to avoid fatal accidents in open carriages; how to dye hair a lustrous deep brown; how to remove stains from

mourning dresses; and how (somewhat alarmingly) to camou-
flage a black eye.[8] The manual also explains how to recognize the
symptoms of drowning, atrophy or gout, and how 'to stop the
Rapidity of Flames when the Female Dress happens accidentally
to take Fire' (wrap yourself in green baize – or, at a pinch, 'a
man's coat will always be useful, and the first man that arrives
ought to supply it').[9]

If a suitable husband was procured, commentators advised
that it was a wife's obligation to look decorative for him.
Whatever the cost to her comfort, the expression of gratification
on her husband's face would make it all worthwhile – as this
young wife disturbingly explained:

> I went and ordered a pair of stays, made very strong and
> filled with stiff bone, measuring only fourteen inches
> round the waist. These, with the assistance of my maid, I
> put on, and managed to lace my waist to eighteen inches.
> At night I slept in my corset without loos[en]ing the lace
> in the least. The next day my maid got my waist to seven-
> teen inches, and so on, an inch every day, until she got
> them to meet. I wore them regularly without ever taking
> them off, having them tightened afresh every day, as the
> laces might stretch a little. They did not open in front, so
> that I could not undo them if I had wanted. For the first
> few days, the pain was very great but as soon as the stays
> were laced close, and I had worn them so for a few days, I
> began to care nothing about it, and in a month or so I
> would not have taken them off on any account. For I quite
> enjoyed the sensation, and when I let my husband see me
> in a dress to fit I was amply repaid for my trouble.[10]

As the nineteenth century progressed, with more and more
British men venturing out into the Empire, there was a surplus
of spinsters in Britain. If no one eligible turned up, nice young

ladies were expected to stay at home looking after needy family members and neighbours – a little like aunts Ju and Dolly, but without the strong opinions. Barbara's cousin Florence Nightingale screamed silently as she sat in the family drawing room evening after evening, waiting for the clock's hour hand to reach ten so she could go to bed. She had the energy and intellect to meet the world on her own terms and improve life for herself and others, yet was condemned by custom to faff her early life away in trivia and boredom. Until she, Barbara and their pioneering friends proved otherwise, women were considered by many to be too nervy, undisciplined, ill-educated and vapid to contribute anything of solid value to society. The Victorian journalist Walter Bagehot reckoned things might change in about two thousand years, but until then 'women will only flirt with men, and quarrel with one another'.[11]

Received wisdom suggested that a woman should be kept institutionally naive, because knowledge of sin to a feeble mind – and all female minds were essentially feeble – was as damaging as sin itself, and liable to plunge her into lunacy. Innocence was an asset, as was beauty, because both brought out the best in men. 'Beauty is to a woman what poetry is to a language . . .' wrote another journalist in 1833, 'for there never yet existed a female possessed of personal loveliness who was not only poetical in herself but the cause of poetry in others.'[12] Ladies were born to be passive.

Although this narrative played throughout the span of Barbara's life, it did not go unchallenged. William Smith's friend Mary Wollstonecraft wrote about the importance of educating daughters and the rights of women as early as 1787. Aunt Ju's – and later Barbara's – friend Anna Jameson made her living as a professional travel writer and essayist who tried to explain to her Victorian readers the injustice of denying middle-class women the chance to earn and spend (or save) their own money. Elizabeth Reid, another friend of Ju's, remarkably managed to garner enough financial and moral support to build a living monument to early feminism in the form of Bedford College, London, in 1849. And the Pater gave his eldest daughter complete financial independence on her twenty-first birthday.

Had the man lost his mind? He was settling a portfolio of investments worth £300 annually (something like £25,000 today, which by 1860 was yielding three times that amount)[13] on a *woman*? Close family members – I suspect Patty was among them – thought the Pater was, indeed, crazy, and forecast general ruination for everyone involved. But the Pater trusted Barbara; presumably he had been educating her and all the Leigh Smith children, who each received the same settlement at twenty-one, boys and girls, in the principles of fair-trade economics. Barbara always maintained that money was a power to do good. The possession of it was not a mark of superiority, but of the potential for generosity. While most middle-class young women – and even not so young women, like 28-year-old Florence – were infantilized by having to ask for pocket money from their fathers or, even worse, their brothers, Barbara strode, chin high, into adulthood: different, and fully in charge. 'I do think you are an unusually happy person in outward things,' her friend Bessie Parkes told her in 1849, 'but half your happiness lies in the tastes your father has promoted.'[14] She might not have been our typical young lady of good breeding, but she had weapons in her arsenal to compensate.

There are other possible interpretations of the Pater's readiness to hand over capital to his adult children. As illegitimate offspring, they had no legal right to inherit automatically, so it could be argued that this decision was a pragmatic way of making sure they were provided for. But he had made a will, so there was no need to worry: as named legatees, they would receive whatever he wished them to receive on his death. Perhaps he felt guilty at depriving them of legitimacy, and this bonus on reaching their majority was a consolation prize. Again, this seems unlikely. The

Pater was not an apologetic man. I cannot help but admire his confidence in his children, especially his daughters, in conferring such a responsibility on them. It was a risky thing to do: they might squander their money, or be preyed upon by unscrupulous suitors or opportunists. This was the Pater's leap of faith.

I closed the first chapter of this biography passive-aggressively angry with the Pater for the way he treated Anne and, by extension, their children. Now he is bidding for heroism. What can you do?

LET HIM BASK IN his glory.

> Men of England! Look at your poor girls, many of them fading around you, dropping off in consumption or decline; or, what is worse, degenerating to sour old maids, envious backbiting, wretched because life is a desert to them; or, what is worst of all, reduced to strive by scarce modest coquetry and debasing artifice, to gain that position and consideration by marriage, which to celibacy is denied. Fathers! Cannot you alter these things?[15]

This passage is from Charlotte Brontë's novel *Shirley*, published in 1849. Barbara's father was already doing what he could to save his daughters from dependence, and his sons from languishing on the lower rungs of whatever ladder they chose to climb in life. He was in so many ways ahead of his time.

It is interesting that Brontë implies a direct link between consumption and languor. Tuberculosis devastated her own family. This deadly infection loomed like an avenging angel over Bessie Parkes's life – her brother Priestley died at the age of twenty-five, despite the blandishments of the Hastings climate – and, in time, over Barbara's. Barbara used to describe her religion as 'sanitarian' rather than Unitarian, and was vocal about the benefits of 'largeness', or unrestricted physical and mental exercise. Like Charlotte (her favourite author at the time), she considered freedom of thought a prophylactic against diseases not only of the body politic, but the corporeal body too.

Some of her earliest correspondence with Bessie and Anna Mary Howitt was about the fear of ill-health and death. This fear was rational, not sentimental. They also spent pages and hours discussing the nobility of usefulness, should they be spared. 'I have a great deal to say to you about <u>work</u>, & <u>life</u>,' Barbara scribbled to Bessie, 'and the necessity of your finding early on a strain of action . . . [W]hat is so sad, so utterly [depressing], as a wasted life, and how common. I believe there are thousands who like you & I <u>intend doing</u> – <u>intend working</u> – but live and die only intending.'[16] Addressing each other as 'Frater' or 'Fellow', they pondered whether it might be possible to combine financial self-sufficiency with a family, and why good governesses, who were really teachers, were paid and therefore valued so very little.

Why should two comfortably off young women, with advantages few could even dream of, worry themselves about work–life balance and the gender pay gap? A happy accident of time, place and personality was responsible for Barbara and her friends' pioneering first-wave feminism. Women like Wollstonecraft, the seventeenth-century educationalist Bathsua Makin and essayist Mary Astell and, more recently, social commentators and reformers Harriet Martineau and Anna Jameson, all wrote about legal and moral injustices to women; their words flared brightly like fireworks in the night sky, but not in any coherent sequence. Caroline Norton's campaign to reform laws governing infant custody and divorce was ultimately constructive, as we shall see, but distractingly personal. More measured voices, like Sarah Mytton Maury's and Clementia Taylor's, quietly raised public consciousness of the rights of women, while the Brontës and the Unitarian Elizabeth Gaskell wrote about heroines who were strong, wronged or both.

All of these women asked questions of a society – functioning under a female monarch – in which women were kept institutionally naive and controlled by low expectation. Barbara, with her radical, dissenting heritage, her clear-sightedness, her energy and optimism, was uniquely positioned to suggest constructive answers. The later feminist movement's best-known motto, 'deeds, not words', was arguably first realized by her. Neither she nor her friends were content to commentate on the action, like the chorus in a male drama about power, strategy and public achievement. They planned to direct their own stories, centre-stage, and inspire other women to do the same.

It was essential, they decided, to find a career. Inherited wealth was undeniably useful, a privilege, but the most valuable currency in life was *earned*. A career brought a man dignity and respect; why not a woman, too, with the added benefit to society and her family of rendering her financially independent? Of course, being financially independent was not much use when a wife lost control of her money and legal identity after marriage, so something would have to be done there, but one thing at a time.

Anna Mary had a role model for a professional woman in her mother Mary, who contributed as much to the Howitts' budget as her husband William, if not more. Bessie's family friends included dyed-in-the-wool Unitarians whose philosophy of reason and tolerance embraced sexual equality (up to a point). They were fine mentors. Barbara, Anna Mary and Bessie, with several of their circle, were members of what Barbara called 'ye newe generation' of radical stock whose concept of human rights was less patriarchal and more meritocratic than their grandparents'. They were proto-socialists, anxious to cooperate in fashioning a new, more just society; idealists (in their youth) and eager to set in motion the alteration of things that Charlotte Brontë so desperately called for in *Shirley*.

What set Barbara apart from her new-generation peers was

her family. The Smiths were merchants as well as philosophers; the Longdens were artisans. Both strands of her family were doers, and so was she. She reminds me of her contemporary Mary Seacole. Mary was the illegitimate daughter of a Jamaican 'doctress' and a Scottish soldier. Again, she honoured both, feeling a kind of liberty in being undefined by the expectations of either her African or her northern European heritage. She found freedom in being an outsider, albeit tempered by the prejudice of her peers, and pride in being useful. 'All my life long I have followed the impulse which led me to be up and doing,' she insisted.[17]

So it was with Barbara: because she did not truly belong in working-class Alfreton or in the drawing rooms of polite society, she created a place of her own. Not a physical place – she lived in family homes until she married, despite her financial independence – but a personal space. She had a strong sense of identity and set her own precedent. This made her 'unhampered', as Bessie enviously put it. A *feme sole*.

Thus armed with the funds to help her generate her own money, like-minded friends, a supportive family and a positive, gregarious nature, Barbara embarked on adult life with a mission. Channelling the social conscience of Grandfather William, the practicality of Grandfather John, the intellectual curiosity of the Pater, and the energy of aunts Ju and Dolly, she was determined to honour Anne's short span on earth by empowering women to open doors locked against them for generations by a jealous and unimaginative Establishment.

To return to the question of a career: what should they *do*, these three female musketeers? Anna Mary worried, at this stage, that she was not entirely normal. She was surely too ambitious to be truly feminine. 'I felt quite angry at being a woman, it seemed to me <u>such a mistake</u>.'[18] Bessie agreed. Women's lives were circumscribed, trivialized. 'How little one can do in a day,' she complained. 'It is very provoking.'[19] Barbara, meanwhile, tended not to waste time in frustration. She was too busy planning an ideal future in which Anna Mary would be an artist and illustrator, Bessie a poet and essayist, and Barbara herself a painter. They would each earn their own living and spend any spare time and money changing the world.

But before all that, they must get themselves properly trained: knowledge itself is power. Bessie had gone to boarding school and scrimped a hand-me-down education from her brother Priestley until he died in 1850. Even so, she fretted that her intellect was undisciplined; that her thoughts incoherently 'dropped about', as she put it. It is obvious from her correspondence that she had an appetite for learning.

Barbara had stashed away whatever James Buchanan taught her, with the barren fruits of her year or two with the Misses Wood in Clapton, and had a taste for debate common to political families. She read widely; in fact her first published work was a letter to the *Birmingham Journal* printed in May 1848 – a month after her twenty-first birthday – about the good one can do 'at little cost' by buying and lending cheap books. 'Think! And resolve never to let dust be on your books; it is as great a reproach as the dust which the Apostles shook from their feet.'[20] The letter is signed RAB – 'Bar' backwards – probably in an attempt to obscure her gender.

Three more letters appeared in June and July, this time in the *Hastings and St Leonards Observer*. They were signed 'Esculapius', the Roman god of medicine whose temple was distinguished by the handy addition of a sanatorium. 'An Appeal to the Inhabitants of Hastings' pleads for more money and attention to be invested in public health; 'The Education of Women' is an argument against treating wives and daughters as angels, 'attendants sent in some way to refine and elevate man'. As many men know to their cost, writes Esculapius, women have feet of clay, so why not teach them to be rational and usefully occupied, along with the other half of the human race? 'Conformity to Custom' is a barely

controlled tirade against the conventional wearing of stays, and
other physical and spiritual constraints on women's natural liberty.[21] All three letters could have been written by Barbara,
especially as the young editor of the paper, William Ransom,
was a personal friend. It is certain that Esculapius was either her
or Bessie Parkes, but unclear which. It hardly matters, as on these
issues they spoke with one impassioned voice.

A new tutor arrived at Hastings during the Christmas holidays in 1849: Philip Kingsford, a 33-year-old barrister and lecturer
in political philosophy. He was a member of the recently established College of Preceptors in London, a professional body for
maintaining standards in teaching. Kingsford was engaged by the
Pater to burnish Willy's academic credentials before his move to
Cirencester, but it was Barbara who learned most from him. He
guided her through the intellectual thickets of political economy, until she emerged into the sunlit uplands of understanding
to write a detailed analysis of John Stuart Mill's *Principles of
Political Economy* (1848). I read Mill's treatise in preparation for
this chapter and, despite starting at a much higher base level of
formal education than Barbara, was addled by page four. The
long exegesis she produced and sent to Bessie for comments is a
lucid, perceptive study of Mill's famous treatise on 'the science
of wealth'. Not only that: she fearlessly points out Mill's omissions, suggesting he turn his attention to the position of women
in society:

> As far as he has let one see his views he thinks nobly, rightly
> and liberally. And I wish with my whole soul that one who
> carries so much weight would put these things before men
> and I do not doubt that they would see the injustice of
> their laws to women and the absurdity of the present laws
> of marriage and divorce.
>
> Philosophers and Reformers have generally been afraid
> to say anything about the unjust laws both of society and

country which crush women. There never was a tyranny so deeply felt yet borne so silently, that is the worst of it. But now I hope there are some who will brave ridicule for the sake of common justice to half the people of the world.[22]

In 1869, Mill did just that, basing his essay *The Subjection of Women* on an article written in 1851 by Harriet Taylor – the woman who became his wife – and on the work of Barbara, who by then had braved considerable ridicule herself for the sake of common justice, by organizing the first mass petition to Parliament for women's suffrage.

That was still to come. There were more immediate matters to address, meanwhile, not least the inconvenient adulation of Kingsford, so struck by Barbara's diligence and radiance that he declared himself in love. Much as she admired him, Barbara did not reciprocate his feelings. He was eleven years her senior, and not strong; indeed, the poor man died of tuberculosis only five years later, in 1854. Illness frightened her. He needed an 'angel in the house' who would tend him, mother him, be gentle. Barbara was no angel.

Before Kingsford arrived, Barbara not only wrote letters to the provincial press, but she also taught herself the Greek alphabet and wrote jokey notes to the Pater in passable Latin (signing herself Barbara Leigh 'Faber', from the Latin word for a smith). She composed a rather dirge-like parable, 'Filia', about the influence of nature and culture on an artistic temperament, which she circulated among her friends, and invested some of her shiny new guineas on college fees.

It would be a while before young women like her were admitted to universities in England – she co-founded the first women's college herself – but an important stepping stone was the establishment in 1849 of the 'Ladies' College' in Bedford Square, London. The person who originated and funded it was a close friend of Aunt Ju, a sister Unitarian and abolitionist, Elizabeth

Jesser Reid. She was even tinier than Ju; a sixty-year-old widow with a wrinkly face, twinkling eyes, and a bizarre ambition to educate young, middle-class girls and women beyond the reach of elementary schools and the average governess.

The Ladies' College soon became known as Bedford College, but was not the constituent university college it later became (now merged with Royal Holloway); it was more like a progressive, non-denominational secondary school for females above the age of twelve, on the model of Queen's College, an Anglican secondary school for girls in Westminster, which had opened the previous year. Its purpose was threefold: to equip its students with experience for future careers in teaching; to offer the discipline and fruits of learning for its own sake; and to demonstrate that they were capable of comprehension and worth educating. It was a statement of confidence in the female intellect.

Barbara and her sisters were bound to go to the Ladies' College as soon as it opened: their Aunt Ju was on its management committee, along with Anna Jameson and a dozen other philanthropic ladies. The teaching staff were all men, assisted by 'lady visitors' (including Ju and possibly Dolly Longden) who acted as chaperones-cum-mentors. The curriculum was more ambitious than any offered to females elsewhere, spanning English literature, moral philosophy, theology, ancient and modern history, mathematics, natural sciences, astronomy, Latin, German, French, music and art. Tutors included professors and Fellows of Oxford, Cambridge and London universities, along with the composer William Sterndale Bennett and the artist Francis Stephen Cary.

Barbara's principal subject at Bedford College was art. She also attended life-drawing evening classes run by her friend Eliza 'Tottie' Fox in the Fox family's library. Tottie was the daughter of a Unitarian preacher deprived of his parish for setting up home with his young female ward; this caused a minor scandal at the time, despite protestations that their relationship was platonic, but does not appear to have worried Tottie. Barbara might have applied to the Royal Academy of Art had women students been admitted, but by the time they were – largely thanks to the campaign she joined a few years later – she had moved on. Bedford College was one of the few places in Britain where women artists could be trained professionally. Another was Sass's Academy in London, run by Cary, which Anna Mary and Tottie Fox both attended, along with Pre-Raphaelites Dante Gabriel Rossetti, William Holman Hunt and John Everett Millais.

Drawing was a compulsory accomplishment for late Georgian and early Victorian young ladies taught by their governesses or peripatetic tutors at home. Subjects in watercolours were suitable for the more adventurous or skilled – think of Queen Victoria – but nothing too . . . *lively*. Misty landscapes were the traditional favourite, or interiors with a vase of flowers, an indeterminate dog or a few well-clad figures. Anything, in fact, that did not call for an understanding of human anatomy, because the study of human anatomy was too dangerous for girls. It corrupted their innocence. That is why most female artists, even the smattering of professionals working during the early nineteenth century like Amelia Long or Maria Cosway, were best known for their landscapes or portrait busts of women and children. Frenchwoman Rosa Bonheur superbly broke the mould by painting animals; she was able to visit abattoirs and dissect dead creatures in private to understand what lurked beneath the skin. Her research was considered disturbingly eccentric, but at least she avoided spending sinful hours gazing in public at live, naked human flesh.

Tottie Fox's pioneering evening classes allowed her friends to do exactly that (without the sinfulness, probably). She unveiled for women exactly what was going on under the fudgy clothing of the period, far more impressively than a marble statue in the

British Museum ever could, though it must be said that Barbara's figures were never numerous or particularly successful features of her paintings. Did Tottie employ male as well as female models, and if so, how did she recruit them? Sadly, history does not reveal.

At Bedford College, students were taught about perspective and the properties of colour, along with composition, focal points and scale. But putting brush to paper was something else: the next step. There, and during those lamp-lit evenings in Tottie Fox's library, Barbara learned the discipline of painting. She was fortunate to have the contacts, through Grandfather William, and the money to develop that discipline by exchanging her pencil for brushes under the tutelage of British watercolourists William Henry Hunt, David Cox, William Collingwood Smith and Cornelius Varley, all of whom became personal friends. Her own talent, with a peculiar eye for strong colour, suggestive line, and dramatic light and shade, did the rest. The first of her watercolours to be exhibited at the Royal Academy were two North Wales scenes painted *en plein air* on a family holiday in 1850, *View near Tremadoc* and *Dawn near Maentwrog*. Her work would make another six appearances there during the next twenty-odd years.

This was heady stuff. She might not be at Cambridge like Ben, or leaving home to learn a career like Willy, but Barbara was already beginning to forge a future unshackled by the traditional restrictions of femininity. She had managed to acquire a comparatively high level of general education, a similar level of specialized training, was romantically unattached, and solvent. She once confessed to being 'one of the cracked people of the world' and how she liked

to herd with the cracked such as . . . democrats, socialists, artists, poor devils or angels; and am never happy in an

English genteel family life. I try to do it like other people, but I long always to be off on some wild adventure . . . I want to see what sort of world this God's world is.[23]

'Cracked' maybe – but then, that's how the light gets in.

BEING YOUNG, FREE AND single is not a state we associate with mid-nineteenth-century ladies, who were traditionally told what to do (be a good wife and mother), where to do it (at home), what to wear (corsets and crinolines) and what to say (whatever the listener wants to hear). But one cannot call what Barbara did during the summer of 1850, aged twenty-three, anything but a joyous celebration of just that.

Barbara's Great Adventure was an unchaperoned excursion to visit Anna Mary Howitt, who was now studying in Munich under the illustrator Wilhelm von Kaulbach. It was virtually unheard of for respectable ladies to travel unprotected by men at this period; those 'globe trotteresses' who did venture abroad, like Lady Hester Stanhope or Ida Pfeiffer, were considered too weird or elderly to worry about. Munich was not exactly at the ends of the earth, but even on the continent it was generally expected that lone ladies were guaranteed to succumb to Latin Lotharios, be relieved of their valuables by unscrupulous fellow travellers, or go rogue through overexcitement and never be seen again.

It says a great deal about the Pater and – when Barbara insisted Bessie come with her – Mr and Mrs Parkes that they trusted their unmarried daughters to travel on their own. Even though Barbara was of age, the Pater still had the power to try, at least, to stop her in her tracks. Anna Mary and her companion in Munich, the artist Jane Benham, both had fiancés at home by now, so they were under some sort of remote control, at least. But Barbara and Bessie were their own mistresses.

Guidebooks were available to tell ladies how to behave and what to take abroad, should they be required to accompany their menfolk. According to Mariana Starke, writing in 1820, the following were but the bare essentials:

> Leather-sheets, made of sheep-skin, or doe-skin – pillows – blankets – calico sheets – pillow-cases – a moschetto-net [mosquito net], made of strong gauze, or very thin muslin – a travelling chamber-lock – (these locks may always be met with in London, and are easily fixed upon any door in less than five minutes) – towels, table-cloths and napkins, strong but not fine – pistols – a pocket-knife to eat with – table-knives – a carving-knife and fork – a silver tea-pot . . . a thermometer – a medicine-chest, with scales, weights, an ounce and half-ounce measure for liquids, a glass pestle and mortar, Shuttleworth's drop measure, an article of great importance, as the practice of administering active fluids by drops is dangerously inaccurate – tooth and hair-brushes – portable soup – Iceland moss – James's powder – bark – salvolatile – aether – sulphuric acid – pure opium – liquid laudanum . . . Epsom salts – court-plaster and lint.[24]

Portable soup, known less appetizingly as 'veal glue', was an ancestor of the stock cube; Iceland moss was a lichen used to treat the common cold; James's Powder was a proprietary medicine sold as a cure for fever; salvolatile was the main ingredient of that Victorian *sine qua non* the smelling salt; and court-plaster a fabric dressing backed with a preparation made from the swim bladders of fish, to help it stick to the skin.

Not much had changed by 1850, though there was more emphasis then on the quality rather than quantity of luggage, and on the importance of keeping up appearances as a patriotic Englishwoman. This meant *never* leaving off your whalebone corset, however hot the weather, and taking every possible precaution – several layers of clothing, a fancy bonnet and a parasol – to avoid unsightly sunburn. But Barbara was having none of it. She deboned; packed Mary Howitt's coloured spectacles; raised the hem of her skirts by a scandalous four inches to prevent them dragging in the mud; plonked a wide-brimmed sunhat on her rose-gold braids; made sure her walking boots had good, thick soles and bright new laces; and turned her face to the East.

Barbara wrote a little song to celebrate the exhilaration of travel. It is dedicated to the Pater, whom she addresses as the patron of 'Liberty Hall, Blandford Square'.

> Oh! Isn't it jolly
> To cast away folly
> And cut all one's clothes a peg shorter
> (A good many pegs)
> And rejoice in one's legs
> Like a free-minded Albion's daughter.[25]

She and Bessie passed uneventfully through Belgium, rejoicing in their legs, before reaching Munich, where Anna Mary welcomed them with near-delirious delight. She and Jane Benham were living just as art students should, hand to mouth in mean little digs down a dingy alleyway with no light or comfort. They were used to this bohemian life by now, but Barbara was appalled. Poor silly creatures, she told them, couldn't they see how dangerous it was to live like this? What would the Pater say if he knew where her friends were holed up? He would have them out of there in a moment. If they looked pale and felt morbid, she warned them, they'd paint pale and morbid pictures. She added (improbably) that whenever she saw a child with its head stuck in a drain, she dragged it out. So no arguments: she must drag them out of their squalor, too. They would all go hunting for better rooms tomorrow, and she would pay the first month's rent herself.

Once they were settled in new quarters, closer to Kaulbach's studio and decorated with a green jug of fresh flowers on the table and one of Barbara's luminous watercolours on the wall, it did not take long for the endearingly bossy Miss Leigh Smith to relax. She unpacked her easel (lugged halfway across Europe), un-crumpled her painting blouse and joined Anna Mary at work. Soon she was 'laughing at the want of salt-spoons and such luxuries',[26] wiping her cutlery between courses on the tablecloth, and swilling quantities of local coffee (traditionally made with chocolate and a kick of schnapps) with gusto.

She and Bessie attracted a good deal of interest from young German gentlemen when they went out exploring. Who were these strange, exotic creatures, the *Herren* must have wondered, stomping around in shapeless clothes and sighing ecstatically over everything? Barbara remained unmoved by their attentions, happy in a bubble of sisterhood. Anna Mary was quite carried away to see her beloved friend, her 'Valkyrie', her 'Justina', so enthralled.

> [Bar] declared again and again that there never was such a delicious, free, poetical life as ours; and she was perfectly right . . . She, the very embodiment of health, soul, and body, without a morbid or mean emotion ever having sullied her spirit – with freshness as of the morning, and strength as of a young oak.[27]

In the evenings, the friends dreamed of the future. Barbara shared something she had been thinking about for a while: her vision of a community of women, not unlike Tennyson's in *The Princess*, where 'sisters' could live who had no homes of their

Ye Newe Generation.

Barbara's cartoon of herself and her free-minded friends shooing away a bull with their paintbrushes, while a more conventional female panics behind them.

own. There would be two sorts of resident. The 'inner sisters' would all be artists, dedicated to their careers, while 'outer sisters' would belong to other professions. Each woman would be self-supporting and contribute to the welfare of the community in a way that was fitted to her particular tastes and talents. Bessie, for example, would mend everyone's stockings, because she loved needlework. I am not sure how thrilled Bessie was by that. Someone else might bake cakes for everyone, or produce pickles and preserves to keep them going through the winter. Once or twice a month there would be an evening meeting when everyone came together: a mass 'show and tell' session to bond them in mutual admiration and support. Barbara explained the idea so well that Anna Mary forgot that this was a mere castle in the air. She could imagine it really happening.[28]

The young women made an excursion from Munich to Switzerland, where overhanging chalet roofs reminded Barbara of her brother Ben's eyebrows, hunched over dark-windowed eyes, and to Austria, still raw with rebellion. She felt a keen sense of oppression there, which confirmed how blessed she was to live in a flawed but flourishing democracy. 'I did not think ... how the sight of people ruled by the sword in place of law, would stir up my heart, and make me feel as miserable as those who live under it.'[29]

Following her return from the continent a few months later, Barbara discussed the state of Europe with a group of Hungarian refugees staying at Blandford Square. It must have impressed them that she spoke not as a drawing-room observer, however sympathetic, but as one who had witnessed some of the effects of political upheaval at first hand. She never forgot how close liberty could come to tyranny.

There was often a group of refugees around from somewhere or other. The Smith household at 5 Blandford Square, Marylebone, welcomed all comers.

On 25 May 1851, Barbara joined them, with a crowd of friends, on a trip to see Ben at Cambridge. It was one of those sparkling days she would always remember. They started early, leaving Blandford Square for Shoreditch station in the most extraordinary vehicle their visitors had ever seen. It was a custom-built horse-drawn omnibus, commissioned and designed by the Pater in 1842 to accommodate his rumbustious family of six, plus two extras. Barbara once drew a cartoon, not of the juggernaut itself, but of three astonished onlookers. 'What a queer turn out,' says the first, a crusty-looking old man. 'What a nasty thing! So ugly!' agrees a prim lady in a bonnet. The third is an earnest young chap in a top hat. 'I don't exactly understand the construction,' he frets.[30] Yet the Smiths and their friends considered it the eighth wonder of the world.

The specification for this omnibus still exists.[31] It was fabulously luxurious, with concealed springs, silver plating and highly varnished paintwork on the body in lake blue and ultramarine. Inside were cane seats and a double sofa stuffed with the finest horsehair, plumped up with pillows of silk and lace. It had blinds, silk curtains, patent-leather trimming and polished silver

The Pater's magnificent family omnibus was a thing of wonder.

handles, and took the combined strength of four horses to move at a respectable pace. The Hungarians' eyes must have been as round as dinner plates.

At the station, they met the rest of their travelling companions, including Mrs Mary Howitt. The poet Richard Monckton Milnes sent his apologies; he said he was too busy planning his forthcoming wedding to a new fiancée. In truth, a day with the Pater might have been a touch awkward. Monckton Milnes had spent the past seven years wooing the Pater's niece, only to be rejected as she finally chose a vocation over marriage to him. The vocation was nursing; her name was Florence Nightingale.

Almost everyone else who had been invited turned up, however, and while the Pater and Willy saw to the business of buying return tickets, twenty-one chattering ladies and gentlemen clambered into reserved railway carriages and set off. 'We were as merry as so many larks,' remembered Mary Howitt. The Pater, now in his late sixties, was 'happy as a boy'.[32]

By ten o'clock they had reached their destination: the fabled university town of Cambridge, where another omnibus and a fleet of horse-drawn carriages waited to collect them. Nothing as grand as the Smiths' mighty chariot this time, but it was still an impressive convoy that made its way to the Bull Hotel in Trumpington Street. Ben met them there, and immediately whisked everyone on a whistle-stop tour of colleges and meadows by the river Cam. A second and very late breakfast followed, served to half the party at the Bull and the other half, including Barbara, in Ben's rooms at Jesus College. Barbara had visited Ben before so she played hostess, serving coffee and ginger beer with great panache while her brother returned to the hotel. She might have been mistaken for an undergraduate herself, were it not for the inconvenient fact that no British university admitted women until almost a generation later – thanks to Barbara.

Mary Howitt was delighted by everything. 'Oh! If you could have seen the fun, freedom, and jollity . . . and what roars of laughter there were!' Breakfast somehow metamorphosed into a vast lunch of pickled salmon, duck, chicken, tongue and pigeon pie. In the afternoon there was further sightseeing to be done before Evensong at King's College Chapel sent them into raptures. Then more food, with speeches by both ladies and gentlemen, the jokes interspersed with moving references to what the refugees' friends and family were going through at home in Hungary. The wife of one of them voiced a startling appeal to 'the ladies of England' to demand the liberation of the nationalist hero Lajos Kossuth, imprisoned by the Austrians in the cause of Hungarian independence.

The *ladies* of England, Barbara must have thought. What influence could ladies have?

All too soon, the carriages returned to ferry everyone back to the station. Ben and his university friends waved them off, proud to have shared their Cambridge lives with these visitors for the day. Conversation was quieter on the way home, the excitement of the morning replaced by a state of happy exhaustion. The omnibus was waiting when the train steamed into Shoreditch at 7.45 p.m. Those who had the energy – and appetite – were invited back to Blandford Square for supper; the rest went home through the late-spring evening, warmed by the wit, generosity and high spirits of the Magnificent Smiths.

ANOTHER UNFORGETTABLE EXPERIENCE DURING this period was a visit to the Great Exhibition in 1851. Like most of its six million visitors, Barbara was bowled over by the opulence of what she saw. The Pater took the whole family along to the Crystal Palace on the opening day on 1 May, to witness Queen Victoria and Prince Albert – whose project this was – making their first official visit. Bessie Parkes was also there and described what she saw. The palace itself looked like fairyland, she said. The glass sparkled and refracted rainbow colours as the royal party arrived in a blast of organ music. The Queen looked splendid in pink silk spangled with silver and a broad blue sash; the Prince, disappointingly bald, was holding one of his 'pale and puny' daughters by the hand as they processed along a red carpet greeting dignitaries from around the world ('a Mandarin included', noted Bessie with excitement).

The Queen made a speech in her 'lovely voice'; then there was a rendition of the 'Hallelujah Chorus', which echoed in the airy vault; finally, the royal couple approached a dais 'and the Queen I supposed said "The Exhibition is opened" and everyone cheered like mad, and Prince Albert waved his plumed hat, and the Duchess of Kent looked so proud; and then they all swept out'.[33]

Barbara made several further visits to the exhibition. Here was the world's most impressive artistry and industry under one fabulous roof half an hour's walk from Blandford Square. It was awe-inspiring to see what wonders humans were capable of. Given the excitement and achievements of the past couple of years, she saw no reason why she, too, might not create something remarkable. *Be* someone remarkable.

She had a ready-made role model in the form of Elizabeth Blackwell (1821–1910), the first British woman to qualify as a doctor. Elizabeth was a cousin of Bessie, and a friend of Florence Nightingale. Born in Bristol, she and her eight siblings emigrated with their parents to America when she was eleven. After her father's death six years later, her mother and eldest sisters opened a school. Elizabeth became a teacher herself, filling various posts around America while gradually saving enough money to fund an unlikely ambition. In 1847 she was admitted to Geneva Medical College in New York State, aged twenty-six, graduating two years later.

Bessie described her progress in a star-struck letter to Barbara after meeting Elizabeth in London, where she had come to further her training at St Bartholomew's Hospital in November 1850.

Language cannot tell you what an exceedingly jolly brick Miss Blackwell [is] . . .

At first we sat down by the fire as we both like unlighted candles, & then she asked my history which I told her in no time, & then I did not like to ask her for hers as I did not know her, but presently the conversation turned that way & then she began

Such a tale! Of energy, & hope; of repulses from men, & scorn of her own countrywomen. (During her 2 years residence in Geneva, the college town, no Geneva lady would call, or speak to her).

Of the glorious day when in a church crowded from ceiling to floor the chief professor after giving the Diplomas to the young men, called her up alone, & rising from his seat & lifting his cap gave her the title of Dr Blackwell. Of the cheers sounding all through the church, & the recanting of all the stupid ladies, who formed in a body at the door & let her & her brother walk thro in a sort of triumphal procession, & of the calls they all paid that afternoon. She left next day. Of the physical hardship of 4 months in the Maternity hospital at Paris, sleeping in a dortoire [dormitory] with 30 coarse girls & women learning to be midwifes, whose noise & vulgarity are beyond description – (Think of that my dainty darling).

Of the terrible opthalmia [sic] caught from a little boy she brought into the world & was attending & syringing, of the 3 weeks all she said [sic] she must be blind; of her Graffenberg stay, her relapse, & a blind journey from Graffenberg to Paris all alone, just able to open one eye for a blink of 5 seconds, of the terrible operation, & her now tolerable sight which will improve.[34]

Barbara was captivated by Elizabeth, one of the few women she knew whose wild intentions had become reality, entirely by her own efforts. If Elizabeth could rewrite history in this age of wonders, then, surely, so could she.

4

Venus Without Corsets

Professional Life, 1852–1855

How charming it would be to organise a regiment of
stay-less, free-breathing, free-stepping girls![1]

I F BARBARA LEIGH SMITH BODICHON IS NOT YET WIDELY
recognized as one of the most influential figures in nineteenth-
century Britain, it must be because she had a finger in so many
different pies (many of which – to stretch a metaphor – she baked
herself, without a recipe). Her name is not associated with a
single cause, like Dr Elizabeth Blackwell's or the politician and
suffragist Millicent Fawcett's, but with several, so it might be
easy to assume that she was something of a butterfly, flitting
gaudily but weightlessly from one campaign to the next. Her
low profile historically owes much to the fact that she never
sought to be a figurehead. To her, success, even acknowledgement, had little to do with fame; it was about liberty, opportunity,
defeating prejudice and enhancing lives. Leadership meant opening doors for others and ushering them through, not elbowing
ahead in front of everyone else. And though praise was 'delicious', she said, too much of it made for an unhealthy diet.

Between 1852 and 1855, in her mid to late twenties, she began
to navigate an already unconventional personal and professional
terrain on her own terms. The personal, tortuous and technicol-
oured, we shall come to in the next chapter. How she had the

time and energy to achieve so much professionally during this period is hard to imagine. She must have been – as more than one of her friends put it – extraordinarily 'large', by which they meant capable, curious, fearless and virtually indefatigable.

Art was always her first choice for a profession, at a time when respectable women simply did not have careers. All three Leigh Smith girls studied painting; Nannie and Barbara were serious about it, particularly Barbara.

Barbara threw herself into her art with all the gusto (vast quantities) at her disposal, because making money, rather than inheriting it, defined her life. 'I should like to give all I had to schools,' she once wrote, 'and earn my own living by painting.'[2] She was good at it; she loved doing it; it had commercial value, unusually for a woman's work, because female artists were assumed generically guilty of amateurism until proven innocent; it made her happy and soothed her soul. What more could one ask? Only the possibility of reinvention. By supporting herself, she could perhaps forget about being an illegitimate offshoot of the family tree. Forget about the cracks. Independence would give her strong, firm roots of her own.

When the Pre-Raphaelite artist and poet Dante Gabriel Rossetti was introduced to Barbara in 1853, he was enchanted. 'Ah! if you were only like Miss Barbara Smith,' he wrote to his pallid sister Christina, 'a young lady I meet at the Howitts' blessed with large rations of tin [cash], fat, enthusiasm, & golden hair, who thinks nothing of climbing up a mountain in breeches or wading through a stream in none, in the sacred name of pigment.'[3] He respected elements of her work, and being something of a hothouse flower himself, could not help but be impressed by her breezy exuberance.

'Large rations of fat' is a little harsh, incidentally. Barbara was robust. Cartoons she drew of herself at work out of doors show her dressed in her usual unstructured outfits (and those sinister spectacles), frightening little children or uninvited animals who come too close to her easel, but she is not corpulent; just shapeless. Had she chosen to conform and dress fashionably, I'd like to believe her figure would have been much admired. But according to her, conformity was evil:

> Beautiful and appropriate dress is a charming thing for the eye to behold; the body is the temple of the soul, and should be well cared for; such care procures us the respect of others and ourselves; but when a false standard, injurious to health, prevails – when those vilest of torture-engines, *stays*, are worn, and it is thought elegant to diminish the graceful and *ample* waist of nature – when the heart, liver, and lungs are compressed into half their natural space – when the beautiful foot is cramped into disease, and the delicate person exposed where it should be wrapped in flannel; then the dress is not lovely . . . and conformity is absurd as well as *wrong*.[4]

She once published a sheet of wonderful drawings illustrating the 'Effects of Tight Lacing', dedicated to Dr Elizabeth Blackwell. It shows crowds of feeble-looking women simpering in wasp-waisted gowns, with diagrams of how their insides are being mutilated by their stays. Cackling skeletons caper around them, while the Venus de Milo looks on with sightless eyes, demonstrating how much more attractive nature is than artifice, even with parts missing. So-called 'rational dress' was a matter of politics; like the wearing of dungarees and the burning of bras during second-wave feminism, it was a statement of anarchy, easily ridiculed and misunderstood.[5] In Barbara's case, it was also a pioneering badge of her profession as both artist and activist. Artists do not wear impractical clothes when they are at work, especially if, like Barbara, they work mostly outside. Nor

Barbara was a vigorous campaigner against the empty-headed dangers of high fashion. She never wore stays herself, thereby preserving her innards in their proper place.

are they judged by their appearance. For them, beauty is at one remove: it really is in the eye of those who behold their art; who see the world newly transformed at their fingertips. And those who are busy trying to make society a fairer place for women cannot do so by spending inordinate amounts of time and money on how they look, or constantly clutching at their skirts to stop them dragging in the mud.

Barbara took lessons in artistic technique well into adulthood. Ever since Grandfather William had taken her as a child to see the great J. M. W. Turner at work in his studio, she had been fascinated by the way a skilled artist transmutes their subject, like an alchemist, from the ordinary to the somehow sublime. 'I wish I could paint as well as David Cox ... I want to do something well, even if it is only an olive tree.'[6] Nature was her inspiration; its shifting light, shade, movement and sensation, as well as basic form and colour. She would sit for hours trying to capture the waves as they broke, or clouds' shadows sliding over cornfields. If her subject was static, *she* would move instead: '[M]y most vivid ideas for pictures are all horseback views, wild and dashy.'[7] Even her botanical studies are dynamic, sprigs of flowers looking as though they are playing a game of grandmother's footsteps, and as soon as you glance away, they will grow a little taller or turn to face the sun.

Correspondence with her friends frequently includes references to good painting weather. Like Barbara, Bessie Parkes loved a high wind, which though inconvenient for anyone working out of doors, 'blows whole years of life into one in a moment'.[8] Barred from the Royal Academy of Art, Barbara prided herself on studying hard at the Academy of Nature, come rain or shine.

She and her widening circle of friends also learned from one another. They pooled their resources. Tottie Fox introduced her to fellow students from her time at Sass's, particularly members of the self-styled Pre-Raphaelite Brotherhood (PRB). They included Barbara, Tottie and Anna Mary Howitt in their professional and personal network. Members of the PRB published a type of house magazine, *The Germ*, from 1850, with the strapline 'Thoughts towards Nature in Poetry, Literature, and Art'. It was a (short-lived) forum for sharing finished work and new ideas; a cooperative in print. During the next few years, Barbara, Nannie,

Anna Mary, Bessie and the poet Adelaide Procter joined first the
Folio Club, founded by Dante Gabriel in 1854, and then the
Portfolio Club, set up by Barbara. This was a similar platform,
but more immediate: regular meetings were held with a given
theme – 'Desolation', for example – when members showcased
pieces of art, poetry or prose for gentle criticism. Christina
Rossetti was a member, but so shy that someone had to read out
her poems for her. This level of mutual support helped to compensate women for the lack of formal training available, and to
coalesce the campaign for their admission to the Royal Academy
in 1859. It also provided a safe space for creative women, where
their work could be considered – for once – without reference to
their gender.

Art historians talk about a Pre-Raphaelite Sisterhood, functioning alongside the PRB. It includes artistic associates of the
Brotherhood like Evelyn De Morgan (wife of ceramicist William
De Morgan), Christina Rossetti, Georgiana Burne-Jones (Edward's
wife), Effie Millais (first John Ruskin's tearful bride, then John
Everett Millais's smiling one), doomed Lizzie Siddal (briefly Mrs
Dante Gabriel Rossetti) and Jane Burden (William Morris's wife
and Rossetti's lover). Although Barbara embraced much that distinguished the art of the Pre-Raphaelites, her style lacks the
hyper-reality and heightened romance of the Brotherhood and
Sisterhood. She is not one of them, though obviously influenced
by their use of colour and reference to nature. Only in an early
self-portrait, a pencil drawing of her looking grumpily like the
Pre-Raphaelites' favourite muse, Jane Burden, could she be mistaken for a Pre-Raphaelite herself. Her paintings are too fluid,
too fugitive, to qualify, and rarely tell a story. But they are similarly luminous and often very beautiful, prefiguring the work of
the Impressionists who – like Barbara – would rather paint *en
plein air* than in the studio.

They are also highly skilled. A scrap of paper serendipitously
saved in her family's archive demonstrates how carefully she *looked*

at things (in this case, a bridge near Edinburgh) and how she thought in terms of pigment.

> Sky slate color [*sic*] with Indian y[ellow] + verm[ilion] clouds distanced green + cobalt & towers of black or nearly so, houses in m[iddle] distance delicious reds & brown with white & blue smoke. Church tower on left beautiful old red sandstone. Foreground a wood going over arches of yellow & grey stone with broken earth ground below, like a picture by Poussin.[9]

(I wonder if she was aware that Indian yellow was a pigment made from the urine of subcontinental cattle fed exclusively on mango leaves? I hope so: it would have tickled her.)

As her confidence grew, so did her appeal. During this period, she exhibited and sold paintings not just at the Royal Academy but at the Royal Society of British Artists and the British Institution, both in London – and she gave scores of watercolours away. They still turn up in unexpected places now and then.

In the summer of 1853, Barbara and Bessie embarked on another sketching trip together. Leith Hill in Surrey was neither as far away nor as foreign as Bavaria, but the jaunt was still something of an adventure. They travelled there by train, lugging capacious carpet bags, and booked themselves into the King's Arms at Ockley, no doubt raising local eyebrows when they revealed that, no, their husbands were not following on: they were unmarried, unprotected and unashamed. It was a point of pride that not only had they no gentlemen to look after them, but they had planned this working holiday entirely without reference to a father, brother or male friend.

The next few days resolved themselves into a cheerful routine. Barbara went out early to pick up the post and gather blossoms to twist into her gleaming hair; after breakfast they packed their paraphernalia – or Bessie's writing notebook and pencil and Barbara's paraphernalia – into a donkey cart; off they trotted with a small boy who called them 'Sir' driving the cart and helping them with Barbara's clobber until they found a suitably inspiring spot. Then everything was unloaded again; Barbara plonked herself and her easel down and surrounded herself with arty chaos, while Bessie wandered about in search of inspiration. Eight hours later, they returned to the inn for a meal and an evening spent reviewing their work, reading the papers and putting the world to rights. I should not be shocked if they ruminatively smoked the odd clay pipe by the fire.

A few visitors came and went while they were there. Aunt Ju stayed for a while; so did a protégée of Joseph Parkes, an austere-looking young woman from Coventry whom he had commissioned to translate a German work on the life of Jesus. Her name was Mary Ann Evans, but Barbara called her Marian. In time, the world would come to know her as the novelist George Eliot. John Chapman, a radical bookseller and publisher, joined them with his wife Susanna (he was a friend of the Howitts), and a close friend of Marian's from home, the governess, writer and translator Sara Hennell.

The landlord of the King's Arms must have been bemused by this unconventional company of friends, but they behaved well enough and were polite. They spent good money and perked up the village with their jolliness. Had he been aware of the complications swirling about beneath this bright surface, he might not have been so accommodating. For Marian was not only Chapman's lodger but – it's generally agreed – his lover, sharing him with Susanna and his children's resident governess Elisabeth Tilley. Barbara was also on the brink of a relationship with Chapman. Bessie was not, and nor was Sara, but both women were passionately devoted to their special friends Barbara and Marian. 'Special friend' is no euphemism; their relationships were simply closer than ordinary friendships. They were spiritual intimates.

Bessie wrote a long and disappointing poem to commemorate the holiday, 'Summer Sketches', published by Chapman with other poems in 1854 ('Ockley is a model village / Planted mainly amidst tillage [. . .] / [Barbara] with a rustic air / Twisting roses in her hair'). The good news is that it was reviewed in the periodical *The Athenaeum*; the bad is that Bessie was described there as 'evidently a strong-minded lady – dealing in every sort of *ism* and *ology*'.[10] 'Strong-minded' was code, at the time, for strident, unfeminine, ridiculous.

Barbara also wrote a long and even more disappointing poem about their customary discussions of the so-called great and good.

To Bessie x x x x x x

You and I have talked apace
Of everything & every place
Of everybody live or dead
On horseback with the leaves o'erhead [. . .]

Wordsworth, Bonaparte & Caesar
I did abuse, & Nebhuchadnezzar [*sic*]
And Statesmen! Oh, I cannot name
The scores of coves we did defame.[11]

This is only a fraction. Mercifully, Barbara's poem was unpublished. But the accompanying pen-and-ink drawing of a country lane 'with the leaves o'erhead' is a little masterpiece.

THE LEIGH SMITH FAMILY left Pelham Crescent in 1853, though Barbara returned to Hastings regularly throughout her life. The Pater still owned various properties nearby. Scalands Farm, surrounded by woodland just outside Robertsbridge on the road to Brightling, was one of Barbara's favourite places. She continued to divide her time between rustic, healthy Sussex and the necessary bustle of London.

The capital was a risky place to live. A digest of fatal diseases present during the week ending Saturday 10 September 1853, published by the *Illustrated London News*, lists 1,015 deaths (in a population of around two and three-quarter million) from causes including smallpox, measles, scarlatina, whooping cough, diarrhoea, typhus and cholera. This number was lower than the average week's toll. Over 10 per cent of the week's deaths were due to tubercular diseases, including consumption. Two people perished of 'Asiatic cholera . . . confined to the poorer and more thickly populated of the metropolitan districts', thus marking the insidious beginning of an epidemic that was to kill more than 10,000 Londoners over the following year. The life expectancy of someone born in London in 1853 was 36.1 years.[12] The air and water were heavily polluted with coal smoke and human and animal effluent. Over 1,000 horses clopped along the streets each day, leaving steaming evidence, and the weekly market at Smithfield processed around 30,000 sheep, 5,000 cattle and 2,000 pigs, all of which were herded through the streets, there and back.[13] Marylebone, where Blandford Square is situated, was right on the edge of the conurbation, close to open fields and fresh air. Still, there is little wonder that Barbara longed for the wholesome countryside of Sussex.

Needs must, however: she had work to do. And there were compensations. The Crystal Palace was dismantled from Hyde Park and re-erected further south in Sydenham in 1854, but several exciting new projects were planned for the original site, including a concert hall and a museum. Waterloo station opened in 1848, King's Cross in 1852 and Paddington in 1854, adding more commuters to the crowds of 20,000 people walking into central London every working day. More significantly for Barbara and her friends, the new termini made travel to the country a spontaneous pleasure, rather than a laboriously planned undertaking involving all the variables attendant on staff and horses. (I can't resist sharing the name of the Pater's coachman at this time: it is Mr Gallop, straight from a game of Happy Families.)

This was the era when shopping became a pastime for those ladies with the money and stamina to withstand a day on their feet without benefit of access to public lavatories. Constrained by what is known as 'the urinary leash', the modest woman could venture only as far from home as her bladder allowed. Her more adventurous sisters relied on strategically placed chamber pots (who knew how useful crinolines could be?), but that was hardly liberating. The Royal British Warehouse – one of the earliest department stores in Britain – opened in 1851 on the corner of Vere and Oxford streets; the zoo in Regent's Park, a short walk from Blandford Square, welcomed the public for the first time in 1847 and was adding new exotica all the time. All sorts of societies held meetings either for their members or the public, including the London Mechanics' Institute (later Birkbeck College) and the 'Lectures to Ladies' series organized by the founder of Queen's College, Professor Frederick Denison Maurice. Construction began on the opulent, domed Reading Room at the British Museum in 1854, and Thomas Carlyle's London Library in St James's Square admitted its first members – and lent them books to take away – from the early 1840s. Barbara was a borrower.

These were all public spaces accessible to women. Meanwhile, cooperative ventures sprang up in private libraries and drawing rooms, including Tottie Fox's art classes; the Folio Club; writer and critic Anna Jameson's famous Thursday-evening get-togethers; and regular soirées held at Blandford Square by Aunt Ju for her literary and political friends. These offered women a chance to talk together, perhaps for the first time without parents or partners, and without fear of sounding silly, naive or hysterical (all of which epithets they were used to being applied to them in mixed company). Such informal discussion groups

paved the way for more publicly organized activism in the years
to come.

Book clubs were popular. Barbara was a keen consumer of
new fiction, poetry and journalism. Elizabeth Barrett Browning
was a favourite (Barbara and the Brownings had mutual friends);
Tennyson, of course; George Sand, the transgressive French
novelist who defied convention at almost every level; Margaret
Fuller, an American journalist and campaigner for women's
rights (a fascinating character: the first female war correspondent
in America and, like Mary Wollstonecraft and Anne Longden,
the mother of illegitimate offspring). Barbara ordered copies of
The Una, a feminist periodical published in Boston, Massachusetts,
between 1853 and 1855 and edited by Caroline Dall, who became
a friend; she also enjoyed the less earnest *Cook's Journal* (1849–54),
a literary miscellany that over time became increasingly political.
Its editor, Eliza Cook, was another contemporary misfit, a self-
educated poet and champion of the rights of working-class
women, who dressed in men's clothes and took female lovers.

It strikes me that the more I research Barbara's cultural and
political circle, the more influential Victorians I find leading parallel lives. Perhaps my perception of the Pater and the women
and children associated with him being unusual in their concur-
rence is wrong. Duplicity, benign or otherwise, is a function of
all social interaction. But it surprises me that libertarianism was
accommodated so readily in an era usually presented to us by historians as stiflingly strait-laced and intolerant. It was not just a
matter of money or power giving high-profile people a pink
ticket to behave as they wished; women like Anna Jameson and
Eliza Cook had neither. Was it more about self-confidence, or a
wider acceptance by society of a redacted persona? Out of sight,
out of mind? That does not work, either; George Sand was an
infamous woman and wildly popular novelist, and Margaret
Fuller was a highly respected commentator while her public
morality remained dubious.

Maybe it was nothing to do with libertarianism at all; just a pragmatic version of hypocrisy, allowing society to ignore taboos when it suited, and professed reformers to remain unreformed. But then, to reform is not to conform. Barbara had to calculate how far she could go, as an illegitimate, steadfastly unfashionable and independent woman, before public censure got the better of her.

BARBARA'S FIRST SERIOUS FORAY into the public eye was anonymous. In October 1854, a pamphlet was published by John Chapman, affordably priced at threepence, entitled *A Brief Summary, in Plain Language, of the Most Important Laws Concerning Women; Together with a Few Observations Thereon*. It was Barbara's admirably rational response to what was at the time a highly emotive issue.

The saga of popular writer Caroline Norton and her husband, erstwhile Tory MP and barrister George Norton, had been the sizzling subject of society gossip for years. They married in 1827, incompatible from the outset, and within a decade were bitter enemies. George legitimately spent the money Caroline inherited or earned, while legitimately depriving her of the custody of their three sons and legitimately drawing up a deed of separation that contained no guarantees and could therefore be defaulted on (which it was) without penalty. In 1836 he legitimately sued for divorce on the grounds of her alleged 'criminal conversation' with the former prime minister Lord Melbourne; though she and Melbourne were close friends – and she does appear to have taken other lovers – no evidence of her adultery with him was forthcoming, so no divorce was granted. Caroline, thus acquitted, was nevertheless imprisoned in a cruel and abusive marriage, without her boys, and with no means of redress or escape unless the rules of legitimacy could somehow be changed to protect her, as a wife, mother and earner, rather than victimizing her.

She asked Barbara's feminist friend Anna Jameson to help her do just that. I have no rights, only wrongs, she complained, expecting Anna's sympathy. Anna was similarly trapped in a miserable marriage in which her estranged husband subsumed her property and refused to share it. She and Caroline were the penniless wives of comparatively rich men; anything they earned or possessed on their own account – including children – was not legally theirs at all, but their husbands'. They were empty vessels.

Anna was more than happy to contribute to the general cause of legal recognition for women, but wary of allying herself too closely with the volatile Mrs Norton. Caroline's was an intensely personal campaign; she professed no interest in widening legal access for her sex, only in retrieving what she considered to be stolen property from George. Her unwieldy, privately printed book on English law relating to women is not objective.

Barbara shared Anna's reservations. While surely sympathizing with Caroline, her analysis of John Stuart Mill's *Principles of Political Economy* had taught her that careful argument was a powerful tool, more effective politically than the most passionately delivered tale of personal grievance. And ignorance was a more dangerous foe than apathy. It was better to educate readers for change than to berate them for complacency. Bessie was already entering the reformist fray with a published essay on the education of girls;[14] that same year, 1854, Barbara did the same.

The previous year, barrister John Wharton produced *An Exposition of the Laws Relating to the Women of England*. It runs to 557 pages and, though he tried to avoid legal jargon, is inevitably abstruse and long-winded. Barbara worked her way through it, with the aim of producing an easily understood precis. No doubt she marked with special interest the passages referring to married women's property (they had none) and illegitimacy. Her mother Anne might have benefited from what some have regarded as the Pater's grand political gesture of refusal to marry, had she much property of her own to keep as a single woman. But she was no heiress. Barbara hoped that, when *she* married, she would be entitled to bestow her fortune as she chose. Her Unitarian ancestors and relations believed in personal liberty, independence and equality, and so did she.

Wealthy brides could afford to have deeds of trust drawn up before marriage to protect various income streams, if their husbands concurred, but that did not help the vast majority who relied for a livelihood on a spouse's common decency. Barbara's conviction that a wife should be encouraged to support herself was compromised completely by the axiom that all that she had was her husband's, while all that *he* had was also his. *A Brief Summary* was therefore more than an explanatory pamphlet on the law. It was about empowerment.

As for illegitimacy: this hit home hard. 'Upon the question of legitimacy depends the legal rights of an infant,' explained Wharton, 'and frequently, the chaste reputation of its mother.'[15] Technically her partner is a paramour, she a concubine and their children bastards. It seemed to bastard Barbara that English law was fundamentally unfair in defining a child, and the adult it became, by the married status of its parents. And why should Anne be assumed unchaste? This burning sense of injustice lies at the root of *A Brief Summary*. Its rationality is all the more remarkable for the depth of her vested interest.

It is likely that Philip Kingsford, the failed suitor who tutored her on John Stuart Mill, also advised her on *A Brief Summary*, though he died in September 1854. But her chief mentor was Matthew Davenport Hill, the Recorder of Birmingham (a senior judicial appointment) and father of Barbara's close friend Florence. He made suggestions, answered queries and went through the proofs for her. John Chapman was a sympathetic publisher, being both feminist and friend.

A Brief Summary is only eighteen pages long.[16] It is arranged under several headings, covering the legal condition of spinsters, wives and widows; 'usual precautions against the laws concerning the property of married women' (complex and expensive settlements, for example); separation and divorce; and 'laws concerning illegitimate children and their mothers'. In the latter section, Barbara states coolly that 'the rights of an illegitimate child are only such as he can acquire; he can inherit nothing, being in law looked upon as nobody's son . . . He may acquire a surname by reputation, but does not inherit one.' Maybe that is why the Pater invented a brand new name for his children.

Each heading is followed by a few short paragraphs, some of which are startlingly direct. I am sure that this was Barbara's intention, despite counsel from Davenport Hill to avoid addressing 'subjects which are considered forbidden to women', such as 'unnatural practices' and adultery. He feared that outspokenness might distract from the cause. '[I]f we wish to reform the world we must be tender of its prejudices or we shall never gain a hearing.'[17]

Barbara, however, would rather be thought unfeminine than mealy-mouthed. She pulls no punches. Then, as now, it must have shocked many to realize that a 'wife's paraphernalia [i.e. her clothes and jewellery] which her husband owns during his lifetime, and which his creditors can seize for his debts, [only] becomes her property after his death'; that when a 'woman has consented to a proposal of marriage, she cannot dispose or give away her property without the knowledge of her betrothed'; that during 'the lifetime of a sane father, the mother has no rights over her children'; that a 'husband is liable for his wife's debts contracted before marriage'; that it 'requires an Act of Parliament to constitute a divorce . . . This divorce is pronounced on account of adultery in the wife, and in some cases of aggravated adultery on the part of the husband'; and that a 'wife cannot be plaintiff, defendant, or witness in an important part of the proceeding for a divorce'.

The last few pages are a commentary on the status quo. Barbara might have let rip here (Caroline Norton certainly would) but, again, she is stark and logical.

> Since all the unmarried women in England are supported either by their own exertions or by the exertions or bequests of their fathers and relations, there is no reason why upon marriage they should be thrown upon the pecuniary resources of their husbands, except in so far as the claims of a third party – children – may lessen the power of earning money, at the same time that it increases her expenses. Of course a woman may, and often does, by acting as a house-keeper and manager of her husband's concerns, earn a maintenance and a right to share in his property, independent of any children which may come of the marriage. But it is evident that daughters ought to have some sure provision – either a means of gaining their own bread, or property – as it is most undesirable that they should look upon marriage as a means of livelihood.
>
> Fathers seldom feel inclined to trust their daughters' fortunes in the power of a husband, and, in the appointment of trustees, partially elude the law by legal device . . . Why should not these legal devices be done away with, by the simple abolition of a law which we have outgrown?
>
> We do not say that these laws of property are the only unjust laws concerning women to be found in the short summary which we have given, but they form a simple, tangible, and not offensive point of attack.

Despite the pamphlet being published anonymously, Barbara's authorship was no secret. It was generally favourably reviewed, but the novelist Margaret Oliphant's piece in *Blackwood's Magazine* was cutting. She accused Barbara of verbal trickery to make her arguments appear cogent, and of jumping on the Norton bandwagon. 'Woman's rights will never grow into a popular agitation,' she declared, 'yet women's wrongs are always picturesque and attractive.' She maintained that independence within a marriage undermined the whole of society. To suggest otherwise was 'the merest nonsense which ever looked like reason'.[18]

Within a year, Barbara had gathered a committee of like-minded reformers, who met in the Leigh Smiths' London drawing room to canvas support in petitioning Parliament for a change in the law concerning married women's property. The publication of *A Brief Summary* – which ran to three editions – marked a metamorphosis from private concern to public activism.

At the same time as she was drafting *A Brief Summary*, Barbara was working on another project designed to offer practical help to the disadvantaged. The Pater had not only settled an investment portfolio on his eldest child when she turned twenty-one, but he had also transferred the deeds of Westminster Infants' School to her. James Buchanan had long gone; Barbara did not have the heart to try to recreate his fairy-tale kingdom in Vincent Square, so she sold that property and rented another in Carlisle Street (now Penfold Street), just east of the Edgware Road. It was only a few minutes' walk from Blandford Square, yet was not a prosperous area, suggesting to the Victorian mind a lesser need for high-quality elementary education. But Barbara had ambitions for what she grandly called Portman Hall School.

The education of girls – and boys, if they were young enough to be able to catch up at a boys' school later – was often associated in the nineteenth century with well-meaning women. So-called 'dame schools' were private establishments usually run by spinsters, impoverished gentlewomen or local philanthropists, ostensibly to teach the young children of the neighbourhood to read and write. They were little more than child-minding services, with only a handful of books between all the pupils. Any boys present were given those, while the girls did needlework. There were exceptions. The author Hannah More and Quaker reformer Elizabeth Fry both ran reputable schools. Before them, pioneering feminists Mary Wollstonecraft, Mary Astell and Bathsua Makin wrote about the importance of educating girls properly. Middle-class girls, that is. 'How can you be content to be in the World like Tulips in a Garden, to make a fine shew and be good for nothing?' demanded Astell of empty-headed young ladies idling in their drawing rooms.[19] She blamed them for a lack of intellectual curiosity, while schoolmistress Bathsua Makin furiously blamed society.

> Custom, when it is inveterate, has a mighty influence: it has the force of Nature itself. The Barbarous custom to breed Women low is grown general amongst us, and has prevailed so far, that it is verily believed (especially amongst a sort of debauched sots) that Women are not endued with such Reason, as Men; nor capable of improvement by Education, as they are . . .
>
> Had God intended Women only as a finer sort of Cattle, he would not have made them reasonable . . . Monkies, (which the Indians use to do many Offices) might have better fitted some men's Lust, Pride, and Pleasure; especially those that desire to keep them ignorant to be tyrannized over.[20]

Barbara's friends Harriet Martineau and Bessie Parkes also wrote about the importance of rigorous schools for girls, pointing out the benefit to a modern society of educated women as workers, wives and mothers. Her cousin Florence Nightingale famously lamented that women had 'passion, intellect, moral activity – these three – and a place in society where no one of the three can be exercised'[21] before opening her school of nursing at St Thomas' Hospital. Barbara herself, however, was less lofty in her approach to Portman Hall. As constructive as ever, she aimed to open a good school to offer local children, both boys and girls,

a sound and useful education at an affordable price to their parents. Like her mentor Buchanan, she considered the relationship
between curiosity and knowledge to be symbiotic. A skilful
teacher imparted both, and as both grew, so did the sum of
human happiness. Happiness was always extremely important to
Barbara; that of others before her own, but her own too.

After securing the building in Carlisle Street (at least during
the day; it was used for Temperance Society and other meetings
after school hours), her next step was to find an exceptional
teacher. She settled on a governess, Elizabeth Whitehead, who
had been a pupil at the Misses Wood's school in Clapton, like the
Leigh Smith girls, and was a friend of Tottie Fox. After meeting
Barbara in 1853, she promptly agreed to leave her current post, in
charge of an unlovely little boy, and to embark on the formal
training Barbara required before opening the school as its headmistress. She was impressed by the research Barbara had done
into pedagogy by observing 'advanced' schools in London and
Edinburgh. The Pater used to deputize his daughter to inspect
the local schools in Hastings that he helped to fund, and his
friend Thomas Southwood Smith (lover of the artist Margaret
Gillies) took her to so-called 'industrial' and 'ragged' schools to
see how they were run. Industrial schools were residential institutions for young vagrants; ragged schools were charitable
organizations, taking in poor and destitute children. Barbara's
conclusion was that William Ellis's philosophy chimed most with
her own. A political economist and friend of John Stuart Mill,
Ellis had recently opened a series of progressive co-educational
schools for working-class children in the suburbs of London,
with carefully trained teachers and a curriculum centred not on
religious education, but on utilitarianism, loosely described as a
practical code of ethics for communal well-being.

Ellis named his schools after George Birkbeck, the founder of
mechanics' institutes for the education of working people
(women as well as men) in 1823. Elizabeth Whitehead spent

much of her training at the Birkbeck School in Peckham, south London, but Barbara encouraged her to observe as many well-run classrooms as she could, to equip her for opening Portman Hall in November 1854. Elizabeth was observed herself, teaching various subjects as a trainee to children of different ages and backgrounds, until Barbara felt her to be sufficiently qualified. Unfortunately, she was not only qualified, but after more than six months of this intensive work, completely exhausted.

Elizabeth would not have let Barbara down, however. The two women quickly became close friends: Barbara called Elizabeth 'my dearest saint'; Elizabeth addressed Barbara as her 'Dear Golden-haired lady' when planning their joint venture to furnish the minds and improve the fortunes of their pupils. Barbara underwrote Elizabeth's expenses, with help from Bella and Nannie, as she would her salary and everything else to do with the school, but Elizabeth had complete managerial freedom. That is what her training was for: Elizabeth was a professional educator by now; Barbara was not. Thus, Barbara empowered Elizabeth to empower her pupils to empower their families at home – and so on.

Portman Hall broke new ground by actively encouraging a cultural mix. Girls and boys were taught the same things in the same classroom (when most co-educational schools separated them). Middle-class children sat next to the working classes: everyone paid just sixpence a week. Since it was a tenet of Barbara's philosophy that we should learn from one another and not judge, there were no rules about religious affiliation, and the children of political refugees were welcome. The son of the Italian revolutionary Garibaldi attended for a while, brought to England for medical treatment; so did Elizabeth Whitehead's delicately brought-up younger sisters, alongside John and Susanna Chapman's children, and boys and girls from some of the meanest streets in London.

Elizabeth recalled the school fondly in later years. The main teaching room had a stage, a slate blackboard and a screen for displaying music. Just as at the Pater's infant school, the walls were covered with beautiful, useful illustrations. There were heaps of books, many provided by the faithful Howitts. Morning assembly was secular. A parable from some world religion might be read, but so might a poem, or some other passage 'putting a fine moral, or stimulating truth, in a form they could appreciate and love'.[22] This was just the sort of thing Buchanan did; it is a safe bet that the *Arabian Nights* was not forgotten. There was very little formal discipline – again, reminiscent of Westminster Infants' School – and pupils' good behaviour or close attention to work were rewarded by trips on Saturday mornings to a museum, gallery or, if they had been *really* good, to the zoo. Barbara was naturally an enthusiastic chaperone and paid for these outings herself.

She also came into school as a 'lady visitor', an idea poached from her alma mater, Bedford College. Other visitors included Octavia Hill, who went on to become a pioneer of social housing and a founder of the National Trust. She taught drawing, having been forbidden by her father to train as a professional artist. Bella and Nannie Leigh Smith were involved, as was Tottie Fox. It may be that the Pater came along from time to time; he was now an elderly figure in his early seventies, but always up for a bit of fun.

The children sang together every day. Exercise and playtime were given as high a priority as desk work. Both Barbara the 'sanitarian' and Elizabeth took advice from Dr Elizabeth Blackwell, who evangelized the importance of healthy minds in healthy bodies for women (a novel concept) and encouraged callisthenics in schools. Elizabeth Whitehead was keen to see her older girls dressed in the sort of loose, flowing clothing Barbara favoured – Venus without corsets – and dreaded the toxic influence of high fashion leaching into Portman Hall. She reported to Barbara after a visit to a pioneer of the keep-fit movement.

> I have been to the Professor of 'Rational Gymnastics' since I wrote to you – seen some of the exercises & practised a few – much to the amusement of 2 of my sisters, who caught me, they say, making unaccountable movements without any apparent cause. The worthy Professor ... declares scholars should practise these movements for at least 2 half hours every day. We cannot find this possible, I fear, but shd. think the gymnastics might soon become popular 'plays.' How charming it would be to organise a regiment of stay-less, free-breathing, free-stepping girls! I must stop! My imagination runs on, & pictures schoolgirls like Grecian water-carriers – but I check it – I fear the sins of the mothers will permit no great amount of grace in English girls of this generation. If we make them abjure stays, it will be doing much for the next at least![23]

It was a nuisance that everything had to be tidied away at the end of the day so that the Temperance ladies and gentlemen could meet over their glasses of water, but that was the only disadvantage Elizabeth could think of, apart from inexorably mounting fatigue. 'In looking back upon the school,' she remembered, 'my feeling is that the children were really educated, rather than merely taught; by this I mean that their minds were developed, and love and interest in knowledge were nurtured, while gentle manners and kindly feelings were fostered by example.'[24]

Barbara was proud of Portman Hall. And the ageing Pater was proud of his dynamic daughter, now beginning to make her mark on the world like a true Smith.

5

Barbara – Whom I Love

Personal Life, 1852–1855

The grave's a fine and private place,
But none, I think, do there embrace.[1]

OF COURSE, A TRUE SMITH IS EXACTLY WHAT BARBARA was not, in the legal sense. She and her siblings were impostors; cuckoos roosting in the family tree. She could campaign all she liked about the inequities of the law, open any number of schools to teach children about love and light, and debate women's rights until her pink cheeks turned blue, but that perceived crack in her integrity would always be there. Professionally, she coped well during a particularly industrious period between 1852 and 1855, but how did the stigma affect her relationships with family and friends?

It is debatable whether cousin Florence Nightingale would have been quite such a national treasure had she been illegitimate. Florence was no less busy than Barbara. Having rejected the Pater's friend Richard Monckton Milnes after a nine-year courtship, she had devoted herself to God, serving Him by training as a nurse in Germany before her appointment in 1853 as the superintendent of an 'Establishment for Gentlewomen During Temporary Illness' in Harley Street, London. That same year she finally persuaded her father William to pay her an allowance instead of irregular pocket money (she was thirty-three). Using her own funds, and with the help of her close friend Sidney Herbert, the Secretary at War, Florence left for the shores of the Black Sea in October 1854 with a corps of volunteer nurses, including Mai Smith, the Pater's sister-in-law and former fiancée, and thus stepped into immortality.

There is barely a mention of Florence in Barbara's extant writing. Barbara very rarely traded on her connection to the living legend but must have admired her cousin's proactivity and determination to be of practical use. Both qualities were inspirational. An article written about the Leigh Smiths much later, in 1899, confidently implies that Ben and Willy both fought in the Crimea, and that the three girls 'took lessons in sick-nursing',[2] but I have found no evidence of this. Bella and Nannie were happy helping out at Portman Hall, painting, visiting friends and travelling. When Willy finished studying at the Royal Agricultural College in Cirencester, the Pater installed him in Sussex as manager of the family estates.

Their brother Ben had left Cambridge with what would have been recognized as a first-class in mathematics were he not a Dissenter and therefore denied a degree. The Pater was keen that his elder son should become a lawyer as a prelude to sitting in the House of Commons as the third generation of Smith MPs. Like his uncle Oc, Ben was more fascinated by mechanics than by abstruse arguments and, if not allowed to spend his time sailing or shooting, would far rather be an engineer. He dreamed of combining all three, by liquidating some of his investments, designing his own yacht and cruising to places where he could hunt unfamiliar creatures and discover new lands.

This was not as outlandish an ambition as we might think. The Pater was himself mildly obsessed by travel and exploration. Britain was gripped by reports of the search for Sir John Franklin, who had sailed his ships *Erebus* and *Terror* into Arctic oblivion on a quest to navigate the fabled North-West Passage between the Atlantic and Pacific in 1845. From 1847, his widow Jane commissioned relief expeditions to try to find Franklin and his crew, alive or dead. An account of the *Prince Albert*'s voyage in 1850 mentions the Pater. Not only did he contribute £100 to the expedition's expenses (no private individual contributed more), but he also donated some cutting-edge technology for improving overland travel in polar regions: a fleet of land kites 'constructed upon scientific principles, by which, if properly managed, very considerable propelling power would be applied . . . [Mr Benjamin Smith] was at infinite pains in the manufacture of these enormous kites, of which he also presented a large number, with the necessary apparatus, to Captain Penny.'[3]

Ben must have witnessed the development of these thrilling contraptions and been caught up in the romance of the whole enterprise. Yet he was not allowed to join in. The Pater's conventional plans for his clever son prevailed and Ben entered the Inner Temple to read for the Bar. His dream was postponed.

There are hints of a major disagreement between Ben and his father in 1852. This could well have been to do with Ben's career. Both men, like Barbara, had strong personalities and a stubbornly independent disposition. They were obstinate, in other words. I think the main source of friction in the family was something else, however; something that rocked the Leigh Smith children to their foundations, and added yet another layer of necessary simulation to their motley lives.

YOU MIGHT RECALL THE Pater asking Barbara and her former governess Catherine Spooner to witness a codicil to his will in 1848.[4] Catherine was aware of its content; Barbara was not. Sometime in 1852, it appears that she found out. What the codicil says is this. To Jane Bentley Smith, at present at Miss Hewlin's school in Emsworth, Hampshire, the Pater leaves £2,000; to Alexander Bentley Smith, at Reverend Briggs's in Bessels Green, Kent, £2,000; and to Henry Bentley Smith, of the same address, another £2,000. That is equivalent to around £170,000 today – each.

A previous codicil, added five months earlier on the day that the original will was drawn up, mentions the same three names. Jane is to have £2,000 when she turns twenty-one or marries, whichever is the sooner; the boys will inherit the same amount when they are twenty-one. If the Pater dies before they reach that age, the interest on the sum is to be used for their maintenance. To Catherine Spooner, currently living at 5 Blandford Square, he leaves £50 (not a vast sum) and asks for her 'care and attention to the above-mentioned children during their respective minorities'.

Each Bentley Smith was therefore in line for £4,000, or around £300,000. Most of the will deals with property to be left to the Leigh Smith children, and *their* children, should they have any. The Bentley Smiths were pecuniary legatees only. The money was all they got.

Who were these children? It is possible to piece together a fractured picture from official documents.[5] On 13 September 1838 – four years after Anne Longden's death – Jane Hannah Smith and Alexander Bentley Smith were baptized together at St Paul's Church, Hammersmith. Later census records suggest they were not twins; Jane was born in 1837 and Alexander the following year. It was not unusual to hold joint baptisms within a family. In the baptism register, their mother is named as Jane Smith and their father as Benjamin Smith. A birth certificate dated 24 March 1839 announces the arrival of Henry Bentley Smith – mother Jane Buss, father Benjamin Smith, a 'Gentleman' – in Fulham.

Buss is a familiar name. Assuming the 'Smith' given to Jane on the baptism record is a courtesy title, I can trace her straight back to the Leigh Smiths' special corner of Sussex. Her half-siblings were Abraham and Kezia Buss, who accompanied the Leigh Smiths to America when Barbara and Ben were young children.

Jane was born in 1819. Her father William lived at Walters Farm House, Poppinghole Lane, near Barbara's own birthplace of Whatlington. If this is the right Jane Buss, and I am convinced it is, then she was just eighteen when her daughter Jane was born, while Benjamin was fifty-four. She must have died within the next decade, before the will was drawn up, as the children were at boarding schools by then and there is no mention of their mother. Only the governess of the natural father's first brood of illegitimate children was somehow deemed close or trustworthy enough to take them on.

The 1851 census shows Catherine Spooner, aged thirty-three, as head of the household at an address in Grafton Villas, St Pancras. She lives with her brother, a civil engineer; a servant; and three others disingenuously described as 'visitors', including Alexander Smith, aged fourteen, and Henry, known as Harry, aged twelve. Ten years later, she is living a few doors down from a friend of Barbara, the artist Ford Madox Brown, in Kentish Town with Alexander, who is now a civil engineer himself.

In 1853 Harry was apprenticed to the Peninsula and Oriental Steam Navigation Company at the age of fourteen. What happened to the Pater's daughter Jane between school and marriage is unknown; by 1861 she was the wealthy wife of a man who worked for the Inland Revenue, with two young daughters of her own.

There are so many questions. When did the Pater embark on the liaison – partly foreseen by prickly Aunt Patty – that would produce his second illegitimate family? How? Why? Why were Jane and Alexander baptized while Harry – apparently – was not? Where did the name 'Bentley' come from? Were they Anglicans or Unitarians? For Benjamin's name to be on Harry's birth certificate, he would have to have been present at registration; otherwise the space for 'Father' would have been left blank. Was he a permanent part of Jane Buss's life? What did she know about the Leigh Smiths? Did the other Busses disown her? What did her children know about their well-read, luxurious half-siblings? And what became of her in the end?

In later life, Alexander vaguely recalled going as a child to see his father conducting weird experiments in Hyde Park; something to do with exploration and the North Pole.[6] That would be the Pater's kite-testing programme for the Franklin expedition. Did the Pater acknowledge Alexander when he saw him? And why choose Catherine as their guardian? It is understandable that the Pater could not quite bring himself to visit another scandal on the accommodating Aunt Ju; certainly not on Aunt Dolly, his sister-in-law (or not in *law*, but you know what I mean). What was his relationship with Catherine?

As for how the news was broken to the Leigh Smith children – who knows? I suspect that something compelled the Pater to reveal to Barbara and Ben in the spring of 1852 that he had named them as executors. Temporary illness might have forced the issue, or simply a weary compulsion at last to tell the truth. Having divulged that much, he could hardly avoid explaining his surprising dispositions.

We have no record of Barbara's reaction. What we do have is a letter to her from her beloved Bessie Parkes, written on 20 March 1852. 'Dearest Bar,' it begins.

> No, no, no; it is not true that these hindrances in youth will prevent your doing all you might. The full promise <u>will</u> come out, when it is great, as I really believe yours is, & what a person <u>is</u> is never lost to the world . . .
>
> I daresay you cannot paint at all now while you are in pain, & grief, darling, but you will find this afterwards. I know it is true . . . I have a degree of faith in your working a very good work in the world which no temporary embarrassments could shape . . .
>
> I don't know how I would bear a great wrongdoing in anyone I loved, because, never having had that sacred love

in an instructive relation, I have chosen love associated
with conscience, & never was pained by seeing sin where I
loved; but I know that if I had loved anyone as long as I
could remember, and found out gradually that they did
very wrong it would be very bad.

Apart from the shock and betrayal she must have felt, Barbara
must have been anguished by the possibility that this might be a
blow from which she could not recover, and that all the passion
she had for art and activism would evaporate in shame and disillusionment. And what about her future relationship with the
Pater? How could that survive? Bessie had more advice.

Barbara . . . is it not better to be linked to those whose
noble natures make you feel the fall with such bitterness,
than to those of whom you would always take a calm and
gentle view because there seemed no high nature to make
the contrast black. Dearest Bar; your father has that
immortal something about him, which so many men are
apparently without: something that will rise, that <u>must</u>
rise; something that I feel vividly when I am with him, &
I know you do too; something that won't die.[7]

We have already seen that Barbara took Bessie's advice. She
refused to judge the Pater, forged ahead with her work and re-
invented herself not as a daughter – bastard or otherwise – but as
a brand-new person, freshly minted and free of precedent. It is
remarkable that publicly she managed to do this apparently
without resentment, preserving her belief in the power of
authenticity and her capacity for joy more or less intact.

This new, defiant attitude to life was encapsulated in a letter
she wrote to Aunt Ju soon afterwards.[8] It describes a partly fan-
tastical visit to Greenwich Fair, held around Easter each year and
famous for its rowdy crowds and general craziness. It was hardly

acceptable for a lady to visit Greenwich Fair in company, never mind on her own, but Barbara did not care. Why the devil shouldn't she, if she liked, she asked Ju. Normal rules didn't apply to someone like her.

The letter is like a tiny, picaresque novella, with Barbara as heroine. She tells Ju about daring to travel to Greenwich by public omnibus. On arrival, after a cheerful journey with the hoi polloi, she decides to buy a fruit seller's entire stock of oranges and sell them on at a profit, which she plans to give to her friend the social reformer Mary Carpenter. But as soon as she settles down to her green grocery, she is thunderstruck to see two familiar faces approaching. One is a Fellow of Ben's old college at Cambridge, and the other a Unitarian divine. So she tosses her oranges to the crowd and bolts for cover.

Her next trick is to borrow a yellow caravan and pose as the Sultana of Constantinople[9] – dressed as she is in orange and black 'trousers' (those newfangled bloomers) and a bright blue bodice. She performs 'the famous carving-knife dance' taught to her in childhood, probably by James Buchanan, and earns enough not only to benefit Miss Carpenter, but to take the friends who had lent her the caravan out to dinner at the British Queen pub in Woolwich Road. Forty people turn up; much fun is had by all, and at the end of the evening Barbara is flattered to be offered £5 a week to perform her act as a permanent circus fixture. After some thought, she declines, finds a boat to take her back home along the Thames, and goes to sleep in her father's house, happy after her adventure.

It is easier to believe Barbara's determination to live and let live than to accept her apparent denial of the Bentley Smiths. As a champion of natural justice she might have sought them out, to welcome them to the hybrid Smith clan, where they had as much right to reside as she did. Alexander gave up engineering and became a watercolourist; he might well have moved in some of the same circles as Barbara and her friends. Harry had a great deal

in common with Uncle Oc, and loved the sea like his half-brother
Ben. Jane settled with her family – Barbara's nieces – in Islington,
barely four miles away from Blandford Square. But perhaps
public familiarity was a step too far. Barbara was occupied
enough in negotiating her own place in the tribe, without com-
plicating matters even further. And there is no doubt that it
would have been deeply divisive of the Pater to acknowledge
openly his clutch of third-class Smiths.

GIVEN THE TURBULENCE SURROUNDING her blood relatives, it
is unsurprising that Barbara valued so highly the steady loyalty
of unrelated friends. Anna Mary Howitt continued to adore her
'Justina', her noble empress who looked so beautiful and was
so good. When commissioned by the philanthropist Angela
Burdett-Coutts to produce a painting of Dante's Beatrice, Anna
Mary chose Barbara for her model. She was later to cast her as
Tennyson's Boadicea: mighty, noble and heroic. Bessie Parkes
was a little jealous, warning Barbara that Anna Mary's blatant
adoration might be considered distasteful, even laughable. Such
fulsomeness threatened embarrassment for Barbara.

Bessie was often a little sharp, as on the occasion when she
upset Barbara by scoffing at milliners. But she was deeply attached
to the Leigh Smiths. Her admiration of the Pater is clear, and
when she visited the Isle of Wight in 1855, describing it unkindly
as 'a hole full of women in brown straw hats',[10] she made sure to
visit Anne Longden's grave. She and Barbara holidayed together,
and dreamed of a golden future when each would be married,
with children (Barbara wanted lots), yet still free to be what
Bessie called blissfully 'daft' in their mission to give women a
voice.

In fact Bessie was right: there was something disquieting
about Anna Mary during this period. In 1853 she and her family
were seduced by the modern craze from America for ghostly

'spirit rapping', holding twilit séances at the Hermitage, their Highgate home, and devouring accounts in the press about mysterious knockings, hovering hats and pieces of furniture skidding around the room. Barbara joined in out of interest, but soon agreed with the pioneer of electromagnetism Michael Faraday, a Smith family friend, that the whole phenomenon was nothing but humbug. The Howitts, however, remained convinced, and Anna Mary began gradually to waft away from Barbara, who was as down to earth as it is possible for a person to be.

It was at the Hermitage that Barbara met several new friends she would keep for life. Among them were the Irish poet William Allingham and art critic William Michael Rossetti, brother of Dante Gabriel. In May 1854, Barbara invited Dante Gabriel and his muse Lizzie Siddal to Sussex for a painting holiday. Barbara found Lizzie fascinating. Like Anne Longden, she was a milliner from a respectable working-class family in the north Midlands; like Anne, her health was poor (possibly due to undiagnosed TB); like Anne, she lived with a man who would not, at this stage, marry her. She was not a 'lady', admitted Barbara, but she was a gifted artist in her own right with a poetic soul; the sort of woman who appealed to Barbara because she defied expectations.

Lizzie would not be strong enough to spend her days painting outside like the others (now joined by Anna Mary). Barbara decided she should take lodgings in Hastings instead, where Dante Gabriel might visit whenever he liked. 'I have got a strong interest in a young girl formerly model to Millais and Dante Rossetti, now Rossetti's love and pupil,' she wrote to Bessie, who was already staying at the Smiths' Scalands Farm.

[S]he is a genius and will (if she lives) be a great artist, her gift discovered by a strange accident such as rarely befalls a woman. Alas! Her life has been hard and full of trials, her home unhappy and her whole fate hard. Rossetti has been

*Dante Gabriel Rossetti's lover Lizzie Siddal, pictured
by Barbara with an iris in her hair. This drawing was
done at Scalands in 1854.*

an honourable friend to her and I do not doubt if circumstances were favourable he would marry her. She is of
course under a ban having been a model (tho' only to 2
PRB's) ergo do not mention it to anyone. Dante R told
me all about her secret then, now you are to know because
you are to help.[11]

Bessie must go down to Hastings, instructed Barbara, and
find a sunny room for Lizzie with a broad-minded housekeeper
for a few shillings a week. Barbara would pay. Lizzie could
remain there for as long as it took to get well, tended by Barbara
and Bessie.

When Lizzie took a turn for the worse, Barbara tried to persuade her to book into her cousin Florence's Hospital for Gentlewomen at Harley Street, but Lizzie refused.[12] Gradually she was coaxed into remission, and, on a visit up the road to Scalands, was proposed to by Dante Gabriel in the bluebell woods, and accepted. One can imagine Barbara peeping from behind a distant tree at the time, like a delighted fairy godmother.

Her friendship with Rossetti and Siddal brought Barbara into contact with such luminaries as John Ruskin — a besotted champion of Lizzie's art — and William Morris; she came to know Ford Madox Brown, another painter 'living in sin', and the rest of the Pre-Raphaelites. Perhaps the most significant friendship of her life was not with another artist, however, but with the woman who was to become one of the greatest novelists in the English language.

Marian Evans (George Eliot, 1819–80) came to London in 1851, a paying guest at the home of publisher John Chapman at 142 Strand. It was an exciting place to be: a little palace of industry where John sold books, edited the liberal *Westminster Review*, published works like Bessie's *Summer Sketches, and Other Poems* and Barbara's *Brief Summary*, held eclectic soirées, dreamed up strange medical inventions (such as 'Dr Chapman's Spine Bag' to cure seasickness and morning sickness) and conducted a series of complicated, concurrent love affairs. Occasionally he took time off, as when visiting Barbara and her party at Leith Hill in 1853.

John was something of a Renaissance man, though more restless and transgressive than most. Friends in his hometown of Nottingham nicknamed him Byron for his good looks and raffish popularity, and were unsurprised when he abandoned his apprenticeship as a watchmaker in Worksop and emigrated to Australia to set up his own business, bankrolled by his brother: he was always an impulsive fellow. Australia did not go well; he was soon home again, having stopped off in Paris for a while to study medicine with an apothecary. By 1843, at only twenty-two, he settled in London, trying to find work as a surgeon, and married 35-year-old Susanna Brewitt, a minor heiress from Nottingham. They had a daughter and three sons in quick succession. One of the boys was born deaf-mute, and the youngest died in infancy.

As well as being an unqualified medical man, John was an aspiring philosopher and political economist. Like James Buchanan and the Pater, he was an apostle of Robert Owen and regarded himself as something of a radical. He bought the publishing business in 1843 as a platform for his own writing, and was an outspoken supporter of what the *Saturday Review* would term the 'isms' and 'ologies' of modern thinking. He was a feminist (before the term existed), a suffragist and a socialist: a man in many ways ahead of his time. Partly because of his native charisma, partly because of a genuine enthusiasm for new ideas and intellectual adventure, he attracted high-profile backers and enjoyed an influential circle of friends.

He was not good with money. When bankruptcy threatened during the early 1850s, he was only wrested from the brink by the generosity of Harriet Martineau, John Stuart Mill, the fabulously wealthy textile manufacturer Samuel Courtauld and – curiously – Octavius Smith. Perhaps Uncle Oc knew John via his sister Aunt Ju, who visited 142 Strand more than once, or his niece Florence Nightingale, also a somewhat unlikely visitor in the company of Aunt Mai.

Marian Evans acted as John's assistant editor on the *Westminster Review*. For a while she is assumed to have also been his assistant mistress. She was temporarily returned to Coventry when the chief mistress, Elisabeth Tilley, his children's governess, saw Marian and John holding hands, and told Susanna. By the spring of 1852 she was back, however. Her friend Bessie was anxious that Barbara should meet her.

I don't know whether you will like Miss Evans. At least I know you will like her for her large unprejudiced mind, her complete superiority to most women. But whether you or I should ever love her, as a friend, I don't at all know. There is as yet no very high moral purpose in the impression she makes, & it is that alone that commands love, every day I feel it more . . . Large angels take a long time unfolding their wings; but when they do they soar out of sight.[13]

This is Bessie at her most perceptive. She introduced her two friends at 142 Strand. They were immediately drawn to one another. At first glance they were opposites: Barbara shiny, beautiful and outgoing; Marian drawn in much more sombre colours, and rather serious. But both loved Perizade in the *Arabian Nights*; both were open-minded and ambitious; they were free-thinking and free-living, believing personal integrity to be more valuable than conformity. To Barbara, Marian was as authentic and incapable of dissimulation as she herself hoped to be one day. To Marian, 'Barbara – whom I love' was large-hearted and true, 'a little draught of pure air'.[14]

When she met Barbara, John Chapman had been replaced in Marian's affections by the philosopher and journalist Herbert Spencer. She had already come across the love of her life, writer George Henry Lewes, but not yet fallen for him. That happened in 1853, after Spencer had extinguished any hope of a relationship. Barbara and Bessie were two of the few people who stood by Marian and George when they decided to elope together to Germany, without benefit of marriage. Like John, George was already a husband and father, though four of the household's seven children were not his, but fathered by his wife's lover. He gave at least one of them his surname in full knowledge of their paternity, perhaps feeling that his wife's infidelity gave him free license to take a mistress in return.

Bessie's father Joseph Parkes – an unfaithful husband himself – forbade her to associate with Marian or George when news of their liaison broke. He told her that there was little doubt that Lewes would tire of Marian 'as he has done [of] others' and that his 'concubinage . . . (not his first amour of the kind)'[15] would ruin her. Bessie was brave enough to disagree, responding to her father that at least Marian was sincere and suggesting that she might even make an honest man of George.

Barbara, with her family background, was disinclined to take the moral high ground. Her first impression of George had not been promising. 'Oh Lewes! Yes, I think I've seen him – a flippant conceited superficial little man but clever.'[16] But they grew to love and admire each other. When Marian asked for her friend's advice before leaving for Germany, Barbara was supremely sensitive. 'What earthly right had I to advise her in such a case?' she wrote later. 'I replied that her own heart must decide, and that no matter what her decision or its consequences should be, I would stand by her so long as I lived.'[17] Meanwhile, ever practical, she put her lawyer's hat on – or wig – and did some homework about the possibilities of divorce, perhaps in another country, for someone in George's situation. The answer was discouraging. Because he had allowed his name to be entered on the birth certificate of a child he knew was not his, he was deemed to be complicit in his wife's adultery. This meant that he was ineligible to divorce her.

Soon after 'Mr and Mrs Lewes' left the country (and Marian had assured Barbara that she was not committing the mortal sin of pretending to be someone she was not: her soul and George's were truly wedded), Barbara embarked on an affair of her own, with none other than the hand-me-down hero John Chapman. Something had been brewing for months. Barbara and Aunt Ju travelled to Rome in December 1854 to stay with Nannie, who was studying art there. It was an unplanned trip, which included the Amalfi coast. The official story was that Barbara was suffering from 'congestion of the lungs' but veiled comments made by friends and family suggest a less concrete complaint. Lovesickness, perhaps.

As is so often the case with Barbara, we only have one side of the story. Her letters to John from Sussex, where she was based after returning from Italy, were destroyed. But over thirty of his remain – and they are astounding.[18] The surviving correspondence starts conventionally enough, on 8 August 1855, with John extravagantly calling Barbara his

> Own Darling . . . haven of spiritual refuge. Anxiety itself is transfigured into a calm feeling of duty under the purifying and ennobling influence of your love . . . Writing to you I feel to be like passing from the din and battle of life into a quiet sanctuary where only sacred music stirs the air.

They have obviously been attracted to one another for a while, and John feels it is time for the relationship to progress. His past history might be . . . complicated, but he perhaps appreciates that Barbara's background is hardly lily-white either.

The letter develops into a variation on the theme of Andrew Marvell's poem 'To His Coy Mistress'. She has told him that she wishes she could cut out of her nature 'the strong necessity of loving' or sexual desire (it is too unsettling), but John disagrees. It is God-given. He realizes it is difficult to enjoy their love 'in its fullness' but they must make use of every moment to find happiness despite 'the crushing sacrilegious hand of conventionalism'. They must be true to themselves. He longs to lay his head on her bosom and is convinced it is natural, not sinful, to express his passionate longing for her in a physical way. 'I know that I shall love you faithfully – entirely until death.' He is sure that she will come to love him in the same way when they get to know each other better.

John Chapman, who so nearly persuaded Barbara to surrender to the 'Master Passion'.

He has no plan for their life together yet (has she asked, I wonder?). For now, it would be best if she found excuses to come to London during the week as often as possible, so they can meet. His wife Susanna and the children will be away from next Monday. They must be careful about alibis. Why not make a confidante of Anna Mary Howitt, to make life easier? Or he could take a furnished room in town for three months, 'where you might paint while we talk, or while I read to you. Could we not spend 2 or 3 hours together most days?' He believes the *Westminster Review* will yield enough money in three years for him to afford to live with her anywhere in the country, but meanwhile the supply of pounds, shillings and pence is problematic. He signs off this long, first letter with 'Yours for ever and ever'.

On 13 August, things begin to get a little surreal. Barbara has obviously taken his medical qualifications at his word and admitted how anxious she is about her irregular periods. '[R]egularity must be restored to your system,' he replies. '[I]t is the primary duty of us both. Yes of us both.' He understands the treatment of cases like hers; she must trust him. So: first, she must fill a hip bath with hot water and a teacup full of mustard, and sit in it for between forty-five minutes and an hour before going to bed; drink a warm sherry with water in bed; and do this every night 'until the flow appears'. Every morning, she must sit over a basin of boiling water (ouch!). She must not wash in cold water until the flow has come and gone. In addition, she should get some horsehair socks and wear them with boots large enough to accommodate them and give the feet 'free play'. It is crucial that Barbara should remember that he has diagnosed a weak heart, so she must never, ever wear tight shoes.

By 14 August, he has had a letter from her 'full of happiness'. Now he is sure of her love. He wants to know exactly how she told Anna Mary the secret (obviously finding the idea rather titillating) and suggests plans for their next meeting. 'Be happy, accept and enjoy the present and the future shall yet look bright to us.'

In the following day's letter, he asks endless intimate questions about how she washes herself. He has been trying to make a good impression on Elizabeth Whitehead (the teacher at Portman Hall) for Barbara's sake. Two days later he has more medical advice for her. She should avoid drinking port. Two baths a day might bring things on. He intends to come to Hastings tomorrow, so perhaps they can go riding together on Sunday?

Sunday comes and goes without a visit. On Monday 20 August, he tells her how much he is missing her. Being away from her 'effects a divorce between my visible and spiritual self'.

He has been talking to a medical man about the best places to settle on the south coast – Ventnor and Torquay are top of the list. He sends her an Etna stove so she doesn't have to bother the servant to warm her wine at bedtime. It is good to sweat . . . Perhaps conscious of the fact that he might be considered to have too subjective an interest in Barbara's reproductive system, John advises her to consult Dr Williams, the Queen's physician. He tells her what to say.

On 22 August, he reveals some doubts about Barbara's feelings for him. She is 'the greatest blessing life has ever conferred upon me'. But if she finds that she can do without him, she must tell him so 'bravely and at once'. She has said that she regrets some of the things she said when they last met, and that 'the veil is very thick between us'. What is she afraid of? Her health will be sorted out as soon as she regularizes her menstrual cycle, and everything good will follow that. He prescribes a purgative and advises her to pay special attention to her bowels. While he's at it: here is a prescription for Anna Mary, because he thinks he remembers Barbara saying that she was irregular too.

The next day, he finally – and verbosely – comes to the point. Of course, he implies, there are other ways than pills and horse-hair socks to sort out women's troubles.

> Sex is certainly not a barrier to the most perfect inter-course of the soul; on the contrary it ensures the fullest intercourse of all and reveals depths in our being which without it are never fathomed. Only because the sexual feeling presses its claims with supreme imperiousness so long as they [*sic*] are unsatisfied do the other parts of our nature shrink for the time from the full operation of them-selves in it[s] presence. But they will gradually become accustomed to associate with it and derive new vigour inspiration and beauty from its influence . . . Complete mutual knowledge of each other would generate complete

mutual trust ... if you really love me – you will ere long wish to have me near you as much as I always wish to be with you – my own dear Angel – my sweet darling love. Oh how intensely, entirely my soul does love you.

Right.

By 24 August, John is on a roll. 'Oh there is in me such a constant welling up of intense loving tenderness towards you that I am ever vibrating and tremulous with deep feeling which yearns to pour itself out in all ways for your behoof.' He even says he feels like waves are breaking on the shore when he thinks of her. Astonishingly, Elizabeth Whitehead has been to Dr Williams for information about Barbara's case, which she has passed on to John. The doctor has recommended a dietary programme, and says she needs to build up her strength. Barbara has confessed a horror of the 'Master Passion' (sexual intercourse) but that will pass, John assures her. He turns mother-hennish, discussing the advisability of residential treatments at Malvern or at a sanatorium in Surrey, and accusing her of failing to love him by sitting outside drawing, when she knows it is not good for her.

John's thirteenth letter in three weeks, written on 28 August, is explicit. He appreciates that Barbara despairs of her health, but she must have patience. John has consulted a 'womb specialist' on her behalf, talking to him for an hour. If you are not 'unwell' in 10–14 days, he tells Barbara, you *must* visit the specialist. 'He inclines to think the womb is distended with blood.' John is business-like.

Exercise – walking on level ground – twice or three times daily – avoiding ascents and stairs, sudden efforts, excitement and standing still in the open air, especially when there is damp. Nutritious diet, with a sufficient admixture of fresh with cooked vegetables. Claret and bitter beer. [T]oo frequent exposure from washing – (particularly in cold water) is to be sedulously avoided.

She must take several glasses of claret a day. He also recommends a 'Chamber Horse'.

> It is a sort of chair elastic [*sic*] with air in which you move up and down and which [the doctor] says has a more direct mechanical action on the womb than has any other exercise ... I consulted him as to the effect of marriage; he eagerly jumped at the idea, exclaiming: 'best thing in the world; best thing in the world!'

He means sex.

Barbara, understandably baulking at the prospect of an elastic horse, asks John to promise – until she is well again – to treat her not as a woman, but a child. Fine, but he is beginning to weary a little of Barbara's insistence on keeping their relationship unconsummated and unacknowledged. He wishes she could be at peace and accept their love. Why does she not take a deep breath and tell the Pater? It might be painful at first, but better in the long run.

> Openness to your family would enable us to be far more effectually secret as regards the world. You would then maintain your right and equal relation towards them, and would be able without fear and undue anxiety and without the knowledge of the world to be really united with me and to look forward with joyous anticipation to becoming a Mother ... [T]he fulfilment of your sexual life <u>may</u> prove the only permanent security of real health.

There is happy news on 30 August: Barbara has started her period. 'God be praised! Oh how full of thankfulness my heart is now,' writes John. 'I mean you to traverse your orbit regularly in 31 days before I have finished your education,' he adds, elliptically.

Until their secret is spilled, John offers to disguise his writing on envelopes to Barbara. While on the subject, he berates her for the state of her own handwriting and for not reading letters before she sends them. 'You rarely send me a letter which does not contain misplaced words or omissions.' She *can* do it, he tells her, but too often her letters 'descend into indecypherable [*sic*] hieroglyphics'. (She did say she wanted to be treated like a child.)

By the beginning of September, John's money troubles are coming to a head. He has moved the family to a house near Barbara's in Blandford Square, but the financial burden is heavy. 'Do you . . . think we might be united in 1856 or 1857?' he asks hopefully. He needs a substantial income for Susanna and the children, he reminds her, and is longing to have a child with Barbara. The future will be expensive. She has skittishly asked him to say what he loves most about her. It is tempting to imagine the pound signs in his eyes as he answers 'everything' and 'all is mine', while asking for a lock of that famous golden hair.

There is good and bad news on 4 September. Barbara has been explaining her financial situation, which has disconcerted John. 'You have at present <u>less</u> money and expect finally to have <u>more</u> than I had been led to suppose . . . I only hope for food sufficiently good to keep me in health, and for clothes that may be called "respectable".' John suggests she might like to paint larger, more finished pictures, to make more money. He asks how she sees their future, practically speaking. He knows she wants to keep her independence. 'As you would wish to be often alone of course your house could not be mine as a permanent residence; do you adopt the idea that I shall continue to occupy, during part of my time, the same house as Susanna, or that I shall take bachelor apartments in town?'

Barbara's reaction to these questions prompts assurances from John. He does not want to 'possess her as English husbands do . . . I would not allow you to surrender yourself legally into my hands by means of an English marriage even if there were no impediments to our legal union.' By 6 September, Barbara is fretting. Stop wondering if we'll still love each other in ten years, he counsels. Just be happy that we love each other now. He has been 'the elect of your <u>heart</u> for nearly 2 years past . . . If there must be any questioning as to whether I shall always love you, you must seek the answer in yourself.' Have faith. Meanwhile, a Rubicon is crossed. Susanna has been told. She will allow John to see the children unhindered but wants to live in a house legally and nominally his. 'She does not so much object to my attachment to you as to its being known.' By the way, if he only had the funds, he could qualify formally as a doctor, then their (perceived) money problems would be over.

Matters intensify on 10 September. John's latest letters have made Barbara ill. Confusingly, she says she is 'angry and disgusted' for giving him so much happiness. All will be well, suggests John, if they can love one another fully. 'God has much happiness for us yet.' After the next dissatisfied letter from Barbara, John becomes irritated. As you mature, he tells Barbara, you will 'appreciate human beings for what they are and not for what they actually accomplish, and will cease to complain that they do not live their lives and do their work after your fashion'.

On 12 September we return to obstetrics. John tells Barbara that for healthy women the menstrual cycle is 28–31 days. She is therefore unhealthy. He discusses poor Anna Mary and comments that nothing but becoming a mother will release her from the period pain she suffers. Every woman should have at least one child . . . He promises Barbara that her system will be reinvigorated by 'a fulfilment of love's physical desires'. It is nature's way . . .

A couple of days later, Barbara has reported that, at last, she has had *the* conversation with the Pater. He was appalled at the idea of her entering a relationship of 'free love' and advised her that if that was the sort of life she wanted to lead, she should go to America. (This is a man who has had two 'wives' and at least eight illegitimate children.) It is evident that the Pater does not approve of John, suspecting him of pursuing Barbara not just for her virtue, but her fortune. That seems a reasonable supposition, which may or may not have been true.

Now John's patience and continence are wearing thin. He implies that as her last period was so scanty, Barbara must either apply leeches to the top of her thighs, or have sex with him. What a choice.

> You have for years been very careless of, and unkind to that precious body, and so you see the gods have given it to me, believing that I shall better appreciate its worth and know how to take care of it. For the future you have only a steward's part in it . . . I do indeed feel myself wedded to you by every fibre in my being.

By 17 September, John is desperate. Barbara has asked him if he really thinks sex will cure her. Yes, he says, yes, yes; and for her to conceive would be even better. The utter relaxation after coitus is completely restorative. We should use 'Raciborski's law' for a time, he suggests, so that you don't conceive straight away. Adam Raciborski was a Polish physician who advocated the 'safe period' for sexual intercourse, but it was a risky means of contraception if one's cycle was as irregular as Barbara's appears to have been. 'We ought to enjoy each other speedily because your unwell time will soon come again, and if we do not before then, we must wait according to [the completely unreliable] Raciborski until about 12 days after it is over.'

Soon John is arguing that Barbara's prevarication is bad for *his* health. She mustn't worry about him, he says, but he has noticed that his left side is weak and he sweats at the least exertion . . . (John used to record multiple episodes of intercourse with the governess/ mistress Elisabeth Tilley during a single night in his diary. By now, Miss Tilley had left and Susanna, presumably, had made herself unavailable.) The Pater is intractable. John comforts Barbara. 'Your father is old and hence will need more time to reconcile himself to the life you have chosen.' He will realize how 'your mind is destroying your body by this terrible contest' and that 'I shall never consent to you being sacrificed to your father's disapproval.' Our duty to ourselves is higher than filial obedience.

The final letter in this extraordinary exchange is undated, but was probably written at the end of September 1855. Barbara has told John that she is frightened of men (I assume she means of sex). In that case, he parries speciously, 'you would be scarcely likely to <u>marry</u> even if I did not exist, hence our mutual love is in no sense an injury to you'. His last words are 'Darling . . . God bless you!' And then, silence.

6

Where Are the Men
Who Are Good?

1855–1857

It will be a dreadful waste of my life if I can't find anyone.
You don't understand the feelings at all nor the desire for
children which is a growing passion in me. Where are the
men who are good? I do not see them.[1]

BARBARA HAD A NATURALLY SUNNY PERSONALITY.
Everyone said so. She was almost invariably described as bonny,
blithe, good and gay: according to the nursery rhyme, the traditional traits of a child born, as she was, on a Sunday. People are
frequently called these things in retrospect, once they are safely
out of the way. But Barbara was complimented all her life for her
'true, large heart', as Marian Evans put it. She was a fortunate
woman. In return, she felt it her duty to share at every opportunity the deep reserves of happiness with which she had arbitrarily
been provided.

After the Pater's shattering revelations, however, and her
intense tussles with John Chapman and the 'Master Passion', it
must have seemed in the autumn of 1855 that those reserves were
in danger of running dry. Her philosophy was always to be
straight and true, like those Scots pine trees the Pater (himself at
times something of a contorted willow) had planted for his first

five children at their farmhouse in Sussex. She was convinced
that health in mind and body was a function of inner harmony
and a clear conscience. But so was John. It bewildered Barbara,
once she had renounced him, that her truth and his were so
different.

There is no suggestion that they were forced apart. The Pater's
disapproval was startlingly obvious, but she was no longer his
responsibility. He had taken considerable pains to give his eldest
daughter a fully sustainable life of her own, once she came of
age. It would have been painful to disappoint him, but he had
disappointed her. And she had forgiven him. Besides, she was her
own woman and had been for quite some time.

Brother Ben's reaction to the relationship was harder to bear.
He knew the extent of John's debts after talking to Uncle Oc and
friends Harriet Martineau and Samuel Courtauld, all of whom
were in danger of losing significant sums invested in the failing
Westminster Review. He was also aware of John's serial infidelities.
He was furious, calling Barbara's affair with the philanderer an
'accursed love' and demanding that she break free.

Barbara herself felt lost. I assume she ended things before it
was 'too late', as Victorian moralists would put it, because she
realized that a hole-in-the-corner partnership like the one John
was suggesting would compromise her as it had compromised
Anne Longden and Jane Buss. Barbara was heliotropic, a creature
born to flourish in the fresh air. She was twenty-eight (the average age for women to marry at this time was around twenty-four);
she wanted a proper family, a solid base, a good man of her own
and children who were confident of their place in the world.
John offered none of these things.

Why, then, was the thought of him so seductive? Barbara
must have questioned her own judgement. She had received two
offers of marriage during the past couple of years: one from a
German lodger of the Chapmans, Joseph Neuberg, who was
nearly fifty; the other from a brilliant mathematician, James

Sylvester, who had been a contemporary of Ben's at Cambridge. Neuberg, a translator and historian, did not attract her. Sylvester *almost* did. He had the unique distinction of having been withdrawn as an undergraduate at University College, London, for attempting to stab a fellow student with a table knife after a fracas in the dining hall (Cambridge obviously did not hold that against him) and was an outsider in Academe, as Unitarians and women were, for, like Neuberg, being a Jew. His intellect was the size of the Crystal Palace and he loved poetry. All this should have made for the perfect romantic hero, but his proposal let him down. It is too generic.

> I am conscious of an ever increasing charm in your society and conversation and . . . I should regard myself as most favoured by Providence were it possible for me to believe that you could accept the offer of my attachment and earnest and lifelong devotion . . . [T]o love you is to love goodness of heart, generosity and all that ennobles our nature. Let me hope that whatever other ill effect this note may produce it may not occasion me the loss of your friendship.[2]

Both men might have made safe husbands, yet she loved neither. John was the one who captivated her, who beckoned her away from that dubious illusion of a 'genteel family life'. Neither Neuberg nor Sylvester ever married.

Along with all those 'happy' adjectives, Barbara was often described as wild. Wild as in close to nature, free-spirited. And, possibly, wild as in loose-haired and uncorseted. Her friend Matilda Betham-Edwards beautifully summed her up as brimming with 'the wild joy of living'. It must have occurred to Barbara around this time that perhaps she was wild in another sense; that her blood was tainted after all, and that behind her open countenance lurked dangerous appetites. She was free to indulge those appetites if she wished: there was nothing but conformity and prurient disapproval to stop her. Or she could add them to an accretion of all the other suppressions in her life. At the end of September, she finally accepted that her personal morality was more conventional than she might have supposed, and let John go. Not conventional enough to accommodate Neuberg or Sylvester, mind you; if that implied a default choice of childless spinsterhood, so be it.

This decision to trust her instincts was courageous, but profoundly unsettling. Her close friends were more or less sympathetic. Bessie Parkes – the recipient of the letter quoted at the head of this chapter about Barbara wanting children and wondering where all the good men were – told her that she must sort out her own life and not expect others to do it for her. Harsh, but probably true, given Barbara's independent spirit. Marian Evans, of whom Barbara had been so supportive over her decision to cross the moral Rubicon with George Lewes, was kinder. She invited Barbara to stay with them a few months later so that they could 'drink in the sight' of her, and promised to 'say nothing of sorrows and renunciations, but I understand and feel what you must have to do and bear'.[3]

Anna Mary Howitt was perturbed by Barbara's unwonted misery, but felt loath to write John off. Perhaps it was something to do with his bizarrely intimate knowledge of her own menstrual cycle, courtesy of Barbara . . . She sent him a letter on Monday 1 October 1855.

I have not seen B[arbara] today but did yesterday & Saturday and Friday – and shall do so tomorrow I trust, when she will I hope now be left quietly with me for some little time – We think of going together quietly down in to the country. Of course she is dreadfully distressed in mind – but seems really pretty well in body – Oh, believe me I shall take the tenderest, tenderest of care of her dear body – and seek to calm – if possible – with God's blessing her dear and troubled spirit – I am thankful to say, that in a long conversation with Ben I have found him much tenderer in feeling towards her than I had dared to hope – and he entirely agrees that she shall be left quite unworried by him – poor fellow! – and by her Father . . . I thought you would like to hear this – God give you strength and peace to come! – Yours in deep sympathy, AM.[4]

I should imagine that the last thing Barbara wanted at this juncture was a spell in the company of increasingly fey Anna Mary, who sounds as though she might think it well worth pleading John's case. But the prospect of going away was attractive; somewhere without associations would be best, somewhere fresh and new, where it would be easier to look forward than back.

It comes as some surprise, therefore, to find her writing to Marian in January 1856 from that go-to destination for Smiths in trouble: the Isle of Wight. She and the persistent Anna Mary were ostensibly on a painting expedition, teaching themselves how to capture the stormy winter waves. Barbara assures Marian that she is feeling much better, though irritated by people's solicitousness (mostly Anna Mary's, I suspect) and still embarrassed. She admits a wish 'intensely to be pelted with rotten eggs or something for a change' and longs for a shift of scene. 'I must go to some wilder country to paint.'[5]

It would be reasonable to suppose – as Marian probably did – that Barbara was staying in Ventnor, in the south of the island, purely for the sake of rest and recuperation. But this was no furlough. Wherever she went, however she was feeling, Barbara worked. Indeed, she painted one of her most successful watercolours there: an expansive and gloriously luminous scene of the coast by Blackgang Chine, just around the corner from Ventnor, exhibited at the Royal Academy the following summer. She was busy on several fronts: with arrangements at Portman Hall, because Elizabeth Whitehead had been laid low for three months with a bad back; following up feedback after publication of her *Brief Summary*; and negotiating the sale of her pictures at prices ranging from £5 to £15 (around £250 to £750 now). Such activity was distracting, even exciting, but also draining.

It was not even her choice to be there: a doctor had suggested her sister Bella was developing TB in her lungs, and though it had patently failed their mother, the first thought of the family was to immerse Bella in the comparatively benign climate of the Isle of Wight. The Pater was approaching his mid-seventies by now; Ben had taken over as head of the family. He put Barbara in charge of Bella's care, instructing her to report regularly to him.

There is yet another layer of complexity in this apparently straightforward episode. It soon becomes chillingly clear, on reading Barbara's letters to Ben, that Bella's crisis was mental as well as physical, and far more deep-seated than anyone had supposed.

> Her unhappiness is of years standing, she told me of it, I cannot tell you as no end would be answered. I hoped she had got over it but it is not so, the less she is in B[landford] Sqre the better ... It is not family unhappiness ... You must not tell anyone there is a mental cause. The Pater must not know ... Her mind runs on the subject of love & marriage & all the force of her long pent up passionate nature has burst forth ... Bell is sometimes happy & gentle as a child then wild & frantic. She was always stronger than me & now is very much stronger. Twice she has seized me & hurt me – today she tried to throw herself out of the window. I caught hold of & pulled her back after she had broken the glass & cut herself.[6]

Poor Bella. Had there been some sort of scandal in London? A damaging case of unrequited love? It seems probable, but family history is opaque on the matter. And poor Barbara, who suspected that Bella was suffering a more acute attack of what John Chapman had suggested was physical and mental atrophy due to sexual frustration. 'I am quite sure,' she wrote to Ben, 'she will never be well unless she marries. All Doctors & all who know what women & men suffer from going against the imperative laws of nature agree.'[7] Did the same fate lie in wait for Barbara?

THE CRISIS PASSED. BELLA was nursed back to something approximating normal health by Barbara and two of Bella and Nannie's closest friends, with whom they had all stayed in Italy the previous winter: the writer Matilda 'Max' Hays and her lover, the American actress Charlotte Cushman. It was only thanks to Barbara that these two unapologetically flamboyant women were allowed anywhere near the sickbed: Ben strongly disapproved of them, but Barbara appreciated the value of love, given and received. 'I know all love is so different,' she once observed, 'that I do not see it unnatural to love in new ways.'[8] Bella had much for which to thank her eldest sister. So did Nannie, who was eventually to choose a woman (despite Ben's misgivings) as her life's partner, with Barbara's blessing.

By now, Barbara was utterly exhausted. In July 1856, she took Marian and George Lewes up on their invitation, and visited them on a seaside holiday in Tenby, Wales. She spent the week sketching rocks and trying to relax. Marian noted in her diary how much she enjoyed Barbara's stay, though she was shocked to find her friend looking so much older and sadder than usual. This languor could partly have been the result of a brave duty-visit by Barbara to Aunt Patty, who had retired to a life of near-seclusion in the resort. Barbara's description of their conversation was hilarious – 'a scene beyond the conception of Molière',[9] according to Marian – but it must have been a trial to sit in Patty's dismal parlour trying not to spill any of the rapidly accumulating family secrets which would no doubt confirm all the elderly woman's doubts and fears about the doomed Leigh Smiths.

Marian and Barbara rarely failed to cheer each other up. They used to go window shopping together in the West End of London, sharing a smug delight in neither needing nor desiring anything they saw. For all Barbara's wealth and love of sharing the good things in life, she was never avaricious. She helped Marian appreciate the joy of spontaneity. Marian's reciprocal gift was to share her concept of wealth as an intangible asset, and of spirituality being distinct from religion. 'I have faith in the working-out of higher possibilities than the Catholic or any other church has presented,' she wrote to Barbara. 'The highest "calling and election" is to do without opium and live through all our pain with conscious, clear-eyed endurance.'[10] Each woman was as resourceful as the other.

Barbara did not depend on organized religion, but could never quite do without the opiate of work. Following the success of *A Brief Summary*, which had now run into its second edition (no longer published by John Chapman), she organized the first-ever committee of women in Britain convened to discuss and promote political change on behalf of their own sex. Women had waged political campaigns before, against slavery and the Corn Laws (Aunt Ju knew that: she had been there). But this is where the women's movement was born: around a table in the drawing room of 5 Blandford Square in December 1855, coaxed into life by a large woman with flowing red-gold hair (and a slightly tired smile), sky-blue eyes, Arthurian garments and a fondness for the underdog. Her vicarious experience of abolitionist and Dissenting politics had taught her that reform was possible if argued for with cogency and conviction. It might take years, but the sooner campaigning begins, the sooner change will come. And many voices speak louder than one, as long as they are in unison. Hence the formation of the Married Women's Property Committee: the logical next step in Barbara's crusade for civil rights.

The Smiths were keen chess players – many a game had been worked out at that same table – so it was natural for Barbara to think in terms of strategy and response. Her first move against the legal status quo had been to articulate its inequities in *A Brief Summary*. The next was to consolidate support for her statements by gathering evidence and demonstrating relevance. That is where the committee came in: to canvass for case histories, political support and necessary funds. Then she could begin a planned and perfectly admissible attack in the form of a petition to Parliament. Public debates would result in resolutions; resolutions in persuasion; persuasion in reform. That is what male activists – male Smiths – had been doing collectively for generations. Why not women? Particularly if by behaving sensibly and responsibly in the process they were able to prove their own argument that females were neither feeble, chaotic nor generically dim.

The original committee inevitably embraced a core of Barbara's most stalwart friends, including Anna Mary Howitt and her mother Mary, Bessie Parkes, Elizabeth Reid, Anna Jameson and Tottie Fox. Aunts Ju and Dolly had supporting roles. Ju was particularly welcomed for her past experience. Barbara drafted the petition; the committee approved it, printed it and sent copies of it to any potential supporter they could think of, to be signed and returned to Barbara. Its text speaks of 'manifold evils' occasioned by the present law granting a husband absolute power over his wife's earnings.[11] 'The sufferings thereupon ensuing, extend over all classes of society.' Barbara explains that though the problem might have been dismissed as theoretical to 'the middle and upper ranks' before – when it was thought vulgar for ladies to seek paid work – it is now a practical problem 'since married women of education are entering on every side the fields of literature and art, in order to increase the family income'. She points out that there are escalating accounts of domestic violence and marital oppression in the newspapers – what we would now call coercive control – and of women forced on to the streets for a living, robbed of their money and dignity by an overbearing spouse.

Nothing was done in a hurry. Wise Mary Howitt advised against a scattergun approach to collecting names. 'I do think it is most needful to have an eye to the moral status of the persons supporting this movement; and that in the fields of science and literature signatures such as those of Mrs Somerville and Mrs Gaskell should be obtained.'[12] Mary Somerville certainly signed; so did Mrs Gaskell, despite her animus towards Barbara. They were joined by about 3,000 other women and men, whether married or single, whose names were all pasted on to a gratifyingly long scroll with the help of eighteen-year-old Octavia Hill.

Not everyone approached by the committee gave their endorsement. Bessie Parkes recalled that many ladies were reluctant to sign because gentlemen did not approve, while many gentlemen assumed the ladies were happy enough as they were. Why rock the boat? Committee members were accused of trying to violate the sanctity of marriage. The *Saturday Review* commented unsympathetically that 'no woman ought to be encouraged in the belief that she has separate interests or separate duties. God and nature have merged her existence in that of her husband.'[13] Despite the final tally of signatures topping 26,000, thanks to Barbara's legal mentor Matthew Davenport Hill bringing it to the attention of the Law Amendment Society, the *Saturday Review* found the whole enterprise laughable in retrospect. 'So long as the petticoat rebellion was confined to a mistaken petition of a few literary ladies whose peculiar talents placed them in a rather anomalous position we really had not the heart to say anything serious about it.'[14]

This reactionary journalist would have been even more scathing had he known who was behind the campaign: the name of the undoubtedly anomalous Miss Barbara Leigh Smith was tactically omitted from the text of the petition and the committee's publicity material, to save the blushes of potential signatories who might approve of married women keeping their own property but heartily disapprove of illegitimacy. Barbara was never one for political prominence, preferring to light the touchpaper and then retire; perhaps this is why.

The petition was brought to the House of Lords in March 1856 by Lord Brougham, the former Lord High Chancellor and veteran of the Great Reform Act, and to the Commons by Whig MP Sir Erskine Perry. Of all the seventy petitions submitted that session, this had the most signatures. But the motion was withdrawn after its second reading in favour of the Matrimonial Causes Act passed the following year, which changed the legislation around divorce. It was not until 1882 that the final Married Women's Property Act received royal assent. The committee kept going all that time (though Barbara's involvement lapsed due to other commitments), propelled by public meetings, tireless campaigning and a level of conviction that eventually won women the vote.

The delay was no failure on the part of novice Barbara and her sister activists; it went with the territory. At least they now had political experience and a growing network to support wider campaigns in the future. She was keen to take advantage of the momentum, and during the winter of 1856–7 planned to write another, longer publication, this time on paid work for women. But she still felt emotionally weary, vulnerable to bouts of anxiety that drained her of energy. She developed 'fetters on her speech'[15] – a stammer – and various low-level physical complaints. She used to feel exasperated when idle women whinged about undefined illness, but no longer. She was never idle, yet here she was, weak and listless. Her malaise was real, and unfamiliar.

Bessie tried to comfort her with the assurance that all would be well because God is wise. Max Hays was more practical, writing directly (and riskily) to Ben about her alarm over Barbara's mood. 'You know that I am very anxious about the coming winter for dear Bar . . . I feel it so important for [her] to be away from London . . . that I shall not think of it, if she has to remain. But she ought not, must not remain – health & Happiness are both at stake.'[16]

SHE DID NOT REMAIN. At the end of October 1856, Ben took his ailing, failing sisters far away from England, far away from the source of their various troubles, to the land of fairy tales.

> The Climate is delicious the sea & distant mountains more beautiful than words & pencil can express and then the new vegetation & the new animals the wonderfully picturesque town and people give one so much to do with one's 6 senses . . . I did not expect anything half so wonderfully beautiful as I find . . . The place intoxicates me![17]

The 'wonderfully picturesque' town was Algiers, where Barbara – writing breathlessly here to Marian – had magically become Perizade, the heroine of a real-life story from the *Arabian Nights*.

It was an inspired choice, made by the Pater. He had never been to North Africa himself – relatively few Englishmen had – but had heard that its warm, bracing climate was ideal for consumptive patients. He must have known how the irrepressibly enthusiastic Barbara would react to its otherness. He remembered the couplet he wrote about her as a child: 'Dear Barbara, your cheerful spirit / Never needs a stick to stir it.' Her spirit *did* need a stick to stir it this time, and he had found just the one: a complete change of scene; a distracting new world of sensation, impression and stimulation. There was a good chance that Barbara would forget Chapman and rediscover her old self there, and Bella might at least survive. No doubt Nannie would enjoy the ride.

Misconceptions about mid-nineteenth-century Algeria were widespread among suspicious, insular Victorians. Was it not once known as Barbary, from which 'barbarian' was derived? Was it not teeming with savages, barely controlled by the French? The *French*, of all people! Was it not a long and dangerous journey, days and days away from home? Rife with lethal fevers? Populated by men and women with dark skin and not enough clothes?

Actually, the name 'Barbary' comes from the same root as 'Barbara': it simply means 'strange', 'far from home'. The pre-Arab Berbers, whose diverse descendants lived there still, took their name from the same source. They were not picture-book 'savages', of course, but a proud people; culturally rich, religiously tolerant and breathtakingly creative.

Algeria had a long history of colonization, having been a precious possession of the Ottoman Empire; the French invaded in 1830, and by the time Barbara arrived it was almost entirely under French administration. In addition to Arabs and indigenous Berber nomads and farmers, its population included European ex-pats of varying provenance, all living in a country ten times the size of Great Britain and functioning more or less peacefully (with notable exceptions) and more or less prosperously. And it was only a couple of days' voyage from the south of France. According to a rather fanciful guidebook written a few years after Barbara's visit, Algiers was 'the Torquay of Africa'.[18] Beat that, if you can.

The landscape was as diverse as its people. Gardens looked like living Pre-Raphaelite paintings, rich with a fragrant, jewel-like profusion of lilies and cyclamen, jonquils, roses, jasmine, peonies and honeysuckle. Barbara feasted on dates, bananas, oranges, apricots and peaches, melons, grapes and figs. And she devoured with her eyes rose-madder mountains and Egyptian-blue hills, rocks coloured bronze and pewter, stretches of cadmium-yellow desert, lapis-lazuli seas, and streets and build-ings in ochre, burnt umber and dazzling flake white. She described it as more heavenly than heaven. 'The more I ride about,' she wrote to Bessie ecstatically, 'the more delighted I am with the country. It is so exquisitely lovely . . . An artist who went to the Atlas range to paint said the country was so beautiful that if he had stayed two months more he should have gone mad.'[19] Insanity due to sensual saturation was not exactly what Ben was looking for: he and Nannie wished simply to restore their sisters Barbara and Bella in mind and body; to revive that famous Leigh Smith buoyancy – and then to return home to normality.

The family's first impressions of Algiers were not over-encouraging. They arrived too late and exhausted to find anywhere to stay after a 47-hour passage from Marseilles in a ship loaded with French soldiers and emigrants. The only food and drink they had between them was an elderly, ant-infested sponge cake saved from the voyage and some brackish water writhing with what Barbara called 'bloodsuckers' (mosquitoes). Taking no chances, they drank champagne instead and immediately things began to improve. They soon found rooms at the Hôtel d'Orient, one of the three 'European' hotels, before renting a house just outside the city walls. Barbara's room was on the roof, with dual-aspect windows by which she positioned her easel according to the time of day.

Whenever she could, she ventured outside – as at home – to paint in the open air. There was a problem trying to source a side saddle (perhaps she had forgotten to pack her bloomers), but once she had fitted up a horse and found a promising spot to spend the day, she was less troubled by onlookers and rude little boys than in England. Muslim women perturbed her: she could not understand why they dressed in white burkas like ghosts and masked their faces with yashmaks. That understanding would come with time. For now, she was content to accept the 'wonderful strangeness' of Algeria and settle down to her default setting of work.

Barbara finished scores of drawings and watercolours during that first season in Algeria. Some look hurried and impressionistic; others are more carefully considered and form the basis of her future reputation as an artist. This was a sustained chance to practise everything she had been taught by tutors and friends at Bedford College and Tottie Fox's classes; to take on board what critics had said about her exhibited work, and consolidate her talent and technique.[20]

As ever, she could not resist the odd cartoon. One of them shows her marching sturdily through clumps of cacti and aloes in a large hat and cape. The sun is setting behind a mountain in the background, and there is a Moorish house in the valley far below. Effortlessly balanced on her shoulder are four enormously long palm leaves, twice as tall as she is. The day has been too short to paint them in situ, so she has hacked them down and is bringing them home to paint in her room. It is a ridiculous, endearing sight.

Art was not Barbara's only occupation. One project at a time was never enough. She had not forgotten that sequel to her *Brief Summary*: a tract about the need for women to earn a professional living without censure or impediment. She drafted *Women and Work* in Algeria over the winter; it was published in the early summer of 1857.

It is something of a curate's egg. The central message is that the 'deconsideration' of women (keeping them institutionally empty-headed and depriving them of useful work for financial reward) is a violation of human rights. Women should be allowed a career – with appropriate training – for the good of their soul, their family and of society.

> To think a woman is more feminine because she is frivolous, ignorant, weak, and sickly, is absurd; the larger-natured a woman is, the more decidedly feminine she will be; the stronger she is, the more strongly feminine. You do not call a lioness unfeminine . . .
>
> If men think they shall lose anything charming by not having ignorant, dependent women about them, they are quite wrong. The vivacity of women will not be injured by their serious work. None play so heartily as those who work heartily. The playfulness of women which makes them so sympathetic to children, is deep in their nature; and greater development of their whole natures will only increase this and all their natural gifts . . . Let women take their places as citizens in the Commonwealth.[21]

This is revolutionary stuff. In retrospect, we can recognize the spirit of *Women and Work* driving forward first-wave feminism from Wollstonecraft to the suffragists and beyond. Unfortunately, however, it is neither cogent nor well written. Barbara is so obviously sincere, but without her usual network of rigorous friends on hand to herd her ideas into neat corrals, she gallops all over the place. One moment she is considering God's purpose in creating women; the next, bewailing the over-sentimentality of the age she lives in. She veers from discussing the basics of political economy to the recalcitrance of the British Establishment. She constantly diverts the reader with apparently unconnected asides, mentioning some of her reforming heroines – cousin Florence, for example, her friend Mary

Carpenter and a French woman, Madame Luce, who ran a school for girls in Algiers – before addressing the iniquities of white slavery, obstinate fathers (she should know) and the misery of being a governess. She appends copies of correspondence about the (non) admission of women to medical schools and information about lunatic asylums in America, all in fewer than sixty pages. Valid arguments lose their vigour in such shallow soil.

The most eccentric passage is about dress. Anyone who knew Barbara would realize that she practised what she preached with some style; others might well be baffled by her remarks on 'disreputable, dirty, and inconvenient' women's skirts. As long as they insisted on wearing floor-length gowns, she said, women deserved to be treated as babies. Far better to hoick up the hems – like she and Bessie had done as 'free-minded Albion's daughter[s]' in Germany – and enjoy the liberty of unimpeded limbs. 'A just medium will be found,' she quipped, 'a little lower than the knee, a little higher than the ground.'[22] Remember, this was the era of pornographic ankles and trousered piano legs.

Barbara appears to have temporarily forgotten the lesson learned from the Married Women's Property Committee's disciplined organization: that collective solidarity is a much stronger political tool than personal outrage, however heartfelt. The *Saturday Review* savaged *Women and Work* as soon as it was published, implying that its author was a fantasist for whom facts were irrelevant and statistics merely ornamental.

Miss Barbara – we cannot bear to speak of so poetical a philosopher as Miss Smith . . . is a lady of large figures [oh, ha ha] . . . If this is a fair sample of what a lady who boasts to have made the subject her own is likely to publish [she never boasted that], we are afraid that the sex is not really so developed as we had hoped. As a piece of 'pretty Fanny's' talk it would be charming, but we should be sorry to trust 'pretty Fanny' with any business more important than the payment of a milk bill.[23]

The *London Daily News* – which had already published a lightly fictionalized account of the Leigh Smiths' arrival in Algiers[24] – was much gentler, calling *Women and Work* 'simple, earnest, vigorous, and yet feminine'.[25] But then, it would: it was founded by Charles Dickens, who shared mutual friends with Barbara's family; it included leading radicals among its contributors, Harriet Martineau among them, and went on to support the women's movement until universal suffrage was won in 1928. Had those two reviews of *Women and Work* been the other way around, Barbara would have worried. As it was, she hardly noticed. Because, by the summer of 1857, she had other things on her mind.

TUCKED AWAY ON PAGE six of *Women and Work* is an extract about nature always favouring the beautiful over the ugly. If two races mix, says the quoted author, the best characteristics of each will dominate the worst, so that gradually humanity will 'perfectionate'. Barbara's two races are men and women; she wants them to mix in society on equal terms and thus create something progressively better than the sum of its parts. She credits the original author, who was writing about ethnology, as 'Bodichon, Docteur Médecin à Alger'.

Dr Eugène Bodichon (1810–85) was a republican from Brittany who arrived in Algeria in 1836 and had been there ever since. He was an intriguing man. Patients flocked to the upper storey of his Moorish house in Algiers, where he treated Arabs, Africans, French, Spaniards and whoever else happened to come along, for free, should they have no money to pay medical bills. One of his first missions had been to campaign for the abolition of slavery in the colony. As corresponding member of the republican

Chamber of Deputies (a political post roughly equivalent to a remote Member of Parliament), another task of his was to extend suffrage to Berber peoples across the country.

Eugène's eccentricity was legendary. He looked extraordinary: tall, with a shock of curly black hair (he never wore a hat) and a noble profile that, according to Barbara, made him look like Caractacus. He thought nothing of walking twenty miles to hear a hyena's cackle, or to seek out rare flowers just for the pleasure of looking at them. He adored animals, protesting at the practice of vivisection during his medical training. He once allowed a homeless mouse to nest unmolested in his hair, and befriended a jackal during a holiday to Algeria while he was a student in Paris. He brought the jackal home with him, donating it to the Jardin des Plantes; it went crazy with joy every time he visited.

He was republican not by birth but by conviction, repudiating his mother's ancestral wealth amassed in the Caribbean island of Saint-Domingue (now Haiti) and refusing to live in the family château near Nantes. As well as an ethnologist he was a philosopher, whose unusual views on the progress of humanity were expressed in a series of printed works. An environmentalist and conservationist, he was well ahead of his time.

But he was best known in Algiers as a colourful local hero who once carried a bishop and two priests over a flash-flooded river, saving their lives (despite not being a practising Catholic himself, it was noted). In 1850 he tried to get an expedition together to trek to Timbuktu – because it was there – but failed to find the battalion of armed Frenchmen and 300–400 'trusty Arabs' he needed for support. Then there was the time he famously rescued Charles Bombonnel, the celebrity French panther-hunter, from disfigurement and probable death. Bombonnel was renowned for his exploits in the field, but was horrifically mauled and almost killed during an expedition in Algeria. Eugène was his saviour, fitting the pieces of Bombonnel's face back together as neatly as a fractured china plate. There used to be two pictures

of the post-operative patient in Eugène and Barbara's home
(where other practitioners might hang their certificates), with a
detailed, handwritten caption:

> The skilful doctor gathering up such pieces as were left . . .
> Here is a list of the wounds:– 5 on the left hand, the ani-
> mal's teeth having pierced it in 3 places; 8 in the left arm; 4
> in the head; 10 in the face; 4 in the mouth, the nasal bone
> being broken, 5 teeth wrenched out; and the left cheek
> below the eyelid torn to tatters.[26]

Bodichon was a surgeon *sans pareil*.

Exactly where or when Barbara met Eugène is uncertain. All
the letters she wrote about him to Bessie, Anna Mary and Marian
have been destroyed. On 14 April 1857, she announced their
engagement, just six months after arriving in Algiers, and a year
and a half after the end of the Chapman affair. They planned to
marry as soon as possible. Given the descriptions of him above,
taken largely from an article in a British periodical,[27] it is easy to
understand why she was convinced that here, at last, was her
'good man', the father of her strong-minded, beautiful children.
He was fiercely independent; passionate about improving the lot
of humanity, especially the dispossessed and the ill; kind to animals; in tune with nature; strong, brave and romantic. She
described him as the most handsome man ever created. There is a
touching drawing of a lily in Barbara's family's collection, with
the name of the place where it was plucked, a date in May 1857,
and a simple note: 'Dr Bodichon gave me. B.'[28]

Anna Mary, Marian and George Lewes were worried that
everything was happening too fast; that Barbara was rashly committing herself to a foreigner seventeen years her senior, and that
they might never see their friend again. Not just a foreigner, but
a Frenchman. *Entente* between the two countries had not been

Barbara kept this sketch she drew of a lily picked for her by Eugène all her life.

cordiale for years; the Battle of Waterloo in 1815 was only a generation ago, and now there were fears that France was planning an invasion of England via the Channel Islands.

On a personal level, Anna Mary thought Eugène looked 'hard' in a sketch she had seen. Bessie Parkes was more positive, certain that her beloved Bar would never forsake the country of her birth. England was like a mother to her. She jokingly wrote to Barbara to ask whether she and the Doctor (people always called him 'the Doctor') were planning to emigrate to Tierra del Fuego or somewhere, expecting an assurance that, no, of course they weren't: they would soon be home. That assurance did not come.

Ben was shocked: who was this weird stranger? Was he after Barbara's money, like Chapman? Bella declined to take sides but Nannie was splenetic. Disinclined to marry herself, she wanted Barbara as an ally, an unattached companion. No doubt supported by the Pater, an attempt was made by Ben and Aunt

Dolly's cousin Jo Gratton to dig up a character reference from somewhere. Barbara was furious, and deeply hurt. She complained to Bessie:

> Ben and Mr Gratton, without telling me, went off and found a Frenchman who gave such an account of Dr Bodichon as to do no end of mischief. I have found out that this man has a bad moral character. And is very ill thought of in the town of Algiers.
>
> Can you think of anything more undignified than that Ben should go to a stranger, and a person who is held in no respect, to ask questions about a man everyone respects?[29]

It must indeed have been mortifying; not quite the family welcome Eugène might have expected, nor the celebration Barbara craved.

Bessie shared Barbara's anger, yet realized the prudence of obtaining a second opinion on Eugène. She and her mother came up with the name of Dr Ange Guépin, the chief physician in Eugène's hometown of Nantes. He was a high-profile medic and author who had known Eugène for nearly twenty-seven years. The socialist Louis Blanc was their mutual friend – and a friend of the Pater's, too. Mrs Parkes wrote to Dr Guépin explaining the situation and asking for his objective opinion of Dr Bodichon. At first, his response was ambiguous. 'Dr Bodichon is too eccentric and too indifferent to what people think of him to be liked ... There is in his character something knightly and something in him both of Diogenes and of Don Quixote. This admixture irritates his adversaries.'

But it got better. 'Miss Barbara would, I think, find in him a suitable husband, especially in view of the fine work to which she is devoting her life. A commonplace woman would be very unhappy with the doctor, and would not know how to guide his curious nature.'[30]

The implication was that Barbara, being anything but a commonplace woman, would match this 'fine and noble' gentleman very well. He was poor, warned Dr Guépin, but never attached any importance to money. He was no fortune hunter.

Good news for Barbara; not so good for the Pater, Ben and others who feared for her future happiness. But in the end, it didn't really matter. She had made up her mind. Bessie reckoned it would be as easy to halt Niagara Falls as to thwart Barbara when she had set her mind on something. Another friend, Jessie Meriton White, was sanguine. 'Well, if he lets dear old Bar get her share of good out of life & does not hinder her being & doing all she was meant to be & to do . . . God bless them both, say I.'[31]

7

Boadicea in America

Personal Life, 1857–1858

Nationality, racial distinction, religion, even colour,
for her were non-existent.[1]

THE HONOURABLE IMPULSIA GUSHINGTON: A NAME TO
conjure with – not unlike Barbara Leigh Smith Bodichon. Impulsia wrote *Lispings from Low Latitudes*, a profusely illustrated
autobiographical account of a journey to Egypt in 1861. The
book opens with her sitting glumly by her English fireside, feeling bilious and bored. When her doctor prescribes travel, she is
delighted: she has always had an 'inclination to go Somewhere'
but never dared admit it. In two shakes of a lamb's tail, she has
put her affairs in order, swept her little lapdog Bijou into a carpet
bag and set off abroad. Not to the comparatively safe surroundings of France, or even newly fashionable Switzerland; instead,
this eccentric middle-aged maiden chooses the mysterious East.

Lispings from Low Latitudes chronicles her adventures en route
to Cairo, where she promptly falls in love with an extravagantly
moustachioed French gentleman, Monsieur Victor-Alphonse de
Rataplan. He proposes within a fortnight of their meeting; she
accepts with alacrity, dazzled by his exoticism and facial hair,
and relieved, at last, to have bagged a husband. The final illustra-
tion in the book shows her swooning decoratively in his arms.

In fact, the comic Miss Gushington was a spoof character,

created by the Irish writer Lady Helen Selina Dufferin to ridicule
the emerging fashion for single ladies to travel abroad. Look
what might happen: you'll be wooed in haste by someone wildly
unsuitable, and then – as is hinted in an epilogue – be left to
repent at leisure.

It is irresistibly tempting to imagine Barbara as a model for
Impulsia, and bearded Dr Bodichon for de Rataplan. Lady
Dufferin was Caroline Norton's sister, so there is no doubt that
she was aware of the larger-than-life Miss Leigh Smith. Despite
their shared interest in the rights of married women, Barbara and
Caroline never collaborated and there is no evidence that they
were friends. That does not mean that they were enemies, of
course, but given that Lady Dufferin patently disapproved of
free-minded Albion's daughters like Barbara (and Impulsia), it
would hardly be shocking to discover that she had chosen her as
the target for satire.

The announcement of Barbara's engagement in April 1857
released a little gust of gossip in London. She was a recognized
figure; most who knew her loved her. The poet Robert Browning
once said that being in her company was like a benediction. But
to others who had only heard of her name and exploits (tagged
with the stigma of illegitimacy) she might easily be written off as
freakishly unorthodox, a highly coloured hybrid of Tennyson's
Boadicea and Dante's Beatrice – both distinctive figures she had
modelled for Anna Mary Howitt. Was this not the woman who
had railed in print against the iniquities of marriage? She was
exactly the sort of cracked person to take herself off to some
pantomimic destination like Egypt or Algeria and make a fool of
herself.

Is that what Barbara did? Intimate friends suggested that she
was emotionally vulnerable, on the rebound from her relationship with John Chapman. Her heart was singed, as Bessie Parkes
put it.[2] Why else choose Eugène? No one seriously suggested
that he seduced or coerced her; Barbara was too proud to risk

that happening a second time. But he was ... unusual. Barbara described him paradoxically as 'ugly and terrific' as well as irresistibly good-looking – ugly as in wild and elemental; 'by temperament sensitive, irritable, passionate, violent and reserved' but with a capacity for 'entire devotion and love to one person': her.[3] Though Marian Evans was circumspect, she was sure he must be a genuine, right-feeling man (which sounds like faint praise). Barbara herself was certain she had found her mate. He was everything she was not, she said; together, they were one.

She wrote to Marian and George Lewes from Algiers before travelling back to London at the end of May, to tell them that the wedding would take place on 15 June. That date came and went, the big day probably delayed by Ben and the Pater's insistence on cementing in place a watertight marriage settlement first. While Barbara naturally stayed at 5 Blandford Square during the negotiations, poor Eugène was farmed out to lodgings off Bishop's Road in Paddington, right next to the recently opened station. The hot, dirty air was filled with clamour and smuts of soot. This was a far cry from the fragrant beauty of Algeria.

From there he sent a long and detailed document to Barbara.[4] It is nothing less than a pedigree, a sort of genealogical curriculum vitae, tracing back an unsullied bloodline from his parents, Dr Charles Théodore Bodichon du Pavillon and Antoinette Le Grand de la Pommeraye, to the mid seventeenth century. As if Barbara cared. It was obviously meant for the Pater's eyes, which is somewhat ironic, given his daughter's confused heritage.

Eugène's body of work spoke more insistently than his ancestry, some of which he had repudiated on political grounds anyway. By the time of their marriage, he had published six works on Algeria, discussing the country's ideology, philosophy, economics, natural history, climate and 'moral hygiene', the latter being a cocktail of subjects addressing sexual, spiritual and mental health. His magnum opus, *De l'humanité*, was not published in full until 1866, but was years in the making. Barbara appreciated the ideals underpinning this behemoth of a book and was impressed by many of them. He considered the universe his country and humankind his family. Though not religious in any orthodox sense, he believed, as she did, in the triumph of good over evil. Humanity's greatest strength in the future would be its racial coalescence, he predicted; a function of miscegenation, meaning (to him) the harmonious genetic mixing of different races. Discrimination would be a thing of the past. To Barbara, she and Eugène embodied the ideal she described in *Women and Work*: they were 'equal in intellectual gifts and loving hearts, the union between them being founded in their mutual work'.[5]

This was all fine and dandy, but the Pater did not yet trust Barbara to judge the man objectively. She was in love, and love – he had good reason to know – was blind. So he and his legal advisers drew up a vast indenture to prevent Eugène from taking advantage of his wealthy, open-hearted bride. It still exists, virtually large enough to wallpaper a modest room, dated the day before the wedding, and signed in slightly wobbly hands by Barbara, Eugène and Barbara's two trustees, Aunt Ju and barrister John Thornely.[6] Trustees were appointed not so much as gatekeepers against extravagance on Barbara's part, as to guard against any stealthy arrogation of funds by Eugène in the future, even after her death. Without this legal document in place, under the terms of the legislation at the time in Britain and France, what had been hers would now be his to do with what he would.

The wedding took place at Little Portland Street Unitarian Chapel on Thursday 2 July 1857. On the marriage certificate Eugène, aged forty-six, is described as an MD, or Doctor of Medicine, and Barbara, aged thirty, as an artist. William H. Channing officiated, nephew of the charismatic American Unitarian preacher William Ellery Channing; he was a friend of the women's rights campaigner Susan B. Anthony and of the Martineau family, completing a three-year stint as a visiting preacher in Liverpool. The signing of the register was witnessed by the Pater, Ben and John Thornely. Barbara was given a lucky rabbit (whether dead or alive, real or pretend, partial or whole is unclear) by Aunt Ju, along with a large black portfolio case for her paintings; Dolly contributed some green ribbons to set off her bonny hair; and Ben, though still angry with Bessie Parkes for encouraging the marriage in the first place – they hardly spoke again – generously gave the couple ownership of 5 Blandford Square.[7]

A quiet note was tucked into the corner of several London and provincial newspapers during the following days, mentioning the wedding of Barbara Leigh, eldest daughter of Benjamin Smith, Esq., but omitting to name her husband. No sense of celebration has drifted down the years. It is almost as though this family's dysfunctional relationship with marriage were compromised by Barbara's choice; as though by becoming Madame Bodichon, a French subject, she had renounced her Englishness and settled for second best.

No doubt her family was mollified by Barbara's very modern insistence on keeping her maiden name. John Thornely told her that it would be incorrect to call herself Barbara Smith Bodichon.[8] She begged to differ. 'Let me say a word about Barbara Smith,' she wrote to her father.

> I believe [Mr Thornely] is wrong as a matter of law. I do not think there is any law to oblige a woman to bear the name of her husband at all, and probably none to prevent keeping the old name. To use it is very useful, for I have earned a right to Barbara Smith and am more widely known than I had any idea of, and constantly my card with my name on it is useful in getting me friends. Dr. says he should think it folly for me to use his name except as a convenience in society, and if we have a line of English descendants they will be Bodichon-Smiths.[9]

That could have been written by a daughter to her father ten years ago. Today, even. Yet again, Barbara is far ahead of her time.

TWO MONTHS AFTER THE wedding, Barbara Leigh Smith Bodichon sailed the Atlantic from east to west for the second time in her life. Just as in 1829, she boarded a record-breaking vessel for the passage: RMS *Persia*, of the Cunard Line, was the largest iron-built ship afloat when she was launched in 1856 and held the Blue Riband for the fastest transatlantic voyage at nine days, ten hours and twenty-two minutes. She and Eugène embarked at Liverpool – the ship's manifest describes her as 'Mrs Bodichan, French' – making landfall in New York on 15 September 1857.

Although this was officially their honeymoon, the Bodichons were in America to work. Each had already had time to broach the idea of sharing life with someone else; of being half a married couple instead of a whole single person; of negotiating the Master Passion. That period between the wedding and leaving for America was the true honeymoon. No letters either to or from Barbara survive from then: their privacy is secure.

Marian commented that this long holiday might be a good opportunity for the reluctant Eugène to learn English. Neither he nor his wife spoke each other's language with any skill, presumably conversing in a sort of hybrid pidgin, or extra loudly and slowly in their own tongue. But his primary mission during their nine-month stay was to collect ethnographical data, to publicize his books and pamphlets, and advertise his reputation as a French abolitionist. He was described in the press – by radical American northerners, at least – as an eminent scientist, a gentleman well known in Europe and America, and a highly respected authority on the theory of miscegenation or racial 'amalgamation'. One of the couple's letters of introduction called him 'really a superior man . . . the least *vaniteux* of Frenchmen' and 'a good deal distinguished in Algeria'.[10]

Reactionaries who sympathized with the Southern states, where the lucrative trade and exploitation of slaves had not yet been outlawed, thought of him differently. His liberal views on the nobility of Africans and the part they had to play in the civilization of the world disgusted the editor of the *Wayne County Herald*, for example, who considered the Doctor's opinions on 'universal fusion' repugnant.

> What a horrible remedy for the evil [of having to live alongside Africans]. This Atheistic French physician and mock philosopher could not conceive of a more abominable expedient. The idea of abasing the Caucasian race by amalgamating it with the negro . . . is unpardonably wretched.[11]

It took courage for Eugène and his wife to speak out against slavery and the treatment of newly free African Americans while in the heartland of the South. Barbara reported that others doing the same had been attacked in the street, tarred and feathered or run out of town. What was it St Paul wrote in his letter to the Colossians? 'Wives, submit yourselves unto your own husbands, as it is fit in the Lord . . . Servants, obey in all things your masters according to the flesh; not with eyeservice, as menpleasers; but in singleness of heart, fearing God.'[12] To many, the abolitionist and subsequent women's suffrage campaigns were sacrilegious, as well as ideologically unsound.

Barbara's grandfather William used to speak of abolitionism with a mixture of pride and horror when she was a child. 'Head, Heart & Hands, have been turned to this subject for the last 40 years . . .' he wrote in the 1820s, 'and, go on to perfection, it will & must – nothing can stop it.'[13] Yet thirty years and more later, the trade in human beings still flourished in southern America.

All that Harriet Beecher Stowe had said about the treatment of Africans in her sensational novel *Uncle Tom's Cabin*, published in 1852, Barbara found – with a shock – to be true. How could she fail to speak out? *Her* mission in America was to ignore the rhetoric surrounding the rights and wrongs; to try to get to know as many of the individually oppressed as she could, and to learn directly from them what they needed to be – and to feel – truly free. And then to tell everyone.

There are some associated problems with all this for a modern audience, however, which it is important to address before setting off with the crusading Bodichons through pre-Civil War America. Firstly, Barbara used the terminology of her day, occasionally repeating the 'n' word herself and thoughtlessly commenting on the different appearance of African Americans. Secondly, to modern ears her identification with those deprived of liberty can sound patronizing. She had been to school with young women of colour; she – of all people – was used to responding to people with an open mind. Yet she found it impossible to empathize with female slaves fully. Their circumstances were almost too terrible to comprehend. She felt frustratingly like an observer, like someone from another world. Her way of trying to overcome this distance, this lack of intimacy, as she described it, was to liken the plight of slaves in their society to the plight of women in hers. We might think this reductive. And thirdly, to those familiar with the later chilling emergence of the eugenics movement, Eugène's ambitions for the blending of races might seem fascist. At the very least, they imply a lack of respect for diversity. But according to Barbara, his 'scientific' theory was enlightened: an abstract construct that all races were 'elevated' when their natural assets and acquired attributes were shared. Social and racial divisions of any kind were unhelpful to the healthy development of humankind. The corollary of distinction is discrimination.

It seems obvious to us that, as privileged Europeans, Barbara's and Eugène's outlook was likely to be riddled with unconscious bias. It is difficult not to judge them, especially with the aid of a modern retrospectoscope. But we are all creatures of our time and place. What distinguishes both Barbara and Eugène from most of their peers is that they tried as hard as they could to change the status quo for the better, for *all*.

To appreciate that, one has only to witness Barbara's utter conviction – not widely current at the time – that liberty was a human right; that no one people was inherently inferior or superior to another (nor any one sex); that everyone deserved opportunity, respect and a voice. She was determined in all she did to shake off the received wisdom of her generation, though stubborn clods of it were bound to stick to the soles of her boots occasionally. Some of her experiences in the slave states made her physically sick, driven to despair of humankind and its hollow religions. She was quick to acknowledge the universal necessity to tolerate and recognize each other as brothers and sisters of equal inheritance (though that recognition appears to have been a lifelong work in progress in the case of her Bentley Smith siblings). She admired many Americans for their demonstrable love of democracy.

> One is so little used to freedom, real freedom, even in England, that it takes time to understand freedom, to realize it . . . Until I came to America, I hardly felt the strange want of rational liberty in England . . . What an incredible amount of humbug there is in England never struck me before. They talk Christianity – all men equal before God – but it is only in the Free States of America that that idea of Christ's about equality is beginning to be understood.[14]

A close friend described Barbara best when she explained that 'nationality, racial distinction, religion, even colour, for her were non-existent'. She tried to take people as she found them, but 'injustice she never could forgive'.[15]

Barbara is identified as a professional artist on her marriage certificate; as well as being something of a sociological field trip, this 'honeymoon' would also prove a rich source of subject matter, and an opportunity to broaden public awareness of her work. Both she and Eugène looked forward to seeing old friends and making new ones along the way (he bumped into people he knew, or who claimed to know him, with staggering regularity). They would enjoy exploring new landscapes, new cultures and each other, away from the demands of committee meetings, clinics, school administration, recalcitrant critics, and high-maintenance friends and family.

Reading Barbara's letters home from America is like eaves-dropping on a fascinating conversation: sometimes we cannot quite catch what is being said, while at other times we can hear every word. She is out of earshot for the first few weeks – all the letters from that period have disappeared – but suddenly, on 6 December 1857, there she is, loud and clear, aboard the *Baltic*, a Mississippi paddle steamer on its way to New Orleans. In her usual style, Barbara is in the middle of deboning an empty-headed American female.

> Miss Juliet was a specimen of a Southern lady. She could not travel alone; she was pale and looked dissipated. She had been brought up in the Great Convent at Washington where fashionable Southerners go for education ... I never heard of a worse system of education in my life, and, according to her account, the girls were as bad as the system – intriguing, lying creatures. Miss Juliet told stories of the way in which lovers were got into the convent in disguise ... She was a horrid animal. She told me her mother was married at thirteen and her sister at fifteen and says it is the custom in the Slave States ... Miss Juliet could

not walk a mile, says few South state American women can; so say all the ladies here in the boat. Slavery makes all labour dishonourable and walking gets to be thought a labour, an exertion.[16]

Barbara thinks nothing of a ten-mile walk (and, indeed, campaigns vociferously for the right to roam at home in Sussex). She tells a companion-piece story of Polly, the slave employed to look after their cabin on the boat.

I said, 'Polly, how many times have you been sold?' 'Twice.' 'Have you any children?' 'I had three. God only knows where two of them are. My master sold them. We lived in Kentucky. One – my darling – he sold south. She is in one of these fields perhaps picking [cotton] with those poor creatures you saw. Oh dear, Mum, we poor creatures have need to believe in God, for if God Almighty will not be good to us some day, why were we born? When I [hear] of his delivering his people from bondage I know it means the poor African.' Her voice was so husky I could hardly understand her, but it seems her master promised to keep one child and then sold it without telling her and when she asked in agony '*Where is my child?*' the master said, 'Hired out,' – but it never came back . . . She said to me on parting, 'Never forget me. Never forget what we suffer. Do all you can to alter it.'[17]

Barbara made quite an impression on the other passengers aboard the *Baltic*. She describes sitting down to write her letters with a flamboyant green feather-pen, occasionally wearing her shirt of glancing green silk, and a green net over her rose-gold hair given to her by Ellen Allen, a teacher at Portman Hall ('Bless me, what hair,' breathes an admirer). Eugène had to fight off the competition – literally, on one occasion, when a general from

Texas took a violent fancy to his wife. The general lurched up to
her when she was sitting on her own one afternoon, leering and
shouting whiskey-scented obscenities about Eugène. He promised that when Eugène died – which the general would soon
arrange – he would marry her 'whether you like or no'. Barbara
was not a woman to be easily frightened, but the drunken general terrified her.

When Eugène appeared, the general 'smashed his hat' on the
Doctor's head, who then leapt to his feet – 'I will not be touched
by anyone!'[18] – and flung the offending hat back in the general's
face. If the Texan came anywhere near Barbara or him again,
hissed Eugène, he would be forced to shoot him. Unfortunately,
the *Baltic*'s captain heard the fracas and took the general's
part, threatening to make Eugène disembark there and then
unless he calmed down. He calmed down.

By 21 December, the Bodichons arrived in New Orleans,
where they stayed for almost two months. They rented rooms
from a shouty Yankee lady who insisted that slavery was a fine
institution, that slaves should not be allowed to marry (though
encouraged to reproduce) and – for the general safety of society –
should *never* be taught to read and write. Slowly, Barbara and
Eugène settled into a routine. Barbara wrote her daily journal for
the Pater and posted batches every week, to be passed around the
close family, and then kept safe for her return. She also wrote
regularly to Aunt Dolly and Mr Gratton. She frequently complained that no one bothered to write back to her, however
interesting she tried to be, but a glance at local newspapers of the
period reveals that on more than one occasion envelopes for her
and for Eugène were lying unclaimed at the post office in New
Orleans. That said, several letters both to and from the Bodichons
appear to have been lost in the post. I dream of them turning up
one day, like those Christmas cards we hear reported every year,
delivered decades late out of the blue.

On most Sundays, Barbara went to church, but not to the

same one. She was curious. It was the Catholics one week, the local 'Black Church' the next; the Unitarians, Methodists and Baptists all got a turn, as did local African-American preachers who gathered ad hoc congregations around the city. She was transfixed by the slaves' celebrations, feeling uplifted and at home in their joyful, heartbreaking company. Good cheer was hard to come by, it was so humid, dank and dreary in that part of the world. She felt as though there were a miasma – physical and moral – perpetually hanging over the town.

She and Eugène were constantly being invited to tinselly parties, concerts and the opera, but loved best to wander out on their own, with Barbara's painting clobber, to explore. Sometimes they would have a target-shooting competition (Barbara having been taught, presumably, by her brother Ben). She was frightened of snakes, and usually sent Eugène ahead to scare them away. She was also terrified of those evil-looking alligators, yet persuaded her poor husband to capture one, tie its jaws together and drag it back to their rooms so that she could draw it. Perhaps it made Eugène feel heroic, like Bombonnel, the panther-conqueror of old. One of Barbara's most famous pictures is of a Louisiana swamp, exquisitely detailed and almost surreal in its grotesque greenery. The *Illustrated London News* published a full-page wood engraving of it. 'How a lady could have realised such a scene with such apparent truth is to me a marvel,' wrote an art critic in *The Express*.[19] It does not occur to him that she was *there*. Others were quick to praise the picture's power and strange immediacy. Only John Ruskin held back, unable to imagine why anyone would want to immortalize such a dismal scene.

How many of the picture's admirers realized that the crouching figure one can just see, almost obscured by the undergrowth, is the artist's husband? He is wearing what appear to be Arabian robes – as Eugène was wont to do – and clutches a rifle, ready to punish any errant alligators threatening Barbara, as she sits in her broad-brimmed painting hat wearing Bessie Parkes's specs in the sweaty sunshine.

The Bodichons preferred renting rooms of their own to staying in a hotel. The dining hall at the St Charles Hotel, for example, was vast enough to accommodate eight hundred chattering people at dinner: to Barbara and Eugène, that would be hell on earth. Having their own place was more relaxing, and cheaper. Housekeeping was never Barbara's forte, and they were hardly likely to acquire slaves of their own, but that did not matter. Eugène was an excellent house husband, 'because, you see, his work is head work and it is good for him to have a little marketing and house affairs to attend to, and my work is hard head work and hard hand work too, and I can be at it all day long'.[20]

This is an example of the pragmatism that hallmarked their early married life. They had different friends – Eugène's a 'codfish aristocracy', according to his teasing wife, all 'flare-up fashionables or political sufferers', and Barbara's 'solid units, rich and quiet or poor and enlightened'.[21] They often went out separately, Barbara to inspect local schools or meet women from as many different backgrounds as she could, and Eugène to network among influential gentlemen. He wrote a letter to the Pater all about politics and economics, as dry as a bone. Only in a single sentence at the end does he touch on the personal. 'Barbara is well,' he says.[22]

Two memorable experiences summed up New Orleans for Barbara. The first was an encounter she had with a 'beautiful but vacant' young white woman near Carrollton (now a fashionable suburb).[23] Barbara had randomly taken a train on her own – something she often did – in search of a good place to sketch. She disembarked at a stop by a swamp in the woods, next to a grand house, and settled down to work. Miss Cecilia and her maid Zoe emerged from the house to watch. Staring Cecilia came so close that Barbara offered her a corner of her outspread mackintosh to sit on. Hardly a word was said. The next day, Barbara returned to the same spot. Out came Cecilia and Zoe again; this time Barbara had brought her a couple of cushions to sit on. As it was difficult to work under such close and silent observation, she tried to engage Cecilia in conversation. Zoe left the young woman in Barbara's care, and disappeared.

It emerged that Cecilia was twenty. She lived with her grandmother in the big house and was never allowed to do anything but crocheting, which she hated. Grandmother would not spend a single cent on teaching Cecilia anything; she dared not go for walks in the woods for fear of runaway slaves and was literally going out of her mind with boredom.

Two years ago, there had been an outbreak of yellow fever in the neighbourhood. The local doctor turned a schoolhouse into a hospital and asked Cecilia to help. Grandmother refused permission, but the doctor defied her and gave Cecilia a rudimentary training as a nurse. She worked from 4 a.m. until midnight every day and was never happier in her life. Barbara suspected that she fell in love with the doctor, but he was already married. When the crisis was over, Cecilia was returned to her grandmother, to moulder.

Barbara asked her if she had read *Uncle Tom's Cabin* yet. No: Grandmother was blind, so there were no books in the house. What was it about? Slaves? Grandmother had owned eight hundred of them once; now only Zoe was left. Even Zoe's four children had been sold. Why was that wrong? Patiently, Barbara explained.

When Grandmother heard about Barbara, she sent for her to come inside immediately and explain what on earth she was doing out there in the swamp on her own. And mind you use the tradesman's entrance. Barbara was incensed and refused to go. Instead, at the end of the day, she calmly walked Cecilia to the front entrance, gently kissed her and promised to be back the following day.

For some reason, Barbara was unable to return the next day, and soon after that she and Eugène left. She wrote to Cecilia, and sent her books, but never heard back. The dull, dull existence of this obviously capable young woman haunted her. What a waste of a life, and what a loss to society. In many ways, Cecilia was a slave, too.

Just before she left New Orleans, Barbara summoned up the courage to visit a slave auction. This was another experience that would remain with her all her life.

I went alone (a quarter of an hour before the time) and asked the auctioneer to allow me to see everything. He was very smiling and polite, took me upstairs, showed me all the articles for sale – about thirty women and twenty men, twelve or fourteen babies. He took me round and told me what they could do: 'She can cook and iron, has worked also in the field,' etc., 'This one a No. 1 cook and ironer –,' etc. He introduced me to the owner who wanted to sell them (being in debt) . . . At twelve we all descended into a dirty hall adjoining the street big enough to hold a thousand people. There were three sales going on at the same time, and the room was crowded with rough-looking men, smoking and spitting, [a] bad-looking set . . . I pitied the slaves, for these were slave buyers . . .

A girl with two little children was on the block: 'Likely girl, Amy and her two children, good cook, healthy girl, Amy – what! Only seven hundred dollars for the three? That is giving 'em away! 720! 730! 735! – 740! Why, gentlemen, they are worth a thousand dollars . . .'[24]

Barbara watched in horror as men opened the slaves' mouths with fat, sticky fingers to examine their teeth, like horses at a fair, and felt them all over before throwing in a bid. The women and girls, for the most part, looked impassive and unemotional. Some even laughed, but as Barbara pointed out, frightened people often laugh 'when they are not merry'. Someone said to Barbara, when she told them she wanted to witness an auction, 'Well, I don't think there is anything to see – they sell them just like so many rocking chairs.'[25] And that is what struck her most forcibly: the mundanity of this trade in human bodies and souls. There was no sentiment involved: no love, no pity, no compassion. Just profit and loss.

The Bodichons left New Orleans on 15 February 1858 for Mobile, Alabama. From there they progressed north via Savannah to Washington, DC, arriving in the middle of March. It was not uncommon for European visitors to drop in on the president, James Buchanan (no relation to Barbara's erstwhile teacher), who seems to have spent a good deal of his time hosting parties. Barbara was game, though Eugène was less keen, preferring to go birdwatching, hunting for 'queerosities' to bring home, or poking about in the Smithsonian Institution. She not only attended a reception at the White House (travelling there by omnibus and walking back), but also a glittering fancy ball, in costume as an Arab Maiden. She fails to mention this occasion in her letters, but it was reported in the Washington papers and even immortalized in a poem published in the city shortly afterwards. Barbara looked exquisite: 'The golden coins which bind her silken hair, / Are far less precious than her beauty rare,' gushed the poet.[26] According to one journalist, hers was 'certainly one of the best sustained characters in the room', though President Buchanan's costume was a tad underwhelming: he went 'as a civilian'.[27]

Some of Barbara's recent sketches and paintings were displayed in a Washington gallery while they were there (it is not clear at whose expense, but probably Barbara's). Fourteen of her paintings were coincidentally on an American tour of their own at the time, being part of a travelling exhibition of British art

visiting northern cities. This notice appeared in a local newspaper in July 1858:

At a late exhibition of paintings in Boston, one of the most
admired pieces was marked 'Bodichon (BARBARA LEE
[*sic*] SMITH).' A gentleman who had known the artist and
some of her previous works, asked, 'Is not that piece by
Mrs SMITH, the English artist?' to which a Bostonian
replied affirmatively. 'What is the meaning of Bodichon,
then?' was next asked, to which the reply was, 'Oh, that is
the name of her style of painting.'[28]

The Pater was keen for his daughter and son-in-law to visit
Niagara and Canada, as he and Anne Longden had done some
thirty years previously. Barbara was not enthusiastic, and planned
to send Eugène on his own, leaving her free to go to Boston and
meet some of the New England suffragist friends Aunt Ju had
come to know during the Anti-Slavery Convention in London
in 1840. As ever, the Pater was hard to resist – even offering a
£250 sub to get the pair over the border – so in the end, they
travelled together. Barbara was glad: the landscape of Canada
was stunning. And the people of Boston were just as delightful as
she had hoped. She borrowed a studio from the landscape artist
Sara Ann Clarke, in which to finish off some of her sketches;
went to see her sisters' friend (and Max Hays's ex-partner)
Charlotte Cushman performing at the theatre; met Ralph Waldo
Emerson (noting despondently that '[n]ot one word especially
Emersonian was said'[29]); and heard the renowned Unitarian
preacher Theodore Parker deliver a spellbinding sermon about
abolitionism. Eugène gave a well-received paper on the races of
Algeria at the Boston Society of Natural History (in French or
English? Despite Marian's optimism, he refused to learn a word
more of the latter than was strictly necessary), and when the

couple embarked on the *Europa* for Liverpool on 30 June, it was
his name the papers chose to highlight from the passenger lists
rather than Barbara's. *Tant pis.*

THERE WAS A LOT to catch up with at home. Aunts Ju and Dolly
were in good form, at fifty-nine and sixty-one respectively. A
love of Ju linked all the twenty-five cousins of Barbara's generation, the most prominent of whom was Florence Nightingale,
once described as looking decidedly 'Smithy'.[30] Not all of them
corresponded with the Leigh Smith branch of the family, though
a single letter from Florence to Barbara does survive – only a
scrap, with neither date nor address, but it is cordial and respect-
ful.[31] Ju was an excellent go-between.

By now, Florence was the most famous woman in England,
next to the Queen, whom she had the honour of meeting at
Balmoral while Barbara was on her way to New Orleans. She had
offered to leave for India (Florence, not the Queen), where a
bloody rebellion against British colonialism had flared up shortly
before the Bodichons' marriage. But the government declined,
on the grounds that she was indispensable at home. She was
heavily involved with writing up her post-Crimean findings on
the health of the British army, while also working on hospital
design and the formal training of nurses. All this while suffering
debilitating illness and exhaustion. We might invoke a diagnosis
of post-traumatic stress disorder today, although it is thought
she may have contracted brucellosis at Scutari. Barbara was
famous among her friends and family for her ability to raise people's spirits, to give them heart. What a shame she could not pop
round from Blandford Square to the Burlington Hotel in
Mayfair, where Florence was based, to give her cousin a hug.
Sadly, I don't think Florence did hugs.

Things were looking brighter for Bella, who had met the man
who was to be her devoted and long-suffering husband. He was

a retired military man, Major-General John Ludlow, twenty-nine years her senior and known to almost everyone simply as 'the General'. Their relationship was at an upbeat pre-courtship stage of taking long (chaperoned) horse rides together and chatting about mutual friends. Willy married his nineteen-year-old wife Georgina Halliday in April 1858, three months after his half-sister Jane Bentley Smith celebrated her wedding. The Pater's ducks were lining up nicely: Ben was obediently (though reluctantly) reading for the Bar; Barbara was married – to an inscrutable foreigner, true, but things might turn out all right; Bella seemed better; Willy was doing exactly what his father intended for him; Nannie was Nannie and not much trouble, if slightly Patty-ish in her egotism; Jane had made a respectable match, apparently unfazed by her future inheritance (did she know about it?); Alexander was nearing twenty-one and training to be an engineer – though he really wanted to be an artist – while Harry, at nineteen, was already four years into his career with the Merchant Navy.

Just before the Pater celebrated his seventy-fifth birthday in April, he sent a letter to Nannie, who was travelling in Europe. His hand is sprawling but strong. 'To let my birthdae [sic] pass D[ear] Nanny, Without a word would not be canny,' he quips. Barbara must have been keeper of the family calendar, alerting people to special occasions; since she was on the other side of the Atlantic, the Pater had to do his own reminding. He tells Nannie the date and asks her to pass it on to Bella. She mustn't forget. 'We live in hope,' he adds, 'that you will not lose any time in your return, for after all, England is the only country where you can be comfortable.' He wants her to base herself in Sussex and Blandford Square – perhaps forgetting it is now Barbara and Eugène's house – and to 'vibrate' between the two. It looks as though Nannie is destined to be the spinster daughter of the family; as such, the Pater implies, he and the aunts need her close. He signs the letter 'Your affectionate Dad'.[32]

There is no doubt that he also wished for his eldest child to settle comfortably in England, but Barbara was born a bird of passage. She was quite happy to 'vibrate', but on a much larger scale between Algeria, where she and her husband planned to spend their winters, and home. Eugène was not overjoyed at the prospect of living half the year in the grubby heat of London or surrounded by Barbara's family in the country, but promised at least to try. In return, Barbara arranged tuition in French, though she was not a natural linguist, apt to giggle disruptively during lessons and maintaining an execrable accent to the end.

Before leaving Blandford Square for Algiers in the autumn of 1858, Barbara found herself busier than she had ever been, catching up with friends, including Dr Elizabeth Blackwell, who had returned to London from New York with her adopted daughter-cum-companion Kitty; working through responses to *A Brief Summary* and *Women and Work*; helping to organize a petition to admit women to study at the Royal Academy; writing up articles on slavery and the state of American womanhood; finishing and arranging to exhibit her American and Algerian artwork; trying to keep Portman Hall School going after the departure of Elizabeth Whitehead in May 1857; and learning to be married. It was around now that she wrote about the pressures of having too much to do and not enough time to do it in, wishing she had 'three immortal lives. I would spend one only with my Eugène, and the other two for art and social life.'[33]

By 'social life' she meant not partying and suchlike, but changing the world for women. If there was one thing her adventures in the Southern states had taught her, it was that institutionalized oppression takes many forms and dehumanizes everyone involved. She tried to explain this point to the Pater.

Some great questions there are which are ever before us. Every hour of the day brings up occasion of action involving these questions, and we have to consider how we shall act and we see what is the result of our action. To hold false ideas on these great questions which are woven in with every-day life perverts, embitters, poisons the soul more than to hold the most monstrously absurd doctrines of religious faith . . . It is bad enough to believe all will be damned but yourself and a few friends, but to believe a man has a right to hold fellow-men as slaves, to breed slaves – to sell his own children, – this doctrine perverts a man infinitely more . . . Every day men acting on this false belief destroy their perception of justice, blunt their moral nature, so injure their consciences that they lose the power to perceive the highest and purest attributes of God. Slavery is a greater injustice, but it is allied to the injustice to women so closely that I cannot see one without thinking of the other and feeling how soon slavery would be destroyed if right opinions were entertained upon the other question.[34]

Barbara had done her research. Now was the time – when she confessed to never feeling better in her life – for action.

8

Women and Work

Professional Life, 1857–1860

There are many ways of doing things, as everyone supposes;
Some folk turn up their sleeves at work, and some turn up their noses.[1]

I CAN IMAGINE BARBARA ON HER WAY TO WORK ON AN ordinary day in September 1860. It is not a long commute: twenty-five minutes at most. She has only to step out of her front door on Blandford Square, walk left towards the Marylebone Road, turn left again, then right at Park Crescent. Just beyond the elegant rotunda of All Souls Church – built only thirty-odd years ago, so still comparatively unblackened – is 19 Langham Place, the headquarters of what Dr Elizabeth Blackwell affectionately calls 'the Reform Firm'. Here, a company of visionary women is laying the foundations of modern feminism, with masonry dismantled – stone by stone – from the hallowed edifices of the British Establishment.

Despite her brisk pace and sturdy boots, Barbara is not the first to arrive at the building. By the time she has greeted the staff, popped her head round the reading-room door to check that it is ready for the day's visitors, scanned the notice board for any forthcoming meetings she might fancy, cadged a cup of coffee from the kitchen and straightened her Algerian watercolours hanging on the staircase wall, the office is already half full.

Bessie Parkes smiles up from her proofreading, her dark eyes frank with enthusiasm. She is editing an article about Sarah Parker Remond, the Afro-American anti-slavery campaigner who is currently lecturing at Bessie and Barbara's alma mater, Bedford College. Bessie asks Barbara whether there are still slaves in New England, where Miss Remond comes from. Barbara's own article revealing the realities of slavery in the South went down well when it was published in the house magazine, the *English Woman's Journal*, a couple of years ago; so did more recent pieces on inspirational slave preachers and the prejudicial education system in America. Abolitionism is one of the journal's core concerns; it is useful to have the expertise of someone like Barbara, who has witnessed its relevance at first hand.

There is something else on Bessie's mind. Opening a drawer, she invites Barbara to slip a slug of something invigorating into her coffee, just as the two of them used to do in Munich. Then she reaches for a manuscript from a pile of submissions and clears her throat. It is difficult to know how to begin this conversation. Embarrassing, even. Barbara has commissioned a series of articles about Algeria from her husband. She and Eugène have recently written a perky guidebook together (*Algeria Considered as a Winter Residence for the English*, favourably reviewed in the *English Woman's Journal*, naturally) and are eager to share the secret of this country's beauty and diversity. Besides, Eugène needs something to do in England; something to forestall restlessness and raise his profile as a social commentator.

The problem is – explains Bessie delicately – that part one of the series, due out next month, is a little . . . unexpected. Has the Doctor perhaps misunderstood his brief? Readers of the *English Woman's Journal* are mostly, if not exclusively, just that: English women. They might travel; they like learning about people and politics, natural history and the wonders of the world. But not *this* :

There is something in the air of Africa which excites the nervous system and predisposes to deeds of violence. Perhaps, too, the intermingling of so many different races is the cause of frequent quarrels and assassinations. Each of these nations has its particular manner of killing, and an experienced physician can tell by inspecting the wound by what hands it was probably inflicted, without asking any questions whatever. The Italians habitually use the stiletto, or a poignard with a straight sharp blade; the Spaniards the common knife, rarely ever fire-arms; the Arabs use guns, knives, but chiefly a large stick, which they handle with amazing dexterity. The number of suicides in Algiers has been prodigious, sometimes two or three in one day. I have remarked that when the wind blows from the south, which wind is here called the sirocco, the increase in the number of crimes is very remarkable; not only are men inclined to commit suicide, but all animals are also more irritable and more inclined to acts of violence.[2]

Barbara takes Bessie's point – Algeria here does sound a little like an extra circle of hell – but the *English Woman's Journal* prides itself on telling the truth, does it not? Eugène always tells the truth (though does have some unusual preoccupations); the article must stay. It does. Though Bessie runs the journal day to day, Barbara has ultimate unspoken authority: it is largely her money behind it. Resigned, Bessie transfers the manuscript to the pile destined for the printer and returns to Sarah Parker Remond.

Max Hays is sitting opposite Bessie, facing a window overlooking Langham Place. She looks so different from Barbara. Both are tall and imposing, but while Barbara's complexion is peaches and cream and her glowing hair flows loose over generously cut gowns, Max has darker skin (some said she was 'half-Creole'[3]) and tightly controlled black hair. Strikingly, she is dressed to the waist exactly like a man. Max is a loyal friend but can be a bitter enemy; both Bessie and Barbara appreciate the importance of keeping on her right side. After all, she was once brave enough to tell Ben what to do, instructing him to get Barbara out of the country following the Chapman affair, and is currently suing her former partner, the actress Charlotte Cushman, for loss of earnings. She sacrificed her writing career for Charlotte, and now wants recompense: a same-sex alimony payment. Sometimes Barbara finds it hard to relax in her company.

Max co-edits the *English Woman's Journal* with Bessie but is working on administration today. Around a thousand copies are printed each month, selling at one shilling each. Running a relatively small-circulation publication is an extravagant business. Many articles are commissioned for a fee; until recently, all unsolicited manuscripts were returned to sender at the journal's expense, which was ruinous. There are printing costs to be paid; staff salaries; advertising budgets. Though the lease on 19 Langham Place is underwritten by one of Max's ardent admirers, Lady Monson, the expenses involved in maintaining it as a private clubhouse, as well as an office headquarters, are challenging.

The *English Woman's Journal* was set up as a newfangled limited company in February 1858, with two hundred shares raising £1,000 capital. Barbara bought sixty shares, not in her own name, as a married woman, but in her sister Nannie's. Bessie and Max bought five each and Maria Rye, a member of the Married Women's Property Committee, bought one. They all serve as directors of the company, along with Smith family friends Samuel Courtauld (one of John Chapman's long-suffering backers at the *Westminster Review*), the barrister James Vaughan and another lawyer, William Strickland Cookson. Nine months later, another two hundred shares were issued; Bella and Eugène bought some this time, with other family members and friends. But even though Helena, comtesse de Noailles – one of

Dr Elizabeth Blackwell's financial sponsors – matched Barbara's haul of sixty, many shares were left unsold. The *English Woman's Journal* is not conspicuously profitable.

The three women look up as Isa Craig comes into the office, hastily unwinding the scarf from her hat and hanging her coat on the stand. They are all fond of her. She is that rare thing, a published woman poet of some renown and no airs and graces at all. Bessie met her on a trip to Edinburgh in 1856 and felt an immediate kinship, even though their backgrounds were so different. Isa is the orphaned daughter of a glover, brought up in Scotland by her grandmother and forced – for lack of money – to leave school at the age of ten. She used to be a seamstress and is now a self-educated professional author: a successful, independent career-woman, and an asset to the office. She divides her working week between the *English Woman's Journal*, the newly formed National Association for the Promotion of Social Science – where, unusually for a woman, she has been appointed assistant secretary – and her own desk, composing lyrical poetry with a social conscience. The journal is lucky to have her.

Each concentrates on her various tasks while the building comes to life. Distant doors open and close, women's voices chatter and call, and the sweet smell of baking swirls up the stairs. And so the working day begins. Later, Barbara has a meeting with Emily Faithfull, who runs the Victoria Press in Coram Street, near the university. From this month's issue onwards, she and her female compositors will be responsible for printing the *English Woman's Journal*.

Like Max, Emily is a slightly inscrutable character. Bessie gets on well with her; they learned the basics of the printing profession together, on a small press Bessie bought when Emily was secretary of another organization based at 19 Langham Place, the Society for the Promotion of Employment for Women (unfortunately known by its acronym, SPEW). Now Emily runs a profitable business of her own, employing sixteen young women as nimble-fingered apprentices, including a deaf-mute girl, proudly supported by the company so that she will excel. Her team works an eight-hour day – two hours shorter than that of most women employees – and has an hour's lunch break. Emily has taken on men to do the heavy lifting, but otherwise this is a female enterprise: just the sort of thing Barbara and Bessie write about each month in the journal.

Emily's success owes a great deal to her strategic skills. She is the youngest of an Anglican clergyman's eight children, so is used to negotiating her own way while avoiding unwanted attention or behaving embarrassingly. Her determination to succeed – which will soon be rewarded by a royal warrant from Queen Victoria – is cloaked by her respectable, old-fashioned appearance and in-offensive demeanour. Printing is a jealous trade, rudimentarily unionized and almost exclusively a male preserve. Barbara admires Emily's spectacular ability to practise what she preaches in terms of women and work. Emily pays her compositors at the same rate as their male counterparts and expects excellence. While others talk, Emily quietly does. Barbara looks forward to seeing her.

At lunchtime Barbara, Bessie, Max and Isa eat at the club – or Ladies' Institute, as it is more formally called. Constantly being asked to explain exactly what goes on at 19 Langham Place – is it *really* a club? Like the Reform or Savage? – they have recently published a prospectus. Barbara collects some extra copies to leave in the lobby downstairs. It reads well:

This Institute comprises the following departments:–

A LADIES' READING ROOM. – (1) The Ladies' Reading Room is open from 11 a.m. to 10 p.m. Leading Daily and Weekly Papers, Magazines and Reviews. Terms, one guinea per annum. A two guinea subscription enables the subscriber to bring with her any lady not a subscriber. N.B. – Professional ladies half price.

Ladies visiting the West End on shopping or other business, will find this a great convenience, as attached to the
Reading Room is a Luncheon Room, and a room also for
the reception of parcels, for the use of subscribers only.

THE OFFICE OF 'THE ENGLISHWOMAN'S [sic] JOURNAL'

(2) The Englishwoman's Journal has now been established for two years, and may be considered as the special
organ for all that relates to the industrial employment, the
education, and the social position of women. Every number
contains four practical articles, a biography of some celebrated or particularly useful woman, a poem, a light paper,
notices of books, open councils (or letters from various
people interested in women's work) and a short summary
of passing events. Its conductors desire to make it at once a
source of accurate information and reference, and a medium
for the expression of opinions on every point relating to its
special objects.[4]

(What the prospectus fails to mention, for delicacy's sake, is that,
here, women are also afforded the luxury of semi-public con-
veniences. It did not escape Barbara's notice that her sex was
discouraged from going about its business in London and elsewhere simply for lack of available lavatories, which were
increasingly numerous for men. This small but much-appreciated
contribution to their comfort thus played its part in the decline
and fall of the British patriarchy.)

At the beginning of this year, membership of the Ladies'
Institute numbered eighty: not a bad tally for a novel concept
viewed with some suspicion by certain journalists (and husbands). It will be interesting to see which of those members is in
today. Maybe Adelaide Procter, the famous poet and protégée of
Charles Dickens, who occasionally writes for the journal and is

an integral member of Barbara's Langham Place circle. Barbara hopes so: she enjoys Adelaide's ready sense of humour. She is a romantic figure, with a noble, aristocratic face and that special luminosity that often accompanies delicate health. In the past she was a close friend of Nannie – *very* close, remembers Barbara; now she appears to be in love with the enigmatic Max. At the moment she is editing a lavish anthology of poetry and prose, *Victoria Regis*, for Emily Faithfull, and working at SPEW with its founder, Jessie Boucherett. So, on second thoughts, she might be too busy for lunch.

Jessie is missing today. She first met Barbara after chancing upon a copy of the *English Woman's Journal* on a railway bookstall at home in Lincolnshire. So captivating did she find the contents that she dropped everything and left for Langham Place, presenting herself at the office and offering to help the cause of women's emancipation in any way she could. She is a curious mixture; the sort of unexpected person Barbara loves to cultivate. Though brought up on a provincial estate, immersed in county society and country pursuits (and a brilliant rider to hounds), she has been allowed to indulge her keen intellect. Her parents sent her to board at the same school Elizabeth Gaskell attended in Stratford-upon-Avon; there she developed an unfeminine fascination for political economy and an ambition to help dignify her sex by campaigning for careers for women.

Now Jessie has set up a women's labour exchange at Langham Place, where registered employers and potential employees can find their match. Barbara has a special interest, as the author of *Women and Work*; she regularly writes articles for the *English Woman's Journal* suggesting potential jobs for readers and their daughters to consider. Some of her ideas are rather recherché: reading to visually impaired visitors to the British Museum's library (Emily Faithfull would be good at that: she has an enchanting voice); copying illuminated manuscripts for anyone who happens to need an illuminated manuscript copying; cutting

high-quality quill pens; designing hair art, like the elaborate
bracelet someone wove from Barbara's tresses; glass painting;
watchmaking; mosaic laying.

It is one of Barbara's pet hates that no one thinks about training women for work; they expect them to qualify solely by virtue
of their natural gifts as domestic creatures. She makes a note to
ask Jessie when she next sees her what SPEW is currently offering. Morning and evening classes in arithmetic and book-keeping
have been available for a while; so have law-copying classes, run
by Maria Rye, who intends to open a business for solicitors who
need detailed documents transcribing in an approved legal hand.
SPEW also awards grants to women who already possess commercial skills but lack capital. It is currently helping a photographer
set up a business that will sustain four female apprentices, and
supports various projects to find work for governesses who have
acquired disabilities such as deafness, failing sight or penury.

Last year the *English Woman's Journal* published a heartbreaking list of case studies highlighting what a precarious career
'governessing' could be. Barbara remembers two in particular:

Miss S. A., aged sixty-eight. Father a large calico printer;
her mother, having impoverished herself to assist her son's
speculations, she gave up the whole of her property to her
and became a governess; and to the same purpose devoted
all her earnings. Is now entirely dependent on the kindness of friends.

Miss M. J. A., aged fifty-nine. One of sixteen children; left
home in consequence at fifteen years of age. With two sisters, supported her father for many years, also an orphan
niece. Impaired sight and infirm health have obliged her to
subsist entirely upon a small legacy, now utterly exhausted.
Mental derangement daily increases under the pressure of
perfect destitution, having no means from any quarter.[5]

A portrait of Barbara sitting resplendently at her easel. It was commissioned from artist Emily Osborn by Girton College, Cambridge, towards the end of Barbara's life.

Stylish Benjamin Smith, known to his children as 'the Pater'.

Grandfather William Smith, politician, abolitionist and art connoisseur, by John Opie.

Barbara's youngest sister, Nannie (right), with her partner Isa Blythe.

Ben Leigh Smith, best known now as a polar explorer.

Beloved Aunt Julia, or 'Ju', a radical role model for Barbara.

Above: *Willy, the youngest of the Leigh Smith siblings, sketched by his wife Georgina.*

Left: *Bella Leigh Smith, looking unusually severe.*

Above: *Pelham Crescent, Hastings, where the motherless Leigh Smiths lived from 1836 to 1853.*

Right: *An inviting glimpse through the front door of Barbara's Sussex home, Scalands. Some of her pottery collection is just visible.*

Barbara asked visitors to sign bricks in the hearth at Scalands. Though faded, many contributions are still legible.

This luminous watercolour from 1856 of
Blackgang Chine, near Ventnor on the Isle
of Wight, is one of Barbara's finest works.

Barbara produced this narrative painting
in 1846 after a visit to Ireland the previous
year during the Great Famine.

Hamet, the Bodichons' servant, waits patiently for Barbara to read a letter in a rather stiff photograph taken in Algiers.

Campagne du Pavillon, the Bodichons' Algerian villa, designed to be simple and unfussy.

Look carefully at Barbara's painting of a Louisiana swamp, and you will see Eugène crouching with a gun, ready to repel oncoming alligators.

Above: *Barbara felt an affinity with sunflowers. Perhaps it was something to do with her own heliotropic personality.*

Top right: *This simple study of a pear by Barbara is a little masterpiece.*

Right: *Hertha Ayrton, another trailblazer, who owed much of her success and happiness to Barbara.*

As she sits down to lunch, Barbara's mind turns to her own governess, Catherine Spooner. She is aware that the Pater commissioned Catherine to look after the interests of his second family, the Bentley Smiths. But why did Catherine agree? Did he pay her a salary on top of the legacy he promised? Did Miss Spooner love that family more than the Leigh Smiths? How long had she kept the Pater's secret, and why did he trust her over his own daughter?

Her reverie is broken by the arrival of Maria Rye, just in time for coffee. She and Barbara have business to discuss. The institute's committee room is free: they move there, away from the constant bustle of 19 Langham Place, and she settles down to work until it is time to go home to Eugène – who at this very moment is preparing part two of his Algerian series for readers of the *English Woman's Journal*, all about the most efficient way to slaughter a wild boar with a hunting knife.

THIS ACCOUNT IS FICTIONAL, of course. I have no way of knowing who went into the office when, and what they talked about, but any resemblance to real-life characters and events is entirely intentional. Nineteen Langham Place hummed with activity during the first few years of its existence as the social and political hub of women's activism in Britain. Some of the era's most remarkable people crossed its threshold and worked to ensure its success: pioneers in the professions, philanthropists, novelists and poets, groundbreaking reformers, defiant iconoclasts. Barbara's co-creation of the Ladies' Institute, with all it embraced, was one of her finest achievements as an influencer and enabler.

It can come as no surprise that she was involved. Her heritage, energy, confidence, money, social circle and past activism fitted her perfectly to be right in the vanguard of change. It all began just before Ben whisked Barbara and her sisters to Algiers in October 1856, when Bessie visited Edinburgh and happened to notice a magazine in a stationer's shop window. The *Waverley Journal*, 'edited and conducted by ladies', addressed precisely the sort of subjects preoccupying Bessie and Barbara. She tracked down the editor, keen to write for it herself. Its premise was noble, she was certain, but its writing lacked energy. Not only did she offer articles to the magazine, but she assumed the editorship of it and, in the summer of 1857, she and Barbara shifted its offices to 14a Princes Street, off Cavendish Square, in London, intending to develop it as an organ of what we would now call feminism.

They also opened a small reading room for ladies on the premises, which they hoped would flourish as a ladies' club. The chance for women to network in print and in person was something they had always been denied. Gentlemen who had gone to school, to university, joined the civil or military services and belonged to a long-established club in Mayfair or St James's, took opportunities for mutual support for granted. So did working men in their guilds, associations and on the factory floor. As in so many things, women, to achieve any coherent progress in improving their lot in society, were forced to start from scratch.

Barbara joined Bessie in contributing articles to the *Waverley* when she had time, which was not often, given her whirlwind courtship, wedding and elongated honeymoon. She planned to buy ownership of it, if the proprietors were willing to sell, so that she and Bessie could work out their own agenda with full editorial control. As this proved problematic, they founded the *English Woman's Journal* instead, along the same lines as the *Waverley*, but less well behaved. In December 1859, they moved its office to 19 Langham Place, where there was much more space to develop the reading-room idea in association with the publishing house.

The *English Woman's Journal* was founded as a platform for Bessie and Barbara to share those 'daft' missions they used to tease each other about in their youth, and to invite others – male and female – to contribute their own ideas about the status of women. Their evangelism was fuelled by their recent experiences with the Married Women's Property Committee and an increasing awareness of women's rights in the radical press. The publication of Barbara's *Brief Summary* and *Women and Work* had raised her profile and that of the issues she covered; it was important to capitalize on this. Although there was no direct precedent for the *English Woman's Journal*, the stars were beginning to align. Women's activism was evolving from the dust and fluff of the drawing room, the school room and the cotton-mill floor. Barbara and Bessie hoped to breathe life into it, put fire in its belly.

The journal never quite managed to break free of the expectation that any periodical written for females must include a quotient of literary prettiness. Therefore, its editors commissioned poems from Christina Rossetti, Adelaide Procter and Isa Craig; fables by the professional writer Eliza Meteyard; frippery features on – for example – the fruits of different nations ('Old Gooseberry and his Currant Relations'); occasional serialized stories and some anodyne travelogues. Marian Evans thought this unwise. The journal needed a strong identity, and pieces like these, most of indifferent quality (apart from the contributions of big-name poets), distracted from its important reformist message. Though Barbara invited her, she declined to contribute.

Its artistic merit might have been dubious, but its political content was extraordinary in scope and usually well expressed, despite Marian's misgivings. Barbara worked like 'a ten horsepower engine' with her team, according to Bessie, to maintain a monthly programme of pertinent and thought-provoking writing – photobombed only occasionally by her eccentric husband. Incidentally, during my research for this chapter I naturally ordered up the entire run of the *English Woman's Journal* and was delighted by the serendipitous discovery that the bound copies arriving for me at the Bodleian Library in Oxford were Barbara's own, with her Sussex library stamp and some hastily scribbled comments in the margins. By the time I reached the end of the six-year run, my head was swimming with shoals of iridescent ideas for progress, reform, inspiration and life-enhancement.

Volume one, number one, came out on 1 March 1858. Its opening article is about the profession of teaching for women. It is significant that the title does not mention the word 'governess': teaching is indeed a *profession*, implies the author (probably Bessie), whether you are a male Oxbridge graduate gently fossilizing in the corridors of some venerable public school or a twenty-year-old girl in charge of a brood of brats in a lonely country house. A governess should not be classed as a servant but properly trained and properly paid. What is more, as Barbara had also pointed out in *Women and Work*, no woman should either be ashamed of or derided for choosing to work for her living, whether that choice be forced upon her or freely made. The author talks about 'social suffrage', demanding emancipation from censure for women who earn their bread. They should ignore anyone who thinks them vulgar or unfeminine, and learn to have the courage of their convictions and enjoy the fruits of their labour, whatever that labour might be.

> And if the worst came to the worst, and one were not asked out to tea – why then one might stay at home by the fire of one's own earning, inside one's own door, and snugly locked up by one's own key . . . holding comfortable conversation with Dickens and Thackeray, Tennyson and Mrs Browning . . . as a compensation for living people whom we have not met because they would not meet us – because we kept a shop![6]

The article closes with a slightly adapted quotation from Byron, which would be taken up with clenched fists half a century later by the suffragette movement: 'Who would be free, herself must strike the blow.'

Another piece in this debut issue reports the (slow) progress of the Married Women's Property Committee's campaign, written in plain language not only to inform, but to engage, for it 'should never be forgotten that all reform originates with the people'.[7] Coventry Patmore's newly published poem *The Angel in the House* is discussed in the book review section. It is so conventional, so reactionary, labelling woman as man's domestic helpmeet, his passive muse, his *thing*. Do not buy it, is the message, unless you like that sort of saccharine stuff. And if you do, you are probably reading the wrong magazine.

Seventy-seven issues followed this one, each highlighting different reasons and opportunities to become involved in reforming the lives of women, and therefore improving their communities and their own self-worth. Barbara's voice carries through them all, even if she is away from home at the time of editing or publication, as was the case until her return from America in July 1858, and thereafter for several months a year in Algeria. One of her most valuable skills was her open-handed ability to delegate. Control was less important to her than empowerment; pioneers less interesting than the pioneering work they did.

While I was making my way through Barbara's bound volumes of the journal, it soon became clear that certain writers were favourites, such as essayist Eliza Meteyard, who used the pseudonym 'Silverpen', and the novelist and travel writer Amelia Edwards. The majority are female, British and obviously in agreement with the Langham Place circle's ethos of equality of opportunity for women – but not all. There are some angry letters in the correspondence pages and excerpts from criticism in the press, quoted to raise discussion. This was what Barbara's old adversary, the *Saturday Review*, had to say:

> [The *English Woman's Journal*] is temperate, indeed, dull –
> it contains one or two rather stupid fictions, and some
> very ordinary disquisitions on political subjects ... It is

simply a fallacy that work is homogenous for both sexes . . . the end of a woman's life is the married state. [No doubt Barbara enjoyed the ambiguity of that final comment.] Humanly speaking, the best sort of British young lady is all that a woman can be expected to be – civil, intelligent, enthusiastic, decorous and, as a rule, prettier than in any other country.[8]

John Ruskin was no kinder. In a private letter to Barbara, after she had asked him to look at some art, he was witheringly dismissive.

Dear Mme. Bodichon,

It has become impossible for me lately to answer above half the letters which I wish to answer, and of those, not above again half in the time I should like to answer, and yet more impossible for me to look at drawings, unless sometimes one or two done by my pupils, and as you know, you are not a pupil of mine, or you would never draw American Swamps, when I have been telling you all, as hard as I could tell you, for years back, the things that really want drawing in our Europe. Do you really seriously think that a drawing of an American swamp is a precious thing to bequeath to posterity?

I don't like your ladies' reading room either, at all, but I am always faithfully yours,

J. Ruskin.[9]

Perhaps he got out of bed on the wrong side that morning. Other commentators were more generous, calling the journal useful, entertaining, admirable and timely, with well-analysed arguments and a refreshing lack of sentimentality.

Certain subjects were favoured, along with certain authors.

There are numerous articles about the relationship between mental and physical health, something in which Barbara took a personal interest following Bella's frightening episode on the Isle of Wight, and her own anxieties ascribed – by Chapman, at least – to the physiological effects of sexual frustration. General malaise is endemic among idle women, according to the journal, and lowness of spirits an apparently direct function of a lack of exercise and useful occupation. More compassionate treatment of the 'nervous' is called for, with some serious scientific research into 'how far the spirit is moulded by the flesh, or how far the flesh is moulded by the spirit'.[10]

It was extremely progressive in the late 1850s to declare, as the journal does, that just as drunkenness can be a symptom of mental distress as well as a cause of physical disease, so 'lunacy' can be a symptom of depression rather than a discrete condition, and depression itself a direct result of poverty or discrimination. It advocates counselling the 'insane' and supporting them in sympathetic communities with an expectation that they might improve. This holistic approach to mental health is something still in development today.

Elsewhere, working-class women are manoeuvred into the soft light of readers' drawing rooms with descriptions of appalling conditions for charwomen, sweatshop seamstresses and match-girls. The deeply unfashionable subject of domestic violence is addressed; how to treat people of 'weak intellect' with kindness (more commonly known as cretins, they were officially classed with criminals and women as unfit to vote); how to make prison the means to an end, not an end in itself. These are risky subjects, liable to put readers off the journal, but demanding serious discussion.

More pleasantly, someone writes about the importance of celebrating 'ordinary things' by preserving them in museums of social history and design – like the newly opened Victoria and Albert (then known as the South Kensington Museum) near the

site of the Great Exhibition. Such objects lift the spirits and make
us proud of who we are and what we do, be it ever so humble.
Barbara was a lifelong admirer of things beautiful and useful, an
arts-and-crafts connoisseur ahead of her time, amassing a collection of patterned pottery, for example, from artisans in Algeria
and Sussex – some of which is now, appropriately enough, in the
possession of the V&A.

The subject of physical exercise crops up regularly. To avoid
accusations of puniness in later life, every young woman should
have access to a public gymnasium and the confidence to use it.
Chronic complaints like curvature of the spine or even TB are
exacerbated, it is claimed, by too much sitting down while doing
brothers' or fathers' mending. Sitting down, like tight lacing, is
bad for you. The journal asks readers to support the idea of
public swimming pools for women, a campaign which comes to
fruition in the summer of 1858 with the experimental opening of
St Marylebone's metropolitan swimming bath for ladies. It is
quite wonderful, writes someone called 'Elleret' fussily, with
crystal-clear water and arrangements of fresh flowers in the
public areas.

We have certainly no wish that St. Marylebone should ever
present such a scene as was customary, not so very long
since, at Bath, where . . .
    'T'was a glorious sight to see the fair sex,
    All wading with gentlemen up to their necks.'
but it would only be an unreasonable prejudice in any lady
to demur at being in the water in the society of respectable
individuals of her own sex, even though strangers; for
albeit a denser medium than air, yet the space here is so
much greater, that, in reality, the atmosphere would be far
less visited by her neighbours than when sitting in close
contact with them in a well filled omnibus. On the continent, where such institutions have been long in vogue, ladies

of high rank do not scruple to enter the bath with their
fellow citizenesses, and in Frankfort [sic] the Baroness
Rothschild may often be seen in the crowded water with
her little one in her arms, teaching it to take part in her
natatorial pastime.[11]

Why not hire a bathing dress and enjoy an unusual outing
with your friends? You are bound to enjoy it, and it will do you
nothing but good.

A piece suggesting that Britain should adopt decimal coinage,
making arithmetic so much easier, concludes with a prediction:
'Oh! We shall never do such things as these!'[12] Another, on the
advisability of life assurance cover for women, is more optimis-
tic. There is no reason why wives, mothers and daughters should
not enter into any kind of financial arrangement, or understand
the simple economics of life, providing that the men in their life
approve. They should have the courage to take responsibility for
managing their own budget, even learn to write cheques (very
daring) and keep accounts. Money is not a vulgar subject. Using
it wisely is a social duty. A privilege.

Annual meetings of the Ladies' National Association for the
Diffusion of Sanitary Knowledge are covered in some depth.
Barbara, as a self-confessed 'sanitarian', was naturally a member.
It was essentially a public health organization, formed to explain
and share principles of good practice in preventative medicine,
including infant and maternal welfare, and personal hygiene. It
was not exactly grass-roots; Florence Nightingale's erstwhile
suitor Richard Monckton Milnes was on the committee, as was
the cleric, author and academic Charles Kingsley, with four
titled ladies, two countesses, a marchioness and an Honourable.
But its aims were basic. Kingsley was starkly direct in a speech at
the first annual meeting in July 1859, the year following the
infamous 'Great Stink' when thousands of Londoners died as a
result of pollution exacerbated by a heatwave. 'It is in the power,

I believe, of any woman in this room to save three or four lives, human lives, during the next six months.' This they could do by encouraging other women to lead healthier, less 'affectional' (or pretentious) lives, and overcoming the taboo of talking about bodily functions.[13]

Scattered throughout the monthly issues of the *English Woman's Journal* are notices of fundraising campaigns, some more relatable than others. Radical ladies are collecting money for the relief of Garibaldi's 'gallant companions in arms' who are fighting for freedom in Italy. Florence Nightingale has donated a hefty £10 to that. There is a collection for those in 'Distress in the North': Lancashire cotton-mill workers laid off due to interruptions in the supply of raw cotton during the American Civil War, and now facing famine. A call goes out for Britons to boycott any imports of cotton or other goods from the Southern states, in protest against the use of slave labour, recalling William Smith's sugar ban years before. A different boycott is going on in Austria: there, society ladies are refusing to wear crinolines – they are *too* ridiculous – and if an actress wears one on stage at the theatre, these ladies are threatening not to buy tickets to see her.

The Nightingale Fund, established in Florence's honour, is asking for subscriptions to subsidize the training of nurses. Would you care to endow a bed in the women's infirmary Dr Elizabeth Blackwell is opening in New York? The Pater certainly would: he offered Elizabeth a loan of £500 to use however she thought fit. Or you could join the campaign started by a woman in service who wants the Post Office Savings Bank to send receipts in plain envelopes, so that greedy members of her family do not realize she is wisely stashing away some of her wages for a rainy day. Support is needed to publicize the perils of overwork and to warn seamstresses and milliners of the danger of working with green dye: it contains arsenic, lethally poisonous over time (Barbara, who loved green, used vegetable dyes instead). And the *English Woman's Journal* could do with considerably more subscribers.

Sometimes the tone of the journal is a little harrying. Don't allow people to wrap you in a cocoon of naivety and ignorance: you have a moral duty to keep yourself informed about the evils of the world, and act accordingly. Don't waste things. Speak plainly – no mealy-mouthing – and don't read too many sensational novels: they are addictive and soften the brain. When you do something – anything – think of the consequences of that deed. Barbara could be prone to bossiness too, but in her case it was often tempered with a sympathetic smile or a joke. The *English Woman's Journal* did not do many jokes. What it did do, with aplomb, is open what has become a fundamental dialogue about women's rights. Nineteen Langham Place was where ideas were hatched, introductions made and the concept of female solidarity found a home.

THE MOST SIGNIFICANT PREOCCUPATIONS of the Langham Place circle – and therefore of the *English Woman's Journal* – can be narrowed down to a quartet: education, specialist training, social reform and, perhaps surprisingly, emigration. Bessie and Barbara both produced pieces on education, ranging from the importance of rigorous examinations in girls' schools to the possibility of university admission for women. (Why are boys cleverer than girls, asks one such article. Simple, comes the reply: because their teachers are paid more.) This is where Barbara articulated some of her earliest thoughts about higher education, which a decade later would take shape in a small Hertfordshire town called Hitchin.

The journal does not confine itself to discussing how the middle classes might learn to think. There are reports of training centres for domestic staff, schools of nursing and a Working Women's College set up in Bloomsbury by Elizabeth Whitehead (Mrs Malleson), Barbara's first headmistress at Portman Hall. It alerts its readers to forthcoming lectures for ladies, and evening classes that have newly opened in mechanics' institutes in London and beyond. Responding to critics' accusations of 'strong-mindedness', or the tendency for females to shout loudly about things they don't understand, the journal is adamant that women have a moral obligation to voice informed opinions.

> It is the work of the ladies of England to inaugurate an age of such strong-mindedness, by using their influence to have the young of their own sex and rank brought under a more strengthening system of education. To discourage mere showy accomplishments, not by cramming with Greek and Latin . . . but by setting the exercise of the reasoning powers above the exercise of the fingers or even the memory, and by earnestly cultivating [a] sense of responsibility, and social as well as individual duty.[14]

Vocational training should be available to those with aptitude. Take, for instance, an area close to Barbara's heart. In April 1859, she helped to organize a petition to the Royal Academy of Art, demanding that women be admitted to its schools. It was good timing: the then president, Charles Eastlake, was a friend. A government project to set up art unions in Britain, with the aim of 'making cheap art good, and good art universal',[15] was developing well; an associated lottery offered its winners vouchers to spend at named art galleries, and in 1858 the recently formed Society of Female Artists (of which Barbara was a founder member) was named as one of the prize venues.

The petition was printed in the *English Woman's Journal*, with the names of thirty-nine signatories, including Barbara and her sisters Nannie and Bella. It argues that when the RA was founded, in 1769, there were not enough women artists to take advantage of its training. But now, no fewer than 120 ladies have already exhibited there, Barbara and Anna Mary Howitt among them. If they are this accomplished without learning about drawing and colour techniques in the depth available to their male counterparts, think what an ornament to British culture they would be if they did receive such instruction!

The Academicians were unconvinced. The RA could not afford to organize separate life-drawing classes for women, they explained, and since there was no question of females being allowed in the same room as males in proximity to a naked body, as far as they were concerned the matter was closed. But when the artist Laura Herford applied in 1859 with only her first initial and surname, and was accepted, they reluctantly capitulated and allowed the aliens in.

Not only are pioneers like French artist Rosa Bonheur and Dr Elizabeth Blackwell presented as role models in a series of mini biographies in the journal, but Dr Blackwell herself writes to encourage others to join her, recommending useful medical text-books and spreading the glad news that even though there are no schools of medicine for women in Europe yet, there are several places in America where they might study (if they have a suitably rich father who is either indulgent or dead). The more women who take the plunge, the better practitioners all doctors will become. Besides, it is lonely being a pioneer, especially when members of the press question your qualification – 'Dr Elizabeth Blackwell, as she calls herself' – and accuse you of wasting patients' time in 'follies and extravagances'.[16]

I have really no medical friend; all the gentlemen I meet seem separated by an invincible, invisible barrier, and the women who take up the subject partially are inferior. It

will not always be so; when the novelty of the innovation
is past, men and women will be valuable friends in medicine, but for a time that cannot be.[17]

The first woman to qualify as a doctor in England was
Elizabeth Garrett, later Mrs Garrett Anderson, in 1865. She was
inspired to do so by hearing Elizabeth Blackwell speak at a lecture organized by Barbara and her friends (the platform decorated
for the occasion with Sussex primroses). The first to co-run a
husband-and-wife general practice, Frances Hoggan, was another
person on the periphery of the Langham Place circle, being a
member of the National Association for the Promotion of Social
Science (NAPSS), an organization for which the *English Woman's
Journal* was something of a mouthpiece.

The NAPSS (or 'Universal Palaver Association', as the *Saturday
Review* dubbed it) played an important part in facilitating constructive networking for women. Though formally non-party
political, it was set up in 1857 by an old friend of the Smith
family, Lord Brougham, as a forum – in his words – 'to aid
legislation, by preparing measures, by explaining them, by recommending them to the community, or, it may be, by stimulating
the legislature to adopt them'.[18] Anyone active or interested in
social reform was encouraged to join, even if they were women.
Bessie credited Barbara as the person who insisted on that latter
point; it would not be surprising to find her behind another,
stipulating that all papers for debate at the fortnightly meetings
(whenever Parliament was in session) and at the week-long
annual meetings should – like Laura Herford's to the Royal
Academy – be submitted blind.

The NAPSS was organized into five divisions: legal reform,
penal policy, education, public health and economics. The pro-
ceedings of each were regularly reported in the *English Woman's
Journal*, where papers presented by members of the Langham
Place circle were sometimes reprinted in full. Each meeting

offered a broad, high-profile public platform for the first time to female reformers like Mary Carpenter, who set up humane reformatories for young offenders; Frances Power Cobbe, a fiery proto-suffragette; and, indeed, Barbara and Bessie themselves. It was like an extension of those weekly drawing-room salons Aunt Ju and her radical friends used to hold, but on an unimaginably larger scale, with hundreds of delegates present.

Maria Rye of the Langham Place circle was a familiar name to members of the NAPSS. Her 'Female Middle-Class Emigration Society' sounds distasteful to a modern audience conscious of the impact of colonization; to Barbara and her colleagues – perhaps naively – it had nothing to do with empire-building, but was an inspired scheme to find useful employment abroad for Britain's so-called 'surplus females'. The idea was born when 810 women applied for a single post at the law-copying office Maria had opened in association with SPEW in early 1860. The money behind it was largely Barbara's – she paid Maria's salary – and when Maria came up with the emigration plan, Barbara again was her most reliable source of moral and financial support. The Pater was also a major donor.

The society operated as follows. Applicants were interviewed by Maria or her staff to see if they possessed the necessary level of education and common sense to leave home and earn a living in a new world. Remarkably, Maria herself travelled to America, Canada, New Zealand and Australia to scope opportunities for work and put in place a support network for emigrants when they arrived. Barbara waved her off on her voyages, wrote to her while she was away, wrote also to wealthy friends to try to raise money for the scheme, and welcomed Maria back when she returned, often tired and disillusioned. She was a stalwart friend.

In theory, the concept of installing gentlewomen where they were needed appeared perfectly sensible, particularly as there were too many of them to earn a livelihood at home. The population imbalance in Britain, exacerbated by the number of single men busy building up the Empire abroad, meant that unless there was some sort of state intervention, tens of thousands of spinsters were likely to find themselves subsisting on, or below, the breadline. So why not export them? That, thought the imperialists of the day, would have the added advantage of helping to consolidate British populations abroad, as any female with a pulse would surely be snapped up by a lonely empire-builder as his wife as soon as she arrived.

Government sponsorship was available to working-class people, but not to 'ladies'. Maria's idealistic ambitions relied on private subsidy and were regularly reported to the *English Woman's Journal*'s readership with an appeal for donations – and for candidates, both as emigrants and as matrons or married chaperones for the voyage. Had Barbara been free, I can imagine her volunteering to escort a clutch of deserving women to the other side of the world, and then staying on to paint what she saw in strange climes, like her itinerant friend the artist Marianne North. But perhaps it is as well that she had other things to do. The enterprise was not a great success. The journal reprinted letters from residents of Australia to explain why. What was *really* wanted in the colonies was a cheap and steady supply of decent domestic staff.

> Any quantities of these, I believe, would be gladly received, but they are just the class that people in England would be glad to keep themselves . . . The voyage itself is in the opinion of all right-minded people a great temptation, and more young girls are corrupted in their passage out than usually imagined. Even matrons themselves are often not to be depended upon.
>
> Our lying-in hospital . . . could tell many a sad tale, and if I were endeavouring to send from England young women of any class (knowing what I do of the colony) I should feel

a deep responsibility to send those of high principle and character.[19]

Women of high principle and character are just the sort of people Maria wanted to send, but there is no work for them. Times are hard; not many families can afford a governess, and shop girls are a luxury most traders cannot even contemplate. Where there are schools, the teaching staff is made up of the master's friends and family. There is no poor law; beggars never used to be seen on the streets of Melbourne but now they are common. Regretfully, so is drunkenness. This, insist Maria's correspondents, is no place for ladies.

It was depressing to realize that gentlewomen were as likely to be as 'distressed' in the new world as they were in the old. But Barbara and her Langham Place friends were rarely disheartened by failure. As strong-minded women they were used to it, generically if not individually. And as the *English Woman's Journal* made all too clear, there was much yet to fight for. An article on female education in the issue for June 1858 includes a phrase that could well stand as the Reform Firm's mission statement:

Let woman put her shoulder to the slowly revolving wheel of progression . . . There is strength in unity, which, as far as the male and female element is concerned, the world has yet to test.[20]

9

Madame Bodichon

1858–1862

Devastators of the day, away, away![1]

BRACING HER SHOULDER TO THE 'WHEEL OF PROGRESSION'
was an exhausting, uphill task for any Victorian woman. It could
easily have become Barbara's full-time occupation during the
first few years of her marriage. But there was too much else
going on involving family and friends; too many pictures to
paint and places to go, and far too little time. She and Eugène
intended to spend the summers in England and the winters in
Algiers, which meant that her life was cloven. For six or seven
months a year, she galloped around London, Sussex and beyond,
cramming as much into her 'Smith' life as she could. Sometimes
the level of activity became too much to manage. 'I am so
worried by people & invitations & parties got up for me,' she
wrote to Marian Evans, 'that I think I shall say I am not married
to Dr Bodichon just to titter the people.'[2] (An interesting
thought, incidentally: did she consider living in sin to be less
socially acceptable than being illegitimate? And did she care-
lessly forget that Marian herself was with a man to whom she
was not wed?) 'Devastators of the day, away, away!' she would
shout at unwelcome visitors when they interrupted her work or
leisure.

Her 'Bodichon' life, reserved for art and marriage in a home

far from home, was altogether different. At the end of October
1858, some three months after returning from America, Eugène
left Blandford Square for the North African coast without
Barbara, to find them a suitable house in which to begin their
married life. In November, his wife followed with her friend
Ellen Allen, Elizabeth Whitehead's successor at Portman Hall.

> If any enterprising English lady or gentleman wishes to
> see another quarter of the globe in addition to their own
> Europe before they die; if they wish to get out of Chris-
> tendom; if they wish to see strange beasts, strange plants,
> and new races; if they wish to ride on camels, to eat por-
> cupine and wild boar; in fact, to be put down without
> much trouble and no danger in a perfectly new world,
> there is only one place within seventy-eight hours of trav-
> elling from London which will answer this purpose.

So wrote Barbara in an article for the *English Woman's Journal*
based on the guidebook to Algiers she and Eugène produced in
1858. The book was essentially a translated rehash of Eugène's
previously published writing on the country, updated, edited
(with less carnage) and made more engaging by Barbara. She
tried to be practical as well as upbeat. Her advice to others is a
useful indication of her own experiences in a colony now considered to be free of the threat of civil war – always a bonus to
the Victorian tourist – and a potential paradise for artists and
invalids. She continued:

> The quickest way of getting out of Europe is to take rail
> from London to Paris, which is twelve hours; from Paris to
> Marseilles, which is eighteen hours; and steam-boat from
> Marseilles to Algiers, forty-eight hours . . . of course the
> journey can be made as long as the traveller likes by stop-
> ping to rest on the road; but a night's rest at Paris and a

night's rest at Marseilles are generally enough for most travellers. Then in four or five days you are in Africa, in ancient Numidia, in Barbary, in Algeria, in the country of the Carthaginians, the Romans, the Moors, the Arabs, the Turks . . .

If you take our advice, and go next winter, you will probably arrive, as we did, on a fiery hot day in November, and be sick and disgusted with everything whilst waiting in the port and going through the horrors of landing; but have patience, and you will be repaid. Even on deck, as we sat under the shade of a great umbrella, which sheltered us from the dazzling sun and the dazzling sea, we began to open our eyes with wonder, and to forget the miseries of the voyage. There, close to us, rose the town, a mass of white walls against a blue-black sky, for it seemed almost black, so deep the colour and so very white and burning the walls stood up against it. To the right and left of the town, hills extend five or six hundred feet in height, yellow, brown, and grey, dotted with dark olive trees and whitewashed Moorish and French houses. Beyond the hills to the left, that is to the east, we see a part of the plain of the Metidja, and beyond the lofty range of the Little Atlas mountains . . .

It is the old town, or the upper town, or the Moorish town, into which the traveller must penetrate to see what is really African, Eastern, and par excellence Algerian; and certainly it is a wonderful place. Enchanting and disgusting; dirty and poetical. Here go with Arabian Nights in your hand, or rather in your head and heart, and you will be transported instantly.[3]

Barbara certainly took her own well-worn copy of the *Arabian Nights*, reminding her of happy days with her beloved teacher James Buchanan, but was *not* transported instantly into the living fairy tale of her imagination. She meant what she said about those 'miseries of the voyage' (seasickness), assuring Marian that 'not an artist's life in Algiers, the gardens of Hesperides or the loving & beloved Doctor are worth this dreadful passage, <u>NO</u>!'[4] She was sorry to leave England, certain that the reform work she had been doing there was worthwhile. She worried that people would think her Algerian work, which was painting, both amateurish and self-indulgent. All the English ladies sketch, noticed a visitor to the country in 1857, plonking their stools and easels down in the middle of a busy street, or the middle of nowhere. They look ridiculous.[5]

But within two days she had forgotten her seasickness and was ready for adventure. Any concern that she was not doing the right thing was dispelled: 'I begin to hope & feel so well & so uncommonly jolly ... I do enjoy living in every pore of my body & soul.'[6] The house Eugène found, Maison Pougnet, was in Mustapha, a suburb overlooking the bay just above Algiers. They bought some chickens and planted violets in the garden, to remind Barbara of Scalands Farm. She was enchanted. 'This place intoxicates me!' she told Marian, delightedly describing the fragrant air synaesthetically in terms of musical dynamics, starting with *pianissimo* heliotrope and *piano* roses, then crescendoing to a magnificent *fortissimo* with citrus blossom, sage, rosemary, thyme and jonquils. 'Such a delicious melody of colour it is ... I wish I had 100 senses!'[7]

They rented Maison Pougnet for six months, during which time Barbara bought another, larger house in fashionable Mustapha Supérieur from the wife of a French horse trader for £800. It had twelve acres of land, and perched on the side of a hill, facing towards the city and the sea. They named it Campagne du Pavillon after Eugène's childhood home in France. It was Moorish in style, a two-storey white-painted villa with graceful arched windows and louvred shutters. It looks cool and elegant in contemporary photographs but, inside, was relatively spartan.

'It is rough . . . and has no luxuries,' Barbara reported to Aunt Ju. 'I am afraid of having a well appointed house. I believe I could not work if I had and I want my money for other things.'[8] Eugène built her a studio on the upper floor, where the light streamed in and rosemary wood burned in the grate. Its fresh, resinous scent mixed with the headier fragrance of cut jasmine and narcissi to create an illusion of luxury. The only other concession to Barbara's concept of civilization was a new kitchen.

She described the view from Mustapha Supérieur as intensely romantic. The blue Mediterranean stretched to the horizon, flecked with lilac shadows. A little to the east, capes and mountains faded into the distance. The waters of the bay looked as though they were kissing the shore, which rose beyond the city into pine woods, olive groves, orchards of orange and lemon trees and rich, russet tracts of earth.

> Over this rough ground, which in three months will be a vast field of asphodel, now browse herds of long-haired goats, and brown sheep with long ears, who look like cousins of the goats, guarded by stately figures all in white, or a little boy in a goat-skin, who amuses himself by playing on a reed pipe as he sits under the great aloe, or with giving his dogs lessons in guarding the flock.[9]

However, as that first autumn drifted into winter, the novelty of living in the *Arabian Nights* disappeared with the sunshine. It was *cold* – as the caption to a cartoon she drew of a couple cantering along in the teeth of a gale makes clear. 'To make an Algerian winter mix 100 icebergs, 50 sheets of lightning, 60 forks of ditto, stirr [sic] up well with the last; shake with 2 earthquakes, add one water spout; a roast by a tropical sun improves this mixture but it is usually [made] without this last.'[10]

The Bodichons' neighbours were an eclectic mix. There was an orphanage next door, run by nuns and frequently visited by

Barbara; the French governor-general had a residence near Campagne du Pavillon for when the heat and bustle of the city got too much, and it was a favourite spot for a growing number of European visitors overwintering in the salutary climate. Barbara admired – and financially supported – a Frenchwoman, Madame Luce, who had set up a school for girls nearby, but otherwise did not feel inclined to mix in local society. She refused to be presented at court in the Algerian equivalent of a super-annuated debutantes' ball, admitting that she proudly belonged to a set of women who never wear low-cut dresses and would therefore feel out of place among the chic European elite, for whom a crinoline and extravagant décolletage were de rigueur. 'Our life here is very quiet and hard-working,' she wrote to her old friend Anna Jameson, '& one would have thought perfectly inoffensive to any one on earth, but it is not so! The little foolish circles of French & English talk in the most absurd manner about us and find us very offensive.'[11] Like Buchanan, they were probably classed as 'queer fish' of dubious pedigree and thus not quite nice. She had not met a single valuable acquaintance among the expat English, she complained. Though she was not really there to meet English people, a little congenial conversation in her own tongue might have helped combat homesickness. She still found speaking French to be a hit-and-miss affair.

Instead of going out in search of more convivial company, Barbara held an open house on Saturday afternoons, and welcomed all comers in the hope of finding a few gems. Several English and French travelogues published during the next few years mention visiting the Bodichons at Campagne du Pavillon. The radical politician and man-of-the-people Richard Cobden, who was a Smith family friend, was particularly taken with Eugène, who led him on a complicated expedition to find the highest point achievable from Campagne du Pavillon, while another tourist, a Mrs Rogers, was treated to a private view of Barbara's sketches when she called, and a well-rehearsed account of how Bombonnel the shredded panther-killer was stitched together again by the Doctor.[12]

Invitations to dinner were something of a lottery. If Barbara considered her guests to be unpretentious and unfamiliar with haute cuisine, she – or the staff in her nice new kitchen – would pull out all the stops and offer them a banquet. But if they were used to fine dining and took it for granted, they were likely to be treated to what she called a 'leg-of-mutton dinner' instead – in other words, anything that happened to be in the pantry. She confessed how much she admired the Canadian-born aristocrat Lady Stanley for serving Prime Minister Gladstone from a half-eaten gooseberry pie.[13] Henrietta Stanley – as we shall see – was Barbara's kind of woman.

Things were not all bad. Luckily, and sometimes embarrassingly, Eugène was not much of a one for social niceties either. When the couple were at home, he was happy to remain behind the scenes, enjoying his role as Campagne du Pavillon's resident housewife. If he must emerge and meet people, he did not always find it necessary to speak to them, or even to get fully dressed. Ideally, both Bodichons would be out roaming among the flowers and hills, on sketching expeditions (for Barbara) or hunting animals to kill, befriend or simply to observe (for her husband). Although Eugène was no longer practising full time as a physician, either for the French military or in a private capacity, he found it hard to refuse requests for medical help and was often consulted by local people on their travels. This was gratifying to them both. As a 'kept' man, essentially, and despite his domestic role, Eugène valued his Gallic pride.

Each was perfectly content to go out alone if necessary. A horse-drawn omnibus, a little like the Pater's, trotted past their door on its zigzag way to and from Algiers below; handsome Arab horses and less impressive donkeys were available to ride into the hills, and Barbara was always a keen and somewhat militant rambler. Photographs – presumably taken at someone else's insistence – show her sitting in the shade outside Campagne du Pavillon in what looks like a painting jacket and a full skirt, looking particularly glum – nothing like a free-minded Albion's daughter – with her fifteen-year-old Arab servant Hamet looking similarly unsmiling at her side. One can imagine a thought bubble hovering above her head expressing a devout wish to be back in her rooftop studio or else out sketching with the dog in the foothills of the Atlas, or on the endless stretches of the Mitidja. Or even back in Blandford Square doing useful things. These reluctant photographic images are entirely static, while her cartoons of being out in the field are dynamic and full of excitement. It is difficult to reconcile the two. But then there are many things hard to reconcile about Barbara and her parallel lives.

Her default state of mind – despite acknowledging herself 'one of the cracked people of the world' – was positivity. 'Nobody ever enjoyed life like Barbara,' said her brother-in-law General Ludlow.[14] She had much to be positive about. But within a few weeks of arriving in Algiers as Madame Bodichon, she felt deeply frustrated. Only mail from home kept her sane. It arrived three times a week. 'I am always rejoiced when I see the <u>facteur</u> [postman] plodding up the asphodel field, and I rush down to seize the fat packet of papers, books, and letters with great delight.'[15]

Her favourite confidantes were Marian and Elizabeth Blackwell. She reported her distress to them after a visit to the wife and daughter of an Arab prince. The daughter was eleven, and therefore of marriageable age: bright, curious and completely uneducated. Barbara wept – literally – at the thought that she would shortly be the property of some unknown man. At the end of the visit, she impulsively clasped the girl to her bosom and kissed her. 'I renewed every vow I ever made over wretched women to do all in my short life with all my small strength to help them!'[16] But what *could* she do, she asked her friends, in a strange land far from 19 Langham Place, when even the swiftest letter took a week to arrive?

Her anxieties sprang mostly from this disconnection between her different worlds. Despite their promises to one another, Eugène refused to commit as much time to England as Barbara needed. They spent most of the summer of 1859 apart. In London she threw herself into work and Smith family life, determined not to have any spare time or energy to think about her husband, but it was hard: she missed him. Harder still when the Pater – of all people – accused her of not caring for Eugène enough to stay with him.

> It is not an easy thing to live 4 months away from the human being I love better than anything on earth & who loves me & thinks of me all the hours of the 4 months. I don't think of him so much because I won't but he never forgets me.[17]

Barbara needed Eugène more than ever at this time. Back in the spring, she had written an ecstatic letter to Elizabeth Blackwell, breaking the news that she was pregnant. Elizabeth wrote straight back. 'Is it really so, dearest Barbara? I have just received your letter, and hold my breath at its contents.' The doctor gave her friend advice about how to take care of herself during the risky first trimester, how to preserve 'this little new life', and suggested she should not attempt to travel home as she had planned, but rest in Algiers for the summer.[18]

Perhaps Barbara realized that she could not possibly rest without coming home, seeing her friends and family, and fuelling up with work in London. Besides, Bella was getting married, and the Pater was growing old. They needed her too. Sadly, the decision was taken out of her hands when, in April, she suffered a miscarriage. For years afterwards she used to sketch the storks that regularly roosted on the chimneys at Campagne du Pavillon, hoping they were there to deliver a baby, just as the old wives' tale promised. She once wrote wistfully to Nannie, 'Did you hear of the storks building on my studio top in Algiers? I hope it is a good omen.'[19]

Instead of uniting them, the loss of their baby seems, temporarily at least, to have isolated the Bodichons. Eugène resented Barbara's long absences, but neither husband nor wife was willing to make the compromises that might have lessened them. He also resented her work. 'He says I succeed at everything – if he does not touch it,' Barbara confided to Marian. 'It is a 1000 pities he can't use the quantity of stuff he has in him. He is full of interesting knowledge. When I see you, I must have some serious talk with you about him. I think you are the most likely person in the world to help me.'[20] He had developed an obsession with Cuba, of all places, and spoke of starting a new life there. But Barbara was aghast at the idea. 'He must not, shall not go.'[21]

When she did eventually return to Algiers in November 1859, she felt shocked – and perhaps guilty – to see Eugène looking old and ill.

> It is very serious to me if he won't always go with me to England. He is the most obstinate being on the face of the earth ... This tenacity of character makes him care about me more than anyone else in the world could, but it is very difficult to manage life with [him] sometimes.[22]

Visitors from home were a welcome distraction. Marian and George Lewes declined Barbara's urgent invitations because Marian suffered so badly from seasickness. But as well as Ellen Allen in 1858, Nannie came in the spring of 1860 and Bessie enjoyed a holiday packed with sketching expeditions, sightseeing trips and picnics in early 1861. Doughty Aunt Ju was another visitor, but Bella was too busy having children and, sadly, relapsing into the mental illness that was eventually to consume her life.

Bessie was a particularly welcome guest. She linked Barbara to her childhood, and to her work; like an anchor in choppy waters, she kept Barbara steady. And she understood how important the separate strands of Barbara's working life were, acting as a liaison between 19 Langham Place and Campagne du Pavillon, and as an unofficial artist's agent. She carried home quantities of Barbara's Algerian paintings and placed them for sale in London galleries; deposited plump little cheques from Gambart's (a prestigious venue otherwise known as the French Gallery); and forwarded press reviews.

Barbara's output certainly attracted notice. Marian reported how thrilling it was to see her friend's name in large letters paraded on a sandwich board through the streets of London during a solo show at Gambart's. During the five years following her wedding, she exhibited at several other galleries, including the fashionable Pall Mall Gallery, the British Institution, the Society of Female Artists, the reading room at 19 Langham Place and in various private spaces accessible by invitation only. She painted almost exclusively in watercolour, enhanced by body colour (which lends depth and opacity), but did submit what she considered to be a 'monster' oil to the Royal Academy in 1862. She wasn't surprised when it was refused.

Tangible success was doubly important to Barbara the artist. It validated her as a professional and gave her an income which was hers by right rather than by dint of the Pater's generosity. Now, given Eugène's truculent state of mind, she needed to earn money for his sake. 'I am very anxious [my pictures] should succeed because if nothing the Doctor writes succeeds & nothing I paint it won't do to stay here. If my pictures succeed he will be content because it is as much his doing as mine if they do.'[23]

At this time, most of her work involved American or Algerian landscapes. Her loyal friends were unstinting in their praise of the way in which Barbara painted – with love and sunshine, said

Marian; powerfully, said William Michael Rossetti; with peculiar freedom, said Elizabeth Blackwell. Many of her critics
agreed. Her technique radiated joy and naturalness, they said; it
was full of purpose, spontaneity, perception and truth. But *what*
she painted was not always to their taste. Her Algerian scenes
were described as 'slaty and opaque', 'glassy and grey', curiously
'cold'.[24] Surely Africa was all about glowing ochres and shimmering bronze? One newspaper even went so far as to accuse her
of painting from the imagination, 'evilly' staying at home while
pretending to be abroad.[25] But I would trust Barbara's eye for
colour implicitly. It informed everything she saw, everything
she described and everything she painted, with unerring authenticity. The Covid pandemic scuppered my hopes of visiting
Algiers during research for this biography, but when I go, I fully
expect it to look glassy, grey and seductively cool.

EVEN THOUGH SHE WAS such a notoriously slapdash correspondent, Barbara managed to remain close to her core friends
while she was away. Elizabeth Blackwell had returned to New
York in 1851 to supervise her sister Emily's medical studies, estab-
lish a private practice and open an infirmary for women. By 1859,
however, she was back in London, greeted with a welcome letter
signed by fifty of Barbara's friends and ready to give a course of
eyebrow-raising lectures on – among other subjects – women's
reproductive organs. She was shockingly candid, explaining the
location and function of the clitoris (a word surely unknown to
most of the people present). 'We find in the special organization
which we are considering, a more abundant provision for exquisite sensation . . . than in any other part of the body.' Slightly less
encouragingly, she described its environs, during sex, as 'something like a great swollen leech'.[26] Bessie worried that audiences
would shriek with horror at such revelations, but most were – or

pretended to be – admirably undeterred, even thanking her for expressing the inexpressible with such confidence and composure.

It is not clear whether Elizabeth understood the backstory behind Barbara's relationship with her cousin Florence Nightingale. Elizabeth corresponded with both women and was Florence's first choice for a professor of sanitation to take charge of training nurses when she opened her school in London. Elizabeth had spent too long, and too much money, on qualifying as a physician, however; she was not about to relinquish the front-line career she had earned. Besides, she found Florence difficult to relate to on a professional level. Florence was a national heroine with a publicly raised fund of £45,000 behind her – a staggering £2.5 million today – and a genius for the administrative minutiae of public health. Elizabeth, on the other hand, relied heavily on Barbara's circle of family and friends to fund her medical ambitions in a hand-to-mouth fashion. Yet Elizabeth was a qualified doctor, from 1858 on the register of the British Medical Council, and already doing great things for her patients and her peers. She resented being treated by Florence as an adjunct to the Nightingale machine. In letters to Barbara, she accused Florence of enjoying 'a little sneer' at the Blackwell sisters' hospital in New York, and of writing an 'ill-tempered, dogmatic and exaggerated' book on nursing.[27] Barbara, meanwhile, she adored. 'I kiss your hands and your beautiful hair – and then your lips.'[28] And Blackwell kisses are hard to come by, she assured her.

Bessie remained constant, and despite suffering from the effects of a blighted love affair with her cousin Sam Blackwell, posted cheerful letters to Barbara about practising a paper for the NAPSS by reading it to her bedpost, for instance, and gently teasing the Bodichons for their endearingly eccentric way of life. She was never afraid to challenge her headstrong friend. For example, just as John Chapman had, she urged Barbara to compromise her artistic ambition a little by trying to be more commercial, and painting what the market wanted. Some of

Barbara's work was impressionistic in tone, even slightly surreal, like the early Irish famine painting, or her brooding *A Hooded Procession* showing fantastic, shrouded figures emerging from shadowed woodland. 'I never can see why . . . you should refuse to paint a certain number of pictures every year representing those elementary & catholic conceptions of nature which the whole world understands. Then you might gain a reputation which would lift your more recondite pictures over the bar of public opinion.'[29] Barbara declined to take her advice.

Unfortunately, Anna Mary Howitt, who married in 1859, continued to reel away from reality. After jolly John Ruskin nastily dismissed her painting of Barbara as Boadicea – 'What do you know about Boadicea? Leave such subjects alone and paint a pheasant's wing'[30] – she refocused on 'spirit drawings' produced, she claimed, by her turbulent subconscious. Even her old friend and fellow Portfolio Club member Dante Gabriel Rossetti began to express his doubts about her creative capacity, describing one of her exhibits at the Royal Academy as particularly miserable, 'involving a dejected female, mud with lilies dying in it, a dustheap and other details'.[31]

Rossetti married Lizzie Siddal in Hastings in 1860. Barbara might not have articulated exactly why, but was intensely sympathetic when Lizzie miscarried the following year. When she died of an overdose of laudanum in 1862, Rossetti's friends were heartbroken for them both. The coroner ruled it an accident, but rumours persisted, and still do, that Lizzie had committed suicide. In a grandly romantic gesture he later regretted – and rectified – Rossetti buried a manuscript volume of his poems in her coffin. Ever afterwards, whenever he needed balm for the soul, he retreated to Sussex; either to Scalands or to other Smith family homes. The modern scholar Mark Samuels Lasner, who knows Dante Gabriel as well as anyone can who never met him, is convinced that he should have married Barbara. Lasner told me during the course of my research that a dose of 'animal spirits' might have done Rossetti good, and his artistic sensibility might have nourished Barbara's confidence and creativity. It's an intriguing thought.

When Barbara was seventeen, she met Robert Ross Rowan Moore, an Irish barrister friend of the Pater who stood (unsuccessfully) for the Liberals on an Anti-Corn Law platform in the Hastings by-election in 1844. Barbara and Moore's Irish wife, Rebecca, got on well, keeping in touch when the Moores moved to Manchester the following year. Their relationship deepened when Moore abandoned Rebecca for another woman during her pregnancy. Baby Norman Moore was born in 1847, and quickly became a favourite of 'Aunt' Barbara. Their fondness was mutual. While other friends of Rebecca might send the child new shirts or edifying books, to help his mother out as she tried to earn a livelihood for them both, Barbara sent him the best present any naturally curious five-year-old lad could ever wish for: a dried-up skate fish attached to a piece of card. That gift kick-started a lifelong interest in natural science, culminating in Norman's presidency of the Royal College of Physicians and eventual baronetcy. When he married one of Barbara's nieces, Barbara was delighted to welcome him into the colourful Leigh Smith clan.

Barbara valued all her friends dearly, but none more than Marian Evans. She made a sketch of her in 1877, a few years before the writer's death; it is very faded now, but utterly truthful and lovingly drawn. This simple portrait is a testament to their deep, unlikely kinship. They had their differences, particularly over religion. Barbara could never come to terms with Marian's insistence that there was no afterlife. 'I told Marian that if I ever felt convinced as she professes to be of utter annihilation,' wrote Barbara to Bessie, 'I should not have power to live for this little scrap of life.'[32] But the sympathy they shared was almost preternatural. Nothing was off-limits. They discussed sex and birth control, Barbara's fear of dying ('I do not like death, I tell you'[33]), Marian's relationship with George Lewes's sons, and appear to have known each other inside out. The only thing they did not discuss, because she hated discussing it with anyone but George Lewes, was Marian's work.

When her breakthrough novel *Adam Bede* was published at the beginning of 1859, it caused a sensation. Everyone naturally assumed its author, 'George Eliot', to be a man. The *Saturday Review* reckoned he was a gifted country clergyman. Barbara was in Algiers when it came out but read an early review and was immediately convinced that this masterpiece was by her dear friend Marian. She was overjoyed, and hastily sent her congratulations. 'I can't tell you how I triumphed over your triumph . . . Now you see I have not yet got the book [she had only read an extract quoted in the review] but I <u>know</u> that it is you.' She recognized Marian's personality in her writing. '[T]here is her great big head & heart & her wise wide views . . . Very few things could have given me so much pleasure 1st that a woman should write a wise & humorous book 2nd that <u>you</u> <u>that you</u> whom they spit at should do it!'[34] Barbara was referring to Marian's extramarital relationship with George Lewes, for which she was reviled by certain self-righteous 'friends' and acquaintances. Public opprobrium was something she shared with Barbara herself, stigmatized for the circumstances of her birth, though, arguably, it was easier for Barbara to conceal her shame.

Marian was astounded. No one else had recognized the book as hers. She wrote in her diary on 6 May 1859:

> Today came a letter from Barbara, full of joy in my success, in the certainty that Adam Bede was mine though she had not read more than extracts in Reviews. This is the first delight in the book as <u>mine</u>, over and above the fact that the book is good. I am not sure that anyone besides Barbara will feel that sort of delight.[35]

Until she had the confidence to acknowledge authorship, Marian begged Barbara to keep the secret – which she did, telling only Eugène. But she was instrumental in persuading Marian to 'come out' sooner rather than later. She should not be a coward and hide behind a male pseudonym, urged Barbara, but instead be proud of her womanhood. By the end of June, everyone knew that George Eliot was a woman. The object of anonymity, insisted Marian, had been to allow the book to be judged without prejudice. But now, no one could unsay their admiration of it. Her literary reputation was safe.

When Marian wrote *Romola*, first published in monthly parts from July 1862 onwards, it was not only the heroine's appearance – tall, noble-looking, with red-gold hair – that recalled Barbara Bodichon. Romola was impetuous, tenacious, loyal, and her love for her father was invincible. When Barbara read it (reluctantly, not being a fan of historical novels) she was overwhelmed. 'I felt more emotions in living in Romola for a week than I have felt in a long time & I am not one who lives like a polyp.'[36] Indeed, anyone less like a polyp than Barbara is hard to imagine.

Reading about Romola and her father reminded Barbara how she had felt two years earlier. Nannie was staying with Barbara and Eugène in Algiers at the time. She was never an easy guest, being one of those defensive people who assume they are being constantly judged, and who consequently live life in a self-indulgent state of umbrage. Barbara found her negativity frustrating, unable to understand how 'a young woman of 29 with near £1000 a year!' could possibly fail to be grateful.[37] In later life, when friendly relations between the two sisters had all but broken down, Nannie claimed that she had only gone to Algiers in the first place because Barbara was frightened to be left alone with her unpredictable husband and was begging for a chaperone. This seems unlikely on several counts, not least the fact that Nannie loved the place so much that she and her partner Isabella (Isa) Blythe bought the house next door to the Bodichons in 1866. Barbara confided to Marian (to whom she always told the truth) and to another friend, the poet William Allingham, that in those early days she loved Eugène dearly and that they were 'unspeakably happy' together. And had she been seriously afraid of the Doctor, she would not have turned to Nannie – or, indeed, to anyone within the family. She was too proud.

Be all that as it may, thoughts were just turning to arrangements for the journey back to England for the summer of 1860, when one of those letters Barbara looked for so eagerly from the *facteur* arrived with terrible news. The Pater had suddenly died on 12 April. She was not even aware that he was ill. He had been suffering from erysipelas, like Grandfather William, and various infirmities of old age (he was seventy-six), but no one suspected him to be in danger.

Barbara and Nannie left immediately for London, while the Doctor closed up the house and followed them. It must have been a grim journey. Barbara was never able to articulate how she felt about her father's death, other than in general terms to friends, telling them what a desperate shock it had been, that she could only cope by thinking of other things, and how she felt his loss more than anyone else, so close were the two of them. Despite his indiscretions and flaws, she admired the Pater above all men for his firmness of principle, his limitless generosity, his (usually) keen sense of justice and of fun, and his love for her. He taught her to be a campaigner, a politician. He also taught her that love conquers all.

The Leigh Smith children decided to bury the Pater next to their mother Anne in the graveyard of St Edmund's Church on the Isle of Wight. Unlike hers, the epitaph they composed for him survives:

He was an ardent advocate of civil and religious liberty and of every measure which could promote the well-being of mankind. He supported for 20 years the first Infant

School in England. He gave hearty and generous assistance to migration. He loved the arts and sciences and was an active friend of their Diffusion among the people.

The misspelled letter her old nurse Hannah Walker wrote to Nannie on hearing the news of his death is more eloquent than the rather stiff memorial: 'it is a sad blow to you all I know it was to me my poor dear old Master I feel very much for you all I new it would be sad wen it did come. The lord has herd my prayers that you are all grow up to do for yourselves.'[38]

The reading of the will must have been exquisitely embarrassing. Was there any contact between the Leigh Smiths and the Bentley Smiths? Barbara's half-sister Jane was a 23-year-old heiress by now; Alexander was twenty-two and Harry twenty-one. Who told them about the Pater's death? Was it Catherine Spooner? If so, did she read about it in the papers before hearing from the solicitor? Did the three siblings feel as though they, too, had lost a loving father? Or just someone who looked after them financially because it was his duty to do so? Did they grieve? Like so many questions about the lives of characters redacted from personal histories, these must, for now, remain unanswered.

By the end of 1860, Barbara, Ben, Bella, Nannie and Willy had settled down to life post-Pater. We know already how busy Barbara was in trying to coordinate her parallel lives. Ben had only trained for the Bar to please his father. Now he was free to devote himself to hunting at home; shooting bears in Albania and other far-flung places; developing a passion, inherited from the Pater, for polar exploration; and keeping an acute eye on his business and property interests. The family was growing: Willy and Georgina's daughter Amy was born in 1859, and her sister Georgina, known as Roddy, two years later. Bella and the General's daughter Amabel, or Mabel, came along in 1860 and her brother Harry in 1862. Barbara took a close interest in them all, especially her nieces. She had high hopes for them. Meanwhile, the storks continued to nest at Campagne du Pavillon, and Barbara continued to long for children of her own.

In June 1861, she and Eugène made a pilgrimage to his native Brittany. They called on Eugène's great-aunt Madame le Grand de la Syraie, the matriarch of his surprisingly Catholic, aristocratic dynasty. It was a strange interlude. Barbara was welcomed warmly but treated very much as a curiosity. She was the first Protestant Great-Aunt had ever seen, reckoned Barbara, and certainly the first 'strong-minded' woman. None of the female members of the family had ever been out of France – barely out of Nantes – and professed no interest in looking beyond the horizon. 'I do not believe [they know] the commonest modern scientific truths,' Barbara commented in the journal she sent round to Aunt Ju and others later; had she stayed in their insular company much longer, she believed she would have 'exploded like the Great Eastern [steamship], having all the safety valves tied down' (let's hope Uncle Oc was not on the round-robin list).[39]

Barbara was heartened by the obvious affection everyone had for Eugène, despite his rampant republicanism and lapsed religion. But as their three-week visit progressed, her patience with these relics of the old order wore thin. 'I am getting tired of hearing these old aristocrats complain, believing firmly as I do that the people suffered more before the revolution than ever they revenged in the revolution,' she wrote. 'It seems to me the Catholics are incorrigible, all the lessons of the past are thrown away . . . I began to get disgusted.'[40]

The Bodichons left Brittany before Barbara's impatience became offensive. They never returned. The rest of that summer was marked by a sketching trip to Wales – though it is unclear whether Eugène accompanied his wife – and a memorable 'Harem Party' in London, which Eugène attended dressed in his favourite outfit, an Arabian burnouse (usually worn, by him at least, with nothing underneath), and where three real-life sheikhs thrillingly turned up as guests.

Eugène's favourite – sole – topic of conversation during this period was eucalyptus trees. He had a grand plan to plant thousands of them in Algeria, to act as they do in Australia as quick-growing screens against harsh winds. We know now that the introduction of an invasive, alien species can have disastrous effects on native flora and fauna, but to Eugène the scheme was irresistibly attractive: it would provide employment for local people; eucalyptus roots stabilized the sandy soil, making it easier to cultivate and more water-retentive; the timber was strong; and the aromatic leaves contained an antioxidant oil effective in reducing fever. He persuaded Barbara to order 'convoys of seed'[41] from Melbourne and, over the next few years, virtually single-handedly set about foresting his adopted homeland. There is now a suburb of Algiers called Les Eucalyptus, and in 2011 riots flared in the Bois des Pins neighbourhood when their local gum trees – 'a symbol of national pride', according to *Al Jazeera* – were threatened by plans to build more tower blocks.

Barbara had a plan of her own, not for Algeria, but for what she had come to think of as her own little corner of Sussex, at Scalands Farm. Ben gave her a three-acre plot of land by the side of the road from Robertsbridge to Brightling, looking south over the farm on his Glottenham estate to the High Weald beyond. It was mostly woodland (she loved her trees, too) and in spring the ground was spread with wood anemones, wild daffodils and violets, like a Renaissance *millefleur* tapestry. Here, Barbara told her husband, she would build him a cottage in which he could relax and learn to love the countryside of her youth, and she could root herself in familiar soil. The next few years were to bring the most difficult and rewarding challenges of Barbara's life. But as long as she had her Sussex sanctuary, she felt safe.

10

Gellie Birds and Deaf-Adders

1863–1866

Scalands is a wonderful place to get un-tired.[1]

WHEN MY HUSBAND AND I GOT MARRIED, SOMEBODY gave us a visitors' book. The idea was that everyone who came to stay with us would sign it, so that in the mellowness of old age we could look back and reminisce about the people and homes we had loved. It was a thoughtful gift, and we were full of good intention, but soon forgot all about it in a flurry of work and children. Sadly, when that mellowness approaches, we shall be forced to rely on fickle memory.

Barbara was more conscientious, and far more imaginative. Instead of a visitors' book for Scalands Gate (to give her new house its formal name) she had the inspired notion to ask her guests to sign one of the bricks around the huge inglenook fireplace instead. Then they would always be close to the heart of her home – the hearth – as visible, ever-present friends.

The house still stands, surrounded by bluebell woods of oak, birch, chestnut (used for local hop-poles) and hornbeam. There is a little tumbledown wooden shed in the garden with a brick chimney and a wall of windows looking towards the farm in the valley, which must be where Barbara or Eugène went to be alone. A towering tulip tree, her pride and joy, still drops its waxen petals on the lawn every spring, and the view of the Weald is still a hazy mallard green fading to peacock blue in the distance. Best of all, the fireplace bricks in the main house are still in place, a russet mosaic of painted names, initials and little vignettes of flowers or birds.[2]

Eugène is there, of course; so are Ben, Bella, Nannie, Willy, aunts Ju and Dolly, Uncle Jo Gratton and various nieces and nephews. Nurse Hannah Walker has signed, as have other domestic staff and tradespeople. Marian and George Lewes are among the more famous names, with doctors Elizabeth and Emily Blackwell and Elizabeth Garrett Anderson, gardeners Gertrude Jekyll and William Robinson, the sculptor Alexander Munro, potter William De Morgan, and artists Dante Gabriel Rossetti, Hercules Brabazon Brabazon (who must surely win the 'best name in a biography' award), William and Jane Morris, Ford Madox Brown, Walter Sickert, Margaret Gillies, Joanna Samworth, Sara Ann Clarke and Emily Osborn, who painted the best portrait of Barbara. The suffragist leader Millicent Fawcett and her husband sit close by Henry Churchill, a British consul in Ottoman Syria; Colin Simson, a sheep farmer from Australia; the dashing military hero Captain Richard Twopenny; several prominent political activists and social reformers (male as well as female); and a host of others whom we shall never know. It is safe to say that the majority of people mentioned in this biography live on in Barbara's parlour. People she liked, that is. 'Some of our friends are roses,' she once commented, 'some are cabbages. Mrs —— is a first-rate cabbage.'[3] Only the roses are immortalized.

Scalands Gate, usually known simply as Scalands, was designed by Barbara to echo the vernacular Saxon manor houses of Sussex. Like her, it was utterly un-Victorian: neither grand nor imposing, but built to be generous. Its rooms were large enough for comfort, lit by wide windows and white interior walls. There were plenty of bookshelves, with space above them to display Barbara's two hundred or so ceramic pots and her collection of paintings. Rush matting covered the floors, and in the same room as the fireplace – the first room you entered on opening the latched front door – was a mural of the Bayeux Tapestry (the scene of the Battle of Hastings being just down the road). Curtains and cushions were bright with Algerian embroidery; there were always bunches of wild flowers in jars or vases on tables, but few concessions to visiting softies, who complained of draughts, no bell pulls to summon servants, of whom there were too few, and a conspicuous lack of heat.

Outside, the garden was developed to flourish in May, when the Bodichons were most likely to arrive home from abroad, with primrose-coloured, early-flowering Banksia roses scrambling up the walls and a profusion of bulbs. The terriers René and Fritz shared their territory with various Leigh Smith pointers, retrievers and beagles, and footpaths wound away through the woods to other family homes, including Brown's, where Barbara grew up. When William and Mary Howitt stayed at Scalands soon after it was built, they were delighted to hear cuckoos, which they noted were locally called 'gellie birds', and sweet-voiced nightingales, and to discover slow-worms or 'deaf-adders' basking lazily in the grass. Mary Howitt declared that she had never witnessed a spring more beautiful than the spring of 1864 at Scalands.

Norman, the son of Barbara's friend Rebecca Moore, loved the place. Barbara once sent him a message asking whether he would care to come over and dissect the nervous system of a dead weasel she had found. On another occasion she invited him to share an 'accidentally shot' roast heron. This was the stuff of an inquisitive young man's dreams. On summer days Aunt Barbara would leave the house on horseback by 8 a.m., and not return from the woods and fields until the light dimmed. Norman knew that, by contrast, most 'ladies' barely ventured out of doors. In family letters, he described waking up in his Scalands bedroom, opening the window and looking through a blissful frame of climbing roses on to the lawn below, where resided two goats, two frisky black pigs and a pampered French partridge with only one leg.

In the evenings, guests sat by the fire in soft lantern-light, aware
of 'dog-music' from the kennels in the background while listening
to readings from Shakespeare or the poets, or to Beethoven and
Schubert inexpertly played on the piano by their hostess. Barbara
dressed less formally in the country than in town (and she rarely
dressed formally *there*); she was liberal with good food – though
less so with drink, diluting wine with water if she thought people
had had enough – and unfailingly welcoming to those she invited
to stay, whether or not she and/or her husband happened to be
resident at the time. It was a true retreat, not just for the Bodichons
but for all their visitors; the perfect place, according to one of
Barbara's colleagues from Langham Place, to 'get un-tired' and
relax. Unless they happened to meet Eugène on one of his naked
walks, of course, when (as family legend has it) he was liable to
wander from behind a bush wearing nothing but a far-away look
in his eyes. Not bothering with clothes made him feel closer to his
dead mother, he said. He enjoyed her spectral company.

Marian Evans described receiving a surprise hamper sent by
Barbara from Scalands. It contained fresh Sussex butter, cresses,
fruit and mushrooms. 'I took it as a hamper full of love,' she
wrote in thanks.[4] That says it all.

AS WELL AS BEING Barbara's sanctuary, Scalands was where the
different-coloured strands of her life were spun together. Friends
and family, Reform Firm work and art, peace and activity, past
and present, thinking and doing, company and solitude; everything belonged there. Except, perhaps, Eugène. He preferred
Scalands to anywhere else in England, and felt comparatively free
of stress in the house and its woods; he did his own laundry,
optimistically spreading his clothes out to dry in the damp morning air on slug-slimy shrubs in the garden; he fed the birds and
found himself jobs to do around the place, but was never completely at home. A guest described his routine.

Dr. B never appears till 11 a.m. when he takes breakfast arrayed in a long garment of white flannel, just like a lady's waterproof sack, with its hood. All day long he wanders about in the wood hatless, umbrella tucked under his arm, & wearing his flannel garment. At 7 we dine – Dr. B then arrays himself in a grey garment made like the white one, puts the hood over his head – also a blanket shawl, & thus sits down to dinner. He always takes eight or nine glasses of wine at dinner.[5]

Despite Barbara's insistence that the house be known as Dr Bodichon's Cottage (it rarely was), and his name appearing in local directories as the owner and occupier, the impression given in visitors' letters and memoirs suggests that he, too, was a guest at Scalands. If he stayed too long he complained of feeling giddy and faint, and often suffered from an unspecified fever which came on promptly at 11 a.m. and lasted for several hours. Barbara suspected that he was only there because of loneliness: there usually came a critical point during their annual separations when he would rather be with her in England than without her in Algeria. In the quiet battle over the ground rules of their marriage – six months here, six months there – Eugène was always the first to blink.

It is true that he was somewhat preoccupied during this period. In 1866 his two-volume doorstopper of a work *De l'humanité* was published in Brussels, to more bewilderment than acclaim. It was reviewed fairly widely in England; most critics were impressed by its scope but baffled by its purpose, such as this journalist from the *Gentleman's Magazine*:

In this age of bookmaking it is positively refreshing to light upon a work that has not been intended for popularity, and could only have originated from severe and solitary thought. Dr Bodichon . . . has not cared to make either the title, style, or subject-matter of his book attractive; he has simply and honestly given the world the carefully sifted opinions of many years, and wishes them to be accepted for what they are worth. The book is difficult to deal with from a critic's point of view. One is startled with the downright sincerity of it. It is not the author or the author's achievement that occupies one's thoughts, so much as the man and the conditions of life, mental and moral, of which his book is a result.[6]

Or this commentator in the *Saturday Review*:

No-one but a Frenchman would sit down to write a book embracing so vast a field of knowledge, with no other preparation than his mother-wit; and no-one but a French-man would extricate himself so cleverly from the undertaking. The book embraces all that could be expected from the title. Beginning with the conditions of the planet on which we live, it treats of the origin of the human species; of the various races, and their geographical distri-bution; of the struggle for existence, and the causes which confer superiority in the struggle; of civilization, of pro-gress, of the future of humanity, of the origin of religions, of metaphysics, of ethics, of the questions of population and subsistence; and of course touches all the political, social, and international questions of the day. Of any pre-liminary studies of these topics there is no trace.[7]

Charles Darwin's *On the Origin of Species* was first published in 1859: after most of Eugène's book was written, but before it was published in full.[8] Eugène diverged from the Englishman's theory of evolution, being a creationist who believed in the cap-ability of humans to engineer a ready-made natural world to their advantage. He advises the successful engineer to develop agriculture; rewrite history, which has hitherto been 'the pan-egyric of the soldier, the priest, the poet'; reduce the function of governors to watchdogs; reduce the population of towns by compelling vagabonds and beggars to emigrate; 'get the Papacy removed to the Isle of Elba'; and finally, hold fast to the belief that life will be improved for everyone in the world, once every-one in the world agrees to make it so.

Although Barbara was undoubtedly proud of her husband's intellectual ambition, some of the precepts in this magnum opus cannot have been easy, as a libertarian, to defend. In the book, he repeats his conviction that *métissage*, or cross-breeding, is the answer to all humanity's problems. A single, mixed race will create 'paradise'. But there's more. Some races are superior to others, he claims, classified not by skin colour but by national characteristics, which inevitably means that the practise of *métis-sage* involves a measure of subjugation. He believes in euthanasia (whether voluntary or involuntary is unclear); in the concept of heritable 'wickedness'; in a 'rational' redrawing of the geopoliti-cal landscape (there is 'no reason to have Portugal', for example); the fatuousness of seeking peace (as opposed to fomenting revo-lution); and a global hierarchy of vegetables.

He also flies the flag for the rights of women, upholding their suitability to be 'kings, popes, archbishops, judges, lawgivers, to fulfil every private or public mission; to do everything as man' – though obviously has no time for kings, popes and archbishops himself. As a famous abolitionist, he urges slaves to fight for their freedom. But again, he goes too far: '[e]very slave, if he has not sold himself, has a right to kill his master'. Priests are the princi-pal obstacle to human progress, he reckons, yet love is what fuels the universe.

In other words, this vast treatise is – like its author – an enigma; deeply eccentric and a paradox of conflicting impulses. Marian Evans heartily congratulated a friend on getting to the end of it: a rare accomplishment. We know how much Eugène cared for animals when he wasn't shooting them. He called them 'our inferior brothers'. He worshipped the immaculate beauty of flowers. And we know that, in his own way, he adored Barbara. He was her noble Caractacus; she his other self. Yet he lacked insight. He did not see himself as others saw him; or if he did, he did not care. It has been mooted that he might not have been neurotypical, coping with life somewhere along the autism spectrum. Some of his later behaviour might well suggest that. What is certain is that he and his wife loved one another. They just found it increasingly difficult to live together, even in the gentle, non-judgemental embrace of the Sussex hills.

For a man who needed no company but that of his wife, the constant stream of visitors to Scalands must have been unsettling. Barbara could seldom resist showing people her country bolthole. She took Rossetti on picnics; demonstrated to her erstwhile suitor James Sylvester how to vault a five-bar gate (what other Victorian heroine can you imagine doing that, at nearly forty? Or at *any* age?); made unlikely introductions – between Marian Evans and Mrs Elphicke, the local baker's wife, for instance (she had been Lizzie Siddal's landlady in Hastings); and offered rest cures to the tired, the ill or the disillusioned, helping them to see that, as she put it, the 'real things' that matter in life are like 'daffodils – poetical things' while the rest is only 'smoke . . . I feel we have a short time to stay, and if I can help any friend to a happier or better life it is a blessed thing.'[9] Scalands was instrumental in that philosophy.

Barbara's friends were unfailingly polite to Eugène, at least in front of his wife. After they got married, barely a letter arrived from Marian, Elizabeth or Bessie without a postscript sending kind remembrances to 'the Doctor'. Later this would change, but while he and Barbara were still spending a reasonable amount of time together, his eccentricities were accommodated for her sake. And his own: Bessie enjoyed talking to him in French, even though she was a little irritated at being asked to do so whenever she visited, while everyone else went out and left them to it. She confided to her mother that it was almost beginning to look as though Barbara was using Bessie's presence at Scalands as a buffer between husband and wife. The writer Matilda 'Milly' Betham-Edwards, who became a close friend of the Bodichons, thought him handsome, invigorating and entertaining, looking thrillingly like a Bedouin with his brown skin and billowing Arab robe. *She* never minded practising her French conversation with him . . .

Members of the family were more circumspect. Nannie did not warm to the Doctor, though he was quick to offer any help he could when she and her partner Isa Blythe moved to Montfeld, a villa next to Campagne du Pavillon, in 1866. He had a soft spot for Isa, once informing her that, should Barbara ever perish, he would marry her next. Ben and Willy rarely sought his company, though do not appear to have consciously avoided it. No doubt they were all civil to one another when they met. The two aunts were non-committal, just wanting their niece – as is generally the way of aunts – to be happy.

Eugène in his outfit of choice, looking brooding and detached.

Distinctly unhappy at this time was another of their nieces: Bella. Barbara obviously felt a special responsibility for her frail sister who tried so hard to be strong (unlike Nannie, the strong sister who tried so hard to be frail, and then lived until after the First World War). Following the birth of Mabel, her eldest child, in 1860, Bella suffered from what was probably postpartum psychosis. It was a terrifying episode for everyone; there were fears she might spiral beyond recall into madness. No doubt influenced by Barbara, whose belief in the healing power of happiness never dimmed, the General immediately dispatched mother and baby to Hastings, the place Bella loved best. And not just to Hastings, but to her old home, 9 Pelham Crescent, fortuitously available for lease. There, they were looked after by the Leigh Smiths' old nurse, Hannah Walker, now in her mid-seventies. Hannah wrote to Nannie to report Bella and Mabel's progress.

> She is sertainly better and will soon be quite well and love her dear little baby she takes a grate deal more notes of it than she did that will come to her when she gets well for she is a dear good baby and very pretty fair blue eyes you wil love her I know . . . I have shed many tears over her and her poor mama to it was very shockin but thank god she had one of the kindes of husbands the ever lived . . . it is many years since I felt so fritened as wen she was taken first and I had care of the baby for 10 day and nights to my self it made me feel as if I 20 years younger.[10]

When Mabel's brother Harry was born thirteen months later, everyone feared Bella might relapse, but she was fine. Barbara invited her to spend her third confinement at Scalands in 1863 with the General and two nurses, just in case. The two older children stayed at Brown's, ten minutes' walk through the woods, where Barbara helped to look after them. Unfortunately, Bella's psychosis returned.

A year later, though her mental health had improved, Bella began coughing up blood. The General took the whole family to Europe, with a nursemaid from Hastings, in search of health and sunshine. It turned out to be the holiday from hell. The children were horribly travel sick and devoured by biting insects; toddler Harry was consumed by tantrums, and the nursemaid threatened to drown herself in the Rhine in the aftermath of an unfortunate love affair. Bella, meanwhile, was tackling some newfangled 'grape cure' for TB, which meant she must eat about three kilos of the fruit each day; unsurprisingly, she did not thrive. Then, to cap it all, war broke out between Prussia and Germany.[11] The family limped home, where, six months later, little Edmund died.

Bella's hold on reality began to disintegrate, but Barbara kept in close touch with the Ludlows, eager to help and veering between hope and despair for her sister's future. She may have wondered, too, whether Bella's madness was further evidence of the tainted blood shared by the Leigh Smiths. Was physical and mental weakness heritable? In *De l'humanité*, Eugène suggested that it was. If so, perhaps it was worth the risk: she still had hopes of becoming a mother herself, telling Bessie what a shame it would be if neither of them had any babies. 'If I can create one in the next three years,' she promised, 'I will.'[12] By then she would be forty.

Uncle Jo Gratton, Anne Longden's cousin, died in 1865 at the age of seventy-seven. He left almost everything to Aunt Dolly, who was now, in her late sixties, a very wealthy woman. He was the nearest thing Barbara had to a father figure on her mother's side. She had been fond of him. His reaction to Marian's *Adam Bede* surprised and moved her: he was no novel-reader, but spent an entranced half-hour on each page of the book and could not help but cry hot tears over the fate of feckless Hetty Sorrel. Both he and Dolly swore the book must be set in their home county of Derbyshire; possibly in Alfreton, where Dolly and Anne

Longden grew up. They were certain they recognized their friend Lisbeth, from the town, in one of Marian's characters.

Another link with the past was severed when beloved Hannah Walker died. The 'old nurse' Aunt Patty used to deride as the lowest of the low was mourned by all her Leigh Smith charges and buried by them in Hastings with a dignified inscription: 'In memory of Hannah Walker who died November 3 1866 aged 80 for many years the faithful and beloved nurse in the family of the late Benjamin Smith Esq. MP for Norwich.'[13]

OF ALL THE PLACES she ever lived, simple Scalands was the one closest to Barbara's heart. Blandford Square was not the same after the Pater died. She described the London air as increasingly 'dead' and, though she relished the conversation of metropolitan friends, was quickly losing her appetite for what she called 'long sojourns in stifling rooms with miserable people'.[14] Travelling was fun — until it wasn't. She describes an expedition through Spain, on the way to Algiers, in a lively series of letters to Marian in 1866 (published in an edited form in the magazine *Temple Bar*). It is all about art: a pilgrimage in honour of her favourite painter Velasquez, and a research trip for her own work. 'I saw more things I should like to paint in one day than I see in 6 months in Algiers but how to do it?'[15] Ever pragmatic, she made sketches on her travels from the train window, some of which still survive. She knew perfectly well 'how to do it', it transpires, dashing down the essence of fleeting new landscapes with spirited skill.

Some of the hotels she stayed in were unbelievably comfortable. She could happily have spent the rest of her days in the one by the divine Alhambra in Granada, she tells Marian; another one in Burgos was so clean that 'I should have thought Florence Nightingale had been there the night before'. The food was usually palatable, except when the chef used too much garlic (which was distressingly often). Nine-hour train journeys were challenging, but she took plenty of luggage with her to provide a few home comforts, including a portable bath. 'I have sworn a solemn oath not to be uncomfortable if I can help it,' she wrote.[16]

Not everything was wine and roses, however. Sitting on a rattling train all day made her bones ache. It was difficult to sleep well in a city hotel when there were so many unnecessary interruptions, like the accursed nightwatchman in Burgos who woke her up every hour just to reassure her that she was being watched. Unlike the bloodthirsty Milly Betham-Edwards, with whom she was travelling, Barbara refused to witness a bullfight, preferring to stand quietly backstage and comfort the wretched-looking horses about to be sacrificed in the ring. After several weeks of adventure, related to Marian with her customary wit and self-deprecation, Barbara crossed the Mediterranean from Gibraltar to Algeria. She was flea-bitten, footsore, exhausted and ready for home. *Real* home, not Campagne du Pavillon.[17]

Of course, Algiers had its attractions, including Eugène when he was well and happy, the climate when it was calm and kind, and endless sketching trips. She enjoyed some of the entertainments got up for Europeans: the occasional ball or boar-hunt, for example; special banquets, like the one at which the novelty menu was composed entirely of horse or asses' flesh; and the opening of an English library. More impromptu diversions were provided by the stranding of a fifty-nine-foot sperm whale near Mustapha corn mill, killed with many axes and left for days as a tourist attraction; the odd earthquake; and a fascinating (though terrifyingly destructive) plague of locusts that razed the countryside like Father Time's scythe. Barbara batted them off her clothes with a furled umbrella.

Milly wrote what to modern eyes is a toe-curlingly patronizing account of her stay with the Bodichons during the winter of 1866–7. It does reveal how Barbara spent her time, however. After commenting on 'dirty little Arabs' and 'the better class of Moors',[18] Milly describes an overnight expedition with Barbara across the Mitidja plain to the cedar forests of Théniet El Had, where Milly could almost fancy herself in Betws-y-Coed, so exotic were her surroundings. Barbara organizes elaborate picnics for twenty people at a time, and regularly shepherds guests to see the major philanthropic ventures in the town, including the orphanage next door and Madame Luce's school. She appears to be her usual buoyant self. 'Madame Bodichon could never have half enough of anything she loved, whether good company, aesthetic impression, or strawberries and cream,' comments Milly.[19] She was one of life's gourmands. But by 1866, good company, aesthetic impression and even strawberries and cream were beginning to lose their appeal in Algeria. And there was so much going on at home. Perhaps it was time to reassess her priorities.

ONE OF BARBARA'S CLOSEST artist friends was her Hastings neighbour Marianne North. Marianne's story was extraordinary. As the spinster daughter of a former MP for Hastings, she looked after her parents until first her mother and then her father died. Then, at the age of forty, she took off, circling the globe twice – in opposite directions – and producing nearly a thousand paintings of the botanical species she found in the tropics. It was her mission to capture these exotica in their natural habitat, which could mean travelling into the jungle for days, or clambering up some steamy mountainside in her black silk gown and bonnet, with a bemused porter in her wake carrying an easel and oils. On her retirement she built a gallery for her pictures in a corner of Kew Gardens. There they hang to this day, flamboyant, gaudy and astounding.

Barbara, however, was not entirely seduced by the exotic. Even in Algeria, she was just as happy painting an iris as an asphodel. What interested her artistically was fidelity. Not realism, necessarily; though she would spend hours training herself to memorize pigment tones, it was only so that the studio paintings she made from sketches in the field were exactly how she wanted them to be, rather than exactly how they appeared in real life. Capturing the spirit of nature – a mass of moving water, perhaps, an illusion of colour, or wind in the trees – was more important to her than producing something pretty. 'Most people like a touching story told badly by painting better than the inside of a dead ox painted by Rembrandt . . . I do not.'[20]

To this end, she insisted on constantly refining her technique. In 1864 she invited artist Tottie Fox (now the newly widowed Mrs Lee Bridell) to Algiers not only to comfort her, but so that Barbara could benefit from her old friend's expertise. That same year Barbara visited Paris, where she was tutored by the sublimely talented landscapist Jean-Baptiste-Camille Corot, and by Charles-François Daubigny, who became a good friend and visited Scalands more than once. Creativity, expressed through art, was the strongest of all the impulses in Barbara's busy parallel lives, and was hard to suppress. But she felt it her duty periodically to forgo what she called 'the Palace of Art' in order to do things for other people, individually and collectively, which meant that she could never reach the heights of her chosen profession. There just wasn't the time.

Nevertheless, there must be hundreds of examples of Barbara's artwork still in existence. Those acknowledged to be hers are in private and public collections principally in Britain (notably Girton College) and the United States. Some are catalogued and hang in spot-lit isolation; others – like those in her family's possession – are carefully stored in folders and ancient wooden chests, forming a cheerful mass of colour and remembrance. Barbara often gave away her paintings as presents, whether for a wedding, a birthday, or just to brighten someone's room when they were feeling dreary. So who knows how many are unacknowledged, taken for granted on descendants' walls or slumbering dustily in the attic? She sometimes signed her work with variations of her full name – Barbara Leigh Smith Bodichon – or her initials, but not always.

Scalands was as much a Palace of Art as anywhere. More so; it features repeatedly, with the surrounding countryside, in her watercolours and sketches. But it was also a Palace of Industry, at a particularly productive period in Barbara the activist's life. At this time, 'she lived from the 1st of January to the 31st of December in a whirl of business', according to Milly.[21] Working from home in Sussex was no problem, given multiple postal collections and deliveries a day, and a direct train line between Robertsbridge and London.

Sorting out the *English Woman's Journal* was a priority. Despite advertising widely, and the support of members of the NAPSS and other sympathetic organizations, subscriptions were not increasing enough to make publication viable. Perhaps this whole enterprise was turning out to be one of what Barbara called her 'benevolent follies'. She would sooner spend her money helping Maria Rye with emigration, or investing in Portman Hall School, than keeping afloat a magazine with a dwindling readership. Here were some lessons to be learned: that good ideas demanded good writing to make an impact; that there was some way to go until women's opinions were considered worth listening to and paying for; and that activists such as the Langham Place circle were more likely to succeed if they thought of some more focused way of getting their reformist message across.

Besides, the circle was fragmenting to an alarming degree. Max Hays was becoming impossible to work with, not least because of her intense but shifting emotional attachments to various women involved with the journal, including Bessie, Adelaide Procter and Lady Monson. Isa Craig and Emily Faithfull would happily have waved Max goodbye in 1861, assuming more editorial control themselves. Bessie wanted her to stay. But Bessie herself divided loyalties in Langham Place, being strongly attracted to Roman Catholicism, which most of her Anglican or

Dissenting colleagues (including Barbara) found inexplicably wrong-headed. It frustrated Barbara that Bessie appeared incapable of averting a looming crisis at the offices of the *English Woman's Journal*; it frustrated Bessie that Barbara held the purse strings and expected everyone else to do the tedious donkey work. It embarrassed both that here was a group of women bickering – just as their critics had foretold – while there was serious work to be done.

The crisis came in April 1862, when Max wrote a furious letter to *The Times* complaining about another correspondent's arrant misogyny. By doing so, she unfortunately played straight into the hands of those who thought any woman who opened her mouth in public to be an unlovely hybrid of harpy, battleaxe and slut. She certainly did not pull her punches:

> What! The Almighty has given us sense, thought, feeling, imagination, patience, long-suffering, and benevolence, a keener sense of right and wrong, deeper intuitions and purer instincts – all that, in the words of the great dramatist, we may 'suckle fools and chronicle small beer;' no platform but the childless hearth or the teeming nursery, and, if these may not be ours, jostled and pushed aside to rot in inaction . . . or, hopeless and helpless, sinking into the ranks of legalized or unlegalized prostitution . . . breeding animals only.[22]

Max was ahead of her time: she should have been a suffragette. Her rage, and the fact that she implied the letter was written on behalf of a 'small band of pioneers', proved too much for her colleagues at 19 Langham Place. The NAPSS committee and the Society for the Promotion of Employment for Women were similarly unimpressed. They had all spent the past five years working patiently and with all the tact necessary to combine credibility with radicalism. But as Eugène pointed out in *De l'humanité*, you can only change the world if the world is ready to be changed. And you can only prepare it for change by persuading or shocking it into action. Not by ranting at it. In swift succession, Max resigned; Bessie took some time out because of ill-health; Adelaide Procter also fell ill and left, having contracted the TB that led to her death in 1864; and a new editor was appointed at the *English Woman's Journal*, in the doughty person of Emily Davies.

Emily (1830–1921) was an Evangelist minister's daughter whose brothers were highly educated but who, while growing up, was not even provided with a governess of her own. Three years younger than Barbara, she was a deep thinker, dissatisfied with the limited reach of the parish work allotted to her, and determined, on discovering the *English Woman's Journal*, to make a difference to the wider world. Who gave her the idea that such influence would be possible for someone like her, the product of a sheltered life and with few material advantages, is a mystery, unless it was Barbara. They met in Algeria when Emily was visiting an ailing brother overwintering there in 1858; coincidentally, another brother had recently been appointed rector of Christ Church in Marylebone (close to Blandford Square), and when Emily moved from Northumberland to London with her widowed mother in 1862, the two became firm friends and close associates. Emily looked neat, precise and grave, with an air of bustling efficiency; Barbara was like a larger-than-life Titian heroine, spontaneous and reactive. They say opposites attract.

Meanwhile, another scandal was brewing, much more damaging to strong-minded women than an impulsive letter to *The Times*. Emily Faithfull had a friend, Helen Codrington, who was married to a senior officer in the Royal Navy. During the Crimean War of 1854–5, while he was stationed in the Mediterranean, Helen asked Emily to come and stay with her in London. Emily was a busy, working single woman who would probably welcome the company of someone beyond her increasingly cliquish circle; Helen was lonely. The arrangement worked well, until Helen left to join her husband on his appointment as superintendent of the Malta Dockyard after the war. When they returned to London, the two women resumed their friendship.

By the early 1860s, it was clear that the Codringtons' marriage was over. Henry – now a rear admiral – sued Helen for divorce, on the grounds of her adultery with a gentleman (or two) in Valletta. Before 1857, when the Marriage and Divorce Act was passed, that would have been the end of the matter. But now, Helen had the right to counter-sue, which she did.

At the trial in 1864, guzzled up by the press, things got very messy, very quickly. Helen accused her husband of refusing sex; when he did manage it, she said, he practised birth control against her will. Most sensationally of all, he was accused of attempting to rape Emily Faithfull while she lay in Helen's bed. Emily signed an affidavit to support the charge. The rear admiral's lawyers retaliated by claiming that Helen now preferred Emily's company in bed to his, which was unnatural and improper. Bessie's father Joseph Parkes was in court. 'There never was a trial in which more falsehoods were told or more *suppressio veri* [suppression of the truth] on both sides,' he reported. 'EF is bold and may try to brazen it out, but the Social Science [Association] can't continue Printing with her.'[23]

Emily later withdrew her affidavit – raising rumours that she had been bribed by the rear admiral to do so – and Helen lost the case, along with custody of her children. Emily was never free of her smutty association with the whole business, though, gallantly, Queen Victoria did not deprive her of the royal warrant awarded in 1861. But just as Parkes predicted, the NAPSS did not employ her again, and nor did the *English Woman's Journal*. In fact the journal folded altogether in September 1864, subsumed by the *Alexandra Magazine*, run by Jessie Boucherett.

It was wearying for Barbara to witness it wither and die. 'The enthusiasm with which I used to leave my easel and go to teach at the school or help Bessie with her affairs is wearing off,' she confessed to a friend, 'and if it were not [that] one has acquired habits which happily cannot be broken I should not go on as I do; I could not *begin* as I used ten years ago at any of these dusty dirty attempts to help one's poor fellow creatures.'[24] Her mention of the school is significant: in 1863 Ellen Allen, Portman Hall's headmistress, married and left, just as her predecessor Elizabeth Whitehead had done. Barbara had not the strength to seek a successor.

> This marriage is a great up-rooting of one of my interests in life because it has made me give up the school; I know no one I can trust to carry it on and so it is wiser to stop. It is the individual that makes the work and I have no faith in Schools, institutions, &c., unless there is a soul in them. It is absurd of people to say they will do good and establish this and that, the great thing is to find a good worker with good head, good heart, & sound health, and then just be contented to help them to do what they best can without any fixed plans of your own which only shackles the real worker.[25]

With the closure of Portman Hall and of the *English Woman's Journal* a year later, it must have seemed as though doors were closing on Barbara's reform work. But she was entirely wrong to think herself beyond initiating something new. When one door closes, runs the proverb, another opens. Or in Barbara's case, is given a determined kick to break the lock and let the fresh air in.

THERE WAS A GENERAL election in Britain in July 1865. Standing as the Liberal candidate for Westminster was John Stuart Mill, whose treatise on political economy Barbara had criticized so confidently at the age of twenty-one. Mill's stock had risen in her estimation since then. The major flaw in his 1848 thesis, in her view, had been a failure to consider the potential contribution of women to the body politic; now he was a paid-up supporter of the Society for the Promotion of Employment for Women and an advocate of equal opportunity in the home, the workplace and at the hustings. Like the Pater, his private life did not bear close scrutiny by public moralists, but he did have firm principles. He had been suspiciously close for twenty years to a married woman; when she was widowed and eventually married him, he baffled his peers by refusing any of the legal and financial privileges due to him as her husband. She was Harriet Taylor Mill, the author of the brilliant essay 'The Enfranchisement of Women', published by John Chapman in the *Westminster Review* in 1851. Harriet died in 1858, but her daughter Helen inherited her political convictions, fully supported by her enlightened stepfather.

Mill stood for election on a platform of universal enfranchisement, believing a person's sex to be as irrelevant to the electoral process as their height or hair colour. Barbara was thrilled. He refused to canvass for votes himself, believing the practice to be distasteful and liable to corruption, but was not averse to others doing it for him. So Barbara leapt into action – forgetting the weariness and disillusionment of the past months – and hired a horse-drawn carriage which she plastered with pro-Mill placards and paraded through the streets of Westminster with Bessie, Isa Craig and Emily Davies on board. Whether this was an asset to Mill's campaign is uncertain. No one was more delighted than Barbara when Mill won the seat. She shared her enthusiasm with the members of a new organization, recently arisen from the ashes of the *English Woman's Journal*: the Kensington Society, founded in May 1865.

One of the most valuable legacies of Langham Place was the concept of networking. There will always be disagreements over means and ends, and personality clashes when people work closely together, particularly if they are pioneers and thus have no precedent to guide them. But those formative years between 1858, when the journal began, and 1864, when it ended, gave Barbara and her companions a hint of the potential power of sisterhood. The Kensington Society developed a sense of cohesion and focus that would stand the future women's movement in good stead.

It was essentially a debating society; the first in Britain formed by and for women. Its numerous members were mostly, but not exclusively, based in London and included the president, Charlotte Manning, an amateur scholar of Indian history in whose Kensington home the meetings were held; Langham Place stalwarts Jessie Boucherett and Emily Davies; the famous headmistresses Frances Buss and Dorothea Beale; Elizabeth Garrett (the elder sister of Millicent Fawcett), inspired by Dr Elizabeth Blackwell to study medicine; Mill's stepdaughter Helen Taylor; Elizabeth Wolstenholme from Manchester, who went on to be a leading light of the suffrage movement in the north-west of England; and Barbara.

According to another founder member, the artist and social reformer Alice Westlake, the object of the Kensington Society was 'chiefly to serve as a sort of link, though a slight one, between persons, above the average of thoughtfulness and intelligence who are interested in common subjects, but who had not many opportunities of mutual intercourse'.[26] This was right up Barbara's street: a vehicle to enable considered activism and to encourage women to express themselves in public.

It all sounds rather serious, as indeed it was – or could be. A list of possible topics for discussion at its first meetings includes several with a subtly hidden feminist agenda, such as 'In what sense is discontent a commendable & exhilarating quality?' and 'Is the love of the beautiful necessarily coincident with, or conducive to, the love of the good?' But as usual with anything connected to Barbara, there was always room for a little levity. 'What feature of the face is the truest indicator of the mind?' is something I have debated with friends (the chin rates consistently highly) and 'What qualities of the national character are expressed in English dress?'[27]

The most significant meeting of the society's rather brief existence was held in November 1865. Barbara was in Algiers at the time, so someone else had to read out the paper she submitted on the enfranchisement of women. Helen Taylor, also absent, contributed another in support of the same subject, while three other members argued against it. At the end of the evening, as was customary, a resolution was put before the audience. Barbara and Helen triumphed almost unanimously, which was particularly gratifying given the initial ambivalence on the part of several other members.

This success gave Barbara food for thought. As soon as she returned from Algiers at the beginning of May 1866, she wrote to Helen.

> I am very anxious to have some conversation with you about the possibility of doing something immediately towards getting women votes. I should not like to start a petition or make any movement without knowing what you & Mr J S Mill thought expedient at this time. I have only just arrived in London . . . but I have already seen many ladies who are willing to take some steps for this cause.[28]

'The Cause' is how the arc of first-wave feminism, designed by Barbara, has been described ever since.

Helen responded positively, assuring Barbara that her stepfather would be happy to present a petition to Parliament at the beginning of June, providing it included more than one hundred signatures. The deadline was linked to the forthcoming debate on a new Reform Bill. Though this left only three weeks to collect them, Barbara was confident of at least that number.

Everyone sprang into action. Jessie Boucherett put up £25 to help cover the costs of canvassing for support, Helen offered another £20 and Barbara, no doubt, met other expenses. A new committee was called into existence (former Langham Place personnel were getting good at committees by now) with Barbara as honorary secretary; the wording of the petition was agreed, along with a covering letter, two thousand copies of each were then printed and either posted or physically delivered to as many potential signatories as possible, all women over the age of twenty-one.

The letter was admirably succinct.

An impression is widely prevalent that the extension of the Parliamentary suffrage to women, whether it would be in itself desirable or not, is at any rate not desired by women. In the hope of in some way removing this impression, it is proposed to present to the House of Commons, at an early date, a Petition briefly expressing the opinion of women on this point . . . The Petitioners do not attempt to enumerate the reasons which might be urged in support of their claim, and by which they are severally influenced. They simply adopt what appears to be the most direct method of expressing their wishes on a matter which they hold to be of great importance.[29]

The response far exceeded expectation. One thousand four hundred and ninety-nine names were collected and laboriously pasted, largely by Barbara, on to an enormous scroll which by the time it was handed over to John Stuart Mill – with another twenty-two additions – was almost too hefty to carry. Sadly the original has long since been consigned to the furnace at the Palace of Westminster, but there are plenty of familiar names on a later printed version, including Bessie, Anna Mary, Nannie, Isabella Blythe, Norman Moore's mother Rebecca, Tottie Fox (as Mrs Lee Bridell), Harriet Martineau and the troublesome Max Hays; some luminaries like Mary Somerville, Josephine Butler and Frances Power Cobbe; and crowds of 'ordinary' women like Rebecca Fisher, the station-master's wife at Battle, Bathsheba Pilbeam, a former grocer also from Barbara's neck of the woods in Sussex, and Emma Tingle, a charwoman from Leeds.[30] Barbara is down as Mrs (rather than Madame) Bodichon. Ironically, as a French subject now, she would not be entitled to vote in Britain even if she were eligible as a woman; for that reason, and given her regular absences from England, she soon stood down from the committee. But nothing could stop her expressing her support for the political ideal. Though she expected no quick result, she was convinced of eventual success. 'You will go up and vote upon crutches,' she predicted to Emily Davies, 'and I shall come out of my grave and vote in my winding sheet.'[31] She was right: Davies *did* vote in 1918 – almost on crutches – at the age of eighty-eight; by then, the bodily Barbara was long gone.

The date fixed for presentation of the petition to Parliament was 7 June 1866. Emily and Elizabeth Garrett handed it over to an excited Mr Mill; Barbara should have been there as its official sponsor, but was mysteriously indisposed that day, so could not join them. Some sources say she was ill; others – including her cousin's daughter Lady Stephen – that it was a 'domestic hindrance' that prevented her. Perhaps she felt awkward as someone who would not benefit directly from the matter in hand, or embarrassed by that old canard, her illegitimacy, and anxious to avoid the spotlight. It might sound unlikely today, but the stigma of being somehow 'tabooed' was not something she could easily ignore, even in her late thirties, particularly if it affected others by association. Or perhaps she, one of the aunts or Eugène really was poorly. We shall never know what caused her to miss being there on the most important day in the history of British feminism.

Barbara's prediction was accurate: nothing happened in Parliament straight away. In fact, the petition was not granted in full until 1928, when women were first allowed to vote on equal terms with men. But that early summer day in 1866 was when it all began; when the battle for the rights of women was officially joined. The quest for equality is a long game, and we are playing it still. Whenever we are flagging, we should perhaps remember the pioneers, and press on.

Outside Parliament, the movement was comparatively quick to gather momentum. Barbara wrote a paper for the annual meeting of the NAPSS, held in Manchester in October 1866, based on her presentation to the Kensington Society. It was published as *Reasons for the Enfranchisement of Women* with a companion piece, also by Barbara: *Objections to the Enfranchisement of Women Considered*. Both essays expanded on the covering letter for the petition: now that it was becoming clear that many women *wanted* the vote, it was important to explain why. Unsurprisingly, she did not mince her words. Women without a voice are discriminated against, she claimed. Plenty run their own businesses – like widowed farmers, who employ male labourers and pay taxes, but have no representation in Parliament. Women of education are denied the chance to influence society; women who run families or charities are dismissed as too busy or too frivolous to engage with the issues of the day.

Meanwhile, any male property owner, or tenant paying more than £10 per year, is eligible to vote, whether or not he is interested in or understands politics; educated men make laws without reference to over half the population; and men who run businesses, belong to clubs, travel widely and maintain simple or complicated family lives are never considered too busy to elect – or, indeed, to become – an MP.

Emily Davies was worried that Barbara's customary forth-rightness would put off potential supporters of the Cause, but Barbara insisted that straight-talking, within reason, was essential. Ambiguity smacked of apology, and *politesse* of deference. As in her *Brief Summary*, her style was admirably articulate and unsentimental:

> There are now a very considerable number of open-minded unprejudiced people, who see no particular reason why women should not have votes, if they want them, but, they ask, what would be the good of it? What is there that women want which male legislators are not willing to give? And here let me say at the outset, that the advocates of this measure are very far from accusing men of deliber-ate unfairness to women. It is not as a means of extorting justice from unwilling legislators that the franchise is claimed for women . . . [I]t is simply on the general ground that under a representative government, any class which is not represented is likely to be neglected. Proverbially, what is out of sight is out of mind, and the theory that women, as such, are bound to keep out of sight, finds its most emphatic expression in the denial of a vote.[32]

People listened to what Barbara had to say. By no means did they all agree. 'To make the natural woman a voter because the epicene woman is an occasional phenomenon would be cruelty to the former,' commented *The Globe*. 'We firmly believe that no greater misery could be inflicted on women generally than to endow them with political responsibility.' The *London Daily News*, on the other hand, considered Barbara's arguments to be carefully reasoned and calm. So much so that they would have 'done credit to any man'. But according to the *Glasgow Herald*, her assertion that it casts a slur on the value of women's opinions

to debar them from voting was like saying it casts a slur on the
intellectual capabilities of men to ignore their opinions on
embroidery and knitting. Not at all, said the *North Wiltshire
Herald*, which praised her intelligence, delicacy and good sense.
She was obviously 'an educated and refined Englishwoman'.[33]

There is an argument that any review is a good review: what
counts is being noticed. Thanks to Barbara and her circle, the
subject of women's suffrage began to gain currency, as more and
more women took courage and formed their own committees to
forward new petitions and debate new resolutions. Even Florence
Nightingale – rarely a joiner-in – was persuaded to sign another
of the original suffrage committee's efforts in 1868, again presented to Parliament by John Stuart Mill. The first one numbered
some 1,500 signatures; this one listed 15,000. There was no going
back now: Pandora's box was well and truly open.

11

Opening Doors

1866–1869

Ever since my brother went to Cambridge I have
always intended to aim at the establishment of a
college where women could have the same education
as men if they wished it.[1]

STRONG-MINDED WOMEN. AMAZONS. EPICENES. BLUE-
stockings. Freaks. According to contemporary reactionaries, these
were the creatures rising on haggard wings from Pandora's box
during the second half of the nineteenth century. They were
monstrous females, treacherous guests in a world that belonged
by inheritance to men, determined to neglect their domestic
duty on an impossible, unnatural quest for equality. People like
Barbara, Emily Davies, Elizabeth Blackwell, Elizabeth Garrett,
Bessie Parkes, Emily Faithfull, Max Hays, Helen Taylor, none of
whom were mothers – or even wives, apart from Madame Bodichon, but she had married a *Frenchman* and, anyway, she was a
bastard. *Quod est demonstrandum.*

Now we regard these people as the pioneers of British feminism, at the vanguard of the modern campaign for human rights
and social justice; not devils, but solid, fleshly angels. Between
1854, when her *Brief Summary* was first published, and 1869, when
she and Emily Davies founded the first university college for
women, Barbara kindled fire in the bellies of so many reformers,

men as well as women. That fire still flares and smoulders. In the heat and light of her family's repudiation of slavery and intolerance, she forged an ideal. One day, perhaps soon, educational, legal, political and professional opportunities for all would be taken for granted.

She would not have put it so sententiously – and she was never a lone operator – but the realization of that ideal is her greatest legacy. There are millions of women today who enter university, enjoy the full protection of the law, cast their votes and earn their own livings, without a backward glance. It does not happen everywhere, of course, nor all the time, but no humanitarian can question a person's right to equality in a fair and just society. If we see open doors to a better future, we feel entitled to step through them. It is amazing how many of those doors were opened by Barbara in her short but wonderfully wild working life.

The Kensington Society petered out following the 1866 suffrage petition and its immediate successors. Former members founded or joined dedicated suffrage societies around the country, notably in London and Manchester. Thousands – *literally* thousands – of copies of Barbara's pamphlets on the enfranchisement of women were printed to inspire and galvanize the campaign, though Barbara herself resigned from the newborn London National Society for Women's Suffrage. She disagreed with the organizers' insistence on an all-female committee, believing that the Cause was relevant to everyone, and that it was short-sighted to snub the sympathy and expertise of experienced, influential men. Why perpetuate division?

However, she continued to enlist as much support for the Cause as she could, cheerfully raising money and public awareness among friends and acquaintances. The diarist Arthur Munby found it hard to ignore 'buxom Mme Bodichon, fresh from Algiers'[2] when she popped up at various addresses in London to explain about women's rights, and he was not alone. With her ready smile and sunny disposition, she had a knack of presenting female enfranchisement as the most common-sensical, least threatening idea in the world.

She also remained involved with Maria Rye's emigration scheme, even though critics considered it nothing more than a wife-export business. Barbara genuinely believed the colonies to be new worlds, where settlers might reinvent themselves as useful members of an equitable society unhampered by gender and racial division. A little like the Utopia envisioned by the Pater when he took his little family to America in 1829, perhaps. When George Lewes and Marian were looking for an occupation for Lewes's teenaged son Thornton, known as Thornie, after he failed to get into the Civil Service in 1863, Barbara suggested they send him to Natal. She persuaded everyone concerned how good an idea it was, made the necessary contacts and waved him off. Tragically, the lad contracted spinal TB while in South Africa and was forced to return. Barbara remorsefully helped to nurse him, sitting and reading to him for hours on end, but he never recovered.

The winter of 1866–7 was spent as usual in Algeria. While the suffrage campaign was gaining ground at home, Barbara felt a mixture of frustration and relief at stepping aside. It was exciting to be in the middle of the action, but not having to be 'good to anyone' made her feel quite jolly, she confessed, and meant that she had more time to devote to art and to her husband.[3] Her career was progressing well; in September 1866, Day and Sons published a large chromolithograph of one of her paintings, *Algiers from Kubah*, which was offered for sale at a guinea as it was, or two guineas framed. This followed a two-woman exhibition of Algerian pictures by Barbara and Tottie Fox at the German Gallery in New Bond Street. She also exhibited during this period at the French Gallery, the Dudley Gallery (or Egyptian Hall), the Corinthian Gallery, the Royal

Barbara Leigh Smith in the pursuit of Art unconscious of small humanity.

Barbara never took herself too seriously, well aware that her eccentricity could make her appear daunting at times.

Academy and with the Society of Female Artists in Conduit Street. According to the critic of the *Penny Illustrated Paper*, her watercolours at the last venue were the best in the entire show.[4] She favoured elongated landscapes now, a format well suited to the wide horizons of Algeria; the most striking images in her sketchbooks are eloquent but economic panoramas in pencil, with a sepia wash and white highlights. They are beautiful, yet the absence of colour gives them a quiet air of melancholy.

It is difficult to ascertain how easy the relationship was

between Barbara and Eugène during the autumn of 1866. They were not conspicuously happy. Eugène's eccentricities were multiplying, and his drinking threatened to become a serious problem, at least to the surprisingly abstemious Barbara. Nannie – now their close neighbour – objected to Eugène's crazy gum-tree scheme and expressed her views, as any Leigh Smith would, in no uncertain terms. His selfish obsession with planting endless eucalyptus was ruining the views from her house. His forest was growing at a ridiculous rate and would soon reach hundreds of feet in height, casting Nannie and Isa Blythe into darkness. Barbara took her husband's side rather than her sister's, which enraged Nannie even further. Campagne du Pavillon was no longer a restful place to be.

In the New Year of 1867, it became hellish. Barbara developed typhoid fever, probably caught from bacteria lurking in the kitchen at Campagne du Pavillon. Typhoid was – and is – potentially fatal, causing headaches, a high temperature, joint and muscle aches, extreme fatigue and painful diarrhoea or constipation. It creeps up on its victims slowly, taking weeks to overwhelm them. Left untreated, there is a danger of internal bleeding, or perforation of the bowel resulting in sepsis. The mortality rate during the Victorian era generally ranged between 20 and 60 per cent. It is usually overcome today with antibiotics; in Barbara's time, rest and spoonsful of quinine, brandy or oil of turpentine were offered in hushed voices, with prayers.

While Barbara languished in bed, Eugène made plans for her to return to England as soon as she was able to do so. Presumably he could not cope with her illness, either physically or emotionally. Nor, apparently, could Nannie. Besides, it made sense for Barbara to avoid the enervating heat of an African summer. Taking a maid with her, she sailed for Marseilles in early spring, where she met loyal Bessie Parkes; together, having dispatched the maid back to Algiers, the two companions travelled up to

Paris by train, where they paused. The journey had taken four days thus far; four days of heat, crowds, noise, nausea and lack of sleep. Barbara was shattered.

What was to be done? She did not feel nearly well enough to face London, where she knew she would be pounced upon by ravening suffragists, nor to stay in a busy, impersonal hotel. So Bessie turned to their friend Madame Mohl, an English Francophile and feminist fondly known as 'Clarkey'. Clarkey had lived in Paris since the age of eight, so was the ideal person to ask for advice. As luck would have it, she had recently spotted an advertisement in the paper: it looked like just the thing for Barbara and Bessie. A small chalet was to let in La Celle-Saint-Cloud, some twelve miles from the capital, standing in lawns and orchards next to the owner's villa – a Madame Belloc – and surrounded by wooded hills. It had two bedrooms, with a veranda, an 'English WC', a small drawing room, a dining room and a kitchen. The views were charming, and there were plenty of gentle walks to be taken through the countryside, right from the door.

Madame Belloc was the French-Irish writer Louise Swanton, recently widowed, whose husband Jean-Hilaire Belloc was a reasonably well-known artist. Barbara had heard of them both and was delighted to have the chance to meet Louise and talk about her career. She was a little old lady now, content to sit among the remains of a diminished collection of paintings and Sèvres porcelain, but in her prime she had translated novels by Dickens and Mrs Gaskell, *Uncle Tom's Cabin* and *The Vicar of Wakefield*, written a biography of Byron and a series of children's books. Once upon a time, she had been famous.

At first, Barbara found the chalet idyllic. It was the perfect place to convalesce in the relaxing company of someone who knew her inside out and loved her dearly, despite their differences over running the *English Woman's Journal* and Bessie's predilection for popery. She bagged the best room, opening on to the balcony with a view of the villa, and soon began to feel strong enough to venture out on sketching expeditions during the day, and to join Madame Belloc and Bessie for dinner in the evenings at least three times a week. Sometimes there were visitors, including a swashbuckling gentleman called Jules Barthélemy-Saint-Hilaire, who was thrillingly rumoured to be an illegitimate son of Emperor Napoleon I. Madame's son Louis came increasingly often, tall, good-looking in a sallow sort of way, but too much of an invalid following prolonged 'brain fever' to work or (it was whispered) to marry and become a father. Poor Louis, thought Barbara. I wonder, thought Bessie . . .

After a while, things started to go awry for Barbara. Her health was improving, but not her stamina or her spirits. Bessie and Madame had become fast friends. They spent hours talking together. Louis livened up remarkably in Bessie's company; so much so that Barbara began to feel as though she were playing gooseberry. Surely Bessie, at thirty-eight, could not be thinking of *marrying* him?

She was. Bessie's mother, now a widow, was appalled when their engagement was announced. Ironically, in trying to explain the situation to Mrs Parkes, Bessie blithely used Barbara and Eugène as examples of unexpected but successful soulmates.

> I believe too firmly in the special leading of Providence not to believe that, in certain cases at any rate, marriages are directed. I even believe that the marriage of Barbara and Dr Bodichon was made in Heaven, and I have never regarded her marriage to that singular man with any regret. Dangers and difficulties would have come with anybody that dear woman had married.[5]

Even those who loved her had to admit that Barbara could be a bit of a busybody, though with the best of intentions. After trying in vain to talk Bessie out of marrying (a) a foreigner (somewhat hypocritical of Barbara); (b) someone Bessie hardly knew and of whom her family disapproved (ditto); and (c) someone who needed constant care and attention (thus depriving the world of an ardent reformer, and Barbara of her on-call company), Barbara took the liberty of writing to Madame Belloc, sending a copy of the letter to Bessie.

> Although you are not aware of it, for after all you do not really know her, Bessie is far too nervous and too delicate to undertake married life under what would be, as I am sure you must agree, unusual difficulties. She is unaware of it, but *I* know that in time she will feel intensely the Abandonment of all she has gained by her noble life of work for others in England. She has built up, though she may not be conscious of it, a position of great distinction. All this she now proposes to give up, apparently without a thought . . .
>
> As for me, her oldest, closest, and most devoted friend, I feel compelled to tell you that I entirely disapprove of this hasty marriage, and I beg you earnestly to ask her to pause, and to think, even now, well over what she is about to do. I was amazed when I heard the news. Indeed, it was a fearful shock. I also feel the terrible responsibility of being the only person who knows both Bessie and Monsieur Belloc. Should the marriage take place, I implore you, Madame, to try and feel – not as a mother-in-law feels, but as a real mother feels.[6]

Bessie was mortified, and furious with Barbara for daring to barge into the most important episode in her life. Madame courteously took Barbara's point, and agreed that the marriage required very careful consideration on both sides, but explained that Barbara did not know Louis as well as she and now Bessie did, and that he was, after all, a good, kind man.

Eugène could be described as a good, kind man, too. Barbara's

impassioned letter to Madame betrays the realization that goodness and kindness were not always enough for happiness. After
her illness she acknowledged that spending half her time in
Algeria had robbed her of a 'good working brain' and left her
feeling helpless. She needed to be at home: 'I can bear anything
in England.'[7] Perhaps she wanted to spare Bessie her own increasingly evident mistake in fragmenting her life beyond repair. But
Bessie was determined.

Though sad, and still convinced that the marriage would not
work, Barbara accepted the inevitable and gracefully offered to
host Louis and his mother at Blandford Square when the wedding took place in London in September 1867, six months after
the two lovers met. That battle was lost, but there were plenty
more to fight – if only Barbara could find the energy.

FAR FROM FEELING REFRESHED after her six-week stay in La
Celle-Saint-Cloud, Barbara was exhausted. She made straight
for Scalands. Friends were alarmed by reports of her decline:
Barbara was *never* ill. She was the very embodiment of health and
high spirits. Mary Howitt wrote to sympathize. 'You have been
for years a sort of ideal person,' she told Barbara mournfully, 'a
strong glorious powerful woman, gifted by God with your
endowments, my living representation of a northern heroine . . .
you remain large and beautiful in my memory.'[8] That remembrance of things past cannot have done much to raise Barbara's
spirits. Marian Evans was a little more upbeat, sending unlimited
love and warning her 'carissima' friend that, for once, she should
stop trying to please everyone else, and think of herself. Dr Elizabeth Blackwell's sister Emily, also a doctor, went to stay with
Barbara soon after her return from France. She reported that
although the patient was improving physically and sleeping
better (with the help of potassium bromide, a powerful sedative),
mentally things were not so good.

Most people laid the cause of Barbara's dejection squarely at the sunburnt feet of poor Eugène. Nannie insisted that it was *she* who had sent Barbara home from Algiers, not the Doctor; he just loafed about being peeved that his vigorous wife had suddenly become enfeebled. Unhappiness, pure and simple, was the cause of Barbara's breakdown in health, she declared; it was all that preposterous Frenchman's fault. In her opinion, Barbara should leave him for good. Except she shouldn't, because Nannie needed her back next door.

Emily Blackwell was less accusatory but suggested similar shortcomings. Barbara was upset, she said, that Eugène had neither accompanied nor followed her to England, ill as she was. It was humiliating for a proud woman to endure speculation that her husband did not care two figs about her. Nevertheless, implied Emily, Barbara was fortunate not to have him around to feed off her. 'I believe she has a much better chance of recovery by herself.' Emily even went so far as to say (privately) that the typhoid was a blessing in disguise; a pretext for 'diminishing the connexion' with Algiers and thus with Eugène.[9]

It was certain that Barbara would not be returning to him in the autumn. No less an authority than Florence Nightingale forbade it, in a message passed to Barbara via their mutual friend Clarkey in Paris. She warned that the only way to ensure a full recovery from the illness was to avoid the place – and therefore the conditions – where it was first contracted. The epidemiology of typhoid was not understood at the time; Barbara referred to it merely as 'the fever of the country' (Algeria) and might not have realized that the same disease claimed plenty of victims on the squalid streets of British cities every day.

The doctors Blackwell agreed with Florence but were anxious about the emotional impact of a prolonged marital separation. 'I believe there will come a hard time in the autumn when there will be gossip probably ... [and] he will be very angry & aggrieved at her not returning – for he will not in the least accept the idea of her not being strong.'[10] Barbara was used to salacious tittle-tattle; all the Leigh Smith children were. But it would be harder to bear when her own moral shortcomings were being discussed behind cupped hands, rather than those of her unmarried parents. 'I told you so,' the gossips would say. 'She *would* marry a foreigner.' Or, worse still, 'I told you so. She's one of those strong-minded women. A harridan, who broke her marriage vows and abandoned her poor husband.' She could not win.

Barbara herself kept quiet about the state of her marriage. Emily worried about her silence in case it was a symptom of serious depression. But it is hardly surprising that she was taciturn. This was a thoughtful period in her life. Ill-health, with its prospect of death, made her contemplative. She told William Allingham that she felt she had a deeper belief now, in middle age, than she had at twenty.[11]

A deeper belief in what?

The answer lies in a letter written to her beloved cousin Hilary Bonham Carter in 1865, a few months before Hilary succumbed to cancer. It is an intensely private document, but I make no apology for transcribing it at length, because it reveals more about the inner landscape of a very public person than any mere biographer could hope to express.

My dearest Hilary, – I was going to write you another letter when your very long and sad letter came. I wish I knew how best to answer it. *I wish that*, with all my heart. As I do not know how best to answer with the *great consolation* which I believe in as existing somewhere, you must take the second best, on which I live myself, always feeling that there is some way of solving the riddle of the suffering world which I cannot see. I have faith, but I am ignorant, and do not live religiously. If I bear troubles and get on in life at all, it is on very second-best expedients which I do not much respect myself – a sort of rough wooden scaffold bridge of life where some day I hope to see a perfect arch. I do not understand God's ways at all in this world. I have not harmonised or made a theory of the facts, I know. I live from hand to mouth. I try to look forward and not backward. *I try never to think of myself*; when I do I am very unhappy. I say 'Cosmos' when little things annoy me.

When I am exaggerating things that happen I say like old Corot, 'il faut chercher les valeurs' [you must look for the positive].

Then every day of my life I remember what the Pater used to say – 'Direct your thoughts and you will save yourself much suffering' – and I make myself think of what is good and noble, or what is to be done at once. In the morning I always plan my day, and I keep my plan unless something more worthy opens, 'mais il faut chercher les valeurs' – and so on.

But you will say, all this is easy if you are strong. If I were ill I should do nothing but grumble. Perhaps so . . .

I send you my poor little experience, which will not be any use to you – though my sympathy may be, I hope, because I think I am as well able as any one in the world to understand suffering and disappointment. I never have succeeded in anything as it seems to me, and I am more often discouraged than exulting. I want so much of so many things, and I can't get what I want. I suppose all our lives are less than our aims. Eternity would not be long enough for all I have had.

I think you have been very happy in having so many good friends; every good friend one has is a fortification against evil, an extra arm for good.

So good habits are all helps, and a routine life if one is dissatisfied or in a weak state of mind. But you know all this.

I don't despise any small means of keeping myself in good cheerful working order. Dress helps me. If I am

going down, I put on a better and brighter gown, and con-
fessing myself a creature of many wants and many
weaknesses, I take anything which can help me.

I hope you will be so well and so strong when you get
this letter that you will laugh at it.

After all, the feeling that others rely on me has given me
most strength of all things. If one leans on one side and one
on another it gives strength to what is weaker than either.[12]

It is worth noting that when Barbara heard the American
preacher Theodore Parker refer to 'the Creator, the Infinite
Mother of us all', she said it was 'the prayer of all I ever heard in
my life which was truest to my individual soul'.[13]

Such were the feelings Barbara explored as she gradually
returned to 'cheerful working order' during the Sussex summer
of 1867. She came to terms with herself, acknowledging her
physical and emotional vulnerabilities yet realizing that they did
not deplete her, nor make friends love her any the less, despite
her name and thus her identity being virtually synonymous with
exuberance. She always said she preferred a stormy sky to sunshine. *Chercher les valeurs.*

Barbara might still be one of the cracked people of the world;
more cracked than ever, perhaps, but that was fine. As the great
Victorian actress Fanny Kemble used to say – and Barbara probably heard her say it – 'Fail not for sorrow, falter not for sin, /
But onward, upward, till the goal ye win.'[14]

BY JANUARY 1868, BARBARA felt stronger, but still wary of
returning to the suffrage fray. She was staying at Willy's place,
Crowham Manor, where she had spent a happy Christmas with
her brother's young family, but now, frankly, she was bored.
This was not the season for a recent convalescent to go out
sketching. Friends were anxious not to tire her, so kept their

distance; besides, it was snowing too hard to travel even the short distance to Scalands. Everyone else seemed to have a job to do but her – including Bessie, who, astonishingly, was already pregnant. Envious Barbara occasionally looked after 'three little chicks' – two nieces and a nephew from Willy's busy family – but otherwise felt she had no one. Never mind; Emily Davies was planning to come to Scalands for a few days when the weather improved, and Emily was always good value. She had stayed with Barbara for a month during the summer, when the two of them had hatched a plan. Built a castle in the air. Perhaps she would have some news of progress, to cheer the dark winter days.

Emily certainly did have news. Unbelievably, their plan was coming to fruition. Each had long dreamed of opening a women's college, making university access available to female scholars for the first time: Barbara ever since that outing to Cambridge to visit her brother Ben back in 1851, and Emily since a Manchester conference of schoolmistresses in 1866. There had been too much going on recently for either of them to do much about it, what with running the *English Woman's Journal*, organizing the suffrage campaign, Barbara's absences in Algeria and her illness. But in the last few years, Emily had found the time to form various committees, with and without Barbara, to investigate the possibility of women students – specifically Elizabeth Garrett – studying medicine; women teachers receiving higher-calibre training; and girls being allowed to sit the same school and matriculation exams as their male counterparts.

Now her efforts had finally resulted in something concrete. Admittedly, Miss Garrett had been refused admission to London University in 1862, and subsequently at Oxford, Cambridge, Glasgow, Edinburgh, Dundee and St Andrews, but four years later her name had been entered on to the British Medical Register by dint of her passing the Society of Apothecaries' qualifying examination. She was now a doctor. And in 1863, girls were allowed to sit Cambridge Local exams for the first time, roughly equivalent to present-day GCSEs; it looked as though they might be admitted to Higher exams – like 'A' levels – in 1869. If females could *prove* their intellectual competence by competing at every level with their male peers, then surely half the battle was won.

Emily's interest in higher education for women was a matter of politics and ideology. For Barbara, it went deeper. She was herself a natural educator. When James Buchanan first opened doors for her, encouraging her to look out at the world in wonder, she longed to share what she saw; hence her involvement with Portman Hall. The Misses Wood's school in Clapton had not added much to her outlook, except to convince her that there must be something better than *this*, but her tutor Philip Kingsford, her stint at Bedford College and, most of all, her long discussions over literature, history and politics with Bessie, all informed her intellect and ambition.

Norman Moore was not the only young person to benefit from Barbara's boundless curiosity and enthusiasm. She always loved to teach her young nieces and nephews about natural history. The kitchen at Scalands was regularly festooned with dissected bits and pieces of deceased wildlife, in varying states of decomposition. How long is the longest earthworm? Find as many as you can and see for yourself. How does a weasel digest its prey? Have a look in his tummy. What are the principles of botany? Here's a bunch of flowers from the garden: *you* tell *me*.

She was not exclusively an empiricist. Her analysis of Mill's *Political Economy* was masterly (or its equivalent, if that seems inappropriate). Her reading was wide and eclectic, and her perceptiveness in divining Marian's hand behind *Adam Bede* almost miraculous. Yet she believed herself to be no more dazzling than the roughest of diamonds – like Mozart's sister Maria Anna, whom she reckoned would have been quite as famous as he was, with a little more respect and attention. Fortunately, it was not in her nature to be resentful. She once said that she would rather be the cause of beauty in others than possess it herself (though, famously, she *did* possess it herself). In other words, though unpolished, she could at least equip the next generations of women to shine.

She was perfectly qualified to do so. In 1858 she gave evidence to a Royal Commission on Popular Education (education for working-class children, that is). She drew on her experiences at Portman Hall, helping the Pater run Westminster Infants' School and acting as an unofficial inspector of the schools in Hastings to which he regularly contributed funds. A year later, her paper on middle-class schools for girls was presented at the NAPSS annual congress and published in the *English Woman's Journal*. It highlights the importance of properly trained teachers; a rigorous system of school inspection; a challenging and relevant curriculum; and formally supervised examinations.

It came naturally to Barbara to agitate not only for a sound, inclusive elementary education for girls, but for that education to extend to secondary-school level and – most radically – beyond. Before the Education Act of 1870, there was no state system. Schools were run by the National Society for Promoting Religious Education for poor pupils aged between seven and eleven. Private establishments of varying efficiency catered to local middle-class children, often run by indigent gentlewomen for girls and by local clergymen for boys. Upper-middle and upper-class boys then progressed to public schools, if their parents could afford it, and to the universities, while their sisters graduated to matrimony or eternal spinsterhood, relying for everything on the men in their lives, if there were any. If there were not, they gently 'decayed' or became servile governesses, babysitting the hundreds of thousands of daughters kept at home by their parents throughout childhood. It was not compulsory to attend any school until 1880, and the school-leaving age was not raised to fourteen until 1918. What did that say about respect for learning?

Especially in females, almost always the last to go to school – if they went at all – and the first to leave.

Emily Davies memorably wrote of intelligent young women being confined to a 'Happy Valley kind of life' by their lack of education.[15] Barbara was of the same mind. According to her, girls were conditioned to be needy. 'The beautiful dependence of woman upon man, upon which novelists and sentimentalists love to dwell ad nauseam . . . is in reality a condition of servitude.'[16] We know what Barbara thought of the stigma attached to young women attempting to earn a living, and the consequent lack of professional training available. We also know how important it was to her that they should play an active role in the body politic. So it can come as no surprise that she set her heart on enabling them to achieve the same qualifications as men at the highest level, by attending university.[17] Education was at the heart of Barbara's philosophy of life, because it opened doors. That is explicitly how she described its purpose to Marian Evans. It was empowering.

While Emily Davies contributed efficiency and thoroughness to the campaign for a women's college, Barbara concentrated on raising moral and financial support. They were in many ways a dream team. 'I am so happy to see any one work with perseverance & good sense,' wrote Barbara of Emily, 'that I feel one cannot do better than help her.'[18] Barbara did not consider herself the originator of the idea, she told Emily, despite having dreamed of it for so long, and she would never have succeeded in realizing it without Emily, being neither strong nor orthodox enough.[19]

That last point was significant. Public perception was a crucial factor in the success of this outlandish venture. Just as Emily tended to hide behind the scenes of the suffrage campaign, lest anyone important should judge her to be unfeminine, wrongheaded or irresponsible, she was anxious that this new enterprise should present an unimpeachable face to the world. She and Barbara chose the committee behind the founding of the college with this in mind. Emily's endearing list of potential members and their assets still survives:

Lady Stanley of Alderley.
Lady Goldsmid – Economy.
Lady Hobart – Sweetness.
The Dean of Canterbury – Greek, Divinity.
James Bryce, Esq.
Mrs Russell Gurney – Drawing.
James Heywood, Esq. – Business.
G. W. Hastings, Esq. – The World.
Mrs Manning – Domestic Morals.
H. J. Roby, Esq. – Latin.
H. R. Tomkinson – Conciliation.
Rev. Sedley Taylor – Music and Mathematics.
E[mily] D[avies] – Principles.[20]

Emily might have added 'Reform' after Mr Bryce's name: he was a Liberal politician, academic and lawyer who was a passionate advocate for including the excluded in British society. A sensible choice. Perhaps Lady Stanley of Alderley was not *quite* as suitable, being once described as

a woman of vigorous but not subtle intelligence, with a great contempt for 'nonsense.' 'Nonsense' included every form of feminine silliness, such as thinking dogs have souls . . . all popular superstitions, of which she had so great a dislike that she always had a dinner-party of thirteen on her birthday; and every kind of enthusiasm except for science, enlightenment, women's education, and Italy. She gave birth to 12 children, and when she died, left her brain to the Royal College of Surgeons 'because it will be so interesting for them to have a clever woman's brain to cut up'.[21]

(Barbara, predictably, thought she was wonderful.)

In fact, Lady Stanley declined Emily's invitation, for fear of embarrassing her husband ('It is not liked to see my name before the public,' she explained regretfully[22]). The novelist Elizabeth Sewell also declined when asked, because the whole idea reminded her depressingly of *The Princess*, Tennyson's serio-comic fantasy about a fictional women's college. Another novelist, Charlotte Yonge, simply disapproved of women aping men; Christina Rossetti said the proposed establishment was not High Church enough for her, and the children's writer Margaret Gatty was sure that such an institution would transform its students into conceited misfits.

Barbara's name is also absent from Emily's roster. She was publicly listed as the principal donor to the fundraising appeal, promising £1,000 (equivalent to more than £62,000 today), but sensitively agreed that her unorthodoxy, as she put it, might repel potential supporters. As Emily pointed out, no doubt with some awkwardness, 'ladylike ladies' were more attractive than – and these are my words, not hers – the illegitimate daughter of a scandalous liaison, married to a mad Frenchman, famous for promoting 'women's rights', whatever *they* might be, and for wearing weird clothes obviously without the decent benefit of stays or corsets. Emily was far too diplomatic to say so, but, as we know, Barbara was described by several of her friends, never mind her enemies, as 'wild'. Imagine what fun the critics would have with the concept of a college for wild women.

The critics had fun anyway, when the fundraising appeal for the proposed women's college went public following Emily and Barbara's meeting at Scalands in March 1868. Inevitably there were plenty of sniggering allusions to *The Princess*, with its reference to a fairy-tale citadel of learning,

> With prudes for proctors, dowagers for deans,
> And sweet girl-graduates in their golden hair.[23]

Any money raised would be better spent on a reformatory for women, thought the *Buckingham Advertiser and Free Press* (the news obviously reached far and wide). The *Sheffield Daily Telegraph* wondered what their degrees would be called. Spinsters of Arts? 'Ladies, bless you,' laughed the *Bristol Times and Mirror* indulgently. Whatever will you think of next? *The Atlas* was a Whig periodical for which George Lewes sometimes wrote; Barbara might have hoped for its support. It did give the appeal publicity by publishing a long and carefully considered discussion of pros and cons, explaining to its readers that the college was projected to cost some £30,000; would house a hundred students 'somewhere in the country' at a cost to each of them of around £80 per year; and that 'Mrs Bodichon' had set the ball rolling with a 'munificent' donation which no one else, as yet, had come even close to matching.

All this was fine in principle, continued the article, but think what would happen in practice. One hundred beautiful and impressionable young women living together in a confined space for months at a time? '[T]he collegiate discipline and residence will simply be an unmixed evil. And this brings us to our great objection to the scheme as it at present stands.' The *Atlas* journalist is pruriently concerned that 'boarding-school friendships' – a euphemistic term for lesbianism – will blossom, rife, rank and unchecked.

> Without stopping to inquire whether, with separate sets of rooms, the 'true collegiate idea' will involve complete isolation – for if it does the Ladies' College will be a prison and not a school – we may ask, how are the boarding-school friendships to be avoided? ... What care will be taken to provide against such intimacies? ... To imagine collegiate rule will stop feminine friendships, and that girls will cease to be either gossipy or intimate, is absurd ...

If, however, this new scheme is, as we fear, only to end in the establishment of a free and easy finishing school, with a rather pretentious name, it is hardly worthy of national support. Any sound plan of feminine education should keep in view the double existence to which most women are born – a life in which intellectual and domestic labour should go hand in hand. For even the most learned and independent of women may one day be conquered.[24]

At least the *Atlas* journalist did prospective students the courtesy of assuming they might marry (or 'be conquered'). Most nay-sayers were quick to warn parents that if they sent their daughters to such a place, they would find themselves paying a great deal of money merely to ensure that they never became grandparents. Bluestockings were sere, sad creatures, too clever to be wives and too selfish to be mothers.

Both Emily and Barbara were used to this sort of thing. They joined members of the committee in giving the college idea as positive a spin as they could, by encouraging local committees to hold meetings, getting supportive schoolmistresses involved, and collaring gentlemen of academic and political influence as advocates. 'We must do this well if we do it at all,' insisted Barbara. 'My whole heart is in the idea.'[25] Not to mention a good chunk of her fortune.

Despite her enthusiastic networking and Emily's hard work, money did not exactly tumble into the committee's coffers. Barbara had a large, elaborate building in her mind's eye; something along the lines of the Assize Courts in Manchester, designed by the go-to architect of the day, Alfred Waterhouse. It must be in or very close to Cambridge, she advised. Not only would that make it easier for tutors and lecturers to visit, but it would be an incontrovertible statement of intent. But by July 1868, only £2,000 had come in. Of that sum, Barbara gave half, Emily £100 and Elizabeth Garrett another £100, with a note that she intended to pay in £20 instalments, in case her patients all got well at once, or something equally calamitous, and left her without any income. Marian Evans gave some books for the library and £50, on the condition that the money be attributed to 'the author' of *Adam Bede* or *Romola* rather than to 'George Eliot' or 'Mary Ann Evans' or 'Mrs Lewes'. This was partly a matter of privacy, and partly to mitigate the persistent stigma of a woman blatantly living in sin. That sort of association – like Barbara's illegitimacy – would not be helpful to conservative supporters.

Two thousand pounds was not nearly enough to buy land at Cambridge, nor to realize the purpose-built design they planned – or not yet. Instead of waiting for more funds, however, Emily took the decision, reluctantly supported by Barbara, to open the college on a much smaller scale. In July 1869, she leased Benslow House in Hitchin, thirty miles from Cambridge. Barbara hastily helped to decorate it, making it as cheerful and picturesque as possible; she also agreed to host entrance examinations at 5 Blandford Square. Charlotte Manning was appointed as – what? Master? Warden? The committee decided the head of the college should be designated the 'Mistress', a less fortunate choice of name, perhaps, than that of Oxford's first women's college, who rejoiced in a 'Principal', but better than 'Duenna', which at one stage was a definite possibility.[26] Charlotte was the amateur scholar who had hosted and presided over meetings of the Kensington Society.

Eighteen young women took the exam that summer; five were accepted to enter Benslow House as Britain's first-ever female university students the following October. One of them was Emily Gibson, the eighteen-year-old daughter of a shipbuilder from London. Her family could not afford to keep her at school, so she worked as a pupil-teacher, encouraged by her employer, a woman who unusually happened to believe passionately in the right of an intelligent girl to be educated without limits. She recommended Emily Davies's *The Higher Education of Women* (1866) to Miss Gibson, who followed it up by reading an article published in *Macmillan's Magazine* by Emily Davies's brother Llewelyn.

As a result of the *Macmillan* article I called on Miss Davies to ask for further information. I told her that my education was very defective and asked her advice as to whether I should attempt the first entrance examination and how soon it was likely to be held. She told me that the examination might probably take place in the following June, and urged me to put my name down for it, saying that it would do me no harm to fail, and that it was very important that there should be plenty of applicants. She advised me to spend the intervening months in studying Latin (of which I knew nothing) and mathematics. This advice was not easy to act on, for money was scarce . . . but I was determined to let nothing interfere with the examination, though I felt quite unprepared for it.

When it came I thoroughly enjoyed it and was immensely interested in seeing the other students . . . I came fifth, I think, in the result. The first scholarship was awarded to Miss Townshend for her essay [but she didn't enter the college in the first cohort after all], and the second to Miss Woodhead [who was even younger than Emily Gibson] for her excellence in Mathematics.

After the examination Miss Davies had a reception or afternoon party for the purpose of introducing the students to the Committee. It was then that I first saw Madame Bodichon, and the little talk I had with her made an outstanding event in my life. Her frank, direct manner went straight to my heart. I felt that the College meant a great deal to her, and that it was a great privilege to have a chance of helping to make it a success. I seem to remember that her face was framed in a cottage bonnet that made a halo for her blue eyes and golden hair.[27]

Emily Gibson's college fees were paid by her brother, though one gets the impression that, had he not been able to help, Barbara would have found it hard to resist putting her hand in her own deep pockets. It was a constant frustration to her, and to members of the committee, that boys' schools and men's colleges never had trouble raising money, with generations of endowment behind them and a host of scholarships available, sponsored by schools, guilds or other institutions or beneficent individuals. Women's colleges – and there would surely be more than this one – had a great deal of catching up to do.

12

Parallel Lives

1869–1877

Madame Bodichon's blue eyes beamed
with the wild joy of living.[1]

A S BARBARA PROGRESSES THROUGH HER FORTIES, I
become increasingly aware of the challenges of writing about
her. Historiography is extremely selective. Women have traditionally operated behind the scenes of history, resulting in
centuries of male chroniclers ignoring – as Barbara put it – 'half
the people of the world'. But I find myself forced to repeat
the same redactive practice when faced with the task of choosing what to include in the narrative of her life and what to
leave out.

If they are lucky, biographers have a mass of material at their
disposal: letters and diaries written by the subject herself; answers
to those letters from different correspondents; contemporary
accounts in manuscript and print; modern interpretations online
or, again, in print; newspaper articles; images; and family memoirs. I have most of these resources in abundance, though I could
perhaps have done with a few more letters from Barbara, in her
very best handwriting, or a virgin cache of private journals. The
trick is to sift through everything, while refining and contextualizing, to reveal what is most important not necessarily to know,
but to understand. This is normally done within academic

guidelines: acknowledge your sources, give relevant dates and other details, and be sparing with the speculation.

But I'm a social historian as well as a biographer; someone who eavesdrops on the quotidian events of the past. As such, I can't avoid speculation. And I can't resist anecdote, rumour and trivia: they all play their part in reimagining the past. So at this point in Barbara's story, I am going to lay aside my stack of diligent notebooks, forget about the footnotes and root around for a while in my bulging box file of undated letters from Barbara (possibly to unknown recipients) and unattributed quotes; hard to justify using when I'm metaphorically wearing my mortarboard, but invaluable in illuminating her character and relationships with herself, with others and the world around her.[2]

What follows, therefore, is a brief, random sample of Barbara's thoughts and comments, for the most part paraphrased by me, from when she was in the prime of her life.

I've been to the College of Surgeons today to look at a narwhal's skull. Do female narwhals have horns as well as males?

I don't mind walking down hills, but walking up? I don't think so. How much strength would it require to lift 10 stone 12 lb up 1,200 feet? That's a sum I can't do.

Could you find me a copy of that book on geometry we were discussing yesterday?

That poor young man's become a Catholic. His family would be more tolerant if he'd become an atheist.

I've spent the last few days in Algiers watching trap-door spiders with a Mr Bird from Cambridge, tutor to the British Consul's family; partly because they are fascinating, but also because there's nothing else to do.

Thank you for sending the pheasants. I never allow them to be killed at Scalands, but if they arrive ready dead, they're welcome.

I only invited her to stay because I felt sorry for her. But I wish I hadn't now: she's so boring.

Would your nurses at St Bartholomew's Hospital like a kitten, Doctor Moore? I have a couple spare.

Would you like a peacock? The one here at Scalands is driving everyone mad with his screeching. I could post him to London for you?

God bless you, my dear child. Whatever you do and wherever you go, I will always be your loving Aunt B.

Thomas Carlyle writes twaddle. Picturesque, irrational twaddle.

Your new book about Dodo is wonderful [this to Marian Evans, referencing Middlemarch and its heroine Dorothea Casaubon].

I'm worried about the drains. I think I'll get the water from the well at Scalands analysed, to see if it's healthy enough to drink. Where should I send it?

Cut those ridiculous high heels off your shoes. You must have healthy feet, for walking in the woods, and if you don't walk in the woods, you'll fall sick.

Please will you go and visit Mr Willetts in Hastings? He's our old riding master, and I hear he's fallen on hard times. Give him £1, if it's obvious that he won't spend it on drink. I'll pay you back.

I'm so sorry my poor pony is nearing the end. Please have him shot before I get to Scalands, as I couldn't bear to let him go if I were there. But if there's a chance he's not suffering, let him live.

Brother Ben is giving one of his Balls, and coming to visit me first with some of his Big Photographs.

Do you happen to have a book bound in viper skin?

I'm very anxious for more daffodils.

Answer all my questions, please.

More strawberries. And cream.

What's that bright green insect called, the one that cocoons himself in spittle?

Miss Davies: here is a brooch for you. It's gold, with a lock of my hair inside, and comes with my love.

Could you send me some toadflax to plant in my new wall?

I was in a hurry to get somewhere the other day, leapt into the hansom cab, but the horse wouldn't start so I had to leap out again . . .

I am quite as full of work and pleasure as ever I can be.

Living with Barbara, *being* Barbara, must have been exhausting at times – but undeniably fun.

WHEN EMILY DAVIES AND Barbara opened the women's college at Hitchin in October 1869, it was an act of faith. There was not yet enough money to secure any kind of future; critics doubted the students' mental and physical stamina, and warned that too much learning could permanently damage not only their own health, but the well-being of the whole country. These arguments were developed by two eminent medical men who later published treatises on the effect on females of higher education. One of them was the pioneering British psychiatrist Dr Henry

Maudsley. In 'Sex in Mind and Education' (1874), he maintained that women had only a finite supply of strength in their (ridiculously over-elaborate) bodies. If they used too much of it to fuel their brains, there would simply not be enough to attend to matters further south.

> When nature spends in one direction, she must economise in another. It is not that girls have not ambition, nor that they fail generally to run the intellectual race which is set before them, but it is asserted that they do it at a cost to their strength and health which entails lifelong suffering, and even incapacitates them for the adequate performance of the natural functions of their sex . . . For it would be an ill thing, if it should so happen, that we got the advantages of a quantity of female intellectual work at the price of a puny, enfeebled, and sickly race.[3]

The American Dr Edward Clarke of Boston went even further. In 1873 he asserted that thinking withered the womb. Every woman who attempted higher education therefore ran a high risk of infertility, inevitably encountering 'neuralgia, uterine disease, hysteria, and other derangements of the nervous system' along the way. 'Educate a man for manhood, a woman for womanhood, both for humanity. In this lies the hope of the race.'[4] Barbara argued just the opposite: that it was enforced idleness that led to physical and mental breakdown. In this lay the curse of the future. Even Emily Davies, usually so timid about offending people, was driven to biting sarcasm when faced with such bigotry.

> [F]or mothers there is nothing like good, sound ignorance. A stolid indifference to the higher interests of life, complete absorption in petty cares, is supposed to produce a placid, equable, animal state of existence, favourable to the transmission of a healthy constitution to the next

generation. We have persuaded ourselves that Englishmen
of the present day are such a nervously excitable race, that
the only chance for their descendants is to keep the mothers in a state of coma. The fathers, we think, are incurable.
Their feverish energy cannot be controlled. We give them
up. But there is hope for the future, if only mothers can be
kept out of the vortex.[5]

It was imperative that the college should not only succeed but
be seen to succeed. There was more than personal pride and credibility at stake for Barbara and Emily. Failure could well result in
the Establishment firmly nailing down Pandora's box again and
sitting on the lid.

Determined to keep up appearances, Emily insisted on there
being a high table at Benslow House. It sat two: Emily and the
Mistress. She required the highest standards of discipline and
deportment. There must be no question of concession. According
to her, it was crucial that the students tackle the same exams as
their male counterparts in Cambridge. This was only possible
due to the good offices of sympathetic male academics who supplied and offered to mark the papers. No doubt Barbara's
relentless positivity helped to persuade them, though it would be
another twelve years before the university formally allowed
women to participate.

Gradually, it became evident that Barbara's optimism was
well founded. When the first two Hitchin students passed the
Tripos, exams qualifying them for a degree (but only theoreti-
cally, in their case), there were wild celebrations. The results
arrived from Cambridge by telegram, whereupon all the young
women climbed on to the roof of Benslow House and rang the
alarm bell, thus activating the local fire brigade. They sang the
traditional academic anthem 'Gaudeamus igitur' ('So let us
rejoice') and tied flags and banners to the chimneys, cheering and
whooping with glee. It was a day to remember.

Barbara loved visiting the college, though was increasingly convinced that it should be in Cambridge, not out in the sticks like a lazaretto. As the number of students slowly rose, she regularly invited them to Scalands for mini breaks. She sent them pictures to hang on their walls; found bright curtains for the windows and rugs for the floors; planted flowers and trees in the garden; and wrote cheery, encouraging letters. She also did her best to raise Emily Davies's spirits when necessary. Emily was appreciative, describing Barbara's influence as invaluable. Madame was clear and firm, yet 'winning and bright',[6] and was beloved of the whole student body. When she was not there – in Algeria, for example, or busy with other things in London or Sussex – the house felt strangely empty. You do not know how much I miss you, wrote Emily to her friend.

Barbara was missed most when there were problems. Mrs Manning had agreed to act as Mistress for one term only (and sadly died in April 1871). Her successor was Emily Shirreff, a writer on girls' education and a friend of Miss Buss, headmistress of North London Collegiate School. But Miss Shirreff resigned after a couple of terms in protest at not being given enough authority by Emily Davies. Next in line was Annie Austin, the sister of a Langham Place alumna, Jane Crow. She lasted another two terms before contracting pneumonia. From the summer term of 1872 until the installation of Marianne Bernard in 1875, Emily Davies herself shared the position with Barbara, stoutly supported by Lady Stanley of Alderley, who had returned to the fold now that her disapproving husband was dead.

None of these appointments were made without a great deal of angst-ridden discussion. Barbara wrote to her family and friends to ask their opinions about various candidates, and occasionally betrayed her own exasperation at Emily's autocracy. She relished her time in charge of what she called her 'flock', while Emily said the pastoral responsibility made her feel like a worn-out widow with multiple unmarried daughters. During their shared interregnum, it became clear that the students favoured Barbara's appropriately collegiate style over Emily's slightly school-mistressy approach, summed up in a truly awful college hymn Emily composed:

> For thee, O dear, dear College,
> Mine eyes their vigils keep;
> For very love, beholding
> Thy happy name, they weep.
>
> O sweet and blessed College,
> The home of the elect,
> O sweet and blessed College,
> Which eager hearts expect [. . .][7]

Admittedly, Emily's tongue was partly in her cheek when she came up with this, but not entirely.

Barbara preferred to teach the young women Sussex folk songs or ballads from Dr Bodichon's Breton childhood. Shared pleasure was a stronger bond, she felt, than anything imposed by authority. She chatted with the young women, listened to their concerns and treated them as welcome guests. To give her her due, Emily appreciated this. Barbara could be a little *too* chummy with the students at times, in her opinion, but when there were any difficulties, Barbara was the one to send for. With her direct yet kindly approach she could say things to the young women that Emily never could.

All of Barbara's diplomatic skills were called upon in March 1871, when Mrs Austin was still in post. The students had decided to amuse themselves by organizing some 'theatricals': a passage from Algernon Swinburne's recently published *Atalanta in Calydon*, and a couple of scenes involving Shakespeare's Benedick and Beatrice, and Olivia and Malvolio. They invited Emily Davies, the Mistress and a few guests to watch rehearsals in the library. Emily was decidedly unimpressed. The Swinburne was just about acceptable, being a pseudo-Greek tragedy in verse, though the poet was known to be fond of a drink and a salacious story. Indeed, one critic had recently called his work pornographic. And Shakespeare was Shakespeare: dangerous, possibly, but glorious too. What really alarmed Emily was the appearance of actresses dressed as men. This was in shockingly bad taste and played into the hands of those who suspected the college of being some sort of den of Sapphic iniquity. The nature of the transgression was not articulated explicitly, but thoroughly understood by those *in loco parentis*, if not by the students themselves.

Mrs Austin asked to see the organizers of the theatricals the following morning. They were nonplussed. What had they done wrong? Used the library without permission? When the Mistress explained, adding that the matter might well be referred to the governing committee, who would decide on a suitable punishment, their bewilderment turned to anger. Emily Gibson was deputed to write to Barbara, to explain why they felt so hard done by and appeal to her sensibilities as an artist and theatregoer. She reminded Barbara of the conversation when they first met, when Barbara spoke loftily of liberty and self-direction. They understood that wearing trousers might not be acceptable in public, and they were sorry to have upset Miss Davies and Mrs Austin, but their performances were usually conducted in private. Why should their conduct behind closed doors be censored if there was no one around to be offended?

Barbara made an appointment to see Miss Gibson, with the full support of Emily Davies and Mrs Austin. Her instinct was to agree that it was a foolish and possibly pernicious idea to get into the habit of aping men, but that it would not be wise to refer the matter to higher authority. She would rather the students realized their mistake, worked out the danger of what they had done for themselves, and thus take responsibility for behaving in a more socially acceptable fashion in the future. A more *feminine* fashion.

After the meeting with Miss Gibson, Barbara melodramatically reported to Emily Davies that she had 'never met such a spirit of revolt, and such self-confidence' but she hoped she had managed to talk some sense into the errant students.[8] Secretly, she must have been glowing. Spirit? Self-confidence? The college was obviously doing its job.

Miss Gibson's recollection of the meeting is interesting.

> To me the most important outcome of the imbroglio was an interview with Madame Bodichon . . . It happened that I had recently gone into mourning and, as a protest against the hideous and fussy fashions of the time, I had contrived a simple little frock of fine Parramatta [a silk and cotton mixture] . . . It was jeered at, at home, as my 'preacher's gown,' but when Madame Bodichon found me in it in my room at Hitchin she was charmed with it. It was a case of the prophet coming to curse and remaining to bless, for she asked me for the pattern and said she would have a gown made like it to paint in.[9]

The squall blew over, but by 1872 it was clear that the college was outgrowing Benslow House. There were twelve students in residence now; some of them had to be put up in uncomfortable, temporary iron huts in the garden, while another student was consigned to the gardener's cottage, the gardener himself presumably having been evicted first. A tight budget meant that their meals were unexciting at best; at worst, inedible. Bread, milk and gristly beef featured heavily, and the puddings were invariably made with dripping instead of butter, and no eggs. They were supplied with cheap candles that spat and sputtered, and in winter the house was so cold that they were obliged to swaddle themselves in blankets.

They complained of boredom, finding the place too isolated. Gymnastics were diverting, and Madame Bodichon insisted they were good for the soul as well as the body, but not everyone could cope with the trapeze. Swimming was fine, but again, some could not manage it. Emily Gibson once rescued one of her peers from drowning, which was terrifying at the time, but exciting in retrospect. Croquet was fun, but it was hard to deliver a good stroke if your mallet kept scuffing your skirts. Someone suggested trying football, but Emily Davies would not hear of it. Theatricals lost their shine after the Shakespeare affair; all that was left was exercise – long walks to gather wild flowers in season – punctuated by glimpses of the Edinburgh express train deftly slipping (deliberately uncoupling) a coach as it paused each day at Hitchin station before manfully steaming away.

The students' tutors were beginning to complain about the journey from Cambridge; one of them had resigned already, while another wrote directly to Barbara to beg her to consider moving the college closer to civilization. Emily was still resistant, suggesting a halfway house between Hitchin and the university city. The governing committee had drastically lowered its fundraising target from £30,000 to £7,000, but even this seemed unachievable, so how on earth could they afford to re-establish themselves in a larger, more convenient location?

By cutting their coat to suit their cloth: erecting a smaller building than originally planned, on a site not quite in Cambridge, but close enough. They could take out loans on the security of friends and family members, providing the college was legally established with a memorandum of association, which it was, with Barbara as a signatory, in 1872. Soon, a parcel of land was bought – sixteen acres on the edge of the village of Girton, two miles from the city centre. A buildings sub-committee was formed with Barbara, handily, as its chairman, and her dream architect, Alfred Waterhouse, was engaged to design the core of what is now Girton College. Here, in October 1873, Barbara's ambition of 'quiet liberty and opportunity'[10] – and a room of her own for every student – was finally realized.

Unfortunately, the builders were still working when the first students arrived. There were tubs of cement and piles of bricks everywhere, no doors or windows on the ground floor, and wood shavings all over, which got swept along in drifts by the women's skirts. Emily Davies flitted about in a white shawl handing out candlesticks and good cheer, like Wee Willie Winkie, and soon everyone got used to navigating the carpenters' benches – and carpenters – in every corridor. One student later remembered how bizarre it was to be wrestling with the intricacies of trigonometry while several men were hammering things in her bedroom.

Gradually, more rugs and pictures appeared (many painted by Barbara) to make the place more homely; the walls were decorated in Barbara's chosen colour-scheme of calming blues and greys; furniture arrived upholstered in gleaming chintz; and her new friend Gertrude Jekyll was consulted about planting the borders. Barbara commandeered young Norman Moore to come to tea with selected students, and invited Marian Evans to visit (though Marian insisted on coming in by the back door to avoid attention); then she asked Norman's friend Charles Darwin for a few of his books for a new library, John Stuart Mill for some interesting exam questions on political economy, and Dr Elizabeth Blackwell for advice on good health and hygiene. Why have friends and not make the most of them? Meanwhile, she resumed her fundraising activities with new vigour and some success, full of work and pleasure.[11] And Eugène remained Eugène, an increasingly distant figure both geographically and, it seems, emotionally.

IN TRUTH, WORK AND pleasure had become one to Barbara, given her semi-detached marriage. Though Girton took up much of her time, she enjoyed the art of plate spinning and pot boiling, always keeping several projects on the go at once. In 1869 the third edition of *A Brief Summary* was published. The proofs she marked up for the printers are buzzing with comments and corrections. John Stuart Mill's feminist essay *On the Subjection of Women* was also published in 1869. Barbara the activist drew confidence from Mill's high-profile support. The fact that women's rights were being discussed more broadly than ever before helped to facilitate networking, and Barbara was an incomparable networker. It was harder for critics to dismiss feminism as the product of hysteria when a *gentleman*, an acknowledged philosopher and political economist, was prepared to argue for it. Even such an unusual gentleman as Mill. Harder still when Parliament chose to credit women with the sense to spend at least some of their money as they wished, which happened the following year when the first Married Women's Property Act was passed. It permitted wives to keep their own earnings and legacies, though any property they might have owned before marriage remained their husband's, unless protected, as Barbara's was, by a trust. Full financial independence would not be possible until a second Act was passed twelve years later.

With the opening of the college and the passing of the Act, two of Barbara's major campaigns came to (limited) fruition within the space of two years. This was also her most productive period as an artist. During the decade between 1867 and 1877, she exhibited at the Royal Academy at least four times, won a gold medal at an international exhibition at Crystal Palace, and continued to show paintings and drawings at the Society of Female Artists' exhibitions in London's Conduit Street and at her usual private galleries. Extraordinarily, one of her paintings – *Cornfield, Sussex* – even impressed John Ruskin. Her work continued to sell well, bringing in between £400 and £500 a year. It would have taken a skilled workman seven years to earn as much.

Barbara liked to keep her 'earned' money and her inherited

wealth separate, tending to spend the former on causes and individuals of her own choice and plough the latter back into the
family or property. It would be interesting to know the source
of 460 guineas she spent in 1863 on a painting by Thomas Creswick:
that was an unimaginably large sum. In 1876 the contents of
5 Blandford Square were insured for £2,390.[12] The purchasing
power of that sum today would be around £160,000 – and that
was just one of her houses. Various income streams included
interest and profit on stocks and shares; the proceeds of sales of
Algerian pottery and photographs (what is now the Victoria and
Albert Museum bought quantities of both in 1868); and rental
payments from leasing Blandford Square and other properties
when she was not in residence herself. She was a canny business-
woman, always bearing in mind her mantra that money might not
guarantee your own happiness, but it could buy other people's.

Elizabeth Blackwell once pointed out that Barbara's commercial success was as much a result of her networking skills as her
popular appeal. It did not seem quite fair to Elizabeth that Barbara
should rely so heavily on rich friends and family to buy her pictures. It deprived struggling artists, who lacked her 'large
acquaintance', of a market, particularly struggling women artists.
But Barbara was so generous with her money, admitted Elizabeth,
that it was hard to begrudge her wealth. Her good nature meant
that she could never refuse any even vaguely reasonable request
for help, and the more she gave, the more she was asked.

Elizabeth had a point, but it is not fair to imply that Barbara
never sold to unknown people. Her exhibitions continued to be
reviewed widely and, for the most part, favourably. Once they
had got used to the coolness of her Algerian scenes, critics praised
her 'dashing pencil', her 'extremely spirited' brushwork, calling
her 'an artist of the rarest gifts, of the closest observation, and
possessing an intimate knowledge of the theory and practice of
art in its highest form'.[13] Having seen scores of her paintings
during my research, for what it's worth I would agree.

Some of her best friends were artists. Charles-François Daubigny, for example, who found himself exiled in England during the Franco-Prussian War of 1870, while his family were besieged in Paris. As a nominal French national herself, by virtue of marriage to Eugène, Barbara felt keenly for all those caught up in the siege, contributing money to relief efforts and suggesting novel schemes to run the blockades and supply what she perhaps surprisingly claimed to be essentials, such as huge consignments of pork pies and 500,000 pots of Liebig's meat extract (an ancestor of Bovril).

When William Allingham married the artist Helen Paterson in 1874, Barbara showered them with presents, including a bookcase, a cupboard, an Arab brass bowl and three pictures which they were welcome to swap for ones of their own choice if they wished. Whether these were cast-offs from Scalands is unclear, but it's the thought that counts. Hercules Brabazon Brabazon – fondly known as 'Brabby' – was another artist devotee, along with the British social realist Frederick Walker, those responsible for the nascent Arts and Crafts movement (like William Morris and William De Morgan) and the old Pre-Raphaelites. Barbara reciprocated their support. When Dante Gabriel Rossetti expressed a need to step aside from the world for a while in March 1870, for instance, Barbara immediately offered him Scalands – temporarily empty – as a retreat, for which he thanked her profusely. He agreed with the poet Robert Browning, who once said that coming across Barbara was one of life's benedictions.

Rossetti was in a bad way. The previous year, he had made a momentous decision, the effects of which had left him reeling. Anxious to develop his literary as well as his artistic reputation, he planned to publish a new collection of poetry. But some of his best work was in that notebook stowed in Lizzie Siddal's grave as a token of his love. It had been a romantic gesture, but totally impractical. He needed the notebook now. So he pulled some strings to authorize an exhumation, and had it retrieved, seven years after Lizzie's death. According to Rossetti's representative at the graveside, when the coffin was opened there were gasps of amazement. Allegedly, Lizzie was whole and still beautiful; her hair appeared to have carried on growing until it swirled around her like rippling water, and she glowed with the same frail pallor that marked her in life. She must have looked exactly like John Everett Millais's *Ophelia* – for which she had been the original model.

Rossetti felt sick with remorse for disturbing her, discomfited by her surreal state of preservation, and guilty for having embarked on an affair since her death with Jane Burden, the wife of William Morris. Morris was a friend; that was bad enough, but now it seemed as though Lizzie had been resurrected to gnaw at his conscience, too. He was already in poor health, enduring chronic insomnia, painful ophthalmia and a tremor probably resulting from his dependence on the sedative chloral hydrate. He needed help.

He accepted Barbara's offer of Scalands and wrote regular letters to her suggesting that he was feeling better, working hard and keeping cheerful. He asked if she could secure the Leigh Smiths' gamekeeper's daughter, Sophy Burgess, to sit for him (which Barbara did; Rossetti sold the portrait for fifty guineas). In reality, he was overworking; not sleeping; drinking too much; and well on the way towards the nervous breakdown he suffered in 1872. To complicate matters, Jane was installed at Brown's, possibly without Barbara's knowledge, and the two of them spent three illicit weeks together. At the end of his stay, Rossetti apologized to Barbara for the damage he had done to her cellar, quaffing bottles of sherry, claret and champagne that he promised he would replace. Though he and Barbara continued a sporadic correspondence, he does not appear to have stayed at Scalands again.

The more she shared her Sussex cottage, the more Barbara loved it. She began to keep bees; never failed to feed the birds (much to the cats' delight); hatched plans for redesigning the garden; and spent hours in her upstairs studio, which was too light for Rossetti – the sunshine hurt his eyes – but just right for her. She was uncomfortable calling the domestic staff 'servants', preferring to treat them as close friends. They appear to have eddied around the various Leigh Smith homes; a few must have known her from childhood and remembered her mother. She certainly relied heavily on her housekeeper in London and Sussex, Henrietta Blackader, and was no doubt upset when Bella and the General's coachman Mr Snoad was sacked for 'improper intimacy' with a housemaid.[14] Smith housemaids had a habit of posing problems, it seems. In 1873 Esther Grealy, in service at Blandford Square, got into trouble. She fell pregnant and, in June 1874, gave birth to baby Alfred. He was immediately consigned by his mother to the Foundling Hospital in London as an unwanted, or unaffordable, burden.

Barbara heard about Alfred, probably via Henrietta, and after fruitless attempts to change Esther's mind, redeemed the baby herself. Historians at the Foundling Hospital cannot account for his being relinquished to a third party, and relevant records are unavailable, but this appears to be exactly what happened. She placed him in foster care in Robertsbridge at her own expense. No one deserved to be disadvantaged by an accident of birth: her personal experience and liberal ideology convinced her of that. Besides, this could be kismet. She and Elizabeth Blackwell – an adoptive mother herself – had discussed the possibility of Barbara adopting a child should she and Eugène fail to produce one of their own. Perhaps the storks were doing their job after all, providing her with a ready-made son.

Alfred was christened at eight weeks old in Brightling church, just down the road from Scalands. Touchingly, he was given the name Alfred Eugène, with his supposed father's surname of Clements.[15] Barbara fretted that if his mother changed her mind about keeping him, she might easily discover where he was and try to take him away. But Elizabeth calmed her fears. Esther had not shown any interest in the baby so far, had no idea what Barbara had done, and even if she did change her mind, she was too poor to support him without help.

The idea of adoption appears to have fizzled out quite quickly. When Alfred contracted cholera at ten weeks old, it was Henrietta Blackader who was his devoted nurse; not Barbara. Elizabeth noticed that Barbara simply did not warm to the child, nor he to her. The next plan was to have him adopted elsewhere, either by her brother Willy and his wife (no thank you, Bar) or by some wealthy acquaintance. But Elizabeth doubted that 'people of position'[16] would be interested in a bastard with an unromantic backstory and a recent history of serious illness. She was right; he remained unclaimed.

Eventually, Barbara appointed herself Alfred's guardian and placed him with a boatman and his wife, Dennis and Alice Breach, along the coast in Eastbourne. She visited him periodically and financed a trust fund for him with £200 of her earnings. His name is there on a brick in Scalands fireplace: an associate member of Barbara's far-reaching family. The episode begs some questions, however. How was Barbara able to redeem the baby from the Foundling Hospital so easily? Why did she not offer to give Esther money so that mother and baby could stay together? (Perhaps she did, and Esther refused.) Why did she not adopt him herself? Their bond might have grown with familiarity.

I get the impression that Elizabeth warned her against hauling the boy out of his social class and inserting him, like the hero in a popular novel, above his station. Elizabeth was perceptive. Barbara prized intelligence, self-confidence, sensitivity and wit. If Alfred grew up to possess none of these qualities, for all her loving-kindness, Barbara might lose interest in him. Then he would be twice rejected. Give him a livelihood by all means, advised Elizabeth (he became a grocer's apprentice), but do not expect more of him than the lad can give. Besides, what would Eugène think? Perhaps we know what Eugène thought. Perhaps what Eugène thought is the reason why Alfred stayed in Eastbourne.

If anyone deserves to be called Barbara's adopted child, it is a young woman she met in 1873, who went on to become one of the most successful female engineers, physicists and inventors in Britain's history. Her name was Phoebe Sarah Marks (1854–1923), but she is best remembered as Mrs Hertha Ayrton. Barbara called her Marquis, a French pun on 'Marky', derived from her maiden name. Her most enduring nickname was Hertha, after the feisty eponymous heroine of a book by the Swedish feminist Fredrika Bremer published in 1856.

Hertha was the daughter of Levi Marks, a Jewish refugee clockmaker from Poland. Levi died in 1861, leaving behind his English wife Alice, Hertha, six other children, a baby on the way and a heap of debt. Alice worked as a seamstress, helped by Hertha as soon as she was able to do so. Hertha was also the principal carer for the younger children. Winnie, unborn at Levi's death, grew up sickly in mind and body, and was particularly demanding. Meanwhile, Hertha gleaned as much education as she could, spending time with her urbane cousins the Hartogs, who were academic, artistic and generous.

When she was sixteen, Hertha became a governess, while still looking after Winnie and the others. She was obviously bright and had an appetite for learning; so much so that, through the friend of a friend of a friend, she was invited to an interview with Barbara in July 1873 as a possible candidate for a Girton scholarship.

Barbara was entertaining friends that evening – artist Helen Paterson and poet William Allingham – and had dressed in a gown of tussore silk for the occasion; not the usual Victorian confection of frills and furbelows with a gigantic bustle, but a simple straight up-and-down shift, like a shimmering column. Hertha thought she looked marvellous. The two immediately took to one another; by the end of the evening, Hertha had committed to working towards a scholarship with reassurance from Barbara that should she fail – her education was hardly comprehensive – some sort of sponsorship would still be available, providing she passed Girton's entrance exam.

Two months later, Hertha arrived at Scalands, equipped with 'mammoth boots'[17] and a serviceable cotton frock for the countryside, as instructed by Barbara. She was there to do academic work, uninterrupted by domestic duties and anxieties, but it felt like a holiday. Eugène was in residence; he taught her French folk songs, which she sang in a sweet, low voice. Other friends of Barbara's came and went, including Marian Evans, whose character Mirah in *Daniel Deronda*, published in 1876, was inspired by this intense, courageous young woman.

Unfortunately, Winnie's declining health and increasing neediness meant that Hertha was unable to sit the scholarship exam until 1875. Her own health was poor and much of her time was necessarily spent earning a living. At least this gave Barbara a chance to find more sponsors for her (Marian Evans and Helen Taylor among them) and commissions for her needlework. In October of that year, despite having failed the scholarship exam, Hertha arrived at Girton to read mathematics.

She told Barbara that she felt like an impostor because of her religion and her poverty. Barbara, who to some extent had felt like an impostor all her life, was quick to counsel her.

> I think you told your friends about yourself too soon. You should have been sure they liked you and called you a lady first! It is quite right to tell, if it seems important; but I think it better to say to some of your true friends . . . that you do not wish to make a secret of your parentage. Yours is an unmixed race; you are not mongrel as we are. Be

content to say you are pure breed and become in yourself
a true gentlewoman.[18]

Dignity is purely a function of integrity, in other words, and
grace comes from within. Neither should have anything to do
with femininity, money or social position. That is a perfectly
reasonable view now; then, in polite society, it was close to
iconoclasm.

DR ELIZABETH BLACKWELL DESCRIBED a visit to Scalands in the
high summer of 1874.[19] Bessie Parkes – now Madame Belloc –
was staying at the time; she and Barbara walked to Robertsbridge
station to meet Elizabeth. Together they all strolled back to the
cottage over a meadow, up a winding path, past a water-lily pool,
across a cornfield, through hop fields and flowering pastures,
along a lane lined with elms, until they came to Barbara's sloping
lawn and eventually to Scalands itself, its red-brick walls glowing in the full sunshine, where they could be glimpsed from
behind the creepers and scrambling blossom. It sounds idyllic.

Yet Barbara's attachment to Scalands did not prevent her from
yearning for another retreat. In 1875 she acquired the old Poor
House at Zennor in Cornwall: a long, low granite house on the
edge of the land and the ocean in one of the remotest spots in
England. To an artist who loved light and shadow, scudding
clouds, vast skies and shifting seas, it was perfect. She hoped it
would become a sanctuary where friends could regularly meet,
paint and learn from one another; a little like the creative community she, Anna Mary Howitt and Bessie Parkes dreamed of
during Barbara and Bessie's trip to Munich in 1850.

Once she had fully recovered from typhoid, Barbara began
travelling again, making visits to Paris and Switzerland with
family and friends. And whenever she could, she made a quiet
pilgrimage to the Isle of Wight to honour her parents. This was

usually close to her birthday in April. Visits to the island had punctuated the Leigh Smiths' emotional lives, ever since Anne's death in 1834. Barbara painted one of her best works – I would say her pièce de résistance – at Ventnor; she nursed Bella there in 1856, buried her father there in 1860, and it was the first place she thought of taking Marian Evans and George Lewes for a restorative holiday in 1870, the year after Thornie Lewes died.

The trip had not been successful. Barbara hired Swanmore vicarage in Ryde from an extremely High Church Anglican priest for three months, including the Christmas period. Presumably the priest, needing the money, found a billet elsewhere. It would be fun, thought Barbara, to have her closest friends with her, like an extended house party where people arrived and left at will, worked separately during the mornings, and were at leisure together for the rest of the day. And the company would prevent her from thinking too much about Eugène, at home alone in Algiers. But a more lugubrious house it would be hard to imagine. It was cold and gloomy. George tried to liven everyone up by making copious cups of tea and playing practical jokes (though it's difficult to imagine George Eliot being pranked). He described his best joke, performed on Christmas Day:

> This parsonage is so intensely ritualistic that there is even a scourge hanging up in the priest's study. [A scourge is a whip with several lashes, used by certain highly religious people to punish themselves for impure thoughts.] I took it down yesterday and arranged the following surprise with the parlour maid. When the soup was removed I told Barbara that I had taken the liberty of ordering a new dish – one only met with at recherché tables. They were all agog to know what it could be. Oysters? Game? Some French entremet? Ann brought in the huge dish and set it before Barbara, then solemnly removed the cover and revealed the scourge lying in a most uncanny aspect – the

thongs which had been pressed inwards by the cover gave
a slight outward movement which startled Barbara as if a
live eel or so were there. Immense laughter.[20]

Despite the alleged glee, this appears to have been Barbara's final
extended holiday on the island.

She continued to invite people to Algiers, including Gertrude
Jekyll, during the winter of 1873–4. The two women met
through their mutual friend Brabby Brabazon. At that time
Gertrude had not yet made her name as a garden designer; she
was primarily an artist and craftswoman. Barbara admired her
creative flair for colour and harmony, and her 'spirit and clever-
ness in contrivances'.[21] But visits to Campagne du Pavillon were
becoming shorter and less frequent. Barbara did not go at all
during the winters of 1869–70 and 1874–5, and only went in
early 1877 because Nannie claimed to be ailing and Barbara was
worried about her. It was no longer somewhere she visited for
pleasure. The journey was exhausting, the fear of a relapse of
typhoid fever ever present, and the promise of time alone with
her husband less and less tempting.

Other members of the family were also proving worrisome.
Aunt Patty died in 1870, at the remarkable age of eighty-eight.
This was sad news, but is unlikely to have broken Barbara's
heart. Much more upsetting was the death of Bella three years
later, at forty-three. After her fourth child, Milicent, was born in
1868, Bella needed two full-time carers to cope with her resur-
gent psychosis. She was violent, hurling things at people, snarling
at them, setting fire to the bedclothes like Mrs Rochester, smear-
ing ashes in her hair (ironically, a badge of illegitimacy in English
folklore) and refusing to eat. The General used to order celebra-
tory champagne for everyone in the house whenever she gained
weight, but towards the end she tipped the scales at only 6 stone
9 lb. That, of course, was fully clothed. Her cousin Florence

Nightingale used to wear five petticoats at a time: imagine the heft of those, never mind everything that went on top or beneath them. The fact that a Victorian woman's clothing could weigh around 14 lb indicates how desperately emaciated Bella had become.

Barbara was devastated. She found Bella's illness unfathomable and could not comprehend why everyone – including Bella herself – seemed incapable of doing anything about it. She would clasp her sister's hand tightly in hers and shoot agonized questions at her, then start crying and have to leave. This helped no one but was surely understandable. Barbara was a pragmatist, someone used to identifying problems, addressing them and making things better. But even she could not help Bella.

Brother Ben was made of sterner stuff. Having left the Bar after the Pater's death, he had taken his Board of Trade master's certificate, qualifying him to command a ship. In 1870 he hired a huge yacht for £500 and sailed it around the British Isles for three months. This was by way of a training exercise: the following year, he headed north on the first of five polar voyages, three of them in consecutive years. These were serious, scientific expeditions, during which Ben filled in blanks on the map around Svalbard and Franz Josef Land, and earned the respect of his peers for his oceanographic research and courage. The photographs he brought home were spellbinding, but even they were not as impressive as the real, live polar bears he gave to London Zoo. In 1873 he famously rescued the Swedish explorer Adolf Nordenskiöld and his crew, beset in the ice; two years later, he was given the singular honour of being a pall-bearer at Lady Jane Franklin's funeral. Lady Franklin knew the Pater, who had contributed to an expedition in search of her husband, Sir John, lost on his quest for the North-West Passage in 1847.

Ben was an exceptionally private man. He never published accounts of his travels, and refused the limelight, despite being acknowledged then, as now, as a significant figure in the history of Arctic exploration. Even members of his family were a little in awe of him. But they enjoyed the regular balls he gave for their entertainment, and respected his inherited role as patriarch of the Leigh Smith clan.

He was particularly fond of his niece Amy. Amy was the eldest of Willy's six children. When she was only ten, she met Barbara's protégé Norman Moore (aged twenty-two) at a party held to discuss the new women's college. They frequently found themselves in each other's company over the next few years, when Barbara asked him to tutor Amy, and by the time Amy was sixteen, Norman was smitten. He waited a year to propose to her, thinking her too young to make an informed decision. Before he asked Amy, he checked with Barbara whether she approved. She did, but Uncle Ben decidedly did not.

The ostensible cause of his opposition was Norman's lack of money and prospects. He was a junior doctor, with a single mother (Rebecca's husband had left her before Norman's birth) and no fortune. He was probably after Amy's money, suggested Ben. Or playing a long game and after the childless Ben's. Descendants of the Leigh Smith family suspect the real reason is more likely to have been jealousy. In any case, Norman was told to wait until Amy was twenty-one, when the situation would be reviewed. Meanwhile, the young lovers were forbidden to communicate.

However, Ben reckoned without his romantic and determined sister Barbara, who was so convinced that Amy and Norman were meant for one another that she agreed – within the bounds of honesty – to act as their secret go-between. Norman wrote to Barbara, and Barbara passed his messages on to Amy. He sent presents, too, including a book of music in 1877 (it still exists) with individual letters subtly underlined in the table of contents. The resulting code spells out a billet-doux:

adieu my own heart true . . . Let Aunt Barbara hear from you often we will not wait three years it is too long when you are

nineteen at latest we must make them let us marry I will do
anything you wish me to do let Aunt Barbara hear & ask her
about me.[22]

It was a dangerous game for Barbara to play. Ben in a good
mood was intimidating enough; imagine what he was like when
he was riled. She was laying herself open to renewed accusations
of interference in business not strictly her own. But she had
always taken an interest in Amy, encouraging her talent for
drawing, and urging her to expand her reading, concentrate on
her schoolwork and possibly try for Girton. When it became
frustratingly clear that the child was not especially academic (she
once managed to dispatch three governesses in the space of a
year), Barbara accepted defeat in that particular battle.

It gratified Barbara to feel that she was facilitating two people's happiness in the face of adversity. That is what 'the wild joy
of living' was all about. And her kindness would be an investment for the future: as Norman said himself, she was

indeed our best friend and one part of our joint duty will
be to love her & to cherish her all her days. We will meet
her enemies in the gate, for every good person has enemies,
& when she grows old we will make her every day gladder
that she did so great a service to each of us.[23]

13

Love in New Ways

1877–1885

I try to do it like other people, but I long always
to be off on some wild adventure.[1]

THE MOST IMPORTANT PHASES OF BARBARA'S LIFE WERE punctuated by journeys. The voyage to America when she was two, for instance, flamboyantly signalling her parents' escape from convention. Expeditions at home and abroad in the family omnibus. Her repeated crossings to the Isle of Wight, meant to heal, but rarely happy. The unchaperoned expedition to Munich when she was twenty-three, in search of art and adventure in boots and blue glasses. That heady trip to Cambridge with the refugees. The first visit to Algiers. Her honeymoon in the Southern states of America. During her first five decades, she seems to have been constantly on the move, constantly progressing. Scalands was the only destination worth lingering at.

In the spring of 1877 she set off again, this time for the Poor House at Zennor, her new painting retreat on the north Cornish coast. It had been a busy few months. The previous Christmas, Barbara held an enormous party at Blandford Square, inviting ninety-eight guests and booking artistes to play instruments, sing and perform dramatic recitations. The music was a touch underwhelming, she confessed afterwards, but the actors doing the readings were marvellous, and well worth the hefty £10 she was charged for them.

Everyone had a splendid time at the party, though poor Henrietta, the housekeeper, was shattered afterwards. None of Barbara's siblings or nephews and nieces came – they were either out of town or out of favour – and it was dreadfully expensive. She did not begrudge the cost, but came to the conclusion that she might not attempt such a large-scale event again. It was too much effort and too diffuse an approach to making people happy. In the future she would stick to more intimate dinner parties instead. Meanwhile, it was time for some work. Before the New Year dawned, she was back in her studio, full of energy and ideas.

She was still acting as fairy godmother to the star-crossed lovers. In January she gave Norman a pair of salt cellars to encourage him not to give up hope of Amy. Not the most obvious metaphor, perhaps, until Barbara explained that a favourite quote of her father's, from a hymn by the Dissenter Anna Laetitia Barbauld, was 'Salt of the earth ye virtuous few'. The Pater used to insist that she, as one of the virtuous few, had a duty to stand up against 'the crowd of worldlings'[2] around her who only *thought* they knew what was important in life. She would have been unwise to call her brother Ben a 'worldling' to his face, but the message was clear.

Conducting the Norman and Amy affair was rather exhausting, but Barbara was skilled at compartmentalizing. As long as she felt healthy and positive, she was usually able to put a temporary lid on problems. Thus, exasperating Eugène, querulous Nannie, bullying Ben and the increasingly tottery Aunt Ju were all firmly shepherded to the back of her mind while she addressed more cheerful matters in London, Sussex and Cambridge. She made time to visit young Alfred Eugène in Eastbourne and spent a few days now and then at Girton – 'my Palace' – where she chaperoned students on outings and invigilated exciting sessions on the microscope. She memorably heard Lord Tennyson give a recital of his poetry in March, before dashing home to Scalands to worship the ten acres of primroses in her woods, then back to London to hear a lecture by Prime Minister William Gladstone at Lady Stanley's house, a concert by the Bach Choir and a piano recital. In April, she was awarded a silver medal at the Crystal Palace Exhibition for her watercolour *The Sea, Hastings*: a gratifying way to mark her fiftieth birthday that month. Her friends continued to complain of the scarcity and carelessness of her letters[3] while revelling in her openness of mind, heart and hand. Life went on.

Barbara described Zennor as one of the most refreshing, inspiring places in the world. It was like a perfect painting, with a background of wide skies and surging seas of azure, violet, cobalt and white; granite rocks in viridian and rose madder in the middle distance; and a profusion of perfectly detailed, gemlike flowers in the foreground: bluebells, anemones, wood sorrel, gorse, milkwort and bilberry blossom.[4] When she heard that the famous British-Italian activist Jessie White Mario needed somewhere to convalesce after injuring her right hand, Barbara invited her to share the Poor House in May. There, Jessie would not only benefit from the bracing climate, but be cosseted by Barbara and Henrietta, Margaret and Charlotte (housekeeper, housemaid and the new cook respectively, all of whom happily accompanied Barbara to Cornwall). She could even continue her journalistic work, thanks to a surprise Barbara had in store for her.

The two women had been friends ever since Jessie's hopelessly ambitious application to study medicine in London in 1855. This was not so much to make a feminist point, as to equip herself to care for wounded revolutionaries in Italy, where she lived and worked as a writer and untrained nurse. She was passionately devoted to the *Risorgimento*, or movement for Italian reunification, and became a friend of Garibaldi, placing his son Ricciotti in Barbara's care at Portman Hall – where she also taught – during the boy's visit to England to treat a badly broken leg. In 1857 Jessie was incarcerated for four months in Genoa as a political prisoner; when freed, she married Alberto Mario, the rebel general with whom she had been jailed. She was an imposing figure, 'rather wild', according to another of Barbara's friends,[5] and given to smoking improbably long cigars. She and Barbara were both strong-minded women who admired each other's moral courage and idiosyncrasy.

The journey from London to Zennor was not easily accomplished. Barbara described it to Norman, whom she also invited to the Poor House, along with the marine artist Henry Moore and Brabby Brabazon (looking worryingly wizened, according to Barbara, and in need of fresh air). Take the 9 a.m. train from Paddington; it gets to Hayle in Cornwall at 9.40 p.m. Then hire a carriage to drive you for nine miles along a wild road via St Ives until you reach Zennor. Barbara advised Norman to travel third class, as she and Jessie had; that cost them only £1 and 6s each, plus 16s and 6d for the carriage and driver. Alternatively, Norman could stay on the train until Penzance and then walk eight miles across the county 'from one sea to the other'[6] but that would mean reaching the Poor House intolerably late in the day. Or early in the morning.

Before the men were due to arrive, Barbara unveiled Jessie's surprise. It was a recently invented 'writing machine' – a typewriter – which meant that, if necessary, Jessie could work with only a single finger of her left hand. Barbara was enchanted by it, using it herself to write to her friend (and Aunt Ju's recent replacement as trustee) the amateur artist Dr Reginald Thompson – who had presumably approved the funds to buy it. A practice draft of the message still survives, bashed out in purple capitals on the back of a discarded letter to Amy. I reproduce it in all its ungainly glory.

MAY 10 18 77   MY DEAR DR THOMPSON

WE HAVE BOUGHT THE WONDERFUL MASHINE
,& CAN USE IT WITH THE LEFT HAND QUITE
AS WELL ASWITH THE RIGHT ,SHE IS
AFACINATESHOUS CREATURE .-I CALL HER
TRYPHENA -SPIPS [SHIPS] &ENGINES HAVE
[NAMES] & WHY NOT THIS? MRIO SIGNORA MARIO
THANKS YOU .HER HAND IS BETTER ALREADY .
HOW YOU WILL LIKE THIS PLACE , IT IS VERY LIKE
BEING AT SEA,VERILY THE SACRED LAND OF
GIANTS TRYHHINA WAS ONE OF THE BEAUTIFUL
LADIES OF KING ARTHUR S COURT ALSO THE
NAME OF MY LOVELY ANCESTRESS .IT IS ENOUGH
PLEASE CORRECT THE PRESS -BLSB[7]

So successful was Tryphena that Jessie was still using her twenty years later, signing off letters to members of the Leigh Smith family with 'Tryphena sends her love'.[8]

Jessie was content to sit indoors in this 'howling wilderness'[9] of a place (her words: it was a far cry from Italy) while Barbara went out and sketched all day, drunk on 'fascinateshous' beauty. But it was unseasonably cold for May: the east wind crept stealthily into Barbara's bones and was reluctant to depart. Norman was not surprised to hear that she was under the weather when he arrived on 24 May. He did not see her that evening, nor the following day, when it became all too apparent that she was seriously ill. He immediately sent for Dr Thompson, who was staying with his family at Scalands. The doctor swiftly diagnosed a stroke, affecting her speech and the right side of her body. His prognosis was grave. 'I have known only one or at most two of such cases recover and only then partially.'[10] He, in turn, summoned Ben on 27 May. No response. Ben was still angry with Barbara for championing Amy and Norman's love affair. The doctor tried again three days later with a greater sense of urgency. Barbara needed to see her brother, and part from him in peace.

This time Ben took notice. He arrived at the Poor House on 3 June, but only for a quick visit. What the two said to each other remains private. There does not appear to have been any dramatic rapprochement.

Norman was allowed to see his beloved Barbara two days after the stroke. He sat by her bed as she lay on her left side and tried to give him her useless right hand. 'Her face had its usual sweet, kind expression,' he noted, and her first concern was not for herself – 'a great fuss about nothing' – but for him and Amy. She wanted their relationship out in the open. She could not stand the duplicity any more; in fact some of her friends reckoned that the stroke was triggered solely by the stress of acting as their go-between. In case this really was the end, she asked Norman to send for the local vicar, to whom she was only able to refer as the 'funny old fellow', not being able to grasp at his name. Then she told him how worried she was about working conditions for Cornish tin miners. What could she do to help them, now *this* had happened? Norman found it almost impossible not to cry. A world without Barbara and her impulsive generosity was unthinkable. If she dies, he wrote in his journal, then God help us all.[11]

By the time Ben arrived, Dr Thompson was a little more sanguine. Barbara was intellectually unimpaired, he said, which was encouraging, but made it more difficult for her to endure her condition, and to manage her expectations. Patience had never been one of her virtues. He did not expect her to be able to articulate clearly, write coherently or paint at all for a very long time. She needed skilled and sympathetic nursing, and not to be bothered by family squabbles and a bevy of best friends jostling to take over her care.

I should love to know whether anyone thought of asking Florence Nightingale for her opinion. There is no evidence of it, though the undated fragment of a letter in Barbara's personal scrapbook proves that Florence grew to respect her cousin. The letter has been cropped around the signature and then pasted down, but a few phrases survive: 'Dear Madame Bodichon . . . excuse my . . . so unceremonious . . . pleasure of writing . . . Permit me . . . Yr. affectionate Florence Nightingale.'[12] This is hardly the sort of letter someone disgusted by her 'tabooed' kinswoman would write. It has always been assumed that Florence never acknowledged Barbara, but it is now clear that they did communicate, even if only sporadically and comparatively formally. It may be that their correspondence was destroyed by both women for the sake of privacy. Indeed, the scrapbook letter is headed 'Private' and Barbara was known to ask people to burn her letters once read.

Hertha Marks was devastated when she heard the news, not only for Barbara's sake, but for her own: because she was not a member of the family, she had no right to rush to Barbara's side, though that was her dearest wish. She had been granted two terms' sabbatical from Girton in January because of her own poor health; since then, she had benefited from Barbara's hospitality and unconditional support. Barbara was her second mother.

Jessie – patient turned nurse – was a fierce guardian of the sickroom, only allowing Barbara those visitors who in her rather arbitrary opinion would be good for her. Luckily, she decided that Hertha should be included in that number; Eugène Bodichon, however, should not. A meeting with him would be too emotionally fraught to do Barbara any good. It might well do her harm. Nevertheless, after he heard and understood how ill his wife was, nothing and no one could stop him making his rickety way from Algiers to see her for himself. When he arrived on 24 July, it almost broke Barbara's frail heart. Not only did he look confused and ill, which worried his wife, but – as she later admitted to Bessie with tears in her eyes – he never even took her hand, until she asked him, as she would ask any doctor, to feel her pulse. Norman was appalled when Bessie told him.

I could have shed tears myself to hear of it & to think that
dear beautiful Aunt Barbara should long, in her illness, for
a caress from her husband long to see him & that when he
came he should not even kiss her ... We have bodies as
well as souls & love permeates & flows through & through
both & kisses are the language of the flesh just as words &
looks are of the soul.[13]

It *is* sad, but perhaps Eugène found it difficult to express or
respond to emotion. We know now that neurodivergent people
sometimes do find it so. At the time, to Barbara, her friends and
family, his behaviour must have appeared bizarre at best and, at
worst, plain cruel. Norman thought it might have been better
had they never separated; Nannie thought it might have been
better had they never met. It is not known how long he stayed on
this occasion before returning to Algeria.

DR ELIZABETH BLACKWELL WAS in Salzburg when news of Barbara's stroke reached her. She immediately offered to return to
England, but Barbara had a team in place by now, including
Hertha. A nurse was engaged, with an amanuensis to transcribe
Barbara's letters when she was able to dictate them, and to read
incoming messages. 'I have been bad for writing,'[14] explains an
undated note in a shaky hand; this must be one of her first
attempts at putting pen to paper. But she was not bad for listening, and asked her friends to keep in touch as often as they could,
on paper if not in person (as long as they didn't write 'crossed'
letters, where each page is filled with writing from west to east,
as it were, and then, to save paper, overwritten south to north).
Any more than two visitors at a time exhausted and unsettled her
so much that she could not sleep. Gertrude Jekyll was a favourite; so was Norman, but she suspected that Amy was too young
and tender-hearted to be of much use. One of her most faithful,

cheerful correspondents was George Lewes, until his death at the end of 1878, when Barbara immediately invited Marian to come and live with her. Marian refused, still stricken by the loss of Lewes.

Three months after the stroke, Barbara consulted the Queen's physician, Sir William Jenner, about managing her convalescence. Dr Thompson was still guarded about her prospects of recovery, but by October 1877 she was considered well enough to make the journey to Blandford Square. The following April, Jenner declared himself pleased with her slow but steady progress. Marian commented that Barbara was now 'completely like herself in everything but strength';[15] a somewhat over-optimistic opinion, given that they had not actually seen each other since the stroke. This could well have been an impression engineered by Barbara herself, who was anxious not to worry those who loved her. She could not fool Dr Blackwell, however, who reported an outing with her in May 1878.

> For the first time she conversed with me rapidly – in the strong clear spontaneous way with which she used to pour forth her ideas – not hesitatingly painfully and with apparent confusion at times. I did not notice one hesitation for words, whilst talking with me – although there was such difficulty when she gave the coachman directions – neither did I observe any exhaustion at the end of the drive. This of course was only a temporary flashing back of the old life – but it was an immense comfort to find it could so flash.[16]

She really was improving.

As soon as she was allowed, Barbara retreated to Scalands. She let Blandford Square from May 1879, and two years after her stroke, dared to look forward to the future. She asked Gertrude Jekyll to draw up plans for alterations to her Sussex home, to include a large ground-floor room and a wide veranda, the latter recommended by Elizabeth Blackwell as health-giving and picturesque. The new room was designed to accommodate Barbara's latest project: a night school for the working men of the locality, with a lending library attached. Its aim was not so much to teach facts and figures, as to educate the students to think for themselves. Aunt Ju would help her run it: though deaf now, and even tinier in old age than she was in her prime, Ju was more than willing to take on 'the big men who can't read'.[17] They must have had some difficulty in seeing her at the head of the class, sitting on a Sheraton chair with the legs trimmed by Barbara so her feet could touch the ground. Enlisting her help was as much about keeping her occupied as anything else. Dearly as she loved her, Barbara was beginning to find her aunt's forgetfulness and increasing neediness a little wearing.

Books still occasionally turn up with the Scalands stamp in them – that run of the *English Woman's Journal* I found in the Bodleian in Oxford, for example; her library was obviously well stocked and popular. The school was never short of students. Barbara was astonished and gratified to hear that one man had walked twenty-two miles to reach Scalands after work one evening. Nevertheless, she was always more interested in universities than schools of any kind, and considered her finest educational achievement to be the co-founding of Girton College.

Emily Davies arrived that summer to bring Barbara up to date with events in Cambridge and was delighted to find her friend and colleague in such good spirits. She could paint a little most days, walk about and even ride without too much trouble, and had retrieved her sense of humour. When Emily told Barbara that she was looking well, and that Scalands was obviously 'a place to grow handsome in',[18] Barbara agreed, solemnly pointing out that Emily was already 20 per cent better-looking than when she had arrived.

All this was good news, but there were some troubling

Barbara's cartoon shows the perils of forgetting the time while out painting, in this instance in Algiers.

undercurrents to life in recovery. Ben was still sulking about Amy and Norman, though the two eventually married in March 1880, as soon as Amy was twenty-one. Barbara lent Amy her wedding veil and gave the happy couple a pair of brass candlesticks and, puzzlingly, a quantity of 'much-mended china'.[19] Willy and Georgina, Amy's parents, were annoyed by the role Barbara had played in brokering the relationship, and refused to communicate with her beyond the minimum required for the sake of family decorum. Barbara fretted about Amy's siblings Roddy and the next in line (of six), 'Willyboy', whom she considered neglected, and said so. That did not help. Nor did an occasional tendency, post-stroke, for Barbara to be petulant or gratuitously rude. It was unlike her, and rather disturbing.

She also developed a few obsessions, revealed by letters in her family's keeping. One was with water quality and drainage (perhaps that was why Willy's family were so odd, she said: they drank impure water, which gave them impure minds and bodies). Another was Amy's future; having resigned herself before the stroke to a life of reflected glory for her eldest niece, she was now anxious again about the girl's lack of premarital experience in the world. Not just the academic world (the Girton horse had bolted by now) but the real world beyond. Even though she was now married, she should travel; learn to speak French like a native; develop her painting; do some good. In other words, she should be the next generation's Barbara. It was unkind of Barbara to repeat what people said about the cause of her affliction: that if it had not been for their affair, she should never have fallen ill. To Norman and Amy, who had indeed loved and cherished her (Amy even took stints as her night nurse), and to whom Barbara had been a figure of almost mythic goodness, this was hurtful. Their closeness cooled slightly.

Amy was not the only member of the family to be criticized by Barbara. Poor Roddy was made to sit the Girton entrance exam, which according to Emily Davies she failed due to 'a general want of [intellectual] strength'.[20] Barbara did not insist, as she had in Amy's case, that she consider trying for Newnham instead. Newnham was the other Cambridge college for women, established a couple of years after Girton, whose founders were less adamant than Emily about achieving academic parity with men. Nor did she suggest Bedford College, her own alma mater. This implied that Roddy was a lost cause, which must have been mortifying for the girl.

To add to this sour mix, members of the family began to take against Barbara's surrogate daughter Hertha, whom they perceived as an opportunistic fortune hunter taking advantage of Barbara's credulous generosity. Nannie, tucked away in Algiers, was the most vituperative, calling Hertha venomous and imagining her cackling with delight at Barbara's dependence on her. There is more than a hint of anti-Semitism about her attitude. Then there was a spat about who was responsible for founding Girton. Emily Davies declined to correct an article about the college's origin, which did not mention Barbara. Barbara was more upset than offended, but Hertha was outraged, describing Emily as 'a vile reptile, viler even than I thought her'.[21] Barbara's life and connections used to sparkle, but illness dimmed everything, so that neither she nor those around her could quite see clearly any more.

But the old Barbara still shone through when really needed. In 1880, Lewes's grieving 'widow' married her financial adviser, John Cross. Marian was sixty, he some twenty years younger. Predictably, many in her social circle – largely the same as Lewes's social circle – were dismayed by the announcement. It was, after all, Marian's first and only 'real' wedding. Why on earth had she done it, when she could have lived out a comfortable and comparatively respectable old age as one of England's most revered writers, her 24-year indiscretion with a married man conveniently forgotten? Was she going senile? That would certainly explain her extraordinary behaviour and his cynical success.

Barbara knew Marian better than that. The letter Marian wrote to inform her of the wedding was never posted, due to an oversight, so Barbara was not aware of the ceremony until she read a notice of it in *The Times*. She immediately wrote to Marian.

> *My dear I hope and I think you will [be] happy.*
>
> *Tell Johnny Cross I should have done exactly what he has done if you would have let me and I had been a man.*
>
> *You see I know all love is so different that I do not see it unnatural to love in new ways – not to be unfaithful to any memory.*
>
> *If I knew Mr. Lewes he would be glad as I am that you have [a] new friend . . .*
>
> *Your loving*
> *Barbara*[22]

This is vintage Barbara: a bright heart in a mutinous body, but learning to love in new ways. Sadly, just six months after her marriage, Marian died. Barbara and her widower exchanged several generous letters afterwards; in one of them, John Cross told her that, of all Marian's intimate friends, Barbara was the one she valued most.

Other friends continued to amuse, irritate or gladden Barbara's days as she slowly surfaced again. Elizabeth Blackwell and her daughter Kitty spent considerable time and energy scouting around Hastings for suitable lodgings for Barbara while building works progressed at Scalands. Her best find was a house right by the sea, with six bedrooms, large drawing and dining rooms, admittedly no piano, but a remarkably 'sweet' WC. 'Kitty particularly sniffed it.' The people who owned the house were very pleasant, and it only cost £4 per week, not including coal, gas and linen.[23] The address? Eight Pelham Crescent.

It was the very house – or one of the two in Pelham Crescent – bought by the Pater in 1836 in which to bring up his motherless family. For Barbara, it was too soon to close the circle of life by returning there; too poignant to remember the days when she would race up the stairs, or be carried by good-natured James Buchanan, squealing with laughter. She declined Elizabeth's suggestion, preferring to float for a while between houses of her own or of family members and close friends, with the occasional rental in Eastbourne, St Leonards or elsewhere in Hastings.

An advertisement appeared in the *London Evening Standard* on 2 September 1879.

North Coast of Cornwall, especially suited to a Landscape Artist – To be sold, furnished, standing on over an acre of ground, containing magnificent granite rocks, giving splendid coast view . . . good water; careful sanitary arrangements; granite walls of house 2 ft. thick; all but walls newly-built, and in perfect order; one large sitting-room, one smaller, five bed-rooms, and offices; new and excellent beds; £800, with immediate possession. Address Madame Bodichon, Scalands-gate, Robertsbridge.

Eight hundred pounds is equivalent to around £52,000 today: not wildly expensive. But the Poor House did not sell. In 1882 she put 5 Blandford Square on the market; this did sell – to Emily Davies's brother Llewelyn – even though it had a scant twenty-six years left on the lease. Only seventeen years later, it was demolished, with half the square, to make way for Marylebone station. I think of Barbara every time I wait for my local train on Platform 6, which is exactly where I estimate her bustling hub of a house to have been.

There was another reason for Elizabeth Blackwell's enthusiasm for settling Barbara in Hastings: it is where she had decided to retire with Kitty, once ill-health made it impossible for her to carry on in practice in New York or London. Other friends of Barbara were also Hastings residents, including the artist Marianne North (who was hardly ever at home, or even in the country). Novelist Milly Betham-Edwards moved there too. Though she and Barbara had spent time together in earlier days, particularly in and en route to Algiers, I get the impression that theirs was a slightly one-sided relationship. Milly was mildly obsessed with Barbara, and wrote particularly perceptively about her after her death, but Barbara did not always reciprocate her warmth of feeling. Barbara was amused at the rumour – which she gleefully spread – that Milly had fallen for none other than Bombonnel, the patched-up panther-killer, who was twenty years Milly's senior and allegedly totally uneducated. Not so funny was Milly's suspected addiction to Dante Gabriel Rossetti's toxic sedative, the drug chloral hydrate, used to treat anxiety and insomnia.[24]

At this stage of her life, one of Barbara's closest Hastings friends was William Ransom, a gentle, sensitive man of firm

Liberal principle. The founder and editor of the *Hastings and St Leonards Observer*, he published some of Barbara's earliest writing,[25] and shared her strong social conscience and kindly determination to enhance the lives of fellow citizens. When Barbara had the notion to open her night school at Scalands, she turned to William for help with the organization, administration and even the teaching.

Barbara's housekeeper and close friend Henrietta Blackader retired in 1880 at the age of forty (she wasn't well) and was replaced by a Derbyshire woman, Eliza Arabella Sanderson, known as Bella, who was in her mid-thirties. Bella was engaged as a companion-housekeeper and stayed with Barbara until the end. It is touching to note that, a few weeks after Barbara's death, Bella married the 68-year-old William Ransom. Barbara would surely have approved, despite the near-quarter-century age difference. This was another happy example of loving in new ways; unusual, but no less valid. The same could arguably be said for the Pater and Anne Longden; come to that, for Eugène and Barbara herself.

THERE WAS PLENTY GOING on to distract Barbara from her precarious health during the next few years. Girton was getting on well, with new buildings and a growing student roll. It felt like a real community now, with a well-established routine. The diary of Bessie Macleod, who arrived in October 1881, reveals a typical day at the college: Barbara's dream of 'quiet liberty and opportunity' come to life.[26]

It begins at 6.30 a.m., when Bessie is woken by her alarm clock and fumbles with chilblained fingers for a match. Those lofty red-brick bedrooms at Girton are never warm, except in highest summer when the students, of course, have gone. Bessie lights a candle, wraps herself up and pads through to her en-suite study to tackle an hour's Latin prose. She has to pick her way through the remains of last night's 'cocoa party', when friends came round at bedtime for the university equivalent of a midnight feast, bravely clad in their dressing gowns and slippers. The 'Gyp', or maid, will tidy up later, when she delivers Bessie's daily ration of coal and a jug of once-hot water for washing.

Compulsory prayers are at eight o'clock, though at the munificent Lady Stanley's insistence (and to Anglican Emily Davies's chagrin), there is, as yet, no chapel. That was a condition of her substantial contribution to college funds. As a first-year, or 'fresher', Bessie must sit at the back of the room, which means she is last to breakfast. By the time she gets to the dining hall there is only cold ham and treacle left. Then it is back to her rooms to complete her Latin before parcelling it up for the ten o'clock postal collection. Her work is mailed to her tutors in Cambridge: it is quicker than physically taking it two miles down the road, with a chaperone, to deliver it by hand.

The rest of the morning is spent on compulsory subjects for all Girton freshers: theology, Greek and maths. Things are improving, but Girton does not yet have enough academic staff to cover entire curricula; that will not happen until the first few cohorts of students have passed through and then re-entered as tutors themselves. Lunch is at 1 p.m., and to signal that she is not in the mood for conversation, Bessie arms herself with a stony expression and a book. Neither works: Girton's (unnamed) dreariest daughter makes straight for her. Everyone is strongly encouraged to take a turn round the extensive grounds after lunch, which Bessie manages to fit in before a lecture at two o'clock. The rest of the afternoon is spent at her desk.

The dinner menu is uninspiring: fish, mutton casserole, potatoes, turnips and sago pudding. Girton students were quite particular about their food from the earliest days, it seems; in 1871 a group of them sent a stern note to the kitchens to request, among other things, that 'the Mentone should <u>not</u> be made so salt as to be almost uneatable' and 'cloves should <u>not</u> be put into apple puddings'.[27] I am not entirely certain what a 'Mentone' was; possibly an onion tart.

Bessie looks forward to some free time after dinner, before remembering that tonight is fire-drill night. Each of the few women's colleges in the country had its own fire brigade, unless it happened to be in a city centre, which for sound, historical reasons, very few were. Girton especially relied on its brigade, being two miles away from the nearest fire station and its horse-drawn tender. The typical brigade boasted buckets, hoses, sturdy ropes and a portable chute down which unfortunate victims were expected to plummet when the flames started licking at their stay-laces. One of the maids at a college in Oxford was so plump that she was excused the chute, for fear of getting stuck. Death rather than indignity.

After fire drill, Bessie returns to her room to do a little more work until the drama society meets at 9 p.m. Happily, the Unfortunate Episode at Hitchin, when Barbara was brought in as peacemaker, is long forgotten. The day closes after the rehearsal, when Bessie returns to her cold bedroom. Breath steaming, her last task of the day is to set the alarm clock for next morning before burying herself in blankets and falling asleep.

There is a photograph of Girton fire brigade's officers in the college archive, taken in 1880, the year before Bessie Macleod arrived. Clutching a pail by a portable water pump is one of its founders: Hertha. She was also a founder member of the choral society and mathematics club, a member of the debating society, and – ridiculous as this might sound – an amateur wrestler, once disposing of a Miss Bennett within a minute. Close by Hertha in the photograph is her great friend Eugénie Sellers, who went on to become an academic with a handicap: she was allegedly so very beautiful that she had to lecture from behind a screen, to concentrate her listeners' minds.

Barbara was thrilled when another friend of Hertha's, Charlotte Angas Scott, achieved the eighth-best result in the whole university in her final mathematics exams in 1880. As a woman she was not eligible to receive a degree; that did not happen at Cambridge for nearly seventy years. But the national newspapers took note, and the college's academic stock rose accordingly. Barbara's commitment to Girton never wavered. After her stroke, she let it be known that she intended to leave it £10,000 in her will; meanwhile, she donated half that amount again in 1884, on condition that the college paid her an annuity of £250 for the rest of her life. That was the year her magisterial portrait by Emily Osborn was unveiled and given to the college. The portrait was commissioned by subscriptions from friends, family members, colleagues and students, and was finished only in the nick of time, according to Barbara. Much later, she joked, and no one would remember who she was.

Every institution experiences ups and downs. It was desperately sad when student Agnes Gosnell contracted peritonitis in 1877 and died at the age of twenty-two. It was frustrating when members of staff bickered, committee members disagreed or students felt hard done by. And it was disappointing when young women did not achieve their academic potential, because of a deficient education before arriving, a lack of application, ill-health or difficult circumstances at home. Hertha had to grapple with all of these (the lack of application being due to distractions, like Barbara's illness, not laziness). So it was perhaps no surprise that she achieved the equivalent of only a third-class degree in 1881. She was mortified and apologized profusely to Barbara for letting her down after all Barbara's efforts on her behalf, and turning out to be a failure. 'My dear, you are not a failure!' insisted Barbara. 'Your life will not be a failure.'[28] How right she was.

Despite an overall improvement in her health, it is likely that Barbara suffered a series of mini strokes following the first onslaught in 1877. Every so often we find that her speech has become difficult again, or she has been forbidden to work. A letter written by her on 21 August 1882 certainly suggests that she is struggling for coherence. It is to Ben. 'We are so happy!' it begins.

> *I hope you are as happy we are.*
>
> *Every feels such a relief. It would do you good to see the pleasure here.*
>
> *One old woman who is dying said 'I should like to live to hear that Mr Smith was safe' She said she did of think him so much – there up in ice & nothing to eat.*
>
> *Dr Bodichon cried with joy, he was always thinking you were dead!*
>
> *Your Barbara.*[29]

The date is significant: Barbara had just heard that Ben and his crew were alive after going missing in the Arctic. He had set off in June 1881 on the *Eira*, a 350-ton ship he commissioned in Peterhead (Scotland) in 1879, with around twenty-three men, Bob the dog (a Newfoundland/retriever cross), Tibs the kitten and a canary. They made good progress north for eight days and spent the next couple of months exploring the coast of Franz Josef Land. But the weather was unusually harsh that summer; on 20 August, the *Eira* started creaking horribly as pack ice trapped and threatened to crush her. She began to rear out of the water, whereupon Ben ordered the men to offload as many stores as they could, with bedding, rifles, ammunition and the lifeboats. Two hours later, the *Eira* – as Ben put it – was 'awa''. She sank so fast they could hear the impact as she hit the seabed.

Ben reckoned they had eight weeks' provisions, but they could not expect to be rescued until the ice cleared after winter. They made a tent from the *Eira*'s salvaged spars and sails, built a stout stone hut with a turf roof, hung up the canary's cage (well away from the kitten) and settled down to wait for fate to decide what happened next.

During September, Ben and the crew shot sixteen walrus, eight polar bears and 1,200 loons (seabirds). On 21 October, the sun set for the last time until the following February and the temperature plummeted to minus 56° Celsius. Everyone ate their monotonous meals in bed, snuggled together like baby blackbirds in a nest. The kitten curled up in Bob's shaggy fur – just as that Algerian mouse did in Eugène's hair – before eventually disappearing, like Captain Oates, into the snow.[30] He was never seen again. The canary fell off its perch on New Year's Eve. But Bob survived.

So – remarkably – did all the men. As soon as cracks appeared in the ice in June 1882, they fitted out their boats with tablecloth sails. The blacksmith canned as much walrus meat as he could by salting it, stuffing it into used tins and soldering lids on with melted metal from a teapot. They left a note in the hut, with six bottles of champagne, and set off, due south. Progress was slow, due to more pack ice and a terrifying storm, but they eventually reached the Novaya Zemlya archipelago forty-three days after setting off in their tiny, makeshift fleet.

Meanwhile, the Leigh Smith family, and possibly their half-siblings the Bentley Smiths, were beside themselves with worry. When it became obvious in the autumn of 1881 that something had gone seriously wrong – Ben should have been home by now – Barbara suggested that Uncle Oc's son Valentine should coordinate a relief mission. The Admiralty contributed £5,000 to the cost; the remaining £9,000 was raised by the family.

A Peterhead whaler, Hope, was fitted out and set sail in June 1882. Coincidentally, the two vessels had met the previous year, when their paths crossed in open waters. Ben had invited the Hope's senior officers aboard the Eira for a drink and a reminisce about their shared home port. One of those officers was the ship's surgeon, a young Scotsman. His name was Arthur Conan Doyle. Astonishingly, Hope was one of the first vessels Ben and his men saw when they limped to Novaya Zemlya. 'There was quite an extraordinary merry meeting in that silent sea,' wrote one of many journalists who chronicled the adventure when everyone got home.[31]

One wonders why this astounding feat of exploration, leadership and endurance is not famous today. It is right up there, surely, with the later heroics of Scott and – particularly – Shackleton. One can only speculate. Scott, Shackleton and their associates needed to raise money for their expeditions, and therefore made deals with the devil, writing books, giving lectures and marketing themselves, to a certain extent, as celebrities. Ben did not need to rely on anyone else to fund him, however, and was never remotely interested in the limelight. He was positively shy: perhaps a legacy of his illegitimacy. So apart from some short-lived attention from the print media, his story was never widely told. But it is a measure of his ephemeral fame – and Barbara's retirement from the public eye – that, in 1882, when the second Married Women's Property Act was finally passed, Barbara was described in one provincial newspaper, writing about the genesis of the campaign, as 'sister of the Arctic navigator'.[32]

Worse than this is a mention in *The Times* at the end of 1883, noting that Miss Osborn's portrait of Barbara is nearly finished, and then going on to remind its readers who Barbara is, or once was, just as she predicted. But she was too preoccupied at the time to mourn the passing of her renown. Eugène was ill and had been for a while. After a visit to England in 1881 Barbara asked the newly wed Norman to accompany him back to Algiers, even though Eugène was known to hate travelling with other people. Norman obliged, setting off in November with supplies of snacks and bags of patience – though not quite the 'enormous mass of food . . . 50 sandwiches & big ones'[33] with which Barbara had urged him to arm himself.

It was obvious to everyone by now that Eugène was fast losing capacity. His eccentricities multiplied, while his physical health declined. He developed nasty abscesses on his neck and suffered increasingly from fevers and seizures. Barbara's anguished requests to Nannie between 1883 and 1885 to keep an eye on him were met by a torrent of complaining letters.[34] No one knows what I've suffered for Barbara's sake, snarled Nannie: I have run myself ragged trying to keep an eye on that wretched man. Twenty-seven years they've been married, and all that time it's been I who have taken responsibility for their happiness and mutual safety. All I get in return is abuse from the Doctor, who belongs in an asylum, and moaning from Barbara, who claims she's too ill to cope with Eugène herself. Too moody, more like. 'Barbara always wants to find the cause of her trouble in the actions of others & not in the Doctor himself – who has always been mad from the beginning & could only make her miserable.'[35]

And how am I ever going to be able to sell the villa Isa and I have been living in for the past twenty years? First the Doctor planted forests of eucalyptus trees to block out the view and light; now he is so empty-headed that he's allowing them to be cut down again by anyone who cares to sell the timber. He's liable to turn up at the door stark naked at any time of the day or night. He can't look after himself any more; the medical men (whom *I* have to summon) have said that he needs a strong man, or two, to care for him twenty-four hours a day. He certainly needs a power of attorney. He frequently uses violence against visitors, but luckily is too weak to cause any damage, even to a woman.

Reading these letters is depressing. For part of the period they span, Ben was missing, presumed (in pessimistic moments) to be dead. Bella had already passed away; so, now, had her genial husband the General, and Aunt Dolly. Aunt Ju died in 1883, much mourned, at the age of eighty-three, and the dear friend of Barbara's youth, Anna Mary Howitt, the following year. Barbara had another fairly major stroke in October 1884, some nine months after her return from a painting trip to the south of France with friends Mary Ewart and Emily Greatorex. The watercolours she produced on her travels – still working *en plein air* – are bound into an album held by her family. Remarkably, their grace and intensity betray little of the frequent bouts she suffered of neuralgia, toothache and congestion of the lungs.

It seems a shame that the surviving Leigh Smith siblings could not come together and support one another as the old order crumbled around them. There is no doubt that Barbara asked a great deal of Nannie, who (according to her own account) visited the Doctor every afternoon towards the end. And no one could deny the challenges of any relationship with Eugène. It is tempting to imagine that things might have been easier for everyone had Nannie been a little less self-righteous and Barbara a little more objective. But that would be patronizing. As we all know, family life is a many-headed beast, full of complex dynamics inexplicable to outsiders – and often to insiders too.

It was always Barbara's hope that the next generation would be as happy as she had been, and more. In the midst of these afflicted years, that hope must have bought her some comfort. So must her conviction, shared with Marian Evans, that a love of life is stronger than the fear of death.

14

Living on Aspiration

From 1885 to the Present

For, when the power of imparting joy
Is equal to the will, the human soul
Requires no other heaven.[1]

BARBARA ALWAYS RECOGNIZED THAT SOMETHING WAS disjointed in her Victorian psyche. That is why she found it impossible to settle for the social status quo; to 'do it like other people'. Far from disabling her, her distinctive attitude to life turned out to be empowering. It allowed her to live every day – as her friend Dr Elizabeth Garrett Anderson once put it – upon aspiration.[2] The dictionary defines 'aspiration' in several ways; it can mean the desire for something unattainable, or the act of reaching out and securing your prize. The first relies on imagination; the second on energy. Until stricken by ill-health, Barbara had plenty of both. Now, however, her reserves were running dangerously low.

Three letters arrived from Nannie in Algeria at the beginning of 1885.[3] They were addressed to Amy, Barbara's niece. The first, written on 10 January, complains that the Doctor is 'not going right' and that the carer eventually provided by the local hospital is leaving, which is desperate news. Eugène is madder than ever. The second letter, written a fortnight later, predicts that he has only about a month left to live, and advises Barbara not to mourn when he dies, but to rejoice. He is not a man any more, 'but an unintelligent semblance of humanity'. Cold comfort for his wife. The final letter is dated 30 January. The Doctor died of pneumonia two days ago. Barbara is lucky, says Nannie: she avoided having to cope with his chaotic final days.

Of course, Barbara did have to cope. She was already mourning what might have been, not only in terms of health and strength (for both of them) but on a deeper level. Eugène was not the kindred spirit she had imagined him to be in her salad days. It was painful to admit that, but Dr Elizabeth Blackwell saw it at once.

> I suppose . . . that the early passionate attachment revives in memory. And the long effort she made to ennoble his life – the hope that she cherished that on his death bed he would open his eyes to the nobility of her affection – all these things I suppose have combined to give her a terrible shock.[4]

To Barbara he was a dear man, an admirable man in many ways, handsome, loving and intriguing. But he was not her soulmate. Even so, he *was* her husband, to whom she was bound in sickness and in health. She bitterly regretted not being with him and sent 3,500 francs during his last months to make his life as easy as possible. Soon after his death, the money was discovered in a hidden corner of Campagne du Pavillon, squirrelled away by Eugène and forgotten.

The funeral arrangements were made by some French officials in Barbara's absence, who buried him in the European Cemetery at Boulevard Bru in Algiers. She donated £10 to the local Anglican church every year, asking them in return to tend Eugène's grave and plant it with flowers 'as if it were situated in the English portion of the Cemetery'.[5] It has since disappeared.

A number of obituaries appeared in the French and British

press, soberly celebrating the Doctor as 'l'honnête Bodichon', whose efforts to rid Algeria of slavery would surely win him an honoured place in the chronicles of the country. According to the eulogies, he fused revolutionary idealism with the old aristocratic traditions of honour, generosity and moral probity. Had he not chosen medicine, he might have been a great politician, said some; he reminded others of a true ascetic: austere, incorruptible and unworldly. All agreed that he was an unusual man of high ideals who meant well, but who never seemed to be on the same wavelength as anybody else. That might have been a choice on his part, or an irrelevance.[6]

Campagne du Pavillon was put up for sale in January 1886. The particulars enthused about its fashionable location, its convenient frontage to the road from Algiers, the fact that it could easily be divided into several lots, and its unusual on-site eucalyptus plantation.[7] Nannie was livid. It added insult to injury that those blessed gum trees should be a selling point: she had hoped, now that the Doctor was gone, that they could finally be felled to return the sunlight and unobstructed view to Montfeld. But Barbara continued to refuse permission, knowing how much the trees had meant to her husband. They stood as a monument to him, just as those five Scots pines stood – and still stand – at Brown's (though they are leaning a little now), in defiant testament of the Pater's love for his motherless children.

NANNIE AND BARBARA WERE never close again. It was not only about the trees; Nannie was accused of intercepting and opening Barbara and Eugène's correspondence: an unpardonable invasion of privacy that in Barbara's imagination cheated her of any final messages from her husband, and Eugène of any words of love from her. Brother Willy and his wife could not quite forget Barbara's interference and implied criticism of their parenting of Amy and her siblings, who grew up (complained their aunt) with

neither intellectual nor artistic ambition. Even Norman Moore –
now married to Amy – lost his lustre as the golden boy. He had
grown too reactionary, according to Barbara. A letter of his in
the family archive is undeniably disconcerting.[8] It is all about
wifely duties; about a woman's mind being free to roam (within
reason) but her body being the property of her husband. A wife
should never appear in society without him; once married, she
ceases to be a separate entity. They are one. Or to put it more
cynically, they are him. This was not the sort of attitude likely to
commend Norman to Barbara, the daughter of Liberty Hall.

Ben remained aloof, easily irritated and slow to show warmth
or affection, until at the age of fifty-nine he miraculously fell in
love. Charlotte 'Charley' Sellers was the nineteen-year-old sister
of Eugénie, Hertha Marks's spectacularly beautiful Girtonian
friend from the fire brigade. Charley was beautiful too, and despite
the chasm of years between them, she accepted Ben and married
him in 1887. Nannie's reaction was, perhaps, predictable, and
recalls Aunt Patty's disgust at the Pater's domestic arrangements.
'Men, certainly about . . . Ben's age, seem to go crazy & I am sure
it ought to be illegal for [them] to marry girls 40 years younger
than themselves . . . I feel that she must be doing it for the money.'[9]
Barbara, on the other hand, was open-minded as usual. She wished
the couple well. After his marriage, Ben softened a little, and his
relationship with his older sister grew gentler.

So much for family. As they had all her life, Barbara's friends
were the ones who raised her spirits and gave her solace, even
when she could no longer reciprocate as brilliantly as she used to.
Loyal Elizabeth Blackwell visited Barbara twice a week whenever she could. She was incensed by what she called the 'crooked'
Leigh Smiths' treatment of Barbara. Whenever Barbara was ill –
which was increasingly often – they ganged together to 'imprison'
her, Elizabeth insisted, driving her friends away and trapping her
in 'a network of minute nursing details which keep me from her,
except by occasional formal appointments'.[10] 'I am amazed that

they did not kill [her].'[11] Exactly who these jealous family members were is unclear. Elizabeth may have judged their natural anxiety for Barbara's well-being a little harshly. It is well known that some of them hated Hertha Marks, but surely Dr Blackwell posed no danger?

Hertha was all that Barbara could have wished for in a daughter. In 1885 she married a widowed professor, the physicist William Ayrton. Their baby, born the following year, was uncompromisingly named Barbara Bodichon Ayrton. Hertha was able to continue her scientific research after the baby's birth because our Barbara helped to pay for childcare – and, incidentally, for the patents taken out on several of Hertha's inventions, such as the line-divider drawing tool she came up with while still at Girton. Such imaginative support reminds me of Dorothy Hodgkin's generosity on becoming the first and, as I write, the only British woman to win a Nobel Prize for science, in 1964. She spent part of her award on establishing a nursery for working mothers like her at Somerville College, Oxford. Barbara was delighted by her young namesake and used to send her little postcards from Scalands telling her, in an increasingly shaky hand, about what birds were singing in the garden, and how many eggs were huddled in their nests. Hertha and 'Barbie' were the lights of Barbara's life.

Bessie Parkes (Madame Belloc) gave Barbara pictures drawn by her children Marie and Hilaire; it was a sweet gesture, but now that Bessie was a doting mother and a Roman Catholic, the two women appear to have grown more distant than they had ever been. Barbara's circle of friends still included Jessie White Mario, Emily Davies, the artists Brabby Brabazon and Marianne North, novelist Milly Betham-Edwards, poets Christina Rossetti and William Allingham, and doctor Elizabeth Garrett Anderson, but – like the Pater and Eugène – Marian Evans, George Lewes, Anna Mary Howitt, Dante Gabriel Rossetti, Bella, General Ludlow and the stalwart aunts Dolly and Ju were all gone.

Marian Evans might not have been conventionally beautiful, but in a few strokes of the pencil towards the end of Marian's life, Barbara illuminates her striking character.

It was typical of Barbara that she chose to express her joy at having known such people rather than her regret at losing them. 'It certainly is a great happiness to have known so many good people in my life,' she wrote.[12] One of her friends' nicknames for her was Queen Mab; not the faintly sinister fairy from *Romeo and Juliet*, but the eponymous heroine of Shelley's epic poem about enlightenment and reform, written in 1813. It includes the snatch of verse at the head of this chapter, which could easily stand as Barbara's epitaph.

A glance through the local Sussex newspapers shows how ready Barbara was to impart joy as she approached her sixties. In July 1887, six hundred local Sunday school members were invited to Scalands for a summer outing. *Six hundred*. Two-thirds of them were children. They processed from Robertsbridge headed by a fife and drum band, just as the children of Westminster Infants' School used to process behind James Buchanan and his pipe. Following an afternoon of revelries, races and a slap-up tea, they all trotted home again, happy after their day out.

On 24 December that year, there was another tea party, this time for sixty children who sat around a Christmas tree in the night-school room and were given presents, donated by Hertha and Barbara's watercolourist friend Henry Moore. Barbara's doctor and trustee Reginald Thompson and some of her nieces played Father Christmas and his helpers. Barbara watched benevolently from her chair while a sawdust pie of colossal proportions was wheeled in, ogled at and consumed. Sawdust pies are American concoctions of pastry, egg white, biscuit crumbs, chopped pecans and shredded coconut. Barbara and Eugène must have enjoyed one or two on their honeymoon.

A 'meat tea' with plum pudding and musical entertainment for 'Madame's boys' (the students of the night school) was held between Christmas and New Year, during which a hearty toast of thanks was raised to Madame Bodichon. There were regular cricket matches at Scalands in season (Willy was a keen player) and occasional 'scholars' dinners' at the night school, enlivened by informal spelling bees and a free book for everyone from Barbara. Millicent and Henry Fawcett enjoyed a choral concert there in June 1883; that is possibly when they signed their bricks in the fireplace.

Alongside reports of events like these in the *Hastings and St Leonards Observer*[13] are frequent mentions of Madame's generosity in other directions: £5 to the local hospital, for example; £5 to Hastings Liberal Association with the gift of some books for the reading-room library; £2 to a fund to help support the impoverished naturalist and novelist Richard Jefferies; ten shillings to a hardship fund for a local man fallen on tricky times; some pottery loaned to the Women's Art, Industries and Inventions Exhibition in London; and use of the grounds at Scalands for a parish picnic, with visitors given guided tours of her house. In July 1888, it is noted that she has added her name to a petition demanding degrees for women. And she is still involved with fundraising for Girton. Once an activist, always an activist.

By the beginning of January 1890, Barbara's health was declining fast. Friends and family continued to call when she could cope with them, but visits were no longer much of a pleasure either to them or to her. (There was still *some* fun to be had, as when an unsuspecting guest plunged his hand into an ancient mortuary jar on Barbara's shelves and swiftly wished he hadn't. It was still full.) Sometimes she forgot Eugène had died and fretted about where he was. Her housekeeper Bella Sanderson was faithful to the last, helped by Amelia Carter, a trained nurse, Mary Morgan the cook, Emma Payton the parlourmaid and Harriet Church and Edith Lewis, both housemaids. 'Her household will not let her die,'13 wrote Hertha to Bessie Parkes Belloc.[14] However, on the morning of Wednesday 10 June 1891, she fell unconscious. Dr Thompson was sent for, and at half past midnight the next day, quietly and without pain, she passed away.

Few letters of condolence to the family survive, but one has been kept, sent by E. Phillpot, who was probably a former member of staff at Blandford Square. Barbara would have treasured it: 'I felt so cast down to think I will never see that dear face nor hear Dear Madam['s] sweet voice again which was like music to me I think it is nearly or quite 32 years I have loved her dearly.'[15]

The funeral was held at Brightling on 15 June. Leading the cortège on the two-and-a-half-mile journey from Scalands to St Thomas-à-Becket's Church were fifty night-school students, mostly dressed in black, quietly marching in step. Twelve carriages for family and friends followed the hearse, and the route was lined from beginning to end by well-wishers, silent except for stifled sobs and the occasional muttered 'God bless her'. After the service, her coffin was committed to the grave in a spot she had chosen for herself years before, because Aunt Dolly was buried there and it was 'so pretty and quiet'.[16] Heaps of flowers surrounded her, some accompanied by grateful messages, but many, touchingly, anonymous. 'Madame Bodichon's whole life was wrapped up in trying to elevate the poor, and alleviate the sufferings of all that were down-trodden,' wrote a local newspaper reporter (possibly her friend William Ransom, who rode in the third carriage); 'never a day passed by that someone was thought of and made all the happier . . . Can anyone then be surprised that the funeral on Monday was such as has never been seen in the place before?'[17]

The local press was not alone in finding the occasion impressive. *The Times* marked the passing of a 'carefully and unconventionally educated' woman whose force of character and catholic sympathies (with a small 'c') set her apart from her peers.[18] The *Englishwoman's Review* considered that with the death of Madame Bodichon 'the Englishwomen of this generation have lost the woman to whom, more than any other, they owe the great change which has taken place in their position and opportunities'.[19] The *Pall Mall Gazette* thought it fitting that the life of such a 'large-souled, whole-hearted woman' should be celebrated, particularly as the many mourners at her funeral came from all denominations and none, united in grief for 'a good citizen, a staunch friend, a fearless reformer . . . a character as magnanimous as it was original'.[20]

Two of Barbara's strapping 'boys' from the night school had emigrated to Connecticut on their graduation from Scalands. One of them confessed to weeping when the news reached him. They owed their new lives to the education and confidence Barbara had given them. They, too, loved her dearly.

It would be tediously repetitive to quote from Barbara's numerous obituaries. A digest, in their words, will do. She was a brave and generous champion with a commanding intellect, large reserves of sympathy and an open mind. Joyous, light-hearted and tender, she was one of the most notable women of the century, to whose staunchness of purpose and sturdiness of character she united the endeavour of a noble nature, wholly unspoiled by the world. She was a woman of ardent faith in individuals and causes; in the middle of a conservative neighbourhood, her house was a beacon of advanced ideas. It was respect for humanity in concrete form that made her life so salutary and stimulating: she strove for liberty under the banner of justice for all. She was truly one of God's good gifts, always seeking to make others happy and better.

Artistically, she was Britain's second-best watercolourist (begging an obvious unanswered question); one of the very few who could paint moving masses of water. 'Her paintings are full of nature and poetry, and power and strong individuality. Years must pass before they cease to bring tears into the eyes of those who can recall the artist in her beautiful prime.' That was Bessie Parkes Belloc's comment, to which she added that of all the remarkable women she had met in her life, Barbara shone the brightest and the best.[21]

The most used words across all of her obituaries are 'friend', 'large' and 'happy'.

Barbara left an estate of over £28,600, equating to more than £2 million today. Her will, drawn up in 1885, is a lengthy document, complicated by no fewer than eight codicils, the last of which was added less than a month before she died. Though she originally left Scalands and most of her effects to Nannie for her lifetime, and thereafter to their cousins-once-removed Rosalind and Margaret (Uncle Sam Smith's granddaughters), following Ben and Charley's marriage she changed her mind and left it all to him instead. Girton got its promised £10,000, with a collection of Barbara's paintings, on condition that the college paid annuities to specified friends, including Elizabeth Blackwell (£40), Jessie White Mario (£40), William Ransom (£50) and a Mrs Clarence Greenfield (£52; she was the young widow of a Robertsbridge carpenter, with seven children to support). Girton was also required to admit Barbara's youngest nieces, Bella and

Dorothy Leigh Smith, as students, neither of whom took up the opportunity (Dorothy died of TB aged thirteen). Bedford College received £1,000, while various friends, family and staff each inherited sums between £100 and £1,000. The Poor House at Zennor was left to Gertrude Jekyll, along with Barbara's cherished collection of Spanish pottery.

It is a mark of Barbara's generosity that there are nearly forty named legatees in the will and its codicils. As far as I can make out from the legal handwriting swarming across the pages like a synchronized legion of spiders, Nannie ended up with a half-share of everything that was left when all the other disbursements had been made. The second half went to one of the people Nannie liked least in the world: Hertha Ayrton. It must have been fun sorting that lot out.

Barbara was only sixty-four when she died. Her three surviving siblings outlived her handsomely. Willy died in 1910 in his late seventies; Ben in 1913 aged eighty-five (he is buried next to Barbara); and Nannie five years later, at eighty-eight. Norman Moore and Amy had three children; when Amy died in 1901, Norman went on to marry her cousin Milicent, Bella's youngest daughter. They settled in Hancox, the house where I spent long, happy hours poring over Barbara's letters and paintings – not to mention Eugène's bloomers – during my research. It is now home to the fourth and fifth generations of Moores: Barbara's great-great-great-niece and her sons. Hancox is minutes away from where Barbara was born, from Brown's, where she lived as a child, and from Scalands.

Alfred Eugène Clements, the foundling Barbara 'rescued' in 1874, happened to be at Scalands the day Barbara died. She left him enough money to set himself up in business as a grocer. Four years after Barbara's death he emigrated to South Africa, where he worked for a 'high class' tea and coffee importer – not unlike the Smiths' old Sugar Loaf in London, but on a smaller scale. He settled in Durban, where he died in 1936.[22] Barbara's governess

Catherine Spooner died before Barbara did, in 1880. She married in 1867 at fifty, but unfortunately her husband died the following year. Her age on marriage might be significant: the Bentley Smiths were all grown up by then, and her duty to the Pater safely discharged.

There is no record of Barbara's reaction to the death of Catherine, but she must have been mourned by her erstwhile charges. Jane Bentley Smith, the eldest, married a civil servant in the Inland Revenue office, and had – according to the 1881 census – nine surviving children. Though her brother Alexander trained as an engineer, he gave that up in favour of watercolour painting (perhaps financed by the Pater's bequest). His wife Lucy Meadows, a sculptor and portraitist, was the daughter of Charles Dickens's great friend the illustrator Joseph Kenny Meadows. (*Surely* Barbara came across Alexander and Lucy? It is almost impossible to believe that their paths never crossed.) They had three children. Alexander died in 1905, celebrated in the local press not just as an artist, but someone dedicated – like his half-sister – to public service and 'good fellowship'.[23] The youngest Bentley Smith, Harry, settled in India, making the occasional visit home to stay with Jane. The *London Gazette* of February 1872 lists his occupation in Calcutta (Kolkata) simply as 'Esquire', so he must have left the Merchant Navy by then. He was still alive in 1901, when he was reported as arriving by ship in Bombay (Mumbai); after that, I can find nothing.

Hertha Ayrton went on to become one of the most distinguished scientists of her age, fulfilling Barbara's assurance while Hertha was a downcast student that she would *not* be a failure and her life would be both meaningful and fulfilling. She was the first woman to be awarded the Hughes Medal from the Royal Society in 1906, in recognition of her work on the electric arc (with a practical application in the first electric lighting) and sand ripples (all to do with the laws of vortices and oscillation). There has been only one other female recipient since. More than 150,000 of the portable fans she invented to dispel poison gas were supplied to soldiers on the Western Front during the First World War. One of her closest friends was Marie Curie, whose discovery of radium was at first attributed to her husband. In the spirit of her beloved Barbara, Hertha wrote to a national newspaper to complain: 'Errors are notoriously hard to kill, but an error that ascribes to a man what was actually the work of a woman has more lives than a cat.'[24] Following in Barbara's footsteps again, Hertha became a committed campaigner for women's votes, investing some of the money she had inherited from her mentor in funding the suffragette movement. Her daughter Barbie, also a suffragette, was elected a Labour MP in 1945.

Hertha's definitive work *The Electric Arc*, published in 1902, bears a moving preface.

> To Madame Bodichon, whose clear-sighted enthusiasm for the freedom and enlightenment of women enabled her to strike away so many barriers from their path; whose great intellect, large tolerance and noble presence were an inspiration to all who knew her; to her whose friendship changed and beautified my whole life, I dedicate this book.

She left her collection of Bodichon watercolours to the Tate in London when she died in 1923; sadly, they refused them. What became of them I don't know, but I like to think they helped to inspire her grandson, the artist Michael Ayrton, who is well represented in the same gallery.

Bessie Parkes Belloc died in 1925, at the notable age of ninety-five. Despite almost living to witness universal suffrage in Britain, her name does not feature in any suffrage organizations. Indeed, her son Hilaire Belloc, the writer, campaigned against votes for women during his short tenure as a Member of Parliament. All those 'daft' missions she and Barbara used to dream and write about in their youth were forgotten.

No doubt this disappointed Emily Davies, who never gave up her crusade for women's education and enfranchisement. She was still taking part in protest marches and signing petitions into her eighties, proudly casting her vote at the first opportunity when the Representation of the People Act was finally passed in 1918. The Act's title is significant: before the efforts of Barbara, Emily and their peers, women were not legally considered 'people' at all. Abolishing what she termed the 'deconsideration' of 'half the people of the world' was a lofty ambition for young Barbara in the 1850s, but she achieved it in the end – with a little help from her friends.

Dr Elizabeth Blackwell retired to Hastings with her daughter Kitty, proud of her influence on medical successors such as doctors Elizabeth Garrett Anderson and Sophia Jex-Blake. 'It was my privilege and pleasure, in some small degree, to encourage these brave workers in their pioneer enterprise in England,'[25] she wrote towards the end of her life – just as it had been Barbara's privilege and pleasure to encourage her. She is now regarded as a true heroine of the medical profession on both sides of the Atlantic.

Gertrude Jekyll sold the Poor House not long after inheriting it from Barbara. She was becoming too busy and successful to use it. But she remained ever grateful to the friend who gave her one of her first commissions (the alterations at Scalands) and whose buoyancy, love of natural beauty and simple pleasures inspired her life and her career.

Campagne du Pavillon is still standing, now part of the American Embassy compound in Algiers with Nannie and Isa's Montfeld. Scalands has had a chequered past. Ben and other members of the Leigh Smith family used it until 1953. Then it was left unoccupied, 'falling with the autumn leaves', as Barbara's great-nephew put it,[26] its contents, including many of her paintings, damaged by fire and water. But now it is alive again as a private home, standing comfortably in its woods and gardens, and watched over by the towering jawbone of a whale brought home from the Arctic by Ben. Barbara's painted bricks around the hearth whisper happily of times past. And almost within sight, the five Scots pine trees at Brown's wait patiently for their long story to come to a close.

IT IS TRADITIONAL, AT the end of a biography, to talk about the subject's legacy. Where do I begin? One of the Bonham Carter cousins wrote an elegy soon after Barbara's death.

> Those curtains where they fall
> Might almost drop apart and she walk through
> And very slight recall
> The robe's line and the slow walk once I knew,
> The face, both sad and bright, the gold hair bound with blue.
>
> The ghosts of sad thoughts press
> On one another in this empty spot
> Of grief for childlessness
> Of sorrow heavy on an innocent lot,
> And of a genius little known and soon forgot.[27]

Though understandably tempered by grief and love, it is relentlessly downbeat. Too downbeat for Barbara. Her name may have been 'little known and soon forgot' for a while – a long while – but her influence greets us every day. Girton College continues to flourish under the benevolent eye of two Barbaras, in portraits by Emily Osborn and Samuel Laurence. She would have found it impossible to believe that women would not be awarded degrees at Cambridge until 1948, but in every other way I suspect she would be radiantly proud of her Palace. In 1976 it opened its doors to male undergraduates. This upset some of its alumnae and supporters but could easily be considered an extension of its founders' campaign for accessibility and equal opportunity.

Barbara's name is very much alive there: scholarships and Foundation Fellowships are named after her, and her paintings still shine down on the light-filled corridors. When I stayed there last, I almost fancied I could hear her solid, reassuring tread on the carpet outside, and the swish of her rough-silk gown. It was not frightening at all. In fact I was disappointed, on opening my door, not to find her there in person.

Barbara is also remembered with gratitude at Royal Holloway, University of London, which merged with Bedford College in the early 1980s. There is a rather worn blue plaque on the wall of her home in Pelham Crescent, Hastings, commemorating her stature as an 'educational pioneer, campaigner for women's rights, and artist'. Art historians are beginning to recognize her originality, and her importance in linking the methods of the Pre-Raphaelites with those of the Impressionists. This is largely thanks to the late John Crabbe, who was an avid collector and careful curator of her work. The scholar Mark Samuels Lasner is another of her champions; his Bodichon collection at the University of Delaware is peerless, complemented by the Delaware Art Museum's possessions, including Barbara's miraculous painting of Ventnor on the Isle of Wight.

It has been estimated that Barbara exhibited nearly three hundred pictures at seventy different events between 1850 and 1881. Her Algerian pictures number around 150.[28] There are scores of watercolours and sketches in the family's keeping, and examples in public galleries and private collections around the country. After her first stroke in 1877, her brush stuttered and slurred a little, like her speech, and never quite regained its former fluency. But her entire output is characterized by a bright spirit of liveliness and spontaneity. As an artist she never shouts. She converses, explains and invites.

A poet I know who lives in New York was delighted when I told her I was writing about Barbara. A panel about her in a recent exhibition at Brooklyn Museum had literally stopped my friend in her tracks. There was something about Barbara's painterliness that was arresting; something synaesthetic about her work, as though she were a poet herself, using colour instead of words. There was an immediate personal connection.

That connection is something I recognize well. I feel as though it is Barbara's gift to me, to keep long after this book is done and dusted. I began writing about her because I wanted readers to meet the person who was responsible for the development of what we now call feminism in Britain. She articulated and campaigned for equal opportunity in the workplace, the law, the polling booth, at home and in the world beyond the kitchen or the drawing room; she founded the first university college for women and the first women's suffrage society; she was fervently against slavery of all kinds, and a committed activist for human rights. Perhaps because her achievements were so diverse, history has not treated her with the respect she deserves. Look in the engine room of every aspect of social change in Victorian Britain, and you'll find Barbara.

Look for the origins of the various inclusivity and kindness campaigns of today, and there she is again. And that, I have come to realize, it what really matters: not what she did, but who she was. Here was an illegitimate, unconventionally educated girl, growing up in a culture dominated by an elite Establishment, where women were defined by low expectation; society was organized along hierarchical lines according to class, education, religion and the old-boy network; defiance was considered dangerous, and difference unsound. Barbara was eccentric. She was 'cracked'. She said as much. Yet she managed not only to challenge all that Victorian traditionalists held dear, but to change things for the better. And to keep smiling, at the centre of an endless circle-dance of genuine friendship.

Her personal qualities were utterly authentic, life-enhancing
and inspiring. They are as valid in today's society as they were in
hers, given our collective struggle for a less judgemental, more
generous world. It was her life's work to combat prejudice and
closed-mindedness in thought, word and deed. Loving and
beloved, she is a very modern heroine.

The last word belongs to Barbara. When she was struck down
in 1877, and feared she might not survive, she asked for a copy of
her favourite poem. It was not by anyone she had met – Dante
Gabriel Rossetti or Robert Browning, maybe; Tennyson or
Adelaide Procter. It wasn't even one of the Shakespeare sonnets
she used to read aloud on summer evenings at Scalands. It was
Dryden's poem from 1685 written in imitation of an ode by the
Roman poet Horace.

Happy the man, and happy he alone,
He who can call today his own:
He who, secure within, can say,
Tomorrow do thy worst, for I have lived today.
Be fair or foul or rain or shine
The joys I have possessed, in spite of fate, are mine.
Not heaven itself upon the past has power,
But what has been, has been, and I have had my hour.

The end of a perfect day.

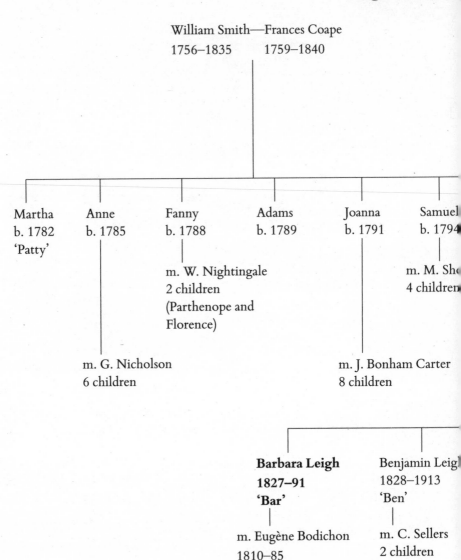

William Smith—Frances Coape
1756–1835   1759–1840

Martha
b. 1782
'Patty'

Anne
b. 1785

m. G. Nicholson
6 children

Fanny
b. 1788

m. W. Nightingale
2 children
(Parthenope and
Florence)

Adams
b. 1789

Joanna
b. 1791

m. J. Bonham Carter
8 children

Samuel
b. 1794

m. M. Sh
4 children

Barbara Leigh
1827–91
'Bar'

m. Eugène Bodichon
1810–85
'The Doctor'

Benjamin Leigh
1828–1913
'Ben'

m. C. Sellers
2 children

Tree (pruned)

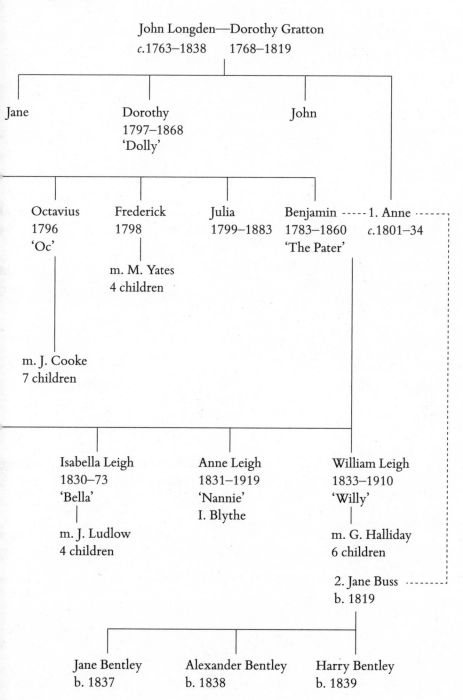

John Longden—Dorothy Gratton
*c.*1763–1838   1768–1819

Jane

Dorothy
1797–1868
'Dolly'

John

Octavius
1796
'Oc'

Frederick
1798

Julia
1799–1883

Benjamin ----- 1. Anne ------
1783–1860   *c.*1801–34
'The Pater'

m. M. Yates
4 children

m. J. Cooke
7 children

Isabella Leigh
1830–73
'Bella'

Anne Leigh
1831–1919
'Nannie'
I. Blythe

William Leigh
1833–1910
'Willy'

m. J. Ludlow
4 children

m. G. Halliday
6 children

2. Jane Buss --------
b. 1819

Jane Bentley
b. 1837

Alexander Bentley
b. 1838

Harry Bentley
b. 1839

Dramatis Personae

A BRIEF GUIDE TO FRIENDS OF BARBARA LEIGH SMITH Bodichon and other key figures most frequently mentioned in the main text, where further biographical details will be found. Cross-references to individuals with their own entry are in bold type.

Allingham, William (1824–89). An Irish poet and journalist who resigned his position as a customs officer in 1870 to earn a living by his pen. He was a close friend of Alfred, Lord Tennyson, and of members of the Pre-Raphaelite circle. He married Helen Paterson (1848–1926) – best known as the watercolourist Helen Allingham – in 1874.

Anderson, Elizabeth Garrett *see* **Garrett, Elizabeth**

Ayrton, Hertha (1854–1923). Born Phoebe Sarah Marks near Portsmouth, Hertha was as close to a daughter as Barbara ever had. Her father was a Jewish watchmaker who died when she was seven; her mother was a seamstress who sent Hertha to be educated at her aunts' school in London. Nicknamed 'Hertha' by a friend, after the eponymous heroine of a feminist novel by Fredrika Bremer, she was mentored by Barbara through the admissions process for Girton and soon became a devoted friend. Barbara supported her financially and emotionally throughout a remarkable life. She became a pioneering electrical engineer, an inventor (of a fan, among other things, to disperse poisonous gas in the trenches of the First World War) and a prominent suffragist. Her daughter was named Barbara Bodichon Ayrton in her friend's honour and was elected to Parliament in 1945. How proud our Barbara would have been.

Betham-Edwards, Matilda (1836–1919). 'Milly' Betham-Edwards was one of Barbara's devotees. She was, unusually, a farmer in her own right as well as a popular novelist and travel writer, who admired Barbara's independence of spirit and tried to perpetuate her memory after her death by originating and contributing to a series of obituaries.

Blackwell, Elizabeth (1821–1910). Elizabeth, a cousin of **Bessie Rayner Parkes**, was born in Bristol, emigrated with her family to America at the age of eleven, and spent the early part of her career teaching, to raise the funds necessary to train as a doctor. Lack of money was not her sole handicap: the only establishment to admit a woman at that time was Geneva Medical College in New York State. When she qualified as an MD in 1849 she became the first British-born woman to do so. Barbara helped sponsor Elizabeth and her sister Emily Blackwell (1826–1919), also a doctor, in their work and on their travels. Elizabeth was one of Barbara's closest friends.

Boucherett, Jessie (1825–1905). A member of the Langham Place circle, Jessie was a Lincolnshire heiress inspired by the writings of **Harriet Martineau** to campaign for women's rights. She worked with Barbara at the offices of the *English Woman's Journal* and developed a special interest in women's employment. She helped organize the first women's suffrage petition in 1866.

Brabazon, Hercules Brabazon (1821–1906). An Irish watercolourist, born in France, who settled in Sussex close to Barbara's home and that of his friend **Gertrude Jekyll**. He and Barbara often painted together, sharing similar styles and artistic sensibilities. Barbara was very fond of 'Brabby', and he of her.

Buchanan, James (1784–1857). An unconventional teacher who ran the infant schools set up by Barbara's father and by Barbara herself, and who tutored Barbara and her siblings during their childhood. A disciple of socialist Robert Owen, his intuitive methods, good humour and kind heart influenced Barbara all her life.

Chapman, John (1821–94). One of Barbara's would-be lovers. Although he enjoyed desultory careers as a watchmaker and a physician, he is best known as the rather bohemian publisher of the liberal *Westminster Review*, as **George Eliot**'s probable lover, and as a political and literary networker whose contacts included Charles Dickens and Thomas Carlyle.

Craig, Isabella ('Isa') (1831–1903). Edinburgh-born Isa was a protégée of **Bessie Rayner Parkes**. She left school at nine; while working as a seamstress, she studied literature and became a published poet in 1856. She was a stalwart of the Langham Place circle as an activist, administrator and champion of women's emancipation.

Davies, Emily (1830–1921). One of the suffrage movement's most influential pioneers, she helped to organize **John Stuart Mill**'s petition to Parliament in 1866, and three years later was co-founder, with Barbara, of Girton College, the UK's first university college for women. She campaigned all her life for equal opportunities for women, and was the only one of the Langham Place circle to survive long enough to cast a vote in 1918.

Eliot, George *see* **Evans, Marian**

Evans, Marian ('George Eliot') (1819–80). Barbara was the famous novelist's closest friend. Each played a vital part in the other's life. Marian's 'husband', the writer George Lewes (1817–78; they never married), was also beloved of Barbara, who never judged their relationship and never failed in her support. Barbara was the first person to recognize the hugely successful *Adam Bede* as Marian's work, and inspired the character of Romola in Marian's eponymous novel. Barbara's surrogate daughter **Hertha Ayrton** was the model for Myrah in *Daniel Deronda*.

Faithfull, Emily (1835–95). Emily was a recent debutante when she met Barbara in the late 1850s and joined the Langham Place circle. Like **Jessie Boucherett**, her special interest was in women's employment; in 1860 she set up the Victoria Press, employing female compositors, and though her credibility was dented by involvement in a scandalous divorce case, her influence on the women's movement was significant.

Fox, Eliza ('Tottie'), later Mrs Lee Bridell and Mrs Bridell-Fox (1823/4–1903). Tottie was a successful painter who campaigned with Barbara for formal art training for women. She ran informal evening classes herself, which Barbara attended. Her friendship with novelist Elizabeth Gaskell and poets Robert and Elizabeth Barrett Browning enriched Barbara's own social circle.

Garrett, Elizabeth, later Mrs Garrett Anderson (1836–1917). Although best remembered as the first woman to be entered on the Medical Register in Great Britain (she qualified in 1865), Elizabeth was also a committed feminist. Inspired by **Elizabeth Blackwell**, she determined to make the medical profession more accessible to women and to win women the vote. Her sister was the suffragist leader Millicent Fawcett (1847–1929).

Hays, Matilda ('Max') (1820?–97). Max was a writer and journalist with trenchant views on women's rights. She was a founder of the *English Woman's Journal*. Her intense relationships with the actress Charlotte Cushman and poet **Adelaide Procter** alienated her from so-called 'polite society' – but not from Barbara.

Howitt, Anna Mary, later Mrs Watts (1824–84). One of Barbara's oldest and closest friends, Anna Mary was the daughter of literary celebrities William and Mary Howitt. She became a professional artist and an impassioned writer on equal opportunities, until poor mental health and an all-consuming fascination for spiritualism isolated her from Barbara and the feminist cause.

Jameson, Anna Brownell (1794–1860). Mrs Jameson was one of Barbara's mentors: a campaigner for women's independence who practised what she preached. Impoverished by the injustices of the divorce laws, she wrote essays, travelogues and art criticism to support herself, and rarely missed an opportunity to capitalize on her fame by publicly protesting against sexism and institutional prejudice.

Jekyll, Gertrude (1843–1932). Barbara gave the artist and pioneering garden designer one of her first commissions, for improvements at her Sussex home, Scalands Gate. Gertrude also advised on the décor of Girton College. The two became close friends; so much so that Barbara bequeathed her house in Cornwall to Gertrude.

Lewes, George Henry *see* **Evans, Marian**

Mario, Jessie White (1832–1906). A journalist, military nurse and activist for Italian unity. Jessie's circle included the Italian general and revolutionary Giuseppe Garibaldi and the poets Robert and Elizabeth Barrett Browning. Barbara found Jessie's personal and political courage inspiring and her flagrant eccentricity delightful.

Martineau, Harriet (1802–76). Harriet came from a family of religious Dissenters whose radical politics informed her copious writing. She was a prominent political economist and social commentator, with influence on both sides of the Atlantic. She refused to allow the dual handicaps of deafness and femininity to confine or define her life.

Mill, John Stuart (1806–73). One of the political economist and philosopher's first tasks on being elected to Parliament in 1865 was to present Barbara and her colleagues' petition demanding votes for women. Barbara first came across him when she and **Bessie Rayner Parkes** studied his work as young women. His wife Harriet Taylor Mill (1807–58) wrote a seminal essay on women's emancipation, and her daughter Helen Taylor (1831–1907) was instrumental, with Barbara, in the foundation of the women's movement in the 1860s.

Neuberg, Joseph (1806–67). The German Jewish writer and translator worked as Thomas Carlyle's secretary. Though twenty years her senior, he asked Barbara to marry him in 1855.

Norton, Caroline (1808–77). Caroline's campaign for mothers' rights was catalysed by the loss of her children (and money) following a divorce. Her activism influenced the Custody of Infants and Matrimonial Causes Acts of 1839 and 1857 respectively. She would not consider herself a feminist, unlike Barbara, but her appetite for reform helped galvanize Barbara's own campaign for women's legal rights.

Parkes, Bessie Rayner, later Madame Belloc (1829–1925). Bessie was Barbara's closest lifelong friend. Childhood neighbours, the two highly intelligent young women encouraged each other's intellectual ambition and determined to dignify their lives by working for a living (unnecessary in both cases) and improving the lives of others. Bessie became a lynchpin of the Langham Place circle, a writer on women's education and work, and a cheerleader for social reform. Both her children, Marie Belloc Lowndes (1868–1947) and Hilaire Belloc (1870–1953), were successful writers.

Procter, Adelaide (1825–64). Like Barbara, this celebrated poet – much admired by Charles Dickens – was loved for her sympathetic nature and sense of humour. She worked at

Langham Place with Barbara, **Bessie Rayner Parkes**, **Max Hays** et al. until ill-health intervened. She died of TB aged thirty-eight. It has been suggested that she and Barbara's sister Nannie had a brief romantic attachment.

Rossetti, Dante Gabriel (1828–82). The Pre-Raphaelite artist and poet was a Victorian celebrity; a complex character whose frank affection for Barbara was reciprocated. He admired her painting and fearless personality, relying on her support to manage his troubled relationship with **Lizzie Siddal**. His sister, the poet Christina Rossetti (1830–94), was another of Barbara's slightly star-struck friends (though Christina's fame has outlived Barbara's); their brother, the art critic William Michael Rossetti (1829–1919), corresponded with Barbara through much of her life.

Ruskin, John (1819–1900). Though the art critic supported certain women's university colleges with gifts of artwork and jewellery, on a personal level he found Barbara's attempts to create equality for women wrong-headed and ridiculous. He was no great fan of her art, either. Unlike **Anna Mary Howitt**, who found Ruskin's criticism deeply traumatic, Barbara appears to have been unruffled by the great man's disapproval.

Rye, Maria (1829–1903). Maria's primary role at Langham Place was to coordinate the Female Middle-Class Emigration Society, supported financially and ideologically by Barbara. Both women viewed emigration not as an instrument of colonialism, but an opportunity for women to play a valuable part in building a new, equitable society in other countries, away from the prejudices of the old world.

Siddal, Lizzie (1829–62). The story of hauntingly beautiful Lizzie's progress from milliner's apprentice to Pre-Raphaelite artist reads like a slightly dark fairy tale. **Dante Gabriel Rossetti** is said to have scooped her into his studio in 1850, and into his heart. Barbara helped enable their relationship by arranging for them to be together in Sussex. They married in 1860, by which time Lizzie had become **John Ruskin**'s artistic protégée. A victim of TB, she suffered a miscarriage in 1861 and died by her own hand at the age of thirty-three.

Spooner, Catherine (1817–80). How this linen-draper's daughter from north London became Barbara and her siblings' governess is unknown. Their father obviously trusted her implicitly, secretly placing her in charge of his second brood of illegitimate children. There is no evidence that she and Barbara kept in touch in later life.

Sylvester, Joseph (1814–97). A brilliant mathematician and noted academic, Joseph fell in love with Barbara and proposed, in a letter that still exists, in 1854. Though she refused him, they remained good friends for the rest of Barbara's life. She taught him how to vault a five-bar gate when she was nearly forty . . .

Taylor, Clementia ('Mentia') (1810–1908). It was around her dining-room table in Aubrey House, London, that the first massed petition for women's suffrage – engineered by Barbara – was put together. Mentia was a governess before she married; afterwards her home became a meeting place for all who were interested in radically improving the lot of women.

Taylor, Helen *see* **Mill, John Stuart**

Walker, Hannah (*c.*1786–1866). Though strongly disapproved of by certain members of Barbara's family, the Sussex country-woman Hannah Walker was beloved of all the Leigh Smith siblings. She was their childhood nurse, or nanny, linking them in adulthood with a mother they could barely remember.

Notes and References

For full details of the sources quoted, please see Select Bibliography, pp. 367–74.

I. NAMES AND NO NAMES

1 Bessie Rayner Parkes, Diary, August–December 1849. Girton College Archive, GBR/0271/GCPP Parkes 1/4.
2 Madame de Staël's opinion of Wilberforce, who was also said to be devastatingly handsome in his youth.
3 Quoted in Handley and Lake, *Progress by Persuasion*, p. 90.
4 Lady Stephen, 'Life of William Smith' (typescript, 1940). Cambridge University Library, MS Add. 7621/IV/71.
5 William Smith to 'Pat', n.d. Cambridge University Library, MS Add. 7621/V/A/147.
6 The original painting (1784) is now in the Huntington Library and Art Museum in California; a Reynolds studio copy painted in 1789 is a star of the show at Dulwich Picture Gallery in London.
7 Copied in 'Notes made by Lady Margaret Verney', 1920. Claydon House Trust, N390 (part).
8 Ibid.
9 Florence Nightingale remembering her youth. British Library, Add. MSS 72832, vol. ix a, p. 79.
10 William Nightingale was born William Shore, assuming his great-uncle Peter Nightingale's surname on inheriting the Nightingale Estate at Lea Hurst in 1815.
11 By Marie Belloc-Lowndes in an unpublished letter quoted by Jacquie Matthews in Spender, *Feminist Theorists*, p. 93.
12 An edition of the *London Tradesman*, directing its eighteenth-century readers towards suitable occupations, warned that 'the title of milliner . . . was a more polite meaning for bawd'. Quoted by Serena Dyer in *Who Do You Think You Are?* magazine, 6 July 2015, pp. 72–3.
13 *Derby Mercury*, 9 May 1838.
14 Patty Smith to Fanny Nightingale, 6 November 1832. Claydon House Trust, N26 (part). This is possibly a contemporary copy rather than the original letter.
15 Patty Smith to Fanny Nightingale, 1 October [1828]. Claydon House Trust, N22 (part).

16 *New York Evening Post*, 5 May 1829.

17 I am grateful to Helen Richards and the co-researchers of her family tree for the information that her kinsman Abraham Buss accompanied the Pater. He was only about thirteen at the time. Searches on www.ancestry.co.uk reveal that Kezia was his elder sister; I am assuming this is the Kezia referred to in the Pater's journal.

18 See Cutler, *Greyhounds of the Sea*, p. 73.

19 Alice Delano fortuitously kept a journal of a voyage on the *Columbia* soon after her marriage to Captain Joseph in 1826. Details of mealtimes are taken from this journal. See Druett, *Hen Frigates*, pp. 25–9.

20 Cambridge University Library, MS Add. 7621/1/11. Subsequent quotations in the rest of this section are taken from this source.

21 https://www.statista.com/statistics/1041714/united-kingdom-all-time-child-mortality-rate/ (accessed October 2021).

22 Patty Smith to Fanny Nightingale, postmarked 30 January 1834. Claydon House Trust, N22 (part).

23 Part of the inscription was recorded by Bar's friend Bessie Parkes years later; it read: 'This stone is placed to commemorate his wife, her patience during years of suffering from a lingering & fatal consumption, by Benjamin Smith.' See Lowndes, *Turning Victorian Ladies into Women*, p. 22.

2. PLANTED IN SUSSEX SOIL

1 Quoted in Burton, *Barbara Bodichon*, p. 13.

2 Patty Smith to Fanny Nightingale, postmarked 3 October 1834. Claydon House Trust, N22 (part).

3 Ibid. The suggestion about going 'over the water' is made in a separate letter written in October 1834 (Claydon House Trust, N22 (part)).

4 Quoted in Gill, *Nightingales*, p. 44.

5 Quoted in Woodring, *Victorian Samplers*, p. 123.

6 Cambridge University Library, MS Add. 7621/1/14.

7 Bostridge, *Florence Nightingale*, p. 31.

8 London Metropolitan Archives, DL/C/513/001/2.

9 Ibid., DL/C/513/001/4.

10 By now the Pater owned Scalands Farm and Glottenham Manor (both near Robertsbridge), as well as the Pelham Crescent houses, Crowham Manor, Brown's, Mountfield Park Farm and 5 Blandford Square.

11 Howitt, *Autobiography*, vol. 2, pp. 34–5.

12 Hancox Archive.

13 *Chelmsford Chronicle*, 19 December 1834.

14 William Nightingale to Benjamin Smith, 15 June 1838. Claydon House Trust, N66 (part).

15 Frances Coape Smith to Benjamin Smith, [25 June 1838]. Claydon House Trust, N66 (part).

16 Buchanan, *Buchanan Family Records*, p. 6.

17 Julia Smith, 'Memoirs' (with copied letters from other members of the family). Cambridge University Library, MS Add. 7621/1/14.

18 Ibid.

19   Quotations taken from James Buchanan's letters (1826). Claydon House Trust, N24 (part).

20   Barbara to Alice Bonham Carter, 28 May 1884. Cambridge University Library, MS Add. 7621/1/14.

21   Quoted in Burton, *Barbara Bodichon*, p. 24.

22   See Hirsch, *Barbara Leigh Smith Bodichon*, p. 18.

23   Anna Mary Howitt to Barbara, 5 January 1848. Transcribed in Beaky, 'Letters', no. 6.

24   Bessie Rayner Parkes to Barbara, 1847. Girton College Archive, GBR/0271/ GCPP Parkes 5/1/1−2.

25   Belloc, 'A Great Englishwoman'.

26   Bessie Rayner Parkes to Barbara, 13 February 1847. Girton College Archive, GBR/0271/GCPP Parkes 5/6/1−3.

27   See Ashton, *142 Strand*, p. 226.

28   Bradbrook, *Barbara Bodichon*, p. 4.

29   Marian Evans to Sara Hennell, 29 June 1852. Quoted in Eliot, *George Eliot Letters,* vol. 2, p. 47.

30   Gaskell, *Letters of Mrs Gaskell*, pp. 606−7. Reproduced courtesy of the Elizabeth Gaskell Family Collection.

31   Julia Smith, 'Memoirs' (with copied letters from other members of the family). Cambridge University Library, MS Add. 7621/1/14.

32   Sarah Mytton Maury, *An Englishwoman in America* (London: Thomas Richardson, 1848), p. 4.

33   Now in the collections of the Whitworth Gallery at the University of Manchester.

3 . YE NEWE GENERATION

1   Barbara Leigh Smith, 'Ode on the Cash Clothes Club'. Girton College Archive, GBR/0271/GCPP Parkes 10/75/1.

2   Buchanan, *Buchanan Family Records*, p. 17.

3   Family legend has it that Oc was trying out some unorthodox experiments at his Scottish home in 1846 when he lost his eye in an(other) unscheduled explosion. He was trying to blast tunnels for smoke to escape, because he didn't like chimneys.

4   *Norfolk News*, 2 October 1847.

5   *The Times*, 11 February 1848.

6   *The Examiner*, 30 August 1851.

7   Anna Mary Howitt to Barbara, n.d. Transcribed in Beaky, 'Letters', no. 8.

8   The full title of the manual by Mrs Mary Holland is *The Modern Family Receipt Book, Containing a Great Variety of Valuable Receipts, Arranged Under Their Respective Heads, Connected with the Art of Social and Domestic Life, Including Many Valuable Original Communications, the Result of Long Experience.* Though it was published in 1825, much of its advice was still pertinent twenty years later. The answers to the problems I list are as follows. How to avoid hysterics: don't slap the patient across the face, like they do in period dramas; give her a mixture of caraway seeds, ginger and salt spread on toast instead. To avoid accidents in open carriages: don't jump over the side, but leap off the back. To

dye your hair a lustrous brown: use silver caustic (or nitrate, well diluted). To remove stains from black clothing: rub them with a liquor made of fig leaves boiled in water. To cure a black eye: gather some red roses and a rotten apple, wrap them in muslin and press the pad against the eye. So now you know.

9   Ibid., p. 180.

10 Quoted in Helene E. Roberts, 'The Exquisite Stare: The Role of Clothes in the Making of the Victorian Woman', *Signs*, vol. 2, no. 3 (Spring 1977), p. 554.

11 Quoted in Virginia Woolf, *Three Guineas*, ed. Lee, p. 277.

12 *Fraser's Magazine*, vol. 7 (1833), p. 601.

13 See Oguri, 'Barbara L. S. Bodichon', p. 92.

14 Bessie Parkes to Barbara, 22 July 1849. Girton College Archive, GBR/0271/GCPP Parkes 5/1/32.

15 Charlotte Brontë, *Shirley* (Oxford: Clarendon Press, 1979), vol. 2, p. 443.

16 Barbara to Bessie Parkes, n.d. Girton College Archive, GBR/0271/GCPP Parkes 5/165.

17 See Robinson, *Mary Seacole*, p. 39.

18 Quoted in Cherry, *Painting Women*, p. 56.

19 Bessie Parkes to Barbara, n.d. Girton College Archive, GBR/0271/GCPP Parkes 5/24/1.

20 *Birmingham Journal*, 13 May 1848.

21 'The Education of Women' was published in the *Hastings and St Leonards Observer* on 7 July 1848, 'An Appeal to the Inhabitants of Hastings' was published on 16 June and 'Conformity to Custom' on 28 July.

22 Girton College Archive, GBR/0271/GCPP Parkes 5/4/2.

23 Barbara to Aunt Dolly Longden, *c.*1857. Quoted in Burton, *Barbara Bodichon*, p. 21. In *A Mid-Victorian Feminist*, Herstein attributes the original letter to the Bonham Carter collection at Hampshire Record Office, but I have failed to trace it.

24 See Robinson, *Unsuitable for Ladies*, p. 13.

25 'Ode on the Cash Clothes Club'. Girton College Archive, GBR/0271/GCPP Parkes 10/75/1.

26 Howitt, *Art-Student in Munich*, vol. 1, p. 90.

27 Ibid.

28 Ibid., p. 91.

29 Barbara to Julia Smith, quoted in Burton, *Barbara Bodichon*, p. 33.

30 Pencil and ink sketch, 1844. Girton College Archive, GBR/0271/GCPP Bodichon 8/2.

31 Hancox Archive, 1842.

32 This and subsequent quotes about the Cambridge trip are taken from Mary Howitt's letter to her husband, 27 May 1851. Reprinted in Howitt, *Autobiography*, vol. 2, pp. 78-81.

33 Quoted in Lowndes, *Turning Victorian Ladies into Women*, p. 38.

34 Bessie Rayner Parkes to Barbara, 13 November 1850. Rare Book and Manuscript Library, Columbia University Libraries, MS 0124, box 1, folder 2.

4. VENUS WITHOUT CORSETS

1   Elizabeth Malleson to Barbara, 25 July [1853 or 1854]. Women's Library Collection at LSE Library, 7BMC/F/12.

2   Quoted in Crabbe, 'An Artist Divided', p. 311.

3   D. G. Rossetti to C. Rossetti, [8 November 1853]. Rossetti, *Correspondence of Dante Gabriel Rossetti*, p. 294.

4   'Conformity to Custom', *Hastings and St Leonards Observer*, 28 July 1848.

5   The only copy of the drawing I have located is in the collections of Delaware Art Museum, ref. 2017–50. It was published as an undated lithograph by the *English Woman's Journal*. Barbara's insistence on healthy clothing prefigured a more formal 'rational dress movement' towards the end of the nineteenth century, although bloomers made their first scandalous appearance in 1851. They may well have been what Barbara was wearing when Rossetti referred to her 'breeches'.

6   Barbara to Beatrice Shore Smith, 28 April [1859?]. Women's Library Collection at LSE Library, 9/08/017. David Cox (1783–1859) was a Birmingham blacksmith's son acknowledged to be England's finest landscape watercolourist at the height of his powers. Barbara was very fond of him, professionally and personally.

7   Barbara to Aunt Dolly, quoted in Burton, *Barbara Bodichon*, p. 75.

8   Bessie Parkes to Barbara, 25 June 1847. Girton College Archive, GBR/0271/GCPP Parkes 5/10.

9   Hancox Archive.

10 *The Athenaeum*, 18 February 1854. Quoted in Worzala, 'Langham Place Circle', p. 59.

11 Barbara to Bessie Parkes, n.d. Girton College Archive, GBR/0271/GCPP Parkes 5/161.

12 See Graham Mooney, 'Shifting Sex Differentials in Mortality During Urban Epidemiological Transition: The Case of Victorian London', *International Journal of Population Geography*, vol. 8, no. 1 (2002), pp. 17–47, at p. 23. The figure is the same from the years 1851–60. My thanks to Dr Richard James for bringing this article to my attention.

13 See Picard, *Victorian London*, pp. 31–2.

14 *Remarks on the Education of Girls*, 1854; revised edition printed by John Chapman in 1856.

15 J. J. S. Wharton, *An Exposition of the Laws Relating to the Women of England* (London: Longman, Brown et al., 1853), p. 15.

16 All quotations that follow are taken from the 1854 edition of *A Brief Summary* (see 'Works by Barbara Leigh Smith Bodichon' in 'Select Bibliography').

17 Florence Davenport Hill (quoting her father) to Barbara, 20 August 1854. Women's Library Collection at LSE Library, 7/BMC/E5.

18 Oliphant, 'Laws Concerning Women'.

19 Mary Astell, *A Serious Proposal to the Ladies* (London: Richard Wilkin, 1697), Part I, p. 9.

20 Bathsua Makin, *An Essay to Revive the Antient Education of Gentlewomen* (London: Tho. Parkhurst, 1673), pp. 3, 23.

21   Florence Nightingale, 'Cassandra', in *Suggestions for Thought to Searchers After Religious Truth* (London: Eyre and Spottiswoode, 1860), vol. 2, p. 402.

22   Malleson, 'Portrait of a School'. I am indebted to Dan Benedetti of Boston University Libraries in the USA for unearthing the original and copying it for me.

23   Elizabeth Malleson to Barbara, 25 July [1853 or 1854]. Women's Library Collection at LSE Library, 7BMC/F/12.

24   Malleson, 'Portrait of a School'.

5 . BARBARA – WHOM I LOVE

1   Andrew Marvell, 'To His Coy Mistress' (published posthumously in 1681, but written much earlier).

2   'Reminiscences of Old Hastings', p. 269.

3   W. Parker Snow, *Voyage of the Prince Albert in Search of Sir John Franklin* (London: Longman, Brown, Green et al., 1851), p. 10.

4   Benjamin Smith's will was proven on 6 June 1860. A digital copy is available to order from www.probateserach.service.gov.uk.

5   I have used church records, census forms and information available on www.ancestry.co.uk, including public and private family trees. Sadly, any records of Miss Hewlin's or the Reverend Briggs's schools have eluded me.

6   See Alexander's obituary in the *Western Morning News*, 6 June 1905.

7   Bessie Rayner Parkes to Barbara, 20 March 1852. Girton College Archive GBR/0271/GCPP Parkes 5/61a.

8   Barbara to Julia Smith, n.d. Girton College Archive GBR/0271/GCPP Parkes 10/46/1. It is unclear how much of Barbara's account is fictional.

9   Embroidered garments commissioned by the Sultana of Constantinople were displayed at the Great Exhibition; perhaps Barbara and Aunt Ju marvelled at them – and at their exotic owner – on one of their visits.

10   Bessie Rayner Parkes to Barbara, 23 August 1855. Girton College Archive GBR/0271/GCPP Parkes 5/72/1.

11   Barbara to Bessie Rayner Parkes, n.d. Girton College Archive GBR/0271/ GCPP Parkes 5/172. Lizzie (1829–62) is said to have been discovered by Rossetti's artist friend Walter Deverell, who allegedly spied her through the window of the hat shop where she worked. He asked her to model for him and other members of the PRB; she later took art lessons herself, but is generally considered a gifted amateur rather than the genius Rossetti, Ruskin and Barbara hailed her to be. She was hauntingly beautiful, with pale skin, strikingly blue eyes and auburn hair. Her surname was originally 'Siddall'; the final letter was dropped at the suggestion of Rossetti, to add distinction and a touch of mystique.

12   It would be fascinating to know Florence's response, had Lizzie agreed to go. Though not a 'gentlewoman', she was undeniably ill.

13   Bessie Rayner Parkes to Barbara, 27 March 1852. Girton College Archive GBR/0271/GCPP Parkes 5/60.

14   Eliot, *George Eliot Letters*, vol. 2, p. 109. Quoted in Stephen, *Emily Davies*, p. 38.

15   Joseph Parkes to Bessie Rayner Parkes, [October 1854]. Girton College Archive GBR/0271/GCPP Parkes 2/53.

16   Barbara to Bessie Rayner Parkes, undated postscript. Girton College Archive GBR/0271/GCPP Parkes 5/179.

17   Quoted in Herstein, *A Mid-Victorian Feminist*, p. 106.

18   Beinecke Rare Book and Manuscript Library, Yale University, GEN MSS 1086. I have used direct quotations, paraphrase and my own commentary in the following account of this correspondence.

6. WHERE ARE THE MEN WHO ARE GOOD?

1   Barbara quoted in Margaret Compton's typescript 'Prelude to Arcadia'. Girton College Archive GBR/0271/GCPP Parkes 15/70.

2   James Joseph Sylvester to Barbara, 21 November 1854. Women's Library Collection at LSE Library, 7BMC/C/01.

3   Marian Evans to Barbara, 13 June 1856. Eliot, *George Eliot Letters*, vol. 2, p. 254.

4   Anna Mary Howitt to John Chapman, 1 October 1855. Transcribed in Beaky, *Letters*, no. 29.

5   Barbara to Marian Evans, 14 January 1856. Beinecke Rare Book and Manuscript Library, Yale University, GEN MSS 963.

6   Barbara to Benjamin Leigh Smith, [1856]. Hancox Archive (original not seen).

7   Ibid.

8   Barbara to Marian Evans (Mrs Cross), 8 May [c. 1880]. Beinecke Rare Book and Manuscript Library, Yale University, GEN MSS 963.

9   Eliot, *Journals of George Eliot*, p. 62.

10   Marian Evans to Barbara, 26 December 1860. Eliot, *George Eliot Letters*, vol. 3, p. 366.

11   Quotations from the petition taken from the *Fife Herald*, 28 February 1856.

12   Mary Howitt to Anna Mary Howitt, [January 1856]. Quoted in Howitt, *Autobiography*, vol. 2, p. 115.

13   *Saturday Review*, 14 February 1857.

14   Ibid., 18 July 1857.

15   *An American Diary 1857–8*, p. 51. (See Chapter 7, note 9.)

16   Matilda Hays to Benjamin Leigh Smith, [1856]. Hancox Archive (original not seen).

17   Barbara to Marian Evans, 21 November and 8 December 1856. Beinecke Rare Book and Manuscript Library, Yale University, GEN MSS 963.

18   See Bencherif, *British in Algiers* (unpaginated).

19   Barbara to Bessie Rayner Parkes, [1856]. Girton College Archive GBR/0271/GCPP Parkes 5/176.

20   Dante Gabriel Rossetti's brother (William Michael) considered Barbara's painting of Ventnor to be 'capital' and 'full of real Pre-Raphaelitism'. Even Ruskin was complimentary, praising an accomplished watercolour of a Sussex cornfield. Bessie was excited by the praise, boasting that her friend was shaping up to be a great artist. See Girton's exhibition catalogue *Barbara Bodichon 1827–1891*.

21 Barbara Leigh Smith, *Women and Work*, pp. 18, 15.
22 Ibid., p. 50.
23 *Saturday Review*, 18 July 1857.
24 *London Daily News*, 8, 12, 24 and 26 November 1856.
25 Quoted in Burton, *Barbara Bodichon*, p. 103.
26 Piper, *History of Robertsbridge*, p. 26.
27 'Eugène Bodichon; A Republican of 1830'.
28 Hancox Archive.
29 Barbara to Bessie Rayner Parkes, April 1857, quoted in Marie Belloc-Lowndes's typescript 'Before She Found Arcadia'. Girton College Archive GBR/0271/GCPP Parkes 16/1/7, pp. 539–40.
30 Dr Guépin to Elizabeth Parkes, n.d. Ibid., pp. 542–3.
31 Jessie Meriton White to Bessie Rayner Parkes, [1857]. Girton College Archive GBR/0271/GCPP Parkes 9/143a.

7. BOADICEA IN AMERICA

1 Betham-Edwards, *Reminiscences*, p. 266.
2 Bessie wrote to Barbara in 1850 that she would not like to marry with a singed heart. Girton College Archive GBR/0271/GCPP Parkes 5/43b.
3 Quoted in Burton, *Barbara Bodichon*, p. 91.
4 This is my assumption; there is no address on the document.
5 Barbara Leigh Smith, *Women and Work*, p. 12.
6 London Metropolitan Archives E/LS/001.
7 See Hirsch, *Barbara Leigh Smith Bodichon*, p. 129, for mention of the rabbit.
8 Barbara calls him 'John Thomas' on this occasion.
9 This and all subsequent quotations from Barbara's letters home from America, which formed her journal, are taken from the originals generously scanned for me during the Covid lockdowns of 2020 and 2021 by the Beinecke Rare Book and Manuscript Library, Yale University, GEN MSS 119, box 1. They were reprinted as *An American Diary 1857–8*, with an introduction by Joseph W. Reed Jr, by Routledge in 1972. Page numbers of the reprint are given for reference. This excerpt appears on p. 134.
10 Barbara's cousin-in-law Arthur Clough writing to Charles Norton, quoted in Clough, *Correspondence*, vol. 2, p. 533.
11 *Wayne County Herald*, 15 July 1858.
12 Colossians 3:18–22, King James Version.
13 Quoted in Bostridge, *Florence Nightingale*, p. 12.
14 *An American Diary 1857–8*, p. 73.
15 Quoted in Betham-Edwards, *Reminiscences*, p. 266.
16 *An American Diary 1857–8*, p. 56.
17 Ibid., p. 65.
18 Ibid., p. 57.
19 *The Express* (London), 14 February 1859.
20 *An American Diary 1857–8*, p. 67.
21 Ibid., p. 91.
22 Ibid., p. 151.

23 Barbara wrote an account of this encounter, 'A Dull Life', published in *Macmillan's Magazine* in May 1867. (See 'Works by Barbara Leigh Smith Bodichon' in 'Select Bibliography'.)

24 *An American Diary 1857–8*, pp. 103–4.

25 Ibid., p. 105.

26 The poem was originally written for *The Star*, a Washington newspaper.

27 Havilland, *Metrical Description*, pp. 13–14.

28 *Charleston Daily Courier*, 7 July 1858.

29 *An American Diary 1857–8*, p. 161.

30 Norman Moore's unpublished 'Casebook', vol. 8 (1887–8), p. 122. Hancox Archive.

31 This fragment is frustratingly stuck down on a page of Barbara's scrapbook of autograph letters at Girton College, GBR/0271/GCPP Bodichon 7/49. It is impossible to read it in its entirety.

32 Hancox Archive.

33 Barbara to Elizabeth Malleson, n.d. Quoted in Stephen, *Emily Davies*, pp. 38–9.

34 *An American Diary 1857–8*, p. 63.

8. WOMEN AND WORK

1 Old Yorkshire proverb.

2 *English Woman's Journal*, vol. 6, no. 32 (October 1860), p. 96.

3 Joseph Parkes described her thus; see Lisa Merrill's entry on Hays, published 23 September 2004 in the online edition of the *Oxford Dictionary of National Biography*.

4 Reprinted in Blackburn, *Women's Suffrage*, pp. 248–9.

5 *English Woman's Journal*, vol. 4, no. 21 (November 1859), p. 145.

6 Ibid., vol. 1, no. 1 (March 1858), pp. 11–12.

7 Ibid., p. 59.

8 *Saturday Review*, 10 April 1858.

9 John Ruskin to Barbara, 14 October [no year given]. Girton College Archive GBR/0271/GCPP Bodichon 7/24.

10 *English Woman's Journal*, vol. 1, no. 2 (April 1858), p. 127.

11 Ibid., vol. 1, no. 6 (August 1858), p. 414.

12 Ibid., vol. 2, no. 10 (December 1858), p. 263.

13 Quoted in ibid., vol. 3, no. 18 (August 1859), p. 380.

14 Ibid., vol. 4, no. 19 (September 1859), p. 14.

15 See Hurtado, *The Company She Kept*, for more information on public art policy during this period.

16 *Saturday Review*, 28 May 1859.

17 Blackwell, *Pioneer Work*, p. 140.

18 Quoted in Lawrence Goldman, 'The Social Science Association', *English Historical Review*, vol. 101, no. 398 (January 1986), p. 97.

19 *English Woman's Journal*, vol. 8, no. 46 (December 1861), pp. 240–41.

20 Ibid., vol. 1, no. 4 (June 1858), p. 227.

9. MADAME BODICHON

1   Bodichon, *An American Diary*, p. 49.
2   Barbara to Marian Evans, n.d. Beinecke Rare Book and Manuscript Library, Yale University, GEN MSS 963.
3   *English Woman's Journal*, vol. 6, no. 31 (September 1860), pp. 21, 23.
4   Barbara to Marian Evans, 2 December [1858]. Beinecke Rare Book and Manuscript Library, Yale University, GEN MSS 963.
5   Davies, *Algiers in 1857*, p. 43.
6   Barbara to Marian Evans, 2 December [1858]. Beinecke Rare Book and Manuscript Library, Yale University, GEN MSS 963.
7   Ibid., early April 1859; 8 December [1858].
8   Barbara to Aunt Ju, [1859?]. Women's Library Collection at LSE Library, 9/08/016.
9   *English Woman's Journal*, vol. 6, no. 31 (September 1860), p. 29.
10 Hancox Archive.
11 Barbara to Anna Jameson, n.d. Quoted in Erskine, *Anna Jameson*, p. 330.
12 Cobden, 'Diary Paris – Algiers'. West Sussex Record Office, Cobden 468; Rogers, *A Winter in Algeria*.
13 I came across this anecdote while researching *Bluestockings* and have to confess that I cannot now locate the source. But I can't resist including it here.
14 Hancox Archive.
15 Barbara to William Allingham, [July 1862]. Quoted in Allingham and Baumer Williams (eds), *Letters to William Allingham*, p. 77.
16 Barbara to Marian Evans, 8 December [1858]. Beinecke Rare Book and Manuscript Library, Yale University, GEN MSS 963.
17 Ibid., 28 September [1859].
18 Elizabeth Blackwell to Barbara, 15 April 1859. Rare Book and Manuscript Library, Columbia University Libraries, MS 0124, box 1, folder 3.
19 Quoted in Burton, *Barbara Bodichon*, p. 138.
20 Barbara to Marian Evans, 25 December 1859. Beinecke Rare Book and Manuscript Library, Yale University, GEN MSS 963.
21 Ibid.
22 Ibid., 27 November [1859?].
23 Ibid.
24 *Illustrated London News*, 20 January 1866; *The Athenaeum*, 3 April 1858; *The Express*, 31 March 1858.
25 *Leamington Spa Courier*, 2 April 1859.
26 Quoted in Nimura, *The Doctors Blackwell*, p. 216.
27 Elizabeth Blackwell to Barbara, 25 April 1860. Rare Book and Manuscript Library, Columbia University Libraries, MS 0124, box 1, folder 2.
28 Ibid., 25 August [1870?].
29 Bessie Parkes to Barbara, 30 August 1859. Girton College Archive GBR/0271/GCPP Parkes 5/90.
30 Quoted in Hirsch, *Barbara Leigh Smith Bodichon*, p. 164.
31 Quoted in Chadwick, *Women, Art and Society*, p. 189.
32 Barbara to Bessie Parkes, 27 December 1861. Girton College Archive GBR/0271/GCPP Parkes 5/178.

33 Barbara to William Allingham, June 1868. Quoted in Allingham and Baumer Williams (eds), *Letters to William Allingham*, p. 84.

34 Barbara to Marian Evans, 28 June 1859. Beinecke Rare Book and Manuscript Library, Yale University, GEN MSS 963.

35 Eliot, *Journals of George Eliot*, p. 301.

36 Barbara to Marian Evans, [July 1863?]. Beinecke Rare Book and Manuscript Library, Yale University, GEN MSS 963.

37 Ibid., 22 December 1860.

38 Hancox Archive.

39 Girton College Archive GBR/0271/GCPP Bodichon 8/4.

40 Ibid.

41 Betham-Edwards, 'Madame Bodichon: A Reminiscence', p. 217.

10. GELLIE BIRDS AND DEAF-ADDERS

1 Emily Davies, quoted in Hunt, *The Wife of Rossetti*, p. 110.

2 I am extremely grateful to the present owners of Scalands for allowing me to see the fireplace, and to Barbara's great-great-great-niece Charlotte Moore for providing me with a list of names, initials and attributions.

3 Betham-Edwards, *Mid-Victorian Memories*, p. 76.

4 Marian Evans to Barbara, 3 October 1859. Eliot, *George Eliot Letters*, vol. 2, p. 171.

5 Kitty Blackwell to Alice Stone Blackwell, 31 October 1870. Library of Congress, MSS 12880, box 73, reel 55, image 26.

6 *Gentleman's Magazine*, February 1867, pp. 215–17.

7 *Saturday Review*, 13 October 1866.

8 Extracts of an earlier draft of *De l'humanité*, translated into English, were published in London in 1859 by Austin Holyoake, who also published the second edition of Barbara's *Brief Summary*. The following quotations are taken from this English translation. No French publisher offered to take it on, though it was published in Brussels in 1866.

9 Barbara to William Allingham, n.d. Quoted in Allingham and Baumer Williams (eds), *Letters to William Allingham*, p. 87.

10 Hancox Archive (original not seen). Quoted in Hirsch, *Barbara Leigh Smith Bodichon*, p. 175.

11 This was the so-called 'Seven Weeks' War' of 1866.

12 Quoted (but unattributed) in Hirsch, *Barbara Leigh Smith Bodichon*, pp. 230–1.

13 The memorial tablet is at All Saints Church, Hastings, half a mile from Pelham Crescent.

14 Barbara to William Allingham, [July 1862]. Quoted in Allingham and Baumer Williams (eds), *Letters to William Allingham*, p. 79.

15 Barbara to Marian Evans, [November 1866]. Beinecke Rare Book and Manuscript Library, Yale University, GEN MSS 963.

16 Ibid.

17 Ibid.

18 Betham-Edwards, *Winter with the Swallows*, pp. 4, 124.

19 Betham-Edwards, *Mid-Victorian Memories*, p. 51.

20   Barbara to Marian Evans, [November 1866]. Beinecke Rare Book and Manuscript Library, Yale University, GEN MSS 963.

21   Quoted in Piper, *History of Robertsbridge*, p. 25.

22   *The Times*, 29 April 1862.

23   Joseph Parkes to Bessie Parkes, 23 January 1864. Girton College Archive GBR/0271/GCPP Parkes 2/79.

24   Barbara to William Allingham, [July 1862]. Quoted in Allingham and Baumer Williams (eds), *Letters to William Allingham*, p. 79.

25   Barbara to William Allingham, 2 August 1863. Quoted in ibid., p. 81.

26   Quoted in Crawford, *The Women's Suffrage Movement*, p. 322.

27   Girton College Archive GBR/0271/GCPP Davies 10/2.

28   Barbara to Helen Taylor, 9 May 1866. Women's Library Collection at LSE Library, Mill-Taylor 12/40.

29   Quoted in Robinson, *Hearts and Minds*, p. 25.

30   For a fascinating discussion of the signatories to this petition, both individually and collectively, see Dingsdale, ' "Generous and Lofty Sympathies" '.

31   Davies, 'Family Chronicle', p. 424. Girton College Archive GBR/0271/GCPP Davies 1.

32   Reprinted in Lacey (ed.), *Barbara Leigh Smith Bodichon*, p. 105.

33   *The Globe*, 11 October 1866; *London Daily News*, 11 October 1866; *Glasgow Herald*, 16 October 1866; *North Wiltshire Herald*, 4 May 1867.

11. OPENING DOORS

1   Barbara to Helen Taylor, 1 August 1869. Women's Library Collection at LSE Library, Mill-Taylor 12/50.

2   Quoted in Crawford, *The Women's Suffrage Movement*, p. 69.

3   Burton, *Barbara Bodichon*, p. 154.

4   *Penny Illustrated Paper*, 1 February 1868.

5   Belloc-Lowndes, *'I, Too, Have Lived in Arcadia'*, p. 52.

6   Ibid., pp. 65–6.

7   Barbara to Emily Blackwell, 28 September [1867]. Schlesinger Library on the History of Women in America, Radcliffe Institute for Advanced Study, Harvard University MC411, folder 185.

8   Mary Howitt to Barbara, 27 June [1867]. British Library, Add. MSS 72832, vol. ix a.

9   Emily Blackwell to Elizabeth Blackwell, n.d. [1867]. Schlesinger Library on the History of Women in America, Radcliffe Institute for Advanced Study, Harvard University MC411, folder 165.

10   Ibid.

11   Barbara to William Allingham, n.d. Quoted in Allingham and Baumer Williams (eds), *Letters to William Allingham*, p. 87.

12   Quoted in Burton, *Barbara Bodichon*, pp. 182–4.

13   Barbara writing home from America, 6 June 1858. Beinecke Rare Book and Manuscript Library, Yale University, GEN MSS 119, box 1. Reprinted in Barbara Leigh Smith Bodichon, *An American Diary*, p. 158.

14   F. A. Butler [Fanny Kemble], *Poems* (Pennsylvania: John Penington, 1844), p. 132.

15 Davies, *The Higher Education of Women*, p. 62.

16 Quoted in Holcombe, *Victorian Ladies at Work*, p. 6.

17 For a closer look at the history of higher education for women and at the experience of early students and educators, see Robinson, *Bluestockings*.

18 Barbara to Helen Taylor, 1 August 1869. Women's Library Collection at LSE Library, Mill-Taylor 12/50.

19 Ibid.

20 Stephen, *Emily Davies*, p. 161.

21 Russell (eds), *The Amberley Papers*, vol. 1, p. 17.

22 Stephen, *Emily Davies*, p. 162.

23 Alfred, Lord Tennyson, *The Princess*, Prologue, line 141, available online.

24 *The Atlas*, 13 March 1868.

25 Quoted in Stephen, *Emily Davies*, p. 162.

26 See Hirsch, *Barbara Leigh Smith Bodichon*, for an account of the committee's deliberations. The Oxford college was Somerville, founded in 1879.

27 Stephen, *Emily Davies*, pp. 214–15.

12. PARALLEL LIVES

1 Betham-Edwards, *Reminiscences*, p. 239.

2 Most of these letters were found in Barbara's family's private collection at Hancox Archive, the house bought by Barbara's niece Milicent in the village where Barbara was born.

3 Henry Maudsley, 'Sex in Mind and Education', *Fortnightly Review*, vol. 15 (January–June 1874), pp. 466–83, at pp. 467, 472.

4 Clarke, *Sex in Education*, p. 18.

5 Davies, 'Some Account of a Proposed New College for Women', p. 552.

6 Quoted in Stephen, *Emily Davies*, p. 280.

7 Ibid., p. 152.

8 Ibid., p. 243.

9 Ibid., p. 244.

10 Barbara to 'Marquis' (Hertha Ayrton), 6 March 1876. British Library, Add. MSS 72832, vol. ix a.

11 See Barbara's undated letter to Bessie Parkes 'To be happy is to work, work – work – for ever!'. Girton College Archive GBR/0271/GCPP Parkes 1/165.

12 The original policy is in Dr Bodichon's name. London Metropolitan Archives, E/LS/004.

13 *Illustrated London News*, 3 February 1877 and 11 February 1871; *Morning Advertiser*, 6 February 1871.

14 Quoted in Moore, *Hancox*, p. 29.

15 In her biography of Barbara, Pam Hirsch names Shadrack Clements as the father, but further research shows him to be married to a different Esther, with a legitimate infant Alfred of his own. On our Alfred's baptism certificate, the father is recorded as unknown.

16 Emily Blackwell to Barbara, 19 July [1874]. Rare Book and Manuscript Library, Columbia University Libraries, MS 0124, box 1, folder 3.

17 Quoted in Sharp, *Hertha Ayrton*, p. 33.

18   Ibid., p. 52.
19   Elizabeth Blackwell to Ellen Blackwell, 8 August 1874. Schlesinger Library on the History of Women in America, Radcliffe Institute for Advanced Study, Harvard University MC411, folder 185.
20   Quoted in Eliot, *George Eliot Letters*, vol. 5, p. 127.
21   Barbara to Norman Moore, [December 1873]. Hancox Archive.
22   Moore, *Hancox*, pp. 109–10.
23   Ibid., p. 113.

13. LOVE IN NEW WAYS

1   Barbara to Aunt Dolly Longden, *c.*1857. Quoted in Burton, *Barbara Bodichon*, p. 21. In *A Mid-Victorian Feminist* Herstein attributes the original letter to the Bonham Carter collection at Hampshire Record Office, but I have failed to trace it.
2   Barbara to Norman Moore, 8 January 1877. Hancox Archive, BLSB 138.
3   Pam Hirsch has estimated that Barbara habitually wrote some fifteen letters each day. It is a testament to the width of her social circle that friends still complained of her negligence.
4   Barbara to Amy Moore, 16 May 1877. Hancox Archive, BLSB 155.
5   She was thus described by Anna Mary Howitt's sister Meggie. Quoted in Lee, *Laurels and Rosemary*, p. 330.
6   Barbara to Norman Moore, 13 May [1877]. Hancox Archive, BLSB 114.
7   Mark Samuels Lasner Collection, University of Delaware.
8   Moore, *Hancox*, p. 117.
9   Jessie White Mario to an unknown recipient, 10 June 1877. Hancox Archive.
10   Reginald Thompson to Norman Moore, 2 June [1877]. Hancox Archive, BLSB 295.
11   Norman Moore's 'A New Journal to Stella', vol. V, 26 May 1877. Hancox Archive.
12   Autograph Letter Collection (scrapbook). Girton College Archive GBR/0271/GCPP Bodichon 7, p. 49. Reproduced by permission of the Trustees of the Henry Bonham-Carter Will Trust.
13   Moore, *Hancox*, p. 129.
14   Hancox Archive, BLSB 306.
15   Marian Evans to Sara Hennell, 16 November 1877. Eliot, *George Eliot Letters*, vol. 6, p. 119.
16   Quoted in Hirsch, *Barbara Leigh Smith Bodichon*, p. 296, and credited to Catherine Barnes, New York.
17   Barbara to Amy Moore, 15 December 1881. Hancox Archive, BLSB 056.
18   Stephen, *Emily Davies*, p. 306.
19   Moore, *Hancox*, p. 141.
20   Emily Davies to Barbara, 25 March 1881. Girton College Archive GBR/0271/GCPP Bodichon 1/174.
21   Hertha Marks to Amy Moore, 21 January 1883. Hancox Archive.
22   Barbara to Marian Evans, 8 May [1880]. Beinecke Rare Book and Manuscript Library, Yale University, GEN MSS 963.
23   Elizabeth Blackwell to Barbara, 3 February [1879?]. Rare Book and

Manuscript Library, Columbia University Libraries, MS 0124, box 1, folder 4.

24 Barbara discussed this possibility in a letter to Marian Evans on 16 July 1874. See Eliot, *George Eliot Letters*, vol. 6, p. 70.

25 See Chapter 3, note 21.

26 The passage that follows in the main text is adapted from Robinson, *Bluestockings*, pp. 57–60, which is in turn based on Bessie Macleod's diary in Girton College Archive (GCRF 4/1/24).

27 18 November 1872. Girton College Archive GBR/0271/GCPP Davies 15/1/5/19.

28 Quoted in Sharp, *Hertha Ayrton*, p. 88.

29 Barbara to Benjamin Leigh Smith, 21 August 1882. Reproduced by permission of the University of Cambridge, Scott Polar Research Institute, MS 653.

30 I'm grateful to Charlotte Moore, Ben Leigh Smith's great-great-great-niece, for the information that before his (or her?) disappearance 'Tibs' survived the winter and accompanied the boats on their escape the following summer. He used to jump out of the boats on to land whenever he could and, on one occasion, he simply failed to return.

31 For a particularly lively account of the expedition, and for this quotation, see Neale, 'Castaways in the Frozen North'.

32 *Nottingham Evening Post*, 21 September 1882.

33 Barbara to Amy Moore, 8 November 1881. Hancox Archive, BLSB 18.

34 These letters are all in the Hancox archive.

35 Nannie Leigh Smith to Amy Moore, 10 January 1885. Hancox Archive.

14. LIVING ON ASPIRATION

1 From Percy Bysshe Shelley, *Queen Mab*, Book III, lines 11–13.

2 This was in an undated letter from Elizabeth Garrett Anderson to an unknown recipient, written from Barbara's house in Blandford Square. 'At present I live upon aspiration,' she said, deliciously. Author's collection.

3 Hancox Archive.

4 Elizabeth Blackwell to Emily Blackwell, 21 March 1885. Schlesinger Library on the History of Women in America, Radcliffe Institute for Advanced Study, Harvard University MC411, folder 48.

5 Ross, *American Embassy Properties in Algiers*, p. 37.

6 I have sourced obituaries in *The Times* (31 January 1885), *The Athenaeum* (7 February 1885), *Journal des débats politiques et littéraires* (12 February 1885) and *La Justice* (13 February 1885).

7 *The Field*, 23 January 1886.

8 Norman Moore to Amy Leigh Smith, 23 April 1878. Hancox Archive.

9 Quoted in Moore, *Hancox*, pp. 178–9.

10 Elizabeth Blackwell to Emily Blackwell, 17 May [c.1885]. Schlesinger Library on the History of Women in America, Radcliffe Institute for Advanced Study, Harvard University MC411, folder 48.

11 Ibid., 21 March 1885.

12 Barbara to Thomas Wentworth Higginson, 13 July 1879. Boston Public Library, MS P.91.37.12.
13 The date range for the information included is 1885–90.
14 Quoted in Sharp, *Hertha Ayrton*, p. 126.
15 E. Phillpot to Amy Moore, 16 June 1891. Hancox Archive.
16 *Hastings and St Leonards Observer*, 20 June 1891.
17 Ibid.
18 *The Times*, 15 June 1891.
19 Bessie Parkes Belloc writing in the *Englishwoman's Review*, 15 July 1891.
20 *Pall Mall Gazette*, 16 June 1891.
21 Bessie Parkes Belloc in *Englishwoman's Review*, 15 July 1891.
22 See Hirsch, *Barbara Leigh Smith Bodichon*, p. 353.
23 *Western Morning News*, 6 June 1905.
24 Mason, 'Hertha Ayrton', p. 210.
25 Quoted in Campbell, *Women in White Coats*, p. 299.
26 An unpublished poem by Alan Moore. Hancox Archive.
27 Anonymous, quoted in Herstein, *A Mid-Victorian Feminist*, p. 191, and attributed by her to a member of the Bonham Carter family whose archive is held at Hampshire Record Office. The Record Office cannot trace it.
28 Catalogue for the University of Hull's exhibition of Barbara Bodichon's work, 9–30 June 1992, p. 2; Hirsch, *Barbara Leigh Smith Bodichon*, p. 132.

Select Bibliography

WORKS BY BARBARA LEIGH SMITH BODICHON

A Brief Summary, in Plain Language, of the Most Important Laws Concerning Women; Together with a Few Observations Thereon [anon.] (London: John Chapman, 1854)

'Life in Algiers' [anon.], *London Daily News*, 8, 12, 24 and 26 November 1856

Women and Work (London: Bosworth and Harrison, 1857)

An American Diary 1857–8, ed. Joseph W. Reed Jr (London: Routledge & Kegan Paul, 1972)

Algeria Considered as a Winter Residence for the English [co-written with Dr Eugène Bodichon] (London: English Woman's Journal Office, 1858)

'Submission to the Report of the Commissioners Appointed to Inquire into the State of Popular Education' (1858), Parliamentary Papers, 21 (London: Eyre and Spottiswoode, 1861)

'Kabyle Pottery', *Art Journal*, February 1865

Objections to the Enfranchisement of Women Considered (London: J. Bale, 1866)

Reasons for the Enfranchisement of Women . . . Read at the Meeting of the National Association for the Promotion of Social Science at Manchester (London: J. Bale, 1866)

'Authorities and Precedents for giving the Suffrage to Qualified Women', *Englishwoman's Review of Social and Industrial Questions*, January 1867

'A Dull Life', *Macmillan's Magazine*, May 1867

'Australian Forests and Algerian Deserts', ed. George Lewes, *Pall Mall Gazette*, May 1868

'An Easy Railway Journey in Spain', *Temple Bar*, January 1869

'A Conversation on the Enfranchisement of Female Freeholders and Householders', *Englishwoman's Review of Social and Industrial Questions*, April 1873

Letters/articles in the *Birmingham Journal*, the *Hastings and St Leonards Observer* and *The Leader*

Articles in the English Woman's Journal

'Female Education in the Middle Classes', June 1858

'Slavery in America', October 1858

'An American School', November 1858

'The Market for Educated Female Labour' [co-written with Bessie Parkes], November 1859

'Slave Preaching', March 1860

'Algiers: First Impressions', September 1860

'Middle-Class Schools for Girls', November 1860

'Slavery in the South', October–December 1861

'Cleopatra's Daughter, St Marciana, Mama Marabout and Other Algerian Women', February 1863

'Of Those Who Are the Property of Others and of the Great Power that Holds Others as Property', February 1863

'Painted Glass Windows Executed by the Carmelite Nuns of Mans', February 1863

'Six Weeks in la Chère Petite Bretagne', May 1863

'Accomplices', February 1864

PRINCIPAL ARCHIVE SOURCES WITH A BRIEF DESCRIPTION OF HOLDINGS

Beinecke Rare Book and Manuscript Library, Yale University (New Haven, Connecticut): George Eliot and George Henry Lewes Collection; John Chapman Collection; Barbara Leigh Smith Bodichon Collection

Bishopsgate Institute Special Collections and Archives (London): Records of the National Association for the Promotion of Social Science

Boston Public Library (Massachusetts): Bodichon and Rossetti papers

British Library (London): Clough–Shore Smith papers

Cambridge University Library: Smith family papers including MS journal by Benjamin Smith and Lady Stephen's typescript 'Life of William Smith'

Claydon House Trust Archives (Buckinghamshire): Smith/Nightingale family papers, letters and reminiscences

Delaware Art Museum (Wilmington): Bodichon artwork and papers

Dr Williams's Library (London): Unitarian records

Girton College Archive (Cambridge): papers of Barbara Bodichon, Emily Davies, Bessie Rayner Parkes, Lady Stephen

Hampshire Record Office (Winchester): Bonham Carter papers

Hancox Archive (private collection): Leigh Smith family artwork, memorabilia and papers

Houghton Library, Harvard University (Cambridge, Massachusetts): Bodichon and Howitt papers

Library of Congress (Washington, DC): Kitty Barry Blackwell papers (1855–1938)

London Metropolitan Archives: Smith and Bodichon legal papers and documents; photographs of the Smith Distillery/brewery

Mark Samuels Lasner Collection, University of Delaware (Wilmington): artwork and papers (Bodichon, Rossetti and their circle)

Massachusetts Historical Society (Boston): Bodichon papers

Morgan Library (New York): Daubigny, Howitt, Lewes, Procter and Rossetti papers

National Library of Scotland (Edinburgh): Jane Burdon Sanderson and Bodichon papers

New York Public Library: Lewes and Bodichon papers

Princeton University Library: Bodichon and Rossetti papers

Rare Book and Manuscript Library, Columbia University Libraries (New York): Elizabeth Blackwell papers

Schlesinger Library on the History of Women in America, Radcliffe Institute for Advanced Study, Harvard University (Cambridge, Massachusetts): Blackwell family papers

Scott Polar Research Institute, University of Cambridge: Bodichon/Leigh Smith papers/photographs

West Sussex Record Office (Chichester): Cobden papers

Women's Library Collection at LSE Library (London): papers relating to members of the Langham Place circle; women's suffrage campaign records

SELECT PERIODICALS

The Germ: Thoughts Towards Nature in Poetry, Literature, and Art (1850)
Illustrated London News (as detailed in 'Notes and References', pp. 360 and 363)
Saturday Review of Politics, Literature, Science, and Art (1856–1917)
The Una: A Paper Devoted to the Elevation of Woman (1853–5)
Victoria Magazine (1863–78)
Waverley [or *Waverly*] *Journal* (1856–7)
Westminster Review (1824–1914)

BOOKS, ARTICLES AND PHD THESES

Allingham, Helen, and E. Baumer Williams (eds), *Letters to William Allingham* (London: Longman Green, 1911)

Allingham, William, *A Diary*, ed. H. Allingham and D. Radford (London: Macmillan, 1907)

Ashton, Rosemary, *142 Strand: A Radical Address in Victorian London* (London: Jonathan Cape, 2007)

Atkinson, Diane, *The Criminal Conversation of Mrs Norton* (London: Preface, 2012)

Beaky, Lenore Ann, 'The Letters of Anna Mary Howitt to Barbara Leigh Smith Bodichon', PhD thesis, Columbia University, New York, 1974

Belloc, Bessie Rayner, 'A Great Englishwoman' [obituary], *Review of Reviews*, vol. 4, no. 20 (1891), p. 162

—*A Passing World* (London: Ward and Downey, 1897)

Belloc-Lowndes, Mrs, *'I, Too, Have Lived in Arcadia': A Record of Love and Childhood* (London: Macmillan, 1941)

—*Where Love and Friendship Dwelt* (London: Macmillan, 1943)

Bencherif, Osman, *The British in Algiers* (Algiers: R. S. M. Communications, 2001)

Betham-Edwards, M., *Friendly Faces of Three Nationalities* (London: Chapman & Hall, 1911)

—*In French-Africa: Scenes and Memories* (London: Chapman & Hall, 1912)

—'Madame Bodichon: A Reminiscence', *Fortnightly Review*, vol. 51, no. 302 (1892), pp. 213–18

—*Mid-Victorian Memories* (London: Macmillan, 1919)

—*Reminiscences* (London: George Redway, 1898)

—*Through Spain to the Sahara* (London: Hurst and Blackett, 1868)

—*A Winter with the Swallows* (London: Hurst and Blackett, 1867)

Birney, Margaret, 'Women's Colleges in Nineteenth-Century Britain: Their Architectural and Social Context', 2 vols, PhD thesis, Stanford University, Stanford, 1993

Blackburn, Helen, *Women's Suffrage: A Record of the Women's Suffrage Movement in the British Isles* (London: Williams and Norgate, 1902)

Blackwell, Elizabeth, *Pioneer Work in Opening the Medical Profession for Women* (London: Longmans, Green, 1895)

Bodichon, Eugène, *Of Humanity* [abridged translation] (London: Holyoake & Co., 1859)

Bostridge, Mark, *Florence Nightingale: The Woman and Her Legend* (London: Viking, 2008)

Bradbrook, Muriel, *Barbara Bodichon, George Eliot and the Limits of Feminism* [James Bryce lecture] (Oxford: Somerville College, 1975)

—*'That Infidel Place': A Short History of Girton College 1869–1969*, rev. edn (Cambridge: Girton College, 1984)

Browne, J. Ross, *An American Family in Germany* (New York: Harper & Bros., 1866)

Bruton, Elizabeth, 'The Life and Material Culture of Hertha Marks Ayrton (1854–1923): Suffragette, Physicist, Mathematician and Inventor', *Science Museum Group Journal*, no. 10 (2018)

Buchanan, Barbara Isabella, *Buchanan Family Records: James Buchanan and His Descendants* (Capetown: Townshend, Taylor and Snashall [printed for private circulation], 1923)

Burton, Hester, *Barbara Bodichon 1827–1891* (London: John Murray, 1949)

Callen, Anthea, *The Work of Art: Plein Air Painting and Artistic Identity in 19th-Century France* (London: Reaktion, 2015)

Campbell, Olivia, *Women in White Coats: How the First Women Doctors Changed the World of Medicine* (Toronto: Park Row Books, 2022)

Capelotti, P. J., *The Coldest Coast: The 1873 Leigh Smith Expedition to Svalbard in the Diaries and Photographs of Herbert Chermside* (Chamonix: Springer, 2021)

—*Shipwreck at Cape Flora: The Expeditions of Benjamin Leigh Smith, England's Forgotten Arctic Explorer* (Calgary: University of Calgary Press, 2013)

Chadwick, Whitney, *Women, Art and Society* (London: Thames & Hudson, 1990)

Cherry, Deborah, *Beyond the Frame: Feminism and Visual Culture, Britain 1850–1900* (London: Routledge, 2000)

—*Painting Women: Victorian Women Artists* (London: Routledge, 1993)

Clarke, Edward H., *Sex in Education; or, A Fair Chance for Girls* (Boston: James Osgood, 1873)

Clough, Arthur, *The Correspondence of Arthur Hugh Clough*, ed. Frederick L. Mulhausen, 2 vols (Oxford: Clarendon Press, 1957)

Crabbe, John, 'An Artist Divided: The Forgotten Talent of Barbara Bodichon, a Very Remarkable Victorian', *Apollo*, vol. 113, no. 231 (1981), pp. 311–13

—'Feminist with a Paintbrush', *Women Artists' Slide Library Journal*, vol. 22 (April/May 1988) [unpaginated]

—'Wild Weather in Watercolour', *Country Life*, vol. 183, no. 9 (1989), pp. 100–01

Crawford, Elizabeth, *The Women's Suffrage Movement: A Reference Guide 1866–1928* (London: Routledge, 2001)

Cross, J. W., *George Eliot's Life as Related in her Letters and Journals*, 3 vols (Edinburgh: Blackwood, 1885)

Cutler, Carl, *Greyhounds of the Sea: The Story of the American Clipper Ship* (Annapolis, MD: Naval Institute Press, 1961)

Davies, Edward, *Algiers in 1857: Its Accessibility, Climate, and Resources with Especial Reference to English Invalids* (London: Longman, Brown, Green et al., 1858)

Davies, Emily, *The Higher Education of Women* (London: Alexander Strachan, 1866)

—'Some Account of a Proposed New College for Women', *Contemporary Review*, vol. 9 (December 1868), pp. 540–57

Dingsdale, Ann, ' "Generous and Lofty Sympathies": The Kensington Society, the 1866 Women's Suffrage Petition and the Development of Mid-Victorian Feminism', PhD thesis, University of Greenwich, London, 1995

Doughty, Oswald (ed.), *The Letters of Dante Gabriel Rossetti*, 4 vols (Oxford: Oxford University Press, 1965–7)

Dredge, Sarah, 'Opportunism and Accommodation: The *English Woman's Journal* and the British Mid-Nineteenth-Century Women's Movement', *Women's Studies*, vol. 34, no. 2 (2005), pp. 133–57

Druett, Joan, *Hen Frigates: Wives of Merchant Captains Under Sail* (London: Souvenir Press, 1998)

Eisenberg, Michelle, 'The Chronicles of George Henry Lewes: 1869: "A wasted year." A Transcription of Diary and Journal Entries with Introduction and Notes', PhD thesis, Northern Illinois University, DeKalb, IL, 2015

Eliot, George, *The George Eliot Letters*, ed. Gordon S. Haight, 9 vols (New Haven, CT: Yale University Press, 1954–78)

—*The Journals of George Eliot*, ed. Margaret Harris and Judith Johnston (Cambridge: Cambridge University Press, 1998)

Erskine, Beatrice, *Anna Jameson: Letters and Friendships 1812–1860* (London: T. Fisher Unwin, 1915)

'Eugene Bodichon; A Republican of 1830', *Temple Bar*, vol. 74 (July 1885), pp. 331–40

Gandy, Frances, Kate Perry and Peter Sparks (eds), *Barbara Bodichon 1827–1891* (Cambridge: Girton College, 1991)

Gaskell, Elizabeth, *The Letters of Mrs Gaskell*, ed. J. A. V. Chapple and Arthur Pollard (Manchester: Manchester University Press, 1966)

—*Letters of Mrs. Gaskell and Charles Eliot Norton, 1855–1865*, ed. Jane Whitehall (London: Oxford University Press, 1932)

Gill, Gillian, *Nightingales: The Extraordinary Upbringing and Curious Life of Miss Florence Nightingale* (New York: Random House, 2005)

Haight, Gordon S., *George Eliot and John Chapman, with Chapman's Diaries* (New Haven, CT: Yale University Press, 1940)

Handley, Jenny, and Hazel Lake, *Progress by Persuasion: The Life of William Smith 1756–1835* (n.p.: H. Lake, 2007)

Havilland, John von Sonntag de, *A Metrical Description of a Fancy Ball Given at Washington, 9th April 1858* (Washington, DC: Franklin Philp, 1858)

Herstein, Sheila R., *A Mid-Victorian Feminist: Barbara Leigh Smith Bodichon* (New Haven, CT: Yale University Press, 1985)

[Higgins, Lee] https://lifeandtimesofflorencenightingale.wordpress.com/family-history-2/leigh-smith (accessed June 2022)

Hirsch, Pam, *Barbara Leigh Smith Bodichon: Feminist, Artist and Rebel* (London: Chatto & Windus, 1998)

Holcombe, Lee, *Victorian Ladies at Work* (Newton Abbot: David & Charles, 1973)

—*Wives & Property: Reform of the Married Women's Property Law in Nineteenth-Century England* (Toronto: University of Toronto Press, 1983)

Howitt, Anna Mary, *An Art-Student in Munich*, 2 vols (Longman, Brown et al., 1853)

—'The Sisters in Art', *Cassell's Illustrated Exhibitor & Magazine of Art*, vol. 2 (1852)

—'Unpainted Pictures', *The Crayon*, January–March 1856, pp. 4–5

Howitt, Mary, *An Autobiography*, ed. Margaret Howitt, 2 vols (Cambridge: Cambridge University Press, 2011)

Hunt, Violet, *The Wife of Rossetti: Her Life and Death* (London: John Lane, 1932)

Hurtado, Shannon, *The Company She Kept: Susan D. Durant, a Nineteenth-Century Sculptor and her Feminist Connections*, MA thesis, University of Manitoba, Winnipeg, 1994

'In Memoriam' [obituary], *Woman's Journal*, vol. 22, no. 30 (1891) p. 242

Jameson, Anna, *Characteristics of Women, Moral, Poetical and Historical*, 2 vols (London: Saunders & Otley, 1858)

Lacey, Candida Ann (ed.), *Barbara Leigh Smith Bodichon and the Langham Place Group* (London: Routledge & Kegan Paul, 1987)

Lee, Amice, *Laurels and Rosemary: The Life of William and Mary Howitt* (London: Oxford University Press, 1955)

Lowndes, Emma, *Turning Victorian Ladies into Women: The Life of Bessie Rayner Parkes 1829–1925* (Bethesda, MD: Academica Press, 2012)

Malleson, Elizabeth, *Autobiographical Notes and Letters* (London: [printed for private circulation], 1926)

—'Portrait of a School', *Journal of Education*, vol. 18 (September 1886), pp. 357–9

Marsh, Jan, *The Legend of Elizabeth Siddal* (London: Quartet, 1989)

—*The Pre-Raphaelite Sisterhood* (London: Quartet, 1985)

—and Pamela Gerish Nunn, *Women Artists and the Pre-Raphaelite Movement* (London: Virago, 1989)

Mason, Joan, 'Hertha Ayrton (1854–1923) and the Admission of Women to the Royal Society of London', *Notes & Records of Royal Society*, vol. 45 (1991), pp. 201–20

Mill, John Stuart, *Principles of Political Economy: With Some of Their Application to Social Philosophy*, 2 vols, rev. edn (London: John W. Parker, 1852)

Moore, Charlotte, *Hancox: A House and a Family* (London: Viking, 2010)

Morris, Jane, *The Collected Letters of Jane Morris*, ed. Frank C. Sharp and Jan Marsh (Woodbridge: Boydell Press, 2012)

Neale, W. H., 'Castaways in the Frozen North', *Wide World Magazine*, vol. 1 (April–September 1898), pp. 100–04

Nestor, Pauline, 'Female Friendships in Mid-Victorian England: New Patterns and Possibilities', *Literature & History*, vol. 17, no. 1 (2008), pp. 36–47

—'Negotiating a Self: Barbara Bodichon in America and Algiers', *Postcolonial Studies*, vol. 8, no. 2 (2005), pp. 155–64

Nimura, Janice P., *The Doctors Blackwell: How Two Pioneering Sisters Brought Medicine to Women – and Women to Medicine* (New York: W. W. Norton, 2021)

Oguri, Setsuyo, 'Barbara L. S. Bodichon as a Pioneer in Girls' Education', https://aichi-pu.repo.nii.ac.jp, 2011, pp. 87–118 (accessed June 2022)

Oliphant, Margaret, 'Laws Concerning Women', *Blackwood's Magazine*, vol. LXXIX (April 1856), pp. 379–87

Parkes, Bessie Rayner, *Essays on Woman's Work*, 2nd edn (London: A. Strahan, 1866)

—*Remarks on the Education of Girls, with Reference to the Social, Legal, and Industrial Position of Women in the Present Day*, 3rd edn (London: John Chapman, 1856)

—*Summer Sketches, and Other Poems* (London: John Chapman, 1854)

Percival, Alicia, *About Vincent Square* (London: Vincent Square Residents' Group, n.d.)

Picard, Liza, *Victorian London: The Life of a City 1840–1870* (London: Weidenfeld & Nicolson, 2005)

Piper, J. J., *History of Robertsbridge: Salehurst Parish and Neighbourhood*, 2nd edn (St Leonards-on-Sea: Belderson, 1906)

Raven, Faith, and Nigel Leask, *Ardtornish: Its Houses, Families and Friends 1830–1930* (Morvern: Ardtornish Publishing, 2018)

Rees, Joan, *Matilda Betham Edwards* (Hastings: Hastings Press, 2006)

'Reminiscences of Old Hastings', *Temple Bar*, vol. 118 (October 1899), pp. 262–74.

Rendall, Jane (ed.), *Equal or Different: Women's Politics 1800–1914* (Oxford: Blackwell, 1987)

—*The Origins of Modern Feminism: Women in Britain, France and the United States 1780–1860* (Basingstoke: Macmillan, 1985)

—*Sexuality and Subordination: Interdisciplinary Studies of Gender in the Nineteenth Century* (London: Routledge, 1989)

Robinson, Jane, *Bluestockings: The Remarkable Story of the First Women to Fight for an Education* (London: Viking, 2009)

—*Hearts and Minds: The Untold Story of the Great Pilgrimage and How Women Won the Vote* (London: Doubleday, 2018)

—*Mary Seacole: The Charismatic Black Nurse Who Became a Heroine of the Crimea* (London: Constable & Robinson, 2005)

—*Unsuitable for Ladies: An Anthology of Women Travellers* (Oxford: Oxford University Press, 1994)

Rogers, Mrs G., *A Winter in Algeria 1863–4* (London: Sampson Low et al., 1865)

Rogers, Rebecca, 'Telling Stories About the Colonies: British and French Women in Algeria in the Nineteenth Century', *Gender & History*, vol. 21, no. 1 (2009), pp. 39–59

Ross, Christopher, *American Embassy Properties in Algiers: Their Origins and History*, https://dz.usembassy.gov/wp-content/uploads/sites/236/2017/04/History-American-Embassy-Properties-in-Algiers.pdf

Rossetti, Christina, *The Letters of Christina Rossetti*, ed. Antony H. Harrison, vol. 1 (Charlottesville, VA: University of Virginia Press, 1997)

Rossetti, Dante Gabriel, *The Correspondence of Dante Gabriel Rossetti*, ed. William E. Fredeman, vol. 1 (Cambridge: D. S. Brewer, 2002)

—*His Family-Letters*, 2 vols (London: Ellis & Elvey, 1895)

—*Letters of Dante Gabriel Rossetti to William Allingham 1854–1870*, ed. George Birkbeck Hill (London: T. Fisher Unwin, 1897)

Royal Commission on Education: Answers to the Circular of Questions, 1860 (London: H. M. Stationery Office, 1861)

Russell, Bertrand, and Patricia (eds), *The Amberley Papers: The Letters and Diaries of Lord and Lady Amberley* (London: Hogarth Press, 1937)

Sharp, Evelyn, *Hertha Ayrton 1854–1923: A Memoir* (London: Edward Arnold, 1926)

Simon-Martin, Meritxell, *Barbara Bodichon's Epistolary Education: Unfolding Feminism* (London: Palgrave Macmillan, 2020)

—*Epistolarity*, https://meritxellsimonmartin.wordpress.com (accessed March 2023)

Spender, Dale, *Feminist Theorists: Three Centuries of Women's Intellectual Traditions* (London: Women's Press, 1983)

Stephen, Barbara, *Emily Davies and Girton College* (London: Constable, 1927)

Strachey, Ray, *The Cause: A Short History of the Women's Movement in Great Britain* (London: G. Bell, 1928)

Swiridoff, Christine, 'Writing for a Cause: The "English Woman's Journal" and Women's Work, 1858–1864', PhD thesis, Temple University, Philadelphia, PA, 2005

Tuke, Margaret J., *A History of Bedford College for Women 1849–1937* (London: Oxford University Press, 1939)

Uglow, Jenny, *George Eliot* (London: Virago, 2008)

Vickery, Margaret Birney, *Buildings for Bluestockings: The Architectural and Social History of Women's Colleges in Late Victorian England* (Newark, DE: University of Delaware Press, 1999)

Wollstonecraft, Mary, *Thoughts on the Education of Daughters*, ed. Janet Todd (Bristol: Thoemmes Press, 1995)

Woodring, Carl, *Victorian Samplers: William and Mary Howitt* (Lawrence, KS: University of Kansas Press, 1952)

Woolf, Virginia, *A Room of One's Own* and *Three Guineas*, ed. Hermione Lee (London: Penguin, 2013)

Worzala, Diane, 'The Langham Place Circle: The Beginnings of the Organized Women's Movement in England, 1854–1870', PhD thesis, University of Wisconsin, Madison, 1982

Acknowledgements

M Y FIRST THANKS GO TO BARBARA'S KINSWOMAN Charlotte Moore, who welcomed me to Hancox, her magical home in East Sussex, and shared the family's collections with such generous enthusiasm. I'm grateful to her and her brothers and cousins for allowing me not only to take notes and photographs, but to reproduce some of them here. I genuinely could not have written the book without their support. Charlotte was also kind enough to read my manuscript and offered invaluable suggestions and corrections.

Hannah Westall at Girton has been unstinting in her help, arranging for me to spend time in the college archives on my own (during Covid restrictions) and cheerfully answering endless queries. I owe her, and the Mistress and Fellows, a great deal.

In September 2020 I was awarded a Hawthornden Fellowship. This resulted in the opportunity for a solid fortnight's work in Italy, pausing only for fabulous meals cooked by the peerless Marilena and Margherita. And to gaze at the view across Lake Como. I imagined I was Barbara on a painting expedition. It happened again in September 2022, when I was able to complete the first draft of the manuscript in blessed peace. I am grateful to the Hawthornden Trustees, David Campbell in particular, for making this possible, and to Marwa Helal, Ricardo Alberto Maldonado and Stephen Walsh for their inspiring company.

Meeting Mark Samuels Lasner in Delaware was a joy. His sympathy for Barbara and her work is matched only by his expertise, and working my way through his collection was one of my research highlights. It was a privilege to be welcomed 'backstage' at the Delaware Art Museum by Dr Margaretta Frederick. She is a connoisseur of Barbara's painting, happy to share her appreciation.

I can't express how thankful I am to all the librarians and archivists in this country and abroad who were kind enough to scan documents for me when the pandemic made it impossible to examine them in person. Several institutions refused to accept payment, which really is above and beyond . . . I'm particularly indebted to staff at Boston Public Library; Boston University Libraries; the Houghton and Schlesinger Libraries at Harvard; Isle of Wight Record Office; Massachusetts Historical Society; the Middle East Centre Library, St Antony's College, Oxford; the Morgan Library in New York; the National Library of Scotland; New York Public Library; Princeton University Library Special Collections; the Scott Polar Research Institute, Cambridge; and the Beinecke Rare Book and Manuscript Library at Yale.

For accommodating visits during a particularly difficult couple of years, I must thank the staff at the Bishopsgate Institute in London; the Bodleian Library, Oxford; the British Library; Claydon House; the Syndics of Cambridge University Library; East Sussex Record Office; the Foundling Museum; Hampshire Record Office; London Metropolitan Archives; the Morgan Library; the Rare Book and Manuscript Library at Columbia University, New York; West Sussex Record Office; and the Women's Library at the LSE.

My dear friend Caroline Schimmel gave me a home in New York during visits to the States – and much more besides. More, in fact, than I could ever thank her for. For other invaluable services rendered I'm grateful to Maria Motúnráyò Adébísí, Sue Baxter, Nathalie Belkin, Dan Benedetti, Jo Blyghton, Carole Bourne-Taylor, Janette Bright, Mrs Chippy, Mark Daly, Madeleine Dickens, Richard Ebdon, Marie Elven, Emmy, Gillian

Gill, Pam Hirsch, Caitlin Kennedy, Filipe Lowndes Marques and family, Cresta Norris, Tom Oliver, Jonathan G. Ouvry, Kate Parker, Sarah Prince of the Elizabeth Gaskell Family Collection, Helen Richards, Mariam Rosser-Owen, Charles Rossetti, the Singer family, Ginny Thomas, Véronique Tison and Katharine Weston Smith. As ever, my agent Véronique Baxter and editor Susanna Wadeson have been and continue to be brilliant. I'm beyond grateful to them both.

This book was commissioned during lockdown. Having something to work on from home was a lifeline during those dark days, and so was the far-flung family's weekly online chat. Thank you so much, Richard, Tammy, Molly, Ed and Gabriela, for all your love, support and high spirits. And Bruce: you mean the world to me. I have dedicated *Trailblazer* to our son, Dr Ed James, who reminds me of Barbara in so many ways. He's a feminist, an activist and one of the kindest (and wittiest) people I know. Go well, Ed.

Picture Acknowledgements

Every effort has been made to contact copyright holders. Any who have not been acknowledged here are invited to get in touch with the publishers.

PLATE SECTION

1 *Barbara Leigh Smith Bodichon* by Emily Osborn, n.d.: The Mistress and Fellows, Girton College, Cambridge (GCPH 11/33/31)

2:1 William Smith by John Opie: courtesy Hancox Archive

2:2 Benjamin Smith, 'the Pater': courtesy Hancox Archive

2:3 Nannie Leigh Smith and Isa Blythe: courtesy Hancox Archive

3:1 Aunt Julia: courtesy Hancox Archive

3:2 Benjamin Leigh Smith: courtesy Hancox Archive

3:3 Bella Leigh Smith: courtesy Hancox Archive

3:4 Sketch of Willy Leigh Smith by his wife Georgina: courtesy Hancox Archive

4:1 Pelham Crescent, Hastings (headed notepaper): The Mistress and Fellows, Girton College, Cambridge (GCPP Parkes 10/112a pt)

4:2 The front door at Scalands: courtesy Hancox Archive

4:3 Signed bricks from the Scalands hearth: courtesy Simon and Katharine Weston Smith. Photograph © Bruce James

5:1 *Ventnor, Isle of Wight* by Barbara L. S. Bodichon, 1856: Delaware Art Museum, F. V. du Pont Acquisition Fund, 2016

5:2 *Ireland – 1846* by Barbara L. S. Bodichon: image © The Whitworth, The University of Manchester. Photography by Michael Pollard

6:1 Barbara and her servant Hamet in Algiers: The Mistress and Fellows, Girton College, Cambridge (GCPP Bodichon 7 pt)

6:2 Barbara's drawing of Eugène Bodichon: Hampshire Record Office (94M72/F648)

6:3 Campagne du Pavillon, Algiers: Hampshire Record Office (94M72/F648)

7 *Louisiana Swamp* by Barbara L. S. Bodichon, *c.*1858: Mark Samuels Lasner Collection, University of Delaware Library, Museums and Press

8:1 *Study of Sunflowers* by Barbara L. S. Bodichon, n.d.: The Mistress and Fellows, Girton College, Cambridge (GCPH 11/33/2)

8:2 *Pear* by Barbara L. S. Bodichon, n.d.: Delaware Art Museum, Acquisition Fund, 2017

8:3 *Hertha Ayrton (1854–1923)* by Helena Darmesteter, 1906: The Mistress and Fellows, Girton College, Cambridge (GCPH 11/33/13)

IN-TEXT ILLUSTRATIONS

frontispiece: Barbara, 1850: The Mistress and Fellows, Girton College, Cambridge (GCPP Bodichon 5/2; image cropped and transposed)

page 33: Sketch of a family performance of *Twelfth Night* by Barbara L. S. Bodichon, n.d.: courtesy Hancox Archive

page 72: *Ye Newe Generation* by Barbara L. S. Bodichon, *c.*1850: The Mistress and Fellows, Girton College, Cambridge (GCPP Bodichon 8/6pt)

page 74: *People Looking at Our Carriage* by Barbara L. S. Bodichon, 1844: The Mistress and Fellows, Girton College, Cambridge (GCPP Bodichon 8/2)

page 82: *Effects of Tight Lacing* by Barbara L. S. Bodichon, *c.*1858: Delaware Art Museum, Acquisition Fund, 2017

page 112: Sketch of Lizzie Siddal by Barbara L. S. Bodichon, 1854: Mark Samuels Lasner Collection, University of Delaware Library, Museums and Press

page 118: John Chapman, January 1895: frontispiece to the *Westminster Review*

page 147: Sketch of a lily by Barbara L. S. Bodichon, 1857: courtesy Hancox Archive

page 227: Eugène Bodichon: from *In French-Africa* by M. Betham-Edwards, 1912

page 250: *Barbara Leigh Smith in the pursuit of Art . . .*, n.d.: The Mistress and Fellows, Girton College, Cambridge (GCPP Bodichon 8/6pt)

page 307: *Too Late* by Barbara L. S. Bodichon, n.d.: courtesy Hancox Archive

page 326: Sketch of George Eliot by Barbara L. S. Bodichon: George Eliot and George Henry Lewes Collection. General Collection, Beinecke Rare Book and Manuscript Library, Yale University (GEN MSS 963, box 62, folder IX.4.j; image enhanced by the author)

page 339: *Bar coming home . . .*, n.d.: The Mistress and Fellows, Girton College, Cambridge (GCPP Bodichon 8/14)

Index

Breach, Alice and Dennis 288
Bremer, Fredrika 43; *Hertha* 289, 343
Brewer, Mr (servant) 19, 21
Bridell-Fox, Eliza *see* Fox, Eliza
Bristol Times and Mirror 266
British Institution 85, 208
British Medical Register 260, 346
British Museum 89, 179
Brontë, Charlotte 59; *Shirley* 58, 60
Brooklyn Museum, New York 337
Brougham, Henry Brougham, 1st Baron
   36, 39, 40, 137, 194
Brown, Ford Madox 106, 113, 220
Browning, Elizabeth Barrett 90, 184,
   346, 347
Browning, Robert 151, 285, 346, 347
Brown's, nr Robertsbridge, Sussex 22,
   28, 31, 221, 228, 286, 323, 331,
   335
Bruce Castle, Tottenham, London 41
Bryce, James 264
Buchanan, Anne 41
Buchanan, Isabella 41
Buchanan, President James 166
Buchanan, James 37–9, 40–41, 46–7,
   49, 50, 62, 96, 98, 100, 109,
   114, 200, 203, 261, 326–7, 345
Buchanan, William 41
Buckingham Advertiser and Free Press 266
Burden, Jane *see* Morris, Jane
Burdett-Coutts, Angela 110
Burgess, Sophy 286
Burne-Jones, Edward 84
Burne-Jones, Georgiana 84
Burton, Hester: *Barbara Bodichon
   1827–1891* 4
Buss, Abraham 19, 21, 105
Buss, Frances 240, 277
Buss, Jane 105–7
Buss, Kezia 19, 21, 105
Buss, William 106
Butler, Josephine 243
Byron, George Byron, 6th Baron 184,
   252

Cambridge University 7, 49, 65, 73,
   75–6, 103, 109, 129, 260, 276,
   308, 315, 336; *see also* Girton
   College
Carlyle, Thomas 89, 273, 345, 348
Carpenter, Mary 109, 142–3, 195

Carter, Amelia 328
Cary, Francis Stephen 65, 66
'Cause, the' 241, 245, 248
Channing, William Ellery 153–4
Channing, William H. 153
Chapman, John 86, 113–14, *118*, 345;
   and Marian Evans (George Eliot)
   86, 113, 114, 115; publishes
   Bessie Parkes's poems 87, 113,
   and Barbara's *A Brief Summary*
   91, *see under* Bodichon, Barbara;
   relations with Barbara 86, 93,
   113, 116–26, 127, 128, 129,
   130–31, 133, 139, 151, 175,
   187, 210; his children 99, 123;
   publishes Harriet Taylor Mills's
   'The Enfranchisement of
   Women' 239
Chapman, Susanna (*née* Brewitt) 86, 99,
   114, 118, 123, 124, 125–6
Chartists 52
Church, Harriet 328
Churchill, Henry 220
Clarke, Dr Edward 275
Clarke, Sara Ann 167, 220
Clarkson, Thomas 9
Clements, Alfred Eugène 287–9,
   298, 331
Cobbe, Frances Power 195, 243
Cobden, Richard 203
Codrington, Helen 236–7
Codrington, Rear Admiral Henry 236,
   237
Coleridge, Samuel Taylor 8–9
College of Preceptors, London 63
Columbia (steam packet) 19–20
Cook, Eliza 90; (ed.) *Cook's Journal* 90
Cookson, William Strickland 175
Corn Laws 12, 29, 47, 134, 212
Corot, Jean-Baptiste-Camille 233, 258
Cosway, Maria 66
Courtauld, Samuel 114, 128, 175
Cox, David 67, 83
Crabbe, John 336
Craig, Isa 176, 177, 183, 234, 239, 345
Creswick, Thomas 284
Cricket (steamship) 50–52
Cross, John 309–10
Crow, Jane 277
Crowham Manor, Sussex 17, 49, 259
Crystal Palace, the 76, 88, 283, 299

About the Author

Jane Robinson is also the author of *Bluestockings: The Remarkable Story of the First Women to Fight for an Education* and *Ladies Can't Climb Ladders: The Pioneering Adventures of the First Professional Women*. She was born in Edinburgh, grew up in North Yorkshire and read English at Somerville College, Oxford. She has worked in the antiquarian book trade and as an archivist, and is now a full-time writer and lecturer, specializing in social history through women's eyes. She is a Fellow of the Royal Historical and Royal Geographical Societies, a Hawthornden Fellow, and a Senior Associate of Somerville College. In her spare time she collects books and designs pop-up Escape Rooms. She lives in Buckinghamshire with her husband and two feline assistants, Emmy and Mrs Chippy. *Trailblazer* is her thirteenth book.